COMPETING VISIONS OF EMPIRE

COMPETING VISIONS OF EMPIRE

*Labor, Slavery,
and the Origins of
the British Atlantic Empire*

Abigail L. Swingen

Yale

UNIVERSITY
PRESS

New Haven & London

Published with assistance from the Annie Burr Lewis Fund.

Yale University Press books may be purchased in quantity for educational, business, or promotional use. For information, please e-mail sales.press@yale.edu (U.S. office) or sales@yaleup.co.uk (U.K. office).

Set in PostScript Electra and Trajan types by IDS Infotech Ltd.
Printed in the United States of America.

Library of Congress Cataloging-in-Publication Data

Swingen, Abigail Leslie.
Competing visions of empire : labor, slavery, and the origins of the British Atlantic empire / Abigail L. Swingen.
pages cm
Includes bibliographical references and index.
ISBN 978-0-300-18754-0 (cloth : alk. paper) 1. West Indies, British—History—17th century. 2. West Indies, British—Economic conditions—17th century. 3. West Indies, British—Commerce. 4. Slavery—West Indies, British—History—17th century. 5. West Indies, British—Historiography. 6. Imperialism—History. 7. West Indies, British—History—18th century. 8. West Indies, British—Economic conditions—18th century. 9. Slavery—West Indies, British—History—18th century. I. Title.
F2131.S94 2015
972.9'03—dc23
2014027080

A catalogue record for this book is available from the British Library.

This paper meets the requirements of ANSI/NISO Z39.48-1992 (Permanence of Paper).

10 9 8 7 6 5 4 3 2 1

To Alan and Ruby

CONTENTS

ACKNOWLEDGMENTS

The creation of a book over the course of several years always results in the accumulation of serious debts of gratitude. This project began as a dissertation at the University of Chicago under the guidance of Steven Pincus, John Brewer, Ted Cook, Tamar Herzog, and Ralph Austen. In addition, Allan Macinnes of the University of Strathclyde came to Chicago as a visiting professor in 2003 and kindly allowed me to sit in on his class on Jacobitism and has remained a stalwart supporter of the project. Their expert supervision helped guide the project from a haphazard proposal into a relatively coherent thesis. I particularly wish to thank Steve, whose guidance has not ceased and who has always made graduate advising one of his top priorities. I aspire to be half the adviser and scholar he is. I would also like to thank my mentors at Swarthmore College back in the 1990s, Pieter Judson, Tim Burke, and Marjorie Murphy.

An amazingly supportive community of scholars at the University of Chicago and beyond has helped shape this book in workshop settings, conferences, and informal arenas. At Chicago, Brent Sirota, James Vaughn, Lisa Clark Diller, Heather Welland, Chris Dudley, Fredrik Albritton Jonsson, Ryan Fracc, Kathrin Levitan, Douglas Kanter, Michael Brillman, Craig Hargett, Lyman Stebbens, Gerry Siarny, Paul Cheney, Dan Riches, and Colin Wilder all sat through numerous chapter drafts in workshops and seminars and offered helpful suggestions and advice. Thanks also go to Josh Arthurs, Cam Hawkins, John Deak, Tania Maync-Daly, and Ben Nickels. I wish to thank scholars who have helped in other ways, by reading drafts of chapters or the entire manuscript, providing support while working in archives, or engaging in lively conversations. These include Rob Hermann, Phil Stern, Rupa Mishra, Carl Wennerlind, Nick Popper, Leslie Theibert, Megan Lindsay Cherry, Ted McCormick, Kristen Block, Ed Rugemer, Bill Bullman, Caroline Boswell, Will Pettigrew, Dan

Carey, Dan Szechi, Tim Harris, Susannah Ottaway, and Rich Connors. I want to give special thanks to Brent Sirota and James Vaughn, who have continued to offer cogent scholarly advice and have contributed significantly to the shaping of the argument of this book.

This book has also been shaped by my experiences teaching at Auburn University and Texas Tech University. In particular from Auburn, I wish to thank Donna Bohanan, Ralph Kingston, Kathryn Braund, Kenneth Noe, Christopher Ferguson, Charles Israel, David Carter, Jennifer Brooks, Tiffany Sippial, and Tony Carey (now of Appalachian State University). At Texas Tech, I wish to thank Gretchen Adams, Zach Brittsan, Stefano D'Amico, Barbara Hahn, Justin Hart, Karlos Hill, John Howe, Allan Kuethe, Randy McBee, Emily Skidmore, and Aliza Wong. I have had the pleasure to work with some fantastic graduate students from both institutions, and would like to thank Josh Barronton, Nick Faucett, Abby Sayers, Matt Kocsan, Robert Weaver, and Katie Snyder. Special thanks to Josh and Abby for their research assistance in the summer of 2009. I would also like to give thanks to my department chair at Texas Tech, Randy McBee, and to Nina Pruitt and Mayela Guardiola for their assistance navigating fellowship leave and other administrative hurdles. I also wish to thank the former vice president for research at Texas Tech, Taylor Eighmy (now of the University of Tennessee), and the former dean of the College of Arts and Sciences, Lawrence Schovenec (now provost of Texas Tech), for their support.

The completion of this book was made possible by the financial and research assistance from a number of institutions. Financial support from Texas Tech in the form of a Humanities Start-Up Grant in 2010 helped the research process tremendously. Spending the 2011–2012 academic year as a Barbara Thom Postdoctoral Long-Term Fellow at the Huntington Library was instrumental in providing me the time and resources necessary to complete the book. At the Huntington I learned from a wonderful community of scholars, including Lisa Cody, Heather Keenleyside, Heidi Brayman Hackel, Carla Zecher, Fran Dolan, Harry Stout, Peter Stallybrass, Elizabeth Allen, Will West, Emily Berquist Soule, Lindsey O'Neill, Mark Hanna, Adam Arenson, Adrian Finucane, Heather James, Lori Ann Farrell, and Peter Mancall. I would also like to thank Roy Ritchie for his warm hospitality, Steve Hindle for his unwavering support of my project, and Juan Gomez and Carolyn Powell for their administrative assistance. That year I had the good fortune of also receiving the Frederick A. and Marion S. Pottle Short-Term Fellowship in 18th-Century British Studies from the Beinecke Rare Book & Manuscript Library at Yale University, which gave me the opportunity to round out research for the final two chapters. I wish to thank Stacy Smith at the Beinecke for her assistance. After completing my fellowship year, the College of Arts and Sciences at Texas Tech generously granted me a Returning Faculty Research Award to allow me the time to finish the book. I also wish to thank the people who work at the following libraries and archives: University of Chicago Regenstein Library; the British Library; the Institute of Historical Research; the National Archives in Kew; the Beinecke Rare Book & Manuscript Library; the Huntington Library; Auburn University Libraries; and Texas Tech University Libraries.

Versions of a number of the book's chapters have been presented at conferences and workshops over the years, where I received helpful comments and feedback. These include the North American Conference on British Studies; the Western Conference on British Studies; the Midwest Conference on British Studies; the New World of Projects Conference of the Early Modern Studies Institute of the University of Southern California; the Institutional Perspectives on Early Modern Britain and Its Empire Conference at Yale; the Economies of Empire in the Eighteenth Century Conference at the Huntington; the British Historical Studies Colloquium at Yale; the British Scholar Conference at the University of Texas at Austin; the German-American Frontiers of the Humanities Symposium, sponsored by the American Philosophical Society and the Alexander von Humboldt Foundation; and the Southeastern American Society for Eighteenth-Century Studies Conference.

Portions of this work were published as "Labor: Employment, Colonial Servitude, and Slavery in the Seventeenth-Century Atlantic" in *Mercantilism Reimagined: Political Economy in Early Modern Britain and Its Empire*, edited by Philip Stern and Carl Wennerlind (Oxford University Press, 2014). I thank OUP for permission to republish these portions here.

At Yale University Press, I wish to thank Laura Davulis for her support and encouragement. Not only is she a fantastic editor, but her prompt replies to e-mails and questions made the process transparent, which is all that an author can hope for.

Finally, I need to thank my family. First my parents, Gwen and Carl Boyington and John Swingen and Anne Willard, who have supported me throughout this endeavor; my aunt and uncle, BJ Scott-Turner and Steve Turner, who share a great sense of humor and a love of history; and my late grandparents, Barbara and Robert Scott and John and Laurette Swingen, for instilling a curiosity about the world in me and my parents. I'd also like to thank my late great-aunt and -uncle, Ellen and Rae Beddington, who hosted me on a number of research trips in their snug house in South East London. I also thank my mother-in-law Judy Cole and brother-in-law Michael Barenberg for maintaining a good sense of humor when things sometimes bordered on the ridiculous. Last but not least, I thank the love of my life, Alan Barenberg, and our daughter, Ruby, for showing me what matters and for giving me all of the support I could possibly hope for. Thank you for letting me drag you guys to London, South Pasadena, New Haven, and other exotic locales. Alan, thanks for editing each and every chapter a million times and for the technological and emotional support. Rubes, thanks for letting Mom work all those Saturdays. I love you both more than I can express.

AUTHOR'S NOTE

All dates in this book are given in Old Style, according to the convention of the Julian calendar, used in England until 1752. The beginning of the year is taken to be January 1 rather than March 25, however. Wherever possible, original spellings and punctuation from primary sources remain in place. However, light editing has been necessary in some places for the sake of clarity. All information on sources can be found in the endnotes.

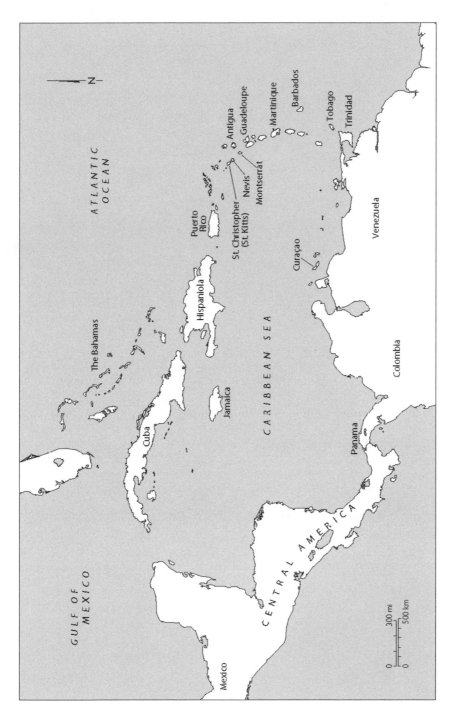

Map of the Caribbean Sea and portions of Central and South America. Map drawn by Bill Nelson.

INTRODUCTION

Why did England establish and maintain an empire in the Americas during the seventeenth and eighteenth centuries? The expansion of the English Atlantic empire during the second half of the seventeenth century was not a foregone conclusion and could even be seen as something of a puzzle, given the strong opposition to colonial acquisition from politicians and economic writers who worried that colonial demand for labor drained England of its own valuable workforce. According to these thinkers, colonies did not supplement the nation's economic prosperity but were in fact detrimental to it. "The Trade of England, and the Fishing Trade," admonished the economic writer Roger Coke in 1670, "are so much diminished by how much they might have been supplied by those men who are diverted in our American Plantations." The political writer William Petyt lamented in 1680, "England never was so populous as it might have been, and undeniably must now be far less populous than ever, having so lately peopled our vast American Plantations."[1]

Despite these warnings, it was during the second half of the seventeenth century that the pace of England's empire building across the Atlantic increased dramatically, as England established and/or fought to maintain Jamaica, Saint Christopher (Saint Kitts), Nova Scotia, New York, East and West Jersey, Carolina, and Pennsylvania, not to mention significant trading outposts in West Africa and India. How are we to account for this apparent discrepancy? Were the critics of empire simply ignored? Or in the end, were they appeased by the widespread use of African slavery in the West Indian colonies? After all, by relying on the forced labor of African slaves, English planters demanded fewer and fewer servants from the home country.

Competing Visions of Empire investigates how disputes over the projected goals and the perceived impact of England's overseas colonial empire were deeply ideological and frequently centered on the issue of labor. It investigates whether or not it was merely coincidental that African slavery became an integral part of English imperial designs at the same time that economic thinkers raised the issue of the empire's impact on England's domestic labor supply. It shows that the establishment and growth of the early modern English empire and the prevalence of slavery in the West Indies colonies were inextricably linked to political and ideological conflicts in England and to political-economic debates on ideas of population, empire, and national wealth that took place throughout the early modern period.

The book focuses on the years 1650–1720, when imperial expansion became a paramount concern of the English state. It concentrates on the West Indies colonies of Barbados, the Leeward Islands, and Jamaica because contemporaries considered these colonies to be most important to England's imperial economy. In addition, it was in these colonies that the transition to African slave labor was the most rapid and entrenched during the seventeenth century. The book focuses on such state-sponsored enterprises as the Western Design and the Royal African Company and illustrates how different groups, especially planters, privateers, merchants, and colonial officials, negotiated with, confronted, and accommodated state policies and institutions. Slavery and the slave trade emerged as key points of contention in these confrontations. The prevalence of slavery in the colonies transformed not only how colonials understood the empire and their place within it, but how metropolitans, particularly state actors, understood the empire and its purpose.

PREVAILING INTERPRETATIONS

Competing Visions of Empire examines the ideological origins of the English empire and its connections to unfree labor systems in the colonies. In doing so it challenges many of the dominant scholarly interpretations of the early English empire. Traditionally, the origins of European colonial endeavors in the early modern period have been described as mercantilist in nature and design. According to this interpretation, most famously articulated by historians George Louis Beer and Charles M. Andrews in the early twentieth century, England's imperial agenda was based on a collection of commercial laws that aimed to restrict foreign access to colonial markets and goods. As Beer wrote, England's early modern empire was managed by a series of "regulations whose fundamental aim was to create a self-sufficient commercial empire of mutually complementary economic parts." This system, of course, came to be labeled "mercantilism," and mercantilist policies included the promotion of state-sponsored monopoly corporations and the Acts of Trade and Navigation. This narrative describes a pervasive, hegemonic "mercantilist mind" that understood such policies governing overseas trade and colonial settlements as natural defenses against foreign economic and military competition. Simply put, if England did not seek out colonies and protect its overseas markets, other European powers would and England would necessarily lose access to wealth and resources.[2]

The idea that mercantilist economic ideas lay at the heart of England's imperial designs in the early modern era has remained the dominant interpretive paradigm for over a century.[3] The overwhelming historiographical acceptance of a static idea of mercantilism has meant that scholars have generally failed to recognize the connections between the rise of unfree labor in the colonies and significant debates about the empire's purpose that took place throughout the period. Although many scholars acknowledge the mutability of mercantilism as a concept, few have explicitly recognized that imperial and commercial policies and the ideas and theories used to support them were highly contested. People in early modern England and the colonies disagreed over how to manage and regulate the overseas empire and whether or not colonies benefited the home country in the first place. One of the major fault lines of the debate was over the issue of labor, particularly the slave trade. *Competing Visions of Empire* uncovers and contextualizes the dissenting voices that complicate the notion of mercantilist consensus and explores the important roles they played in shaping English imperialism.[4]

One of the consequences of this overreliance on the mercantilist interpretive framework is that it has resulted in the prevalence of the idea that England's colonial endeavors of the early modern period were not imperial. Indeed, when compared with the brutal regimes of the British empire in places like India and Africa in the nineteenth century, the small islands and coastal settlements that made up the so-called "first" empire hardly seem noteworthy. But it was during the seventeenth and early eighteenth centuries that the economic exploitation of colonial settlements was developed and perfected. The transatlantic slave trade grew in astonishing proportions at this time, and England and its colonies reaped the economic benefits of this oppressive labor system. If a regime is labeled imperial when it relies on territorial conquest and is militaristic and brutalizing to its subjects, then England's early modern exploits in the Atlantic World were absolutely imperial. The fact that contemporaries sometimes failed to fully understand the implications of these exploits and did their best to maintain myths about the empire being "Protestant, commercial, maritime, and free" does not diminish its imperial nature.[5] Colonization, genocide, slavery, and exploitative plantation agriculture made England's transatlantic exploits imperial from a very early stage.

Rather than focus on the construction of the mythology of empire, this book considers how different contemporary constituencies understood England's empire to uncover its ideological origins. Planters, merchants, privateers, trading companies, imperial authorities, and colonial officials all articulated their own imperial agendas, often in confrontation with, or at least in conversation with, one or more of the other groups. Slavery and the transatlantic slave trade played a significant role in shaping these imperial ideals. It is in these agendas that competing ideas about the purposes of empire, and how (or whether) England could best benefit from an overseas empire, emerged and evolved. By considering the ideas expressed by the people and institutions intimately involved in the highly contested process of empire building, the book illustrates that imperial ideologies existed at a variety of levels of English and colonial societies.[6]

Many historians have attempted to add more-nuanced interpretations of the origins of the English Atlantic empire than the traditional mercantilist narrative, with its primary emphasis on metropolitan concerns, has usually allowed. Richard S. Dunn's pathbreaking book *Sugar and Slaves* has become perhaps the most influential interpretation of the social and economic development of England's West Indies colonies. Rather than focus on metropolitan commercial policies and their implementation, Dunn is concerned with how "the early English planters in the West Indies responded to life in the tropics." He argues quite convincingly that in Barbados, the Leeward Islands, and eventually Jamaica, a cohesive class of powerful and wealthy planters emerged during the seventeenth century. These men, motivated by the desire for personal profit, established large sugar plantations worked by thousands of African slaves, thereby creating a "social mode" that was "totally without precedent in the English experience." For Dunn, the origins of the English empire and the centrality of African slavery to it lay in the motivations and socioeconomic needs of colonial planters first and foremost, which resulted in colonial societies diverging dramatically from English models.[7]

Central to the idea that the English colonies were culturally and socially distinct from England was the astronomic growth of African slavery during the seventeenth century. But how and why did it become acceptable for the English and other Europeans to enslave Africans? Generally speaking, the framework for understanding the prevalence and longevity of African slavery in the Americas centers on the issues of race and contemporary European understandings of racial difference. Some historians, especially Eric Williams, have maintained that the motivations behind the widespread use of enslaved Africans in European colonies were purely economic and that racism inherent in the slave system was an ex post facto justification. Williams argues that it was simply cheaper to rely on the labor of enslaved Africans, and that was all the justification European planters and merchants needed. Other scholars, such as Winthrop Jordan and David Brion Davis, have traced engrained European cultural prejudices against "others" to ancient and medieval precedents to explain the rise of African slavery in the New World. They describe how over the course of the seventeenth century in English colonies, blackness came to be equated with slavery, which had its starkest expression in colonial laws and slave codes. Jordan argues that these ideas were so engrained in the European mind-set that the choice to enslave Africans was effectively an "unthinking decision."[8]

Other scholars have taken on the idea that the decision to enslave Africans and sustain the transatlantic slave system for centuries was somehow accidental or "unthinking." Taking an explicitly "cultural and ideological" approach, David Eltis has not only attempted to answer the question of why Europeans enslaved Africans, but argues that it would have made more economic sense for Europeans to have enslaved other Europeans. He determines that economic "motives operated under the aegis of fundamental non-economic values, in part socially constructed in the modern terminology, which created the Atlantic slave system and the slave trade that sustained it, just as much as the drive to consume and produce plantation produce." Racist ideologies and pervasive notions of who lay "outside" of acceptable European society shaped these ideas. Eltis argues that the development of a particular kind of possessive individualism that valued property rights above all else sustained this binary construction and, in turn, the transatlantic slave system. As a result, he concludes that slavery was implemented in the colonies "without much reference to the metropolitan authorities." Similarly, Susan Amussen has emphasized that imperial authorities were often confused about the legal implications and meanings of slavery in the colonies, thus accentuating a disconnect between metropolitan and colonial concerns.[9]

Investigating the lived experiences of the enslaved is another approach scholars have taken to understand how and why Europeans constructed concepts of racial difference, superiority, and inferiority. Stephanie Smallwood has uncovered, in moving and vivid detail, just how deliberate the process of commodification of human beings was, encompassing capture in Africa, captivity in Royal African Company forts, the horrors of the Middle Passage, and finally slave markets in the Americas. Each step was aimed at dehumanizing the African captive, and she concludes that in consequence the Middle Passage was a trauma that never ended for those who made it to the New World. It was a calculated, violent, and purposeful system. Trevor Burnard has investigated the development of white mastery in colonial Jamaica and how it was practiced and sustained in its most raw, brutal forms by a slave owner named Thomas Thistlewood. Using Thistlewood's diaries, Burnard has vividly described the violence inherent in a system that was based on oppressing the vast majority of the population. He argues that the structures of power in colonial Jamaica emphasized the stark contrast between slavery and freedom, which whites desperately tried to maintain through the use of brute force and sexual violence. Although Jamaican society in some ways resembled contemporary British society in its structures of power, it "deviated" in a crucial way by "abandoning the principle that property was paramount in favor of doctrines that increasingly emphasized race in all matters. Race was the foundation of the social system—white skin meant freedom, dominion, and power; black skin meant slavery, submission, and powerlessness."[10]

These analyses of cultural constructs of race and racial superiority and of the deliberate and violent nature of the slave system have provided tremendous insight into how the system was sustained for centuries. Jack Greene has explored some of the implications of these constructions of racial superiority by whites in the West Indies in the development of what he calls "West Indian political thought" during the eighteenth century. Historians of colonial British America have long recognized that colonists regularly articulated ideas of English legal guarantees of liberty when negotiating with and confronting metropolitan authority. These concepts had particular resonance for white colonists in the West Indies, who wished to emphasize their "English liberties" in order to draw the sharpest contrast possible from the legal status of their slaves. According to Greene, by the mid-1700s this "West Indian political thought" stressed "metropolitan complicity" in creating and maintaining colonial slave societies. According to this position, imperial authorities and metropolitan consumers were just as responsible for the expansion of slavery in the colonies as West Indian planters were and reaped just as many, if not more, of its economic rewards.[11]

Competing Visions of Empire explores the seventeenth-century origins of these ideas, especially the notion of metropolitan responsibility for the expansion of slavery in the colonies. In 2002, Christopher Brown expressed concern that the extensive scholarship on slavery in the early English empire did not yet provide "a connected account of the political history of slavery." He suggested a number of approaches historians could take, considering the numerous ways the establishment of slave regimes informed issues of state building, war, and political thought.[12] *Competing Visions of Empire* provides a step in this direction, by focusing on the ways that the expansion of slavery and the English state's desire to dominate the transatlantic slave trade contributed to the shaping of imperial policies and directives. This often resulted in confrontations over the place of slavery and the slave trade in English imperial designs. For those invested in constructing societies built on white mastery of black slaves, these confrontations informed how they articulated and explained their own imperial ideals. It illustrates that over time, a variety of colonial interests used the institution of slavery to justify the very existence of the empire.

Rather than focus solely on how human networks built the empire on the "periphery," *Competing Visions of Empire* argues that in order to determine how and why slavery became so important to English imperialism, one must take into account the fact that empire building involved transoceanic networks of individuals and, just as importantly, the institutions they served, patronized, confronted, and resisted.[13] It was in these confrontations and negotiations that imperial ideals emerged and evolved and translated into rival interpretations about the purpose of empire and its proper management and administration. They also reveal the variety of ways that English people, both at home and in the colonies, perceived the central role that unfree labor, especially African slavery, played in the overall imperial economy. The book illustrates the extent to which the English state was intimately involved in the growth and development of slavery in the colonies.

SCOPE OF THE BOOK

The question of unfree labor was central to English imperialism as it evolved during the early modern period, even before the English became heavily involved in the slave trade. Chapter 1 begins with a consideration of one of the earliest justifications for overseas colonization: the need for England to unburden itself of its apparent "surplus" population. It explores the development of indentured service and convict transportation in places like Virginia and Barbados. It pays particular attention to the colonial merchants who profited from and promoted the servant trades, many of whom became key players in the transatlantic slave trade by the mid-1600s. The chapter considers why in the long run neither indentured service nor convict transportation became viable alternatives to slave labor in the West Indies by connecting the issue of unfree colonial labor to contemporary debates over population and political economy. Just as these debates became heated, the English government became involved in overseas imperial designs in earnest.

Chapter 2 focuses on the imperial projects of the English state beginning in the 1650s, paying particular attention to the campaign authorized by Oliver Cromwell that resulted in the capture of Jamaica from the Spanish in 1655, the Western Design. This military and commercial campaign, organized by many of the same colonial merchants at the center of the indentured servant, slave, tobacco, and sugar trades, was a plan to conquer territory from Spain in the New World. Coming on the heels of Cromwell's successful subjugation of Scotland and Ireland, these men easily convinced the notoriously Hispanophobic Cromwell of the necessity to embark on a transatlantic imperial plan. In addition to territorial conquest, the Western Design was specifically aimed at bringing the existing English Caribbean colonies of Barbados and the Leeward Islands under closer control of the government by enforcing the new Acts of Trade and Navigation, which outlawed trade with non-English merchants. Although the conquest of Jamaica was considered a disappointment to some contemporaries, this campaign marked a significant turning point in English imperialism. In the end, the merchants who had been so heavily involved in the Western Design were disappointed by the Protectorate's lack of enthusiasm for Jamaica's development. They were optimistic, however, about the imperial direction of the restored monarchy, of Charles II's decision in 1660 to hold on to Cromwell's conquest.

The same month the Privy Council chose to keep Jamaica, Charles II issued a charter establishing the Company of Royal Adventurers into Africa. Chapters 3, 4, and 5 survey the influence of this and the two subsequent African Companies over imperial administration and colonial governance as a means to investigate the company's centrality to the Restoration imperial agenda. The company was a joint-stock corporation that was closely controlled by the Stuart family (specifically Charles II's brother, James, Duke of York, who served as its governor) and that held a monopoly on all African trade.[14] The African Company embodied the Stuarts' economic and political vision of empire. It was created with the explicit purpose of siphoning trade away from other European powers, which reflected an inability to envision a world in which economic prosperity could be shared among nations. In addition, the company's monopoly rested firmly in the authority of the royal prerogative through its charter granted by the king. Belief in the unconditional power of the royal prerogative was one of the most consistent ideologies held by the late Stuarts. Starting in the mid-1660s, the African Company played a central role in implementing the Crown's imperial agenda by influencing colonial appointments and shaping imperial policies. And as English politics became increasingly ideologically driven in the late seventeenth century, so did the politics of empire. Conflicts frequently arose over the company's political, economic, and military jurisdictions. Colonial planters were some of the most vocal critics of the company's monopoly. They frequently argued that an open, though still regulated, slave trade would be the most beneficial for their economic livelihoods. Privateers, a powerful constituency in Jamaica, resented the company's attempts to maintain peaceful trade in slaves with the Spanish, the usual target of buccaneers' plundering. In confronting the company and by extension the Crown, these groups articulated their own imperial agendas. In response, the Crown frequently had to compromise over issues of colonial governance and learned that one of the best ways to keep colonial interest groups happy, and therefore more compliant to imperial directives, was to make sure they had steady supplies of enslaved Africans. These chapters illustrate how these competing and overlapping imperial ideologies from a variety of constituencies played a significant role in shaping early modern English imperialism.

The final two chapters of the book consider how, by the turn of the eighteenth century, African slavery and the slave trade were understood to be in the national interest by a wide portion of English society. After the removal of James II in the Glorious Revolution of 1688–1689, the African Company effectively lost its monopoly as well as its position at the center of imperial affairs. Over the next two decades, heated debates took place in Parliament and in dozens of published pamphlets over the proper management of the slave trade. Some argued for a continuation of the company's monopoly, while others clamored for an open slave trade. But it became commonplace for all sides to portray the enslavement of Africans as essential to the economic functioning of the empire, which had emerged to buttress and sustain the white mastery West Indies planters had so carefully constructed in the colonies. This emphasis on the perceived economic importance of those colonies with slaves to the empire required a fundamental reimagining of the colonies as fully integrated components of the realm. Slavery thus became a justification for the empire itself. Chapter 6 pays particular attention to the two immediate effects of the Glorious Revolution on the Atlantic empire: war with France and the removal of the Royal African Company from the center of English imperial designs. The constant threat of warfare threw a particular dilemma in England's Caribbean colonies into sharp focus: the diminishing number of white people in those colonies. Throughout the 1690s officials in the West Indies complained to imperial authorities that they desperately needed white servants to fill their militias in case of foreign attack or slave revolt. Yet there were only feeble attempts to fulfill these requests, and it was generally left up to individual merchants and governors to fix the haphazard indentured servant and convict trades. The African slave trade, however, continued to be expanded and promoted, despite the increased dangers of trading during wartime and apparent fears of slave uprisings in the colonies.

The book ends with an exploration of how slavery and the slave trade came to be understood as being in Britain's national interest by the early eighteenth century by investigating Britain's winning the *asiento*, the exclusive contract to supply the Spanish American colonies with slaves. As part of the Treaty of Utrecht, which ended the War of Spanish Succession in 1713, Britain was granted the long-coveted *asiento*. Queen Anne gave the contract to the South Sea Company, which had been formed by her trusted adviser and Lord Treasurer, Sir Robert Harley, Earl of Oxford, in 1711. The company had been created with the *asiento* in mind and was given a monopoly on all trade to Spanish America. Chapter 7 explores how the South Sea Company's emergence with the promise of managing the *asiento* occurred at a time when slavery and Britain's participation in the transatlantic slave trade had been at the center of national debate for two decades. The establishment of the South Sea Company and the *asiento* indicated that by the turn of the eighteenth century, slavery and the international slave trade were perceived to be completely interconnected with the national interest.

Competing Visions of Empire provides a new framework for understanding the origins of unfree labor and the English empire, one that focuses on conflict rather than consensus. It is neither an isolated colonial nor a narrow metropolitan history but is an integrative narrative of the ideological origins of the British empire. The project emphasizes that the overwhelming acceptance of African slavery by the English was by no means inevitable, or something that only mattered in the colonies. Ultimately, the events described in this book were crucial in laying the foundations for Britain's domination of the slave trade for the remainder of the eighteenth century.

UNFREE LABOR AND THE ORIGINS OF EMPIRE

In June 1677, the English Privy Council, in the presence of King Charles II, held a meeting to discuss the state of the Leeward Islands. The Caribbean colony, made up of four islands—Saint Christopher (Saint Kitts), Nevis, Antigua, and Montserrat—was in desperate need of laborers to work a growing number of plantations as well as to fill the militia rolls. In response to a number of pleas from the colony's governor and leading officers, the Privy Council approved a plan to help populate Saint Christopher, which involved sending "malefactors," or convicted felons, to the colony. According to the report, colonial merchants indicated that three hundred convicts would be "requisite" for the island, "provided they might not bee obliged to pay for them att the Gaols in regard of the great fees demanded by the Keepers." The report indicated that the sheriffs of London should tell jail keepers to pass along their accounts to the Exchequer, and the merchants were told to "enter into Bond" with the Recorder of London (one of the judges at the Central Criminal Court, the Old Bailey) as a promise that the prisoners would not make their way back to London once out of jail. The case was then forwarded to the Treasury to begin the process of paying the jailers, who would release prisoners to the merchants.[1]

The plan seemed straightforward. There were a number of problems it intended to solve, especially the need for people in the Leeward Islands. But the plan's success was far from certain. In April 1678, ten months after the initial proposal, the Lords of Trade indicated to the king that nothing had yet been done to implement the scheme, "yet the way lyes open." In July 1680, three years after the Privy Council's approval, the governing council of Saint Christopher wrote that they still awaited the arrival of the prisoners. In March 1682, nearly five years after the original proposal, the Lords of Trade indicated to Sir William Stapleton, the governor of the Leeward Islands, that they were ready to proceed but still needed to find a merchant willing to transport the prisoners to the colony and offer enough security. Although Stapleton suggested a friend of his for the job later that year, in February 1684 the deputy governor of Saint Christopher still wondered when the convicts would be sent to his colony.[2]

Why were there so many delays and disruptions getting the "300 malefactors" to Saint Christopher? In what ways might this story have been typical? This chapter will show how this episode was indicative of the overall failure of convict transportation and indentured servitude to become reliable sources of coerced labor in the English Caribbean colonies during the seventeenth century. Demand for colonial unfree labor increased throughout the century, growing especially acute in Barbados by the 1640s and 1650s, and in later decades in the Leeward Islands and Jamaica. But the supply of indentured servants and convicts from England was never enough for the West Indies colonies. This chapter explores the multiple reasons why the transatlantic servant market established during the earliest decades of colonial expansion no longer served the needs of the colonies by the second half of the century. This diminishing servant supply reflected both demographic shifts in England as well as changing cultural attitudes about the kinds of people who tended to go to the colonies as servants, especially the poor and criminals. This chapter considers why in the long run neither indentured service nor convict transportation became viable alternatives to slave labor in the West Indies by connecting the issue of unfree colonial labor to contemporary debates over population and political economy. The turn toward African slavery in the Caribbean colonies was not driven entirely by colonial labor demand but was closely tied to political, economic, and social concerns in the metropolis.

ORIGINS OF UNFREE LABOR IN THE ENGLISH COLONIES

During the late sixteenth and early seventeenth centuries, an overseas colonial empire was promoted as a remedy for England's perceived population woes. Colonial projectors exploited a widespread fear that there were far too many poor and unemployed people in England and that the country did not have the resources necessary to provide shelter, food, and work for its increasing multitudes. The idle poor were a dangerous group that threatened social stability, and it was widely believed that poverty and unemployment led naturally to vagrancy, begging, and criminality.[3] This idea was most famously utilized by the promoters of transatlantic colonial expansion during the late sixteenth century, especially Richard Hakluyt the younger. "The frye of the wandering beggars of England that grow up idly and hurtful and burdenous to this realm," he wrote in his

Discourse of Western Planting, "may there [in New England] be unladen, better bred up, and may people waste countries to the home and foreign benefit, and to their own more happy state."[4] Colonies seemed to provide much needed territory for an expanding population and were promoted as places where the unemployed and vagrant could be put to work for their own good and for the good of the realm.

Pamphlet literature promoting the early settlement of Virginia justified colonial expansion in these terms. "There is nothing more dangerous," warned one writer in 1609, "for the estate of common-wealths, then when the people do increase to a greater multitude and number then may justly parallel with the largeness of the place and country: for hereupon comes oppression, and diverse kind of wrongs, mutinies, sedition, commotion, rebellion, scarcity, dearth, poverty, and sundry sorts of calamities." One sermon ominously declared the same year, "Look seriously into the land, and see whether there be not just cause, if not a necessity to seek abroad. The people, blessed be God, do swarm in the land, as young bees in a hive in June, insomuch that there is very hardly room for one man to live by another." To ease these burdens, Virginia was promoted as a land of opportunity and advertised in utopian terms, "well ordered," where a family could live "rent free." Promoters argued that moving poor people to a new colony and to "a harder course of life, wanting pleasures, and subject to some pinching miseries, and to a strict form of government, and severe discipline, [they] do often become new men, even as it were cast in a new mould, and prove good and worthy instruments and members of a Common-wealth." New transatlantic colonies were also seen as places where England could rid itself of undesirable and dangerous elements of society. According to one contemporary, England was "abounding with swarms of sole persons, which having no means of labour to relieve their misery, do likewise swarm in lewd and naughty practices." Poverty was understood to be an infectious disease, and by sending the poor and vagrant to the colonies, England would become a healthier nation. "So that you see it no new thing, but most profitable for our State, to rid our multitudes of such as lie at home, pestering the land with pestilence and penury, and infecting one another with vice and villainy, worse than the plague itself."[5]

During the first half of the seventeenth century the idea that colonies could be used as dumping grounds for prisoners and political and religious troublemakers also gained traction. Colonial convict transportation has often been interpreted in terms of legal transformations in England and changing attitudes about crime and punishment. When considered from a colonial perspective, prisoner transportation is usually presented as a source of class antagonism in colonial American society, or as an extension of English law across the Atlantic.[6]

But transportation can also be understood as a source of coerced colonial labor and therefore part of a larger imperial project, intimately connected to both indentured servitude and slavery. In the 1580s, Richard Hakluyt lamented the fact that many potential laborers were wasted when petty criminals were executed for their offenses. In 1611, four years after the initial settlement of Jamestown, Governor Thomas Dale of Virginia sent a request to Lord Treasurer Salisbury asking for two thousand men. "On account of the difficulty of procuring men in so short a time," Dale suggested, "all offenders out the common gaols condemned to die should be sent for three years to the colony." In 1614, James I granted his Privy Council the power to sentence convicted felons to transportation to the American colonies "as that in their punishment some of them may live and yield a profitable service to the Common wealth in parts abroad."[7]

This narrative, of course, has a long history and is a key component of traditional historiographical interpretations of the origins of the English empire. It is not without its critics. In 1960, Mildred Campbell argued that many contemporary thinkers felt that overpopulation in and of itself was not England's problem, but rather the real crisis was the need for people who could contribute to the commonwealth in meaningful ways. The primary concern, therefore, was "the proper handling of labour."[8] Ted McCormick has argued that contemporaries feared changes in population of certain groups or "multitudes," not increases in overall population numbers. Enclosures and other disruptive practices seemed to drain entire regions of laborers while creating new populations of unemployed people. Total numbers were not as important as perceptions of various subgroups in this early phase of theorizing about population.[9] Sending vagrants and other problematic multitudes to the colonies was an outgrowth of these concerns, regardless of whether or not population actually increased.

The idea of shipping poor and dangerous people to the colonies was not limited to promotional rhetoric. Sending criminals, vagrants, and even potential offenders was officially adopted by the Virginia Company as a means to supply the colony with a labor force. Despite these early efforts, the first decade of Virginia's settlement was disastrous. Of the approximately six hundred men who came in 1607, barely sixty were alive by 1610. Disease and harsh living conditions combined with the infamous mistakes of the first settlers, who were better prepared for military expeditions than agricultural work, left the colony on the brink of extinction by 1615. The following year, however, the company adopted a "headright" system of land allotment, in which colonists were given fifty acres of land for each person they transported to the colony. This encouraged potential planters to seek their own sources of labor and allowed merchants who were willing to send servants the opportunity to obtain land grants and develop their own plantations.[10]

Led by its governor, Sir Edwin Sandys, the Virginia Company in 1619 embarked on an ambitious program of transporting servants in order to exploit the profitable possibilities of the crop that flourished in the Virginia soil, tobacco. Under this system, the company contracted with private merchants who took advantage of this new labor market by delivering shiploads of servants and supplies to North America and shipping cargoes of tobacco back to England. The servants were then bound to company lands or sold to individual planters for a certain number of years in exchange for the cost of transportation across the Atlantic. According to Sandys, the combination of an endless labor supply from England and abundant land in Virginia would result in prosperity for all who survived. He promoted the colony by financing the publication of pamphlets and sermons that presented Virginia as a land of opportunity. Sending orphans and children of convicted felons also became Virginia Company policy, and in 1620 the City of London bound one hundred such children to be sent to Virginia. Attuned to popular attitudes of the time, the governor hoped that "in Virginia under severe Masters they may be brought to goodness."[11] As Edmund Morgan has shown, the implementation of Sandys's program during the 1620s coincided with a "boom" economy in which demand for agricultural labor to grow tobacco reached such heights that this program transformed into a brutal system of involuntary servitude, in which men and women bought and sold others and masters treated servants with levels of violence that would not have been tolerated in England. In further contrast to other forms of servitude in England, such as apprenticeship, colonial servitude tended to last for longer periods of time, often for several years. Sandys's program delivered nearly four thousand people—children and adults—to Virginia in four short years. Terrifyingly high mortality rates contributed to this insatiable demand for bodies.[12]

The Virginia Company was never able to raise enough revenue to support itself, however, and in 1624 it was officially dissolved. But this system of indentured servitude laid the foundations for the transatlantic servant trade that lasted with varying degrees of success and intensity for most of the seventeenth century. Although labor was not necessarily cheap on the ground in the colonies, it was widely understood that there were always more servants to be had from England or possibly Scotland and Ireland. This was especially true during the earliest decades of colonial expansion, when it seemed that colonial labor demand could only be met through channeling undesirable subgroups into indentured service. This of course did not always reflect reality. Historian David Souden has pointed out that the perception that the American colonies were peopled by "rogues, whores, and vagabonds," especially by the mid-1600s, is an inaccurate picture. The typical indentured servant, usually young and male, was far less likely to have had a criminal or vagrant background and instead probably had some experience working as a farm laborer or even a craftsman in a provincial English town. Such servants also tended to be highly mobile and had probably moved within England before departing for the colonies.[13]

It is worth considering whether popular concerns about England's multitudes that contributed to the use of indentured servants and convict laborers reflected any demographic reality. Historical demographers have determined that contemporary observers were probably correct that England's population increased for most of the sixteenth and into the early seventeenth centuries. E. A. Wrigley and R. S. Schofield estimate that England's population grew from roughly 2.8 million in 1541 to about 5.1 million by 1641. Cities and towns expanded rapidly during this period, especially London, which grew from about 70,000 in 1550 to roughly 400,000 in 1650. As Keith Wrightson has demonstrated, overall population growth, shifting domestic migration patterns from rural settings into urban centers, and changes in agricultural practices combined to raise food prices and increase poverty rates over the course of the sixteenth into the seventeenth centuries. There were many more poor people living in close quarters in cities and towns than ever before, which alarmed many contemporaries. London seemed especially susceptible to the disease of poverty, which was extremely troubling to many observers. "Who seeing this City to be mightily increased, and fearing lest the over-flowing multitude of inhabitants should, like too much blood in the body, infect the whole City with *plague* and *poverty*." The cure, this pamphlet continued, was "the transporting of their overflowing multitude into *Virginia*."[14] Early modern anxieties about limited resources translated into worries over unchecked population growth and the perception that England had too many of the wrong sorts of people. As a result, during the first half of the seventeenth century, few if any people seemed concerned about the prospect of sending large numbers of poor people to the colonies. Even fewer were troubled by the brutal systems of unfree labor that the colonies seemed to require.

THE WEST INDIES, SUGAR, AND INDENTURED SERVITUDE

The establishment of unfree labor systems in the Chesapeake colonies directly influenced similar developments in the English West Indies. Efforts to populate these islands started almost as soon as the earliest English settlements were established on Saint Christopher (1624) and Barbados (1627). The Barbados venture was financed by a private trading company operated by Sir Peter and Sir William Courteen, Anglo-Dutch merchants with experience trading in the Caribbean. Planters were to provide their own labor to clear and cultivate land owned by the Courteen "syndicate," and in exchange the proprietors provided equipment and wages to the planters. The uncertainty of profit inherent in this system left many hesitant to invest much of their own capital in any significant numbers of servants, however. The Courteens soon lost control over the island to James Hay, Earl of Carlisle, who successfully petitioned Charles I for a patent on the "Caribee Islands." Under Carlisle's proprietorship, planters were granted large tracts of land in exchange for an annual quit rent to be paid to the earl. Planters increasingly relied on colonial merchants who took advantage of this burgeoning market for indentured servants. The system of sending indentured labor established in Virginia was adapted in Barbados and the Leeward Islands by many of the same colonial merchants who had transported servants to the Chesapeake. Approximately 836 indentured servants were sent to Barbados in 1634, and the following year, at least 985 people, mostly servants, left London for Barbados.[15]

The transformation of Barbados over the course of the 1630s and 1640s reflected similar developments in Virginia during the 1620s. As in the Chesapeake, the colony's planters turned their attention to growing staple crops, including tobacco, cotton, indigo, and eventually sugarcane. In other ways, however, the North American and Caribbean experiences were markedly different. One major divergence was land scarcity: Barbados is a small island of approximately 166 square miles, and the four Leeward Islands make up approximately 370 square miles. As a result, from early on, land was much more expensive in the islands and tended to be concentrated relatively quickly in the hands of large planters. Carlisle's tenure system in Barbados allotted large plots of land (usually over 50 acres) to planters, and frequently such planters were able to receive more than one land grant. As early as 1647, Carlisle proclaimed that "by reason of the great number of people who repaired thither, and who by the blessing of God have multiplied there; the land is now so taken up as there is not any to be had but at great rates too high for the purchase [by] poor servants." Hilary Beckles has discovered that in the decade from 1628 to 1638, over 74,000 of the island's approximately 106,000 total acres had been allocated. Almost from the beginning and in stark contrast to Virginia, therefore, there was little opportunity for servants sent to Barbados to establish their own plantations after their terms of service had expired.[16]

Another major difference from Virginia was the eventual choice of cash crop grown in the Caribbean, sugarcane. Over the course of the middle decades of the 1600s, Barbados planters turned with increasing regularity to growing sugar, largely abandoning other crops. But the successful cultivation of sugarcane necessitated a much larger initial investment of capital than tobacco required, and it needed a much longer time to grow and harvest than tobacco did (approximately eighteen months from start to finish). In the seventeenth century, sugarcane needed to be cared for intensively by a significant number of agricultural laborers. In addition, large plantations were necessary in order for sugarcane to flourish and be successfully processed and for the large capital investment to be worthwhile. The work was extremely tedious and difficult, and parts of the process, such as grinding and boiling the sugarcane, were dangerous. In contrast, tobacco grew much more quickly and needed far fewer people to maintain a healthy crop. As a result, as Caribbean planters embraced cultivating sugar, they required constant supplies of both capital and unfree labor.[17]

Many of the same merchants who transported servants and tobacco back and forth from England and Virginia also found success shipping servants, slaves, and sugar to and from the West Indies. Men such as Maurice Thomson, William Pennoyer, and Martin Noell made fortunes selling servants and slaves in the West Indies and frequently reinvested their profits into sugar plantations. According to Russell Menard, at least seventy-five English merchants owned land in Barbados by the mid-1600s, and twenty-two of them acquired over 10,000 acres during a nine-month period in 1647. Maurice Thomson and Martin Noell were particularly successful colonial merchant-planters involved in both the servant and slave trades. Thomson settled in Virginia in 1617 and became involved in delivering servants to the colony on behalf of the Virginia Company, eventually becoming an owner of a 150-acre tobacco plantation. By the mid-1630s, Thomson was exporting nearly 25 percent of the colony's tobacco. He also was intimately involved in the settlement of the Leeward Islands by helping to finance a plantation on Saint Christopher in 1626. That same year he and his partner Thomas Combes transported 60 African slaves to the new colony. Thomson had been connected to the African slave trade as an interloper against the Guinea Company since the 1630s and became a prominent director of the East India Company when its monopoly was disestablished in 1647. Similarly, Martin Noell and his three brothers invested heavily in at least five Barbados plantations during the 1640s, and two brothers, Stephen and Thomas, moved to the colony to handle business affairs. They not only invested in plantations but also imported indentured servants and an increasing number of African slaves to the colony. Merchant-planter families like the Thomsons and the Noells helped transform the English Caribbean colonies into sugar-producing islands dependent upon coerced labor. By 1650, there were approximately 12,800 African slaves in Barbados, and one contemporary source claimed that by 1652, there were 20,000 slaves on the island.[18]

Despite initial successes, however, these merchants increasingly found it difficult to keep up with colonial labor demand. Just as the Barbados plantation economy transitioned to sugar cultivation in the mid-1600s, colonial merchants were unable to take full advantage of this burgeoning labor market as war broke out in England, Scotland, and Ireland in 1642. Colonial planters attempted to take advantage of the confused political situation at home by trading with foreign merchants. Scholars have traditionally argued that Barbados planters turned especially to Dutch traders, who dominated the carrying trade and transatlantic slave trade by mid-century and supplied Barbados with provisions, capital, and labor in the form of African slaves. Although English merchants had been supplying the English Caribbean colonies with slaves and Barbados's transition to a "sugar and slave" economy was well under way, the influx of foreign traders increased the number of slaves coming to Barbados by the late 1640s and 1650s. By 1660, the number of slaves on the island had more than doubled in ten years, to 27,000.[19]

War and political upheaval in England not only disrupted transatlantic trade, but coincided with significant demographic and economic changes that made it far less likely for people to migrate voluntarily as indentured servants. This established a pattern that continued for the remainder of the century. A number of historians have noted that voluntary migration to English colonies peaked during the 1650s, when approximately seventy thousand people migrated. Thereafter, the numbers of English and all European migrants diminished, especially after 1660.[20] Other historians have agreed that there was a general decline in the number of people leaving England for the colonies after the Restoration, and especially by the early eighteenth century. In striking contrast, the percentage of Africans arriving in English colonies increased exponentially during these decades. During the 1650s, Africans made up about 65 percent of all migrants into Barbados, and for the remainder of the seventeenth century, Africans always remained above 78 percent of the total. By the eighteenth century, English men and women were not simply forgoing the West Indies colonies where slavery had taken root as the main source of labor; they were also no longer going to the North American colonies in significant numbers, either. Instead, servants settling in the growing mid-Atlantic colonies of Pennsylvania, East and West Jersey, and New York increasingly came from places like Germany and Ireland.[21]

This decline in voluntary migration from England was the result of a number of factors, including war as well as accounts of hard work, disease, and death in the tropics, which had made it back across the Atlantic and diminished the appeal of such a voyage. It was also likely related to a slight but tangible downturn in population in England during the mid-1600s. According to Wrigley and Schofield, from 1656 to 1671 England's population diminished by approximately 400,000 people, from 5.3 million to 4.9 million. Population decline during the middle of the seventeenth century resulted in higher wages for laborers, especially in rapidly growing urban areas. Although population decreased overall, urban centers in England continued to grow significantly. With wages rising, people were less likely to leave the country.[22] These factors combined to make it increasingly difficult if not impossible for planters in Barbados to rely entirely on indentured servants from England for their labor needs.

CONVICT TRANSPORTATION, KIDNAPPING, AND SERVANTS' REGISTRIES

Many scholars have noted that the drop-off in voluntary migration to the colonies during the mid-1600s coincided with a shift in the kinds of unfree labor being delivered to the colonies. Rather than relying on indentured servants, merchants with increasing regularity sent convicted felons sentenced to terms of labor in the colonies by the middle of the 1600s. The direct relationship between the decline in voluntary servant migration and the use of convict labor remains unclear, however. Richard Sheridan has suggested that the English Civil War slowed voluntary migration, and might have contributed to the use of convict labor in the colonies. In his study of forced labor in Barbados, Hillary Beckles argues that a dwindling supply of English servants by the late 1640s contributed not only to the increased use of African slaves but also to the turn toward convict transportation. Russell Menard, on the other hand, has argued that servant migration did not decline significantly during the 1640s, but that colonial labor demand, at least in Barbados, simply outpaced supply by the end of the decade. This in turn contributed to the use of convict labor and the rapid increase in slavery.[23]

Although convict labor had been part of England's imperial project since the early 1600s, the widespread use of transportation by the English state did not take place until the 1650s. Many of the same merchants who had been involved in the indentured servant trade were also at the forefront of transporting prisoners across the Atlantic. The Barbados planter and merchant Martin Noell was charged with transporting war prisoners from Ireland and Scotland in 1655, and planters in Barbados claimed to have received thousands of war prisoners from 1649 to 1655. Plans to populate Jamaica frequently included proposals for transporting prisoners. In 1657, Noell and his associate Thomas Povey proposed the formation of a joint-stock West India Company, which would "take aboard such servants, or such as by commissions given to Justices of the Peace [as] shall be collected of vagabonds, beggars or condemned persons, & proceed with them to Jamaica, which is to be a principal rendezvous of all the English interests there."[24] Although this proposal was rejected by the English government, the idea that prisoners could be used as a source of coerced colonial labor had taken root.

After the Restoration there were at least three attempts to pass legislation codifying transportation to the colonies as punishment for certain offenses. In addition, in the aftermath of political uprisings in London in 1661 and in the north of England in 1663, political prisoners were systematically sentenced to transportation. Laws against religious nonconformity, including the Quaker Act of 1662 and the Conventicle Act of 1664, also subject violators to labor sentences in the colonies. Most famously, over eight hundred men captured in the aftermath of Monmouth's Rebellion in 1685 were sentenced to ten years' labor in Barbados and Jamaica at Judge Jeffreys's "Bloody Assizes."[25] The increased willingness to use transportation as a form of punishment and as a source of colonial labor reflected a number of social and cultural transformations. In the first instance, it represented the further intertwining of imperialism and violence and the use of the empire as corrective "tool" of the state. Just as important, there seem to have been more convicts available for transportation by the mid-to-late 1600s. Cynthia Herrup has shown that over the course of the seventeenth century, increasing numbers of felons received a pardon of transportation to the colonies rather than a death sentence for certain noncapital crimes. But convict transportation never became a reliable source of coerced colonial labor during the seventeenth century. It has been estimated that only about forty-five hundred prisoners were sent to Virginia and the West Indies colonies between 1655 and 1699. This number does not include prisoners of war, which are much harder to quantify, but it is likely that the number of prisoners of war sent to the colonies during the second half of the seventeenth century did not amount to more than five thousand to ten thousand.[26]

There were a variety of reasons for the limited numbers of convicts sent to the colonies during the late 1600s, mostly having to do with how the trade was organized and structured. Its failure was also directly related to the increasing reliance on African slaves on the part of West Indies planters, which the English government hoped to exploit. The following case study of one colonial merchant's attempt to send convicts to Saint Christopher in the 1680s illustrates many of the problems in the convict servant trade and helps to explain why convict labor never became widespread during the seventeenth century. In contrast to Barbados and to a certain extent Jamaica, the Leeward Islands were scarcely populated and underdeveloped by the late 1670s. Only Nevis, the smallest island (thirty-six square miles), had any significant sugar plantations or population.[27] Saint Christopher had been the first island settled in the Caribbean by the English in 1624, and its population grew steadily in the middle decades of the century. But it lagged behind its neighbors because it was extremely vulnerable to attacks by the French, who occupied half the island. The colony was devastated by the Dutch and French wars of the 1660s, and after the hostilities, many English chose to leave the colony altogether.

A primary concern for the imperial authorities, then, was maintaining and increasing the English settler population against the threat of French incursions. In addition, the assemblies of the four islands frequently lobbied the Lords of Trade for servants to fill the militias and work the colony's plantations. Christopher Jeaffreson, a sugar planter on Saint Christopher, wrote in 1677, "wee grow weake by depopulation." He continued, "Nor is there any great hope of the contrary, seeing soe few white servants are sent hither." Men with skilled trades were especially coveted, and according to Jeaffreson, those making the journey could expect a life of prosperity at the end of their term of service. That same year he wrote to his agent in London, "I confess all servants are very acceptable here; and if any laborious and industrious men would transporte themselves, I should gladly receive them and allow them the customs of the country, with meate, drink, lodging and clothing, as are necessarie." But skilled men were extremely hard to come by. William Freeman, a Leeward Islands merchant based in London, indicated in 1678 that although he would do his best to provide the colony with servants, "tradesmen are very scarce. I could not gett one this 2 yeares to send, and those I sent formerly on high wages."[28] The difficulties in attracting skilled laborers to the colony reflected the fact that voluntary servant migration to the English Caribbean colonies had significantly declined by the late 1600s.

In response to a number of letters and reports from the colony's governor and leading officers, the King-in-Council in June 1677 approved a plan to send "malefactors," or convicted felons, to the colony. Despite the endorsement of imperial authorities, as outlined at the beginning of this chapter, the case of the "300 malefactors" was beset with repeated obstructions and delays, which illustrate many of the problems related to the trade in convict labor. The scheme awaited a merchant not only willing to deliver the prisoners but to take full legal responsibility for them by paying an up-front security bond that would be forfeited should any of the malefactors escape (these bonds were usually paid by investors, who would get their money back after the convict's term had ended and if the convict had not escaped). In June 1681, three years after the initial proposal, the deputy governor of Saint Christopher, Colonel Thomas Hill, let the Lords of Trade know he was willing to take the prisoners; the Lords of Trade asked for £10,000 in bonds. Three months later, they were still searching for someone to pay the bonds. In September 1682, the Lords of Trade issued an order that each of the three hundred convicts would require £100 security.

It is unclear why what had once been £10,000 now cost a whopping £30,000, but the order did elicit a response. In November 1682, the Lords of Trade heard from Christopher Jeaffreson. The Saint Christopher planter now lived in London, and he petitioned the Lords of Trade requesting that the security bond be lowered, assuring them that planters would keep close watch over the convicts because it was not in their interest to let their laborers escape. He also requested that once in the colony, the convicts serve eight-year terms rather than the customary four. The Lords of Trade agreed to lower the bond to £20 per prisoner and to the increased term of service. Jeaffreson soon reported to his plantation steward that despite "the charge and trouble of sending malefactors over, which are greater than ever I could imagine," he was hopeful that the scheme would work.[29] He was joined in a partnership in the venture with Deputy Governor Hill and a merchant named Mr. Vickers.

Jeaffreson soon ran into a number of difficulties. A few weeks after issuing his petition, he and his associates sent out inquiries to prisons in and around London in search of convicts. That search revealed "very few men, and *those* not worth sending." And his prospects for the near term did not look hopeful, because he learned that the order for the "300 malefactors" was restricted to London and Middlesex jails. As a result, he realized, "it will take up some tyme to ship off the full complement, because 300 men are not condemned [to trans-portation] in one or two counties in two or three years tyme." In addition, Jeaffreson reported, "The keepers of the prisons oppose us, and must be bribed." Upon trying to collect some convicts sentenced at the Old Bailey in March 1683, Jeaffreson was stopped by Captain Richardson, the keeper of Newgate Prison, who claimed that "the prisoners were [already] disposed of." Two days later, the Privy Council heard a petition from some Jamaica merchants offering to take both female and male prisoners to their colony; Jeaffreson had agreed only to take the men. The Old Bailey judges had "disposed" of the prisoners to these merchants, whom Jeaffreson suspected were friends with Richardson. Jeaffreson appealed to the Lords of Trade, but they were "of opinion that the men and women ought to be taken promiscuously out of the gaols in order to be transported." In the following months, Jeaffreson remained adamant that women and children not be included among the three hundred prisoners sent to Saint Christopher. In the wake of the revelation of the Rye House Plot against Charles II and the Duke of York in the summer of 1683, Jeaffreson hoped that large numbers of plotters would be sentenced to transportation, which "will make the number of men that fall under that sentence, exceed far that of the weomen."[30] But it appears no new groups of prisoners included only men.

Eventually, Jeaffreson relented on the issue of female prisoners, and after presenting imperial authorities with a list of twenty-one prisoners he intended to deliver, in June 1684 the Lords of Trade issued an order, later approved by the king, that all male prisoners condemned to transportation "as shall bee hereafter transported be sent to Saint Christopher till ye number of three hundred be compleated."[31] Almost immediately, however, Jeaffreson ran into further obstructions. Sir Thomas Jenner, Recorder of London, one of the justices at the Old Bailey and a loyal Tory servant to the Crown, seemed uncertain about the new order requiring that all men condemned to transportation be sent only to Saint Christopher until three hundred had been delivered. In addition, he and Jeaffreson squabbled over the "quality" of the convicts to be sent. Jeaffreson wanted to choose the healthiest possible prisoners, but Jenner argued that merchants could not pick and choose. In August, the king issued a letter to the Sheriffs of London, indicating that the convicts should be "transported indifferently & without choice," and if Jeaffreson continued to "refuse to take them in that manner, Our Will and Pleasure is that they may be delivered to such other Person for their transportation." Jeaffreson finally relented and on September 8 sent twenty-eight prisoners—twenty-three men and five women—to Saint Christopher. He had to provide his own armed guards to help march the convicts from Newgate to the docks, having been refused assistance by officials "because the soldiers, as the officers say, must not intermeddle with the civil power, unless upon a very special occasion."[32]

Jeaffreson's problems did not end with this shipment of convicts, however, and he continued to have difficulties with London politicians and officers. Captain Richardson, the keeper of Newgate who had obstructed the first batch of prisoners, in early 1685 accused Jeaffreson and his partners of not landing the prisoners at Saint Christopher, because he did not have any confirmation of their arrival. Jeaffreson and his associate Vickers were called before the justices at the Old Bailey, where "the Lord Mayor seemed much dissatisfied with us." A frustrated Jeaffreson concluded "the whole business is that the persons whose interest it is to oppose us, spare no clamours, raise all objections, and make all interest they possibly can against us, to prevent our taking off the present parcel." It did appear he faced a fairly united opposition to his plan, but nevertheless in April 1685 he and Vickers sent a further thirty-eight prisoners—thirty-one men and seven women. The merchants had to purchase handcuffs and shackles themselves, and Jeaffreson led the guard marching the prisoners to the ship. Despite "a guard of about thirty men, they committed several thefts, snatching away hats, perrewigs, &c., from several persons, whose curiosity led them into the crowd." Jeaffreson warned Hill that "they certainly are a parcel of as notorious villaines as any that have been transported in a long tyme." Adding to Jeaffreson's woes, it soon became apparent that his business partners in the scheme, Hill and Vickers, had cheated him out of his third of the profits (such as they were) from the sale of the convicts. He still awaited payment from Hill well into 1686.[33] Needless to say, this appears to have been Jeaffreson's final foray into the business of sending convicts to the West Indies. Of the three hundred originally planned in 1677, fifty-six had been delivered by 1685.

There were obviously fairly specific reasons why this scheme to bring three hundred convicts to the Leeward Islands failed, and it is true that Jeaffreson seems to have had more than his share of bad luck. As the work of historian John Beattie has demonstrated, convict transportation as it was organized in the seventeenth century was beset with difficulties, many of which Jeaffreson encountered. Jeaffreson's experience confirms that merchants could choose the prisoners they thought would yield the highest prices in the colonies, and that they had to pay exorbitant fees to jail keepers in order to get the prisoners they wanted. Merchants were also not paid up front for their services and often had to purchase their own handcuffs and shackles as well as pay private guards to assist delivering convicts from jails to the shipyards. These costs made the trade in convicts expensive and risky. In addition, colonies became less receptive to receiving convicted felons by the late 1600s. For example, Virginia and Maryland passed laws against receiving convicts in 1670 and 1676, respectively.[34]

It is likely that Jeaffreson's difficulties were also related to a crackdown by the government on the kidnapping of servants by unscrupulous merchants in the 1680s. Jeaffreson himself was well aware of this problem. In November 1682, he wrote to friends in Saint Christopher expressing concern about a case recently heard at the King's Bench involving the kidnapping, or "spiriting," of servants to the colonies. Such people had been either deceived into serving as indentured servants (sometimes while intoxicated), or had been forced to board a ship heading to the colonies. Although instances of outright kidnapping were probably rare, historians have uncovered the existence of complex "spiriting" networks in places like Bristol and London, and the few court cases that resulted gave the servant trade a bad reputation and seem to have hurt business in a number of ways.[35] In the wake of the 1682 case, the Lords of Trade issued proposals to try to prevent kidnapping, which included creating a servants' registry, into which all indentured servants leaving port cities had to be entered. They also suggested requiring servants to be bound in the presence of local magistrates as well as new restrictions on binding children under the age of fourteen. Jeaffreson felt that because of these new regulations it would be even harder for merchants to procure servants. "This is a general discouragement to the merchant," he wrote, "[and] the procurer, and the masters of ships, who are very scrupulous of how they carry over servants."[36]

Although it is perhaps difficult to understand his sympathy with merchants who might have been willing to kidnap unsuspecting young people, often children, to a life of drudgery in the colonies, Jeaffreson did have a point. The presence of servants' registries seemed to limit the total number of servants leaving England, which might have been why they were implemented. A later effort to revive a servants' registry illustrates this point. In April 1689, the merchant Edward Thompson, an MP and alderman from the city of York, petitioned the king to hold the patent on an office for registering servants. This agency, versions of which had been established in 1664, 1672, and 1686, existed to ensure that each indentured servant sent to the colonies was sent legally and not under duress. "To that end that neither any of your Majesty's subjects may be liable to be unduly spirited away from their masters or parents," his petition read, "nor any persons exposed to undue prosecution, after they shall bind any such as shall be sent over, in the said office, and have their names registered in a book publicly kept in the office for that purpose." After some legal squabbling with others who claimed to already hold the patent, Thompson was granted a license, which he held until 1699. There is little evidence, however, that, other than holding the patent, Thompson ever accomplished anything with his license.[37] Nevertheless, the revival of the servants' registry indicated a number of interesting developments in the servant trade by the late 1600s.

As Thompson argued in his petition, the registry was supposed to serve as a deterrent to kidnappers who "spirited" servants to the colonies. Stories and rumors of being "spirited" to the colonies had detrimental effects on the servant trade. First, it made people wary of going to the colonies because of the hardships they might face, and it also had the effect of discouraging merchants from participating in the servant trade for fear of being falsely accused of kidnapping. As a result, servants' registries limited the number of merchants involved in the servant trade, and therefore the number of servants leaving England likewise diminished. David Harris Sacks has shown that the city of Bristol's *Registry of Servants to Foreign Plantations* was only ostensibly an attempt to stop kidnappers from "spiriting" servants to the colonies. According to Sacks, the rules surrounding the *Registry* were revised in 1662 by the Bristol Common Council, dominated by men sympathetic to the generally Anglican and Royalist Society of Merchant Venturers. The Merchant Venturers were an exclusive trading company that had been slow to enter the transatlantic colonial trade and had grown jealous of the success of Bristol's colonial traders, many of whom were religious nonconformists. The limits that the Bristol *Registry*'s regulations placed on the servant trade in the form of fees and oaths were designed to exclude these smaller independent merchants, many of whom were Quakers unable to swear oaths. Interestingly, there was a significant drop in the number of servants sent from Bristol after 1662.[38] Fewer merchants, it seems, meant fewer opportunities for people to leave and might have contributed to the drop-off in voluntary migration to the colonies during the second half of the 1600s.

Servants' registries not only discouraged merchant participation but also served as a potential barrier to emigration because they added an extra layer of bureaucracy to the process. In 1690 the colonial merchant Dalby Thomas wrote that the presence of servants' registries "Occasions new Offices, new Fees, new Methods, for sending Servants thither, all which increases their price in the *Indies* very considerably, and falls as bad as a Tax on the Industry of the Planter; besides makes Servants so scarce, that a universal languishing of such plantations that are growing happens thereby." It is also possible that attempting to register servants indicated a certain amount of anxiety on the part of imperial authorities that perhaps too many people were leaving England. By registering servants, officials could keep better track of just how many people were leaving the country. Edward Thompson's attempt to revive the registry office in 1689 and Jeaffreson's difficulties sending convicts to the colonies the previous decade were indications that by the late seventeenth century, the English government was not interested in sending its own people to the colonies. In fact, convict transportation did not become systematized and organized by the state until the passage of the Transportation Act of 1718/19. The act allowed certain offenses to be punishable with seven years labor in the colonies and granted an exclusive contract for transporting all prisoners to one merchant, with costs paid directly by the Treasury. The vast majority of British convicts sent to the American colonies, nearly fifty thousand people, came in the aftermath of this legislation. They mostly arrived in the North American colonies rather than the West Indies, where African slavery had become widespread.[39]

It was also significant that Jeaffreson's scheme faced problems and obstructions from a number of London Tories, such as Sir Thomas Jenner, the Recorder of London. By the 1680s, for a variety of reasons explored in chapter 6, Tories dominated City politics, including the office of sheriff, a number of judgeships, and the office of Lord Mayor. Jeaffreson's difficulties with London Tories might have had something to do with their commercial interests, specifically their involvement with the Royal African Company. Shortly after the departure of the first shipment of convicts in 1684, Jeaffreson issued a new proposal to the Commissioners of the Treasury for money to transport another one hundred "malefactors" to Saint Christopher. After "several months," Jeaffreson reported, the petition was rejected, "By which I am debarred of any hope of expectations to have the prison-fees discharged by the Sheriff, as was proposed." Jeaffreson had been thwarted by the new Tory Sheriffs of London, Peter Daniel and Sir Samuel Dashwood. Dashwood and his brother Sir Francis were original subscribers to the Royal African Company, and Samuel regularly served on the company's Court of Assistants. The company, which held a monopoly on all trade to and from Africa, including the slave trade to the colonies, had been founded by royal charter in 1672 and was closely run by its governor, the Duke of York. By the 1680s, the African Company was almost exclusively a Tory commercial bastion.[40] It is possible that Samuel Dashwood (who later became Lord Mayor in another Tory ascendancy in 1702), loyal to the company and the Crown, was simply not interested in promoting the servant trade to the West Indies in any form. Servants, even those coming as convicts, could have potentially limited the colonial demand for African slaves.

CHANGES IN POLITICAL-ECONOMIC ATTITUDES

What triggered this apparent anxiety about migration to the colonies in the late 1600s? How did colonial planters and merchants, not to mention the state, address these concerns? The heightened concern with kidnapping, coupled with the general failure of convict transportation as a source of colonial unfree labor in the seventeenth century, was likely related to changes in attitudes about the various "multitudes" that seemed to plague English society in the earlier part of the century. By the mid-1600s, the poor, vagrant, and even criminal populations were not necessarily considered to be threatening to society. Paul Slack has indicated that by the middle of the seventeenth century, concerns about vagrancy decreased and therefore the drive to send the unemployed out of the kingdom diminished. Overall population contraction by the middle of the seventeenth century, outlined above, was a major factor in this generalized shift in thinking about the poorest members of English society. In contrast to the earliest decades of the century, by the mid-1600s the poor were no longer considered a threat to social stability, but rather an economic resource to be better managed and exploited. Therefore, rather than sending convicts and other dangerous elements to the colonies, perhaps they could be rehabilitated into laborers at home. Instead of shipping out its problematic "multitudes," the English state should instead work to maintain and increase overall population levels and focus on how to best employ the population for England's economic "improvement."[41]

As mentioned above, utilizing servants' registries and discouraging the widespread adoption of convict transportation might have been attempts to control emigration. John Beattie has traced the failure of convict transportation to take root in the seventeenth century to changing ideas of labor and wealth, and the notion that emigration of any potential workers out of England was increasingly thought to be against the national interest. This was reflected in contemporary political economic literature. Whereas earlier in the century there was widespread concern that England had too many people and that colonies could help relieve these burdens, by the second half of the 1600s a number of political and economic writers grew concerned that England did not have enough people to sustain economic growth. As we have already seen, historical demographers have determined that England's population declined during the middle decades of the 1600s by as many as four hundred thousand people. A number of writers blamed migration to the colonies for this phenomenon. In 1670, the political writer and economic theorist Roger Coke warned that England's Atlantic empire was detrimental to the nation's prosperity. "Though England be the most excellent and convenient place for Trade of all others," Coke admonished, "yet our practice and ordering it, is contrary to the nature of it." He continued, "the abundance of our people . . . are diminished in peopling our Plantations, and in re-peopling Ireland."[42] Colonies, rather than relieving England of its overabundant multitudes, actually drained England of its most precious economic resource, its people.

Coke was not alone in his criticism of England's overseas empire. "You find fault because some of our people go to Ireland, and the Plantations," wrote the pharmacist, economic thinker, and future Royal Society member John Houghton in a fictional dialogue in 1677, "and say we want people at home to fill out Cities and Countrie-towns." Samuel Fortrey, a place-seeker from a Dutch merchant family, argued in 1663 that those colonies that could enable England to substitute goods it had usually imported from foreign rivals were generally beneficial. But he added the strong caveat that "otherwise it [colonial expansion] is always carefully to be avoided, especially where the charge is greater than the profit, for we want not already a countrey sufficient for double our people, were they rightly employed." The political and economic writer William Petyt despaired in 1680, "England never was so populous as it might have been, and undeniably must now be far less populous than ever, having so lately peopled our vast American Plantations." Instead of focusing on acquiring overseas territory to ship excess poor and indigent people, these commentators emphasized the value and importance of keeping a well-managed population at home for England's economic prosperity. Many writers even urged the state to ease immigration laws and allow legal toleration for all Protestants to encourage people to come and do business in England.[43] Colonies, it seemed, directly competed with England for wealth and other resources.

Scholars of early modern natural philosophy and scientific thought have often considered these perspectives as part of a general trend in the literature of "improvement" that emerged in the mid-1600s. Philosophers of the Hartlib Circle, for example, focused on harnessing nature's infinite potential for improvement by investigating and experimenting with agriculture, husbandry, industry, and credit as ways to increase resources and therefore national wealth. They became interested in gathering accurate information and organizing concrete "facts" in order to better control the natural world. Population was part of this natural world to be harnessed and promoted. By the middle of the seventeenth century, economic literature reflected this shift in opinion in terms of the economic potential of well-managed populations. Many writers and theorists, such as Sir William Petty, who was also skeptical of colonial expansion, no longer concerned themselves with dangerous multitudes and subgroups, but rather with the economic potential of the population as a whole. This desire for accurate data informed writings on trade and wealth creation and represented a turn away from viewing the world's resources in the realm of human endeavor as naturally limited.[44] If properly managed, human labor could improve natural endowments and thus create wealth. The state should therefore do its utmost to promote domestic population growth.

In addition, there was a shift in thinking about the relationship between the economy and the state during the early modern period. In order to successfully compete on the international stage, states needed money, and some argued that governments should focus on promoting the economic welfare of their people. Economic interest, in other words, should be the reason of state, and population should therefore be encouraged. The idea that colonies could be used as dumping grounds for undesirable populations from England did not entirely recede, however. Colonial promoters and officials continued to argue that colonies could benefit the home country by easing domestic population.[45] However, as the remainder of this book will show, this argument decidedly diminished over time as the West Indies colonies in particular became increasingly reliant on the labor of enslaved Africans.

Did the colonies contribute to England's population decline of the mid-1600s, as so many of these contemporaries suspected? Through an analysis of colonial population estimates, Henry Gemery has projected that about 378,000 people left England, Scotland, and Ireland for the American colonies from 1630 to 1700 (the vast majority were from England). More than half, or about 210,000 people, emigrated during the early part of the period, from 1630 to 1660.[46] So it is plausible that the critics of empire were reacting to a material reality that there were actually fewer people in England, and it seems equally likely that emigration to the colonies played an important role in these downward demographic trends.

CONCLUSION

The failure of indentured servitude and convict transportation as viable sources of coerced labor in the English Caribbean colonies during the 1600s was the result of a number of factors, including changing domestic demographic and migration patterns, as well as shifting attitudes about the economic possibilities of a well-managed domestic population. Although there is no denying the role of colonial labor demand, these political and cultural changes in England played a significant role in the transition to the widespread use of enslaved Africans as the main source of unfree labor in the West Indies. Just as popular debates over population, labor, and colonial expansion became more heated in the mid-1600s, the English state became increasingly involved in overseas imperial conquest as well as a desire to profit from the slave trade to English and other European colonies. The remainder of the book seeks to answer the question of how and why slavery and English imperialism became so deeply intertwined during the late seventeenth and early eighteenth centuries by exploring the competing interests and imperial agendas of colonial planters, merchants, and the English government. It will show that the triumph of African slavery in the colonies had as much to do with political, economic, and social concerns in England as it did with labor demand in the colonies.

COMMONWEALTH AND PROTECTORATE IMPERIALISM: THE WESTERN DESIGN AND ITS CONSEQUENCES, 1654–1660

In April 1655, nearly eight thousand English soldiers and sailors, under the command of General Robert Venables, landed on Hispaniola with the intention of capturing the island from the Spanish in a plan known as the Western Design. They hoped to take the city of Santo Domingo, but Venables and his regiments accidentally landed nearly thirty miles from the city and had to march for days though difficult terrain in extreme drought conditions. Almost immediately, the undernourished and ill-trained forces began to drop dead from heat exhaustion, thirst, and dysentery. After two failed attempts on Santo Domingo, in which at least one thousand soldiers lost their lives, Venables and the other leading officers held a council of war to decide how to proceed. In May, the English fleet left Hispaniola and made its way to the Spanish colony of Jamaica, where they initially met little Spanish resistance. Although Spain refused to admit defeat for nearly two decades, by June it was clear that the English intended to stay. But the capture of Jamaica was barely considered a consolation prize by contemporaries. Hoping for bigger glory in Hispaniola, Lord Protector Oliver Cromwell was deeply disappointed when he learned of the conquest. And although Jamaica proved much easier to overpower, the island's early years as an English territory were uncertain at best. Disease and guerilla attacks by remaining Spaniards and Maroon communities of former slaves combined to make settling a permanent colony no small task. And it seemed the Protectorate governments were not up to the challenge: by 1661, the island had approximately three thousand white inhabitants and about five hundred black slaves.[1]

Despite these precarious beginnings, however, the conquest of Jamaica was a defining moment in English imperial policies and projects in the New World. Previously, colonial acquisition in the Americas had been the reserve of trading companies and individual entrepreneurs. But the Western Design was the result of a bold imperial plan on the part of the Protectorate's Council of State, one that had an enormous impact on the course of English imperial expansion during the second half of the seventeenth century. As this chapter will show, the plan itself embodied a brand of imperialism that emerged during the middle of the seventeenth century, especially among an influential group of colonial merchants and their political allies. Many of these merchants had made their fortunes selling servants and slaves to Virginia and the West Indies and wanted to expand their presence in the growing transatlantic market in servile labor. They also hoped to use the military campaign against Spain to bring existing colonies under stricter metropolitan control, which meshed with the Cromwellian state's desire for territorial expansion and firm military hegemony. Such plans met resistance, however, in places like Barbados, where planters had developed their own imperial ideal, in which metropolitan authorities by and large did not interfere with the political or economic life of the colonies. This chapter begins with an investigation of Commonwealth imperial policies and the ideals of those men who financed and orchestrated the Western Design. It continues with the Design's implementation and the problems experienced orchestrating the plan in Barbados. Finally, it considers the conquest of Jamaica and its first years as an English colony and explores the imperial ideologies behind its development. It will show that at the heart of the Western Design was the idea that empire building through territorial acquisition and strict commercial regulation was necessary to expand servant and slave markets and increase England's national wealth.

COMMONWEALTH IMPERIALISM

The Western Design represented a turning point in English imperial designs because for the first time the English government was directly involved in a plan that aimed to expand the realm across the Atlantic. Many of the same merchant-planters and their allies who had created, sustained, and expanded the transatlantic servant and slave trades to Virginia, Barbados, and the Leeward Islands helped to plan and organize the scheme known as the Western Design. According to the historian Robert Brenner, many of these merchants reached an apex of political influence during the period of the Commonwealth (1649–1653). Many were named to important government committees charged with reorganizing the navy, customs collection, as well as determining Commonwealth commercial policies. These men included the colonial merchant Maurice Thomson and his brother Robert, who was involved in the slave trade as well as interloping ventures in the East Indies; their brother George, who was a member of the Council of State and the head commissioner of the navy; the longtime colonial trader William Pennoyer; his brother Samuel, another merchant; and Martin Noell, who had significant business and family connections in Barbados, and was one of Maurice Thomson's key business partners. Brenner describes this group as an association of political independents with close connections to radical Puritan elements in and around London, many of whom were involved in colonial endeavors, especially in the Massachusetts Bay Colony and the Providence Island Company. They attempted to take quick advantage of the political power they gained in the wake of the execution of King Charles I in 1649.[2]

This group had a two-pronged imperial strategy, with both commercial and military elements. Throughout the Commonwealth period, these men and their political allies were instrumental in influencing legislation that specifically sought to remove the Dutch and other foreigners from carrying English colonial produce and provisioning English colonies with supplies and African slaves. They wanted to reestablish English trades and manufactures that had been disrupted during the 1640s.[3] In addition, they aimed to bring those colonies that refused to recognize the legitimacy of the new government under stricter metropolitan commercial, military, and political control.

The plans of this merchant group meshed well with those of the Commonwealth government, which had a strong imperialist agenda, including the desire to conquer territory in the Caribbean and the submission of semiautonomous regions within Britain to its authority through land confiscation, forcible settlement, and revenue extraction geared for the benefit of the metropolis. This imperial ideal was apparent in the first instance in Ireland and Scotland. Cromwell's determination to put an end to the uprising begun in Ireland in 1641 led to brutal attacks on the cities of Drogheda and Wexford in the fall of 1649. In the coming years, the New Model Army under the leadership of Henry Ireton and Charles Fleetwood would exact atrocious assaults on the Irish. After the military conquest of the country was complete in 1652, the English Parliament passed the Act of Settlement, which outlined a policy of forcibly removing not only Catholic Irish but Catholic Old English landowners to designated settlement areas, mostly west of the river Shannon. About three thousand Catholic landowners were forced to surrender their land, which was then handed over to New Model Army officers and personnel in lieu of pay. Land was also designated for English settlers deemed "worthy" by the government to settle in Ireland. In conquering Ireland and orchestrating a massive transfer of landownership based on forced removal and migration, the Commonwealth made its aggressive vision of empire evident.[4]

After subduing Ireland in late 1649, Cromwell turned his attention to Scotland. Since James VI of Scotland became James I of England in 1603, the English had contemplated with varying degrees of seriousness schemes to incorporate Scotland and England into a British polity. Scotland had of course played a crucial role in the Civil War, and when news of the regicide reached Edinburgh, the Covenanters proclaimed Charles II king of the Scots and king of Great Britain and Ireland in February 1649. Fortunately for the English, the Scots were continuously plagued by ideological disunity, and Charles II proved a woefully inadequate military leader and diplomatic strategist. Two crucial defeats of Scottish forces—first at Dunbar in September 1650 and then at Worcester a year later—triggered the Cromwellian occupation of Scotland and the transportation of prisoners of war to the American colonies. After years of negotiations, Scotland was politically incorporated into England in April 1654. Unlike Ireland, it was not subject to a policy of massive resettlement and plantation, but the subjugation of Scotland stemmed from a similar imperial impulse.[5]

The Commonwealth's treatment of its American colonies also reflected this imperial agenda of conquest, submission, and settlement. After the execution of Charles I, colonial governments were uncertain about the direction of the government in England. Many colonists in Virginia and the Caribbean were deeply ambivalent if not overtly hostile to the new regime. Virginia was the first colony to proclaim for Charles II in the autumn of 1649. Sir Philip Bell, the governor of Barbados, remained neutral for as long as possible but was eventually forced to declare for the monarchy after a coup by planters claiming royalist sympathies in the spring of 1650. A number of planters who supported Parliament's cause then fled for London, where they attempted to drum up support to suppress the rebellion. The response by the Council of State to this insubordination in Virginia and Barbados illustrated the Commonwealth's forceful imperial policy. After learning of the rebellion in Barbados, the committee of the navy, directed by George Thomson, Maurice's brother, drew up an act establishing an embargo on all trade to and from the disloyal colonies. This "Act Prohibiting Trade with the Barbada's, Virginia, Bermuda's, and Antego" of 1650 was designed to punish disobedient colonies by blocking access to all foreign merchants and markets. Not surprisingly, colonial governments were not happy with the law. The council and assembly of Barbados issued a declaration that innovatively argued that because they lacked representation in Parliament, they should not be "bound by [its] regulations." It also emphasized the important role Dutch merchants had

played in supplying the colony and in helping establish and maintain planta-
tions in recent years, something also emphasized in Virginia's official reaction.
Even the colonial bastion of Commonwealth political and religious ideals,
Massachusetts Bay Colony, was dismayed by the act.[6]

In addition to the embargo, the English government decided that military
force would be necessary to ensure colonial compliance with the new regime's
imperial and commercial policies. In 1651 the navy sent a small fleet under the
command of Sir George Ayscue to Barbados to force its submission to the
Commonwealth. Ayscue, who had led the English naval forces in Ireland, arrived
in Barbados in the fall of 1651, and proceeded to blockade the island for three
months. There were a few skirmishes, but the royalist governor, Francis, Lord
Willoughby, surrendered to Ayscue once the commander of one of his largest
regiments, Colonel Thomas Modyford, defected to Parliament's cause after
being promised a place in the island's new government. By flexing its military
muscle, the Commonwealth had won the obedience of a colony on the brink of
civil war. The English government also sent a small fleet to Virginia in late 1651,
which quickly won submission in early 1652. Although the terms of the surrender
granted Barbados the freedom to trade with foreigners, as Robert Bliss has argued,
"it was made clear that these [colonial] governments did not exist by virtue of
local mandates," but instead through Parliament's authority and grace.[7] The
Commonwealth had a strong imperialist agenda in which colonies were commercially, politically, and militarily subordinate to the metropolitan government.

Traditionally, the 1650 embargo and the subsequent passage of the first
Navigation Act in 1651, which prohibited all colonial trade with foreign merchants,
have been interpreted as some of the earliest examples of the mercantilist policies
that came to define early English imperialism. But they should also be understood as representing a clear vision of empire espoused by the colonial merchants
and their political associates on the Council of State and the newly created
Council of Trade. There has been a long-standing scholarly debate about the
exact influence, if any, of the colonial merchants over the creation and passage of
the Navigation Act. I argue that a variety of interests, including the colonial
merchants, political and religious radicals, as well as those in charge of diplomatic affairs, orchestrated and supported the Navigation Act and its provisions
limiting foreign access to English markets. What unified this disparate group was
hostility toward the Dutch for a variety of political, economic, and ideological
reasons.[8] In his defense of the Navigation Act, Benjamin Worsley, who served on
the Council of Trade and had financial interests in Virginia, explained that the
act was designed to promote colonial trade in the national interest at the expense
of "the Hollanders." Closely associated with the colonial merchant group,

Worsley made the familiar mercantilist argument that because of Dutch commercial success, England had necessarily lost wealth and treasure. To reverse these fortunes, England had to be prepared to fight the Dutch for empire as well as trade, "by weakening their shipping and draining them by degrees of their treasure and coin." This could be achieved through commercial restrictions, war, or a combination of both. In fact, the Navigation Act of 1651 became law only after the Dutch had rebuffed English overtures to form a political union, which would have eliminated commercial competition between the two countries. Because of this failure, the Council of State and the Council of Trade felt that they were left with little choice but to retaliate, and in addition to passing the 1651 act, war was declared against the Netherlands the following year. The Navigation Act was a clear indication that the English state was now directly concerned with how to promote overseas trade and empire for the benefit of the country using restrictive commercial policies. The willingness of the Commonwealth to utilize strict commercial legislation and military force, or at least the threat of military force, indicated a new imperial direction for the English government.[9]

THE WESTERN DESIGN: PLANNING AND IMPLEMENTATION

It is in this context of an aggressive foreign and imperial policy that the desire to wage war against Spain in 1654 must be understood. This overarching strategy—so apparent in the decisions to conquer Ireland, occupy Scotland, and send naval fleets to subdue the American colonies—also influenced the decision to attack Spain in the New World. The government's imperial agenda became more belligerent in the aftermath of the creation of the Protectorate in late 1653. In becoming Lord Protector, Cromwell effectively became a monarch in all but name, but one equipped with a well-trained modern army and navy and a growing fiscal-military state. One of Cromwell's first goals as Lord Protector was to end the ongoing war with the United Provinces. He and his allies felt that the Spanish were a much more serious threat to the stability of Europe in general and to England in particular. Although Cromwell was probably personally motivated by strong anti-Catholic prejudice and a sense of religious providentialism, declaring war with Spain was not simply a resurrection of the Elizabethan desire to advance the Protestant cause. For many, Spain had to be defeated because of its desire to establish a universal monarchy and hinder England's political and economic prosperity.[10]

While the terms of the Dutch peace were worked out in the winter and spring of 1654, Cromwell and his Council of State turned to discussing the

potential costs and benefits of war with Spain. In order to hobble Spain economically, it was decided that it had to be cut off from its supply of bullion from its
American possessions. According to notes written by Edward Montagu, the
future Earl of Sandwich, at a meeting of the Protector's Council on April 20,
1654, the possibility of intercepting the Spanish plate fleet carrying New World
bullion was one of the major motivating factors for "undertakinge the Designe
of Attempting the Kinge of Spaine in the West Indies." Evidence from this
meeting revealed there was also a clear desire, even at this early stage, for empire
building. Naval Captains Henry Hatsell and William Limbery, both experienced merchants who had traded in the Caribbean, indicated that it was "very
feasible" to take both Hispaniola and Havana, Cuba, from the Spanish in a short
amount of time in order to "have command of the Spaniard's fleet." In addition,
in taking Hispaniola, "our people from New England, Virginia, the Barbadoes,
the Summer Islands, or from Europe," could then settle on that island. Such a
plan would also help to pacify Scotland by providing territory to forcibly remove
Scots, "being not in our view to be setled without a transplantation of 8 or 10000
bodies of men every yeare." Although those opposed to the mission, most notably
General John Lambert, warned that in retaliation Spain would cut England off
from European trade, Hatsell and Limbery replied that "notwithstandinge our
warr with the Spaniard in America, it is possible, if not reasonable to expect that
wee may have peace and trade in Europe." In fact, it seemed that the Protectorate
was counting on Spain's inability to finance such a war or maintain any real
allies while engaged in hostilities with England.[11]

It is revealing that the Protectorate Council turned to Hatsell and Limbery
for expert advice. Both men, in addition to being naval officers, had traded with
the Spanish in the New World and had ties to the colonial merchant community in London. Others known to have been supportive of waging war against
Spain in the New World included Secretary of State John Thurloe and the
colonial merchant-planter Martin Noell, who was Thurloe's brother-in-law.
Attacking Spanish America was not a new idea for these men and their associates. Maurice Thomson and the merchant William Pennoyer had orchestrated
extraordinarily successful privateering raids against the Spanish at the behest of
the Puritan Providence Island Company from 1638 to 1641. In 1641, the year the
Spanish recaptured Providence Island from the English, Sir Benjamin Rudyerd,
a director of that company with known connections to Thomson and a long
history of anti-Spanish prejudice, called for the creation of a "West Indie
Association" establishing a merchant marine that would have aimed directly for
the Spanish possessions in the Caribbean. According to Rudyerd, Spanish colonies were the king of Spain's "[gold] mines in the West Indies, which minister

fuel to feed his vast ambitious desire of universal Monarchy." Fears of Spanish aspirations for universal monarchy had by the 1650s blended with apprehensions that England was losing the empire game to its European rivals and the vast wealth that went along with it. In order to catch up, England had to conquer territory, gold, and trade routes from its enemies in the New World. Jealousy of other nations' economic and imperial prosperity dominated the political-economic discourse of the 1650s. For some, like the Parliamentarian army officer and pamphleteer Samuel Lambe, war and trade went hand in hand as "chief ways that make a nation rich and flourishing."[12]

Although the navy began to provision ships for the expedition to Spanish America, the debate in the council continued on July 20, 1654. Lambert persisted in raising objections about cost and feasibility, but Cromwell insisted that he had been informed "that this designe would cost little more then laying by the shipps, and that with hope of greate profitt."[13] Although the folly of Cromwell's desire to fight Spain in the New World would soon become apparent, as the historian Timothy Venning has argued, the design made perfect sense for the Protectorate. It would be cheaper and more effective than a continental war; it would utilize soldiers and sailors idled by the end of the Dutch war; and previous experience had shown that relatively small forces could inflict serious damage in the Caribbean. In addition, Cromwell seemed to believe that English merchants were effectively prohibited from trading with the Spanish in the New World and had suffered from Spanish reprisals. Although trading with the Spanish was illegal, plenty of English merchants (presumably Hatsell and Limbery included) managed to trade surreptitiously in Spanish America with a significant level of success. Whether or not Cromwell knew this and chose to ignore it, or was genuinely unaware of the local situation, he embraced the idea that Spain had to be forced to allow Protestant English traders access to their goods and markets. The idea that Spain had regularly broken peace treaties and trade agreements both in Europe and in the New World was utilized as a major justification for the war and might have been encouraged by merchants who wanted even greater access to Spanish wealth.[14]

Indeed, many colonial merchants were directly involved in the planning and implementation of the Western Design against Spain. John Limbery (William's brother), Martin Noell, and Maurice Thomson served on an advisory committee organized in August 1654 for planning and financing the Western Design. Other merchants appointed to this committee included Andrew Riccard, William Williams, and William Vincent, who were all involved in the Levant and East India Companies; Riccard and Williams were also both aldermen in the City of London in the 1650s. The fact that such men were involved in the Western

Design suggests that some "traditional" merchants were by the mid-1650s also interested in colonial trades. Although many of these merchants were religious Independents or Puritans, they were not necessarily interested in religious reasons for fighting Spain. They wanted to attack Spanish colonies and establish new English ones for their own personal profit and to increase England's national wealth.[15] As merchants, they all hoped to expand English markets in the colonial trades of sugar, servants, and slaves.

The role of colonial merchants in supporting war with Spain in the New World seems apparent. Historian Stephen Saunders Webb, however, has argued that the London-based merchants in fact opposed the war against Spain at first and only came to support it after they received contracts for provisioning the naval fleet. He argues that the vision of empire espoused by these men, in which English colonies would develop large plantations manned by "servile labor" producing agricultural goods for the home market, was emphatically not imperialist. Yet the merchant agenda he outlines was very much imperialist, albeit amorphous and subject to shifting political and ideological allegiances. It was this ideal of conquering new colonies and creating new markets for unfree labor that the Western Design sought to promote. Colonies conquered from the Spanish would provide English merchants with new opportunities to profit from the trade in servile laborers, including an increasing number of African slaves. In fact, the question of the imperial nature of the Western Design seems to have been a concern of some in England during the planning stages. Some worried that Cromwell's aspirations for overseas territorial conquest would undermine Parliament's fragile authority and that he even hoped to be crowned "emperour."[16] The politics of the Protectorate and its imperial designs were understood as interconnected by contemporaries.

The influence of the Western Design's planning committee, made up of so many colonial merchants, also seems to undermine Webb's assertions. In August 1654 the committee made suggestions for personnel in the existing colonies to oversee and help plan the expedition. Among their proposed commissioners in Barbados were Governor Daniel Searle and Colonel Thomas Modyford, who had switched sides from royalist to parliamentarian during Ayscue's submission of the colony in 1652. Modyford, who was serving as speaker of the Barbados Assembly, had made a fortune with a five-hundred-acre sugar plantation with nearly one hundred slaves and over two dozen servants, and was connected to both Noell and Thomson through the sugar trade. As early as 1652, Modyford had offered his services to the Commonwealth "to enlarge the English dominions in the West Indies," and that year had been instrumental in the English plan to colonize Guiana on the northern coast of South America.

He envisioned the development of plantation colonies driven by the labor of indentured servants and African slaves as necessary to increase England's (not to mention his own) power and profit. Other commissioners suggested by the committee included Martin Noell's brother Thomas, the secretary of Barbados, and Maurice Thomson's brother Edward, also resident on the island.[17] It was partially through such kinship and business connections that men like Noell and Thomson were able to exert so much influence over imperial designs. They had valuable, firsthand information from the colonies, which the Protector and the Council of State took seriously.

In addition to choosing commissioners, the committee selected military officers to lead the expedition. They chose General Robert Venables to take charge of the army, and General William Penn to control the naval forces. Venables was a long-serving Parliamentarian army officer whose regiment was instrumental in the bloody siege of Drogheda, Ireland, in 1649. Venables was then stationed in Ulster from 1649 to 1654, where he oversaw the suppression of Irish and Scottish Presbyterian resistance to the English army and state. He was also a close associate of Martin Noell's. Penn was a naval officer who had also been involved in the conquest of Ireland and led forces in the First Anglo-Dutch War. The son of a Bristol merchant, he also had connections to England's growing colonial merchant community and was known to have radical religious tendencies and a strongly militaristic and providential view of contemporary politics.[18] The selection of Venables and Penn to lead the forces in the West Indies expedition made sense, as they would have been well versed in the agenda of conquest, land confiscation, and forcible settlement espoused by the Cromwellian state.

Throughout the summer and fall of 1654, the planning committee also set about organizing the provisioning of the fleet with food, weapons, and men. This was not without its difficulties, for there were problems finding enough men for the expedition, as well as resistance from those impressed into service. In November 1654, a group of sailors presented Cromwell with a petition complaining that being impressed to serve in this latest expedition was not only unfair to those who had "sacrificed themselves" in previous conflicts, but it was "inconsistent with the Principles of Freedom and Liberty, to force men to serve in Military imployments, either by Sea or Land." They demanded to be "as free as the Dutch Sea-men" as well as to receive the payment of arrears, which had been delayed for many months. On November 8, Martin Noell agreed to advance £16,000 "at instance of the Protector and Council for two fleet and forces," presumably to help pay off some of this debt.[19] Noell's advance indicated not only his financial power over the expedition, but his willingness to support the design to the utmost.

To help plan the overall strategy of the Western Design, the advisory committee turned to Colonel Thomas Modyford, the wealthy plantation owner and speaker of the Barbados Assembly. He argued that ultimately the Spanish Main should be the primary goal of the design. To attempt the sparsely populated Spanish islands, as had been suggested at the Council of State meetings, would bring years of arduous work to the English, "whereas on the main you will meet with good towns, well peopled, with a few Spaniards and many Indians, whom they keep in slavery, and who very probably will be faithful to milder masters." In addition, relatively deserted islands would require constant supplies of English settlers, "which may too much exhaust our native country of men, and render us weak at home." He continued, "but on the main you have Indians to practice on, whom without dispute, will be politic and rational means be as so many hands gained to the commonwealth." The primary reasons for attacking "Terra Firma," however, were financial and strategic. "By settling the islands you provoke the Spaniard, but do not at all disable him of his revenge; but by settling on the main, you do not only take from him the benefit of his pearl, and the mines of gold and silver already open, but also hinder the passage of his treasure from Peru, and lay Peru fairly open to an invasion." Modyford's final point elucidated his own opinion about how the plan should be put into effect. "Lastly, it will be necessary, of the person who shall command in chief of these forces, have a power to command all the governors of the English in any part of America; and that his highness's orders be directed to them to that purpose: and though I verily believe, that every man will be forward to embark on this design, yet it is wisdom to have a power of pressing, which on some extraordinary occasions may be made use of."[20]

Modyford's imperial plan did not mention any religious or providential reasons for going to war. By purposely understating the strength of Spanish forces and population, Modyford portrayed an empire-in-waiting, one that could be developed on the cheap, something that intrigued Cromwell, his ministers, and their merchant allies. It was a plan that would not require moving people from England in the short term, nor would it require many resources to help pay for such a venture. Instead, Native Americans as well as the residents of Barbados and the other existing English colonies would provide the necessary labor in the form of displaced small planters and former servants. But Modyford knew that planters in Barbados might not be willing to allow their own labor force to leave and settle in other colonies. Therefore it was necessary that those in charge of the expedition had total power over local colonial governors and officers to raise forces. Modyford's suggestions were especially important because much of what he insisted upon was included in the commissions and instructions for those placed in charge of the expedition. Cromwell's commission to Venables gave him "full power and authority to command the several and respective governors of the islands of Barbadoes, Bermudas, Antegoa, and other the Caribbee islands, and of all other English plantations in America; and all other officers and ministers whatsoever in the said islands and places." Venables was authorized to implement martial law whenever and wherever he felt necessary and was given the power to impress all people and "such carriages, draughts, boats, and other vessels, as in your discretion shall be thought needful for the conveying and conducting of the said army and forces, or any provisions, or utensils or war, necessary or requisite for the same army."[21] The willingness to grant the officers such extraordinary military powers indicated that the regime was not simply interested in diverting Spanish bullion to England or in religious justifications for fighting a Catholic enemy. It was attracted to the idea of expanding English dominion, trade, and markets across the Atlantic through extensive military force.

Venables was also given broad planning powers over the operation. His official instructions left it up to him to "levy and raise such numbers of souldiers [at Barbados] as shal be found necessary for the better carrying on of this design." It was also left up to him, in consultation with Penn and the other commissioners, to decide the best plan of attack. One option was to attempt to take one or more of the Spanish islands first, most likely the city of Santo Domingo on Hispaniola, "not being considerably fortifyed may probably be possest without much difficulty, which being don, and fortifycd, that wholc Island wil bc brought under obedience." This would have had the benefit of attracting English settlers, and providing a springboard for other conquests, including Havana, Cuba, "which is the back doore of the West Indies, and will obstruct the passing of the Spaniards Plate Fleete into Europe." The second option was to go for the South American continent first, as Modyford had urged, "in one or more places between the River Orinoque and Porto Bello, aymeing therein cheifly at Cartagena, which we would make the seate of the intended design." Modyford's vision of empire on the quick and cheap was clear in this second possibility, which provided "houses ready built, a country ready planted, and most of the people Indians, who will submit to you, there being but few Spanyards there as is informed." Venables's instructions continued, "You wil be able to put the Country round about under Contribution for the maintenance of the Army, and therewith by the Spoile and other wayes probably make a great present returne of profit to the Commonwealth." Ultimately, and presumably with the advice of the other commissioners, Venables chose the first option.[22] This decision, however, does not diminish the imperial underpinnings of the

Western Design as a whole. Both possibilities demonstrated that the campaign was not meant to be a purely military enterprise but was understood as a way to expand English commercial and imperial interests through territorial acquisition, the creation of plantation colonies, and the expansion of the servant and slave trades into new colonial markets.

BARBADOS AND THE WESTERN DESIGN

In December 1654, a fleet of thirty-eight ships with about three thousand soldiers and sailors left Portsmouth for Barbados to begin the Western Design. Although the governor of Barbados, Daniel Searle, had been made one of the plan's commissioners, the arrival of the fleet in January 1655 triggered serious tensions in the colony. As the island's planters were about to learn, the Western Design reflected the regime's aggressive imperialist agenda by bringing existing English colonies under stricter control of the Protectorate's commercial laws and political authority. Venables and Penn were sent with instructions not only to seize military control if necessary, but to rein in illegal trading with foreigners by enforcing the 1651 Navigation Act and condemning foreign ships. Soon after they arrived, the commissioners established a Prize Office in the colony to handle such seizures. The ever-present Colonel Modyford was placed in charge of the office to send the benefits of condemned ships and cargoes back to England. This was an extremely contentious issue for the Barbadians, who claimed they relied on Dutch and other foreign merchants for capital investment in their plantations and to export the island's sugar, as well as to provide them with provisions and African slaves. English colonial merchants had wanted to end Dutch dominance of trade in the West Indies for years, and the Navigation Acts had been designed to do just that.[23] But enforcement had been a serious problem. They wanted Barbados brought into line for the benefit of English merchants, and the Western Design seemed a perfect opportunity to try to achieve this goal. This addition to the commanders' instructions revealed the aggressive imperial ambitions of the state.

Almost immediately after the arrival of the English fleet, there were significant conflicts between the Western Design's commissioners and Barbados planters, many of whom were in the colony's assembly. Commissioner Edward Winslow reported to Secretary of State Thurloe from Barbados that in accordance with his instructions, General Penn had seized and condemned for prize sixteen Dutch ships in February 1655. This resulted in a "tryall at comon law," where all the island's lawyers "were taken up for the strangers [the Dutch], and none could be procured for the state." Not surprisingly, the local jury found for the Dutch merchants who had traded illegally "grounding all upon the articles of Barbadoes," ignoring the theoretical reach of the Navigation Acts. "The Dutch were courted, and highly prized," Winslow continued, "and sent home in a triumphant manner, to invite them freely to the trade of Barbados; by which means many more of them are expected before the end of May next."[24]

This conflict between competing authorities and jurisdictions established a pattern of confrontation that lasted for the remainder of the century. The Barbadian planters in the assembly were by and large willing to pledge political loyalty to England and the Protector, but they were loath to allow that to extend to the commercial realm. They had been living without significant imperial control or interference over their commerce for nearly thirty years and were both resentful and fearful of what the Western Design represented militarily and economically. This confrontation in 1655 represented a key moment in the evolution of the colonial planter imperial ideal, which embraced a plantation empire based on servant and slave labor but not the state's attempts at subordinating the colonies to its commercial and political control. The Barbados planters fully understood the imperial implications of the design. "Some of the planters," reported one commissioner, "being of malignant spiritts (as indeed most of them are) signifie their follyes in venting their calumnious words against not onely the designe, but the powers by which we come and the parties employed in it."[25] On the other hand, the Western Design's planners equally resented the autonomy of the Barbados planters and their blatant disregard of commercial laws. Their vision of empire was one in which colonies existed to supply England with agricultural raw materials and serve as markets for servile labor and English manufactured goods. For the merchants behind the Western Design, imperial authorities had to do their utmost to remove foreigners from English colonial trade in order to make sure that profits made it to England and English merchants.

Governor Searle and the men of the Barbados Assembly resented the commissioners' attempts at limiting their established means of conducting trade and commerce. But this was only one area of conflict. As Modyford had urged, Venables was given absolute authority over Searle and local officers in all military affairs. Not only could he impress men into the expedition's forces without interference from the governor or assembly, but he was also charged with reorganizing the island's militia as he saw fit, and he had the authority to confiscate the colony's excise duties for his own use. The most contentious issue was recruiting forces for the expedition. Modyford reported that before any troops had been raised, Venables informed the assembly "that they expected 4,000 men from hence, and did desire, that to avoid the inconveniencys, which might happen by their soldierly way of raysing them, that the assembly would present them with a list of names of the freemen and unengaged." Modyford continued that "Instead of a fayre complyance, I found such a willfully imbittered party, that instead of debatinge calmely, they fell a clamouring against the quarteringe soldyers in ther houses . . . and would come to no conclusion but this, [to] let them [the commissioners] beat up drumes and take ther owne course, we wil not assist them." This is precisely what Venables and the other commissioners set about doing.[26]

The island's planters were outraged by the way they were forced to allow four thousand men to leave as soldiers for the Western Design. One officer sent with the expedition, Lt. Col. Francis Barrington, admitted that because recruitment was "left to the discretion of our officers, who endeavoured to gett as many men as they could not valuing who was undone, such was the irregularitie of this carriage that many lost all their servants." He went on to explain that many recruits who left Barbados had significant debts on the island and used the chance to serve in Cromwell's army as a means to escape the island's creditors. Even Modyford acknowledged this had occurred. The men of the assembly placed the blame for their losses squarely on Modyford, who because of his past willingness to switch political allegiances did not have the best reputation on the island.[27] One member of the commissioners' service wrote to Thurloe: "Here's in the island one Collonel Moodiford and Mr. Nowell, secretary to the island's affairs, who are hugely distasted by this island; for that they two, as the islanders say, did invite our forces over hither, which our islanders are generally against." Thomas Noell was "Mr. Nowell," the brother of the London-based merchant Martin, a close ally of Modyford's. The actions of both men, with their kinship and business connections to those who had orchestrated the Western Design, alarmed many in Barbados. Modyford's insistence that the officers in charge of the military expedition have supreme authority over local officers left Governor Searle and the assembly offended and worried for the future. Searle explained to Cromwell that many on the island were concerned that as a result of Venables's commission, "two powers, the one for the military, the other for the civil, should be here extant, as two distinct authorities over them."[28] Bringing Barbados under the firm grasp of the Protectorate government caused a significant rift in an already fragile relationship between the colony and England. It represented a major turning point in English imperial policy, as the Protectorate tried to bring existing colonies under firmer control. It was also a defining moment in the evolution of the planters' imperial ideal, which in contrast depended upon a more flexible relationship to metropolitan authorities.

THE CONQUEST OF JAMAICA AND
PROTECTORATE IMPERIALISM

The English fleet, supplemented by about four thousand men from Barbados and another twelve hundred from the Leeward Islands, headed for Santo Domingo on Hispaniola in April 1655. In their hurry to begin the expedition, Venables and Penn left Barbados without sufficient provisions of arms and food. After missing their target of Santo Domingo, Venables and his regiments had to march for days through rough and unfamiliar territory, and within a few short weeks at least one thousand soldiers were dead. After regrouping, Venables, Penn, and the other commissioners decided to head for another Spanish island, and in May the fleet made its way to Jamaica, where they met little Spanish resistance. Upon taking Jamaica, Venables and his officers immediately set about defending their actions to Cromwell and the imperial authorities. Rather than focus on the disaster of Hispaniola, they attempted to describe Jamaica as a desirable acquisition. Three weeks after landing on the island, Commander Daniels wrote to Thurloe that Jamaica "far exceeds all others in America for fertility in all manner of things, fruits and cattle, horses so good as any in England." Similarly, Venables and Captain Gregory Butler explained that Jamaica "lyeth more advantageously for the annoying the Spaniard on every side, than Hispaniola; neither is it inferiour in itself, for we find it to abound with store of fish, fowls, cattle, fruits of all sorts usual in these parts." They optimistically added they had heard there was a silver mine on the island. Major Robert Sedgwick, a commissioner and Puritan who had lived in Massachusetts, wrote from Barbados, "Many think Jamaica a more considerable island than Hispaniola." Thomas Modyford joined the chorus supporting Jamaica's prospects. "It hath an excellent harbour," he explained, "and is accounted the most healthful and plentiful of them all. It will be sooner filled [than Hispaniola], and is far more convenient for attempts on the Spanish fleet . . . And believe it, this will more trouble the court of Spain than ten of the other."[29]

Jamaica's geographic position in the center of the Caribbean Sea and apparently boundless potential, however, could not disguise the fact that English soldiers and sailors could barely survive on the island. Many of the same letters that explained how Jamaica could be transformed into an important and successful colonial settlement also described the hunger, disease, and death that accompanied the English troops there. Supplies were slow in coming and those that did arrive were woefully inadequate and at the point of rotting. The results were disastrous. Major Sedgwick wrote to Cromwell shortly after arriving on the island in November 1655, "Soldiers die daily, I believe 140 every week;

and so have done ever since I came hither. It is strange to see young lusty men, in appearance well, and in three or four days in the grave, snatched away in the moment with fevers, agues, fluxes and dropsies, a confluence of many diseases." Sedgwick offered by way of explanation: "The truth is, God is angry, and the plague is begun, and we have none to stand in the gap . . . there hath been, I fear, in all this design nothing but wrath and heavy displeasure." Adding to his misery, Sedgwick complained that the soldiers were unwilling to plant food for their own survival. "I believe they are not to be paralleled in the world," he later wrote, "a people so basely unworthy, lazy and idle, as it cannot enter into the heart of any Englishman." Venables similarly lamented in a letter to Martin Noell, "Our wants [are] great; our difficulties are many; unruly raw Soldiers, the Major part, ignorant; Lazy dull Officers that have a large Portion of Pride, but not of Wit, Valour, or Activity." Circumstances were so dire that both Penn and Venables left Jamaica for England separately in June, Penn because he felt there was nothing more to be done, and Venables because his own health had deteriorated.[30]

Despite the horrendous circumstances on the ground, the commissioners had little choice but to hold out hope for Jamaica's future and felt it was of the utmost importance to transform the island from a military garrison into a permanently settled plantation colony. This had been the goal of the Western Design from the beginning. Although not nearly as large as Hispaniola, Jamaica's size of 4,411 square miles, twenty-six times the size of Barbados, made it all the more promising to its promoters. From Barbados, Modyford urged "his highness and the council to send speedy and great supplies of men, arms, ammunition, and clothes [to Jamaica] . . . I hope our nation will not draw back, having thus far entered." Even the pessimistic Sedgwick expressed hope that the island not be abandoned because "if some good encouragement were given to increase planters here, [Jamaica] might be well." Many of the officers set about making this transition a reality. After the departure of Venables and the death of Major General Richard Fortescue in October 1655, Colonel Richard Holdip was left in charge of the island. He managed to turn his army regiment into a functioning plantation at Liguanea, near Spanish Town. Sedgwick, who had worked as a merchant in Boston, was also active in advocating a plantation future for Jamaica and did his best to encourage civilian immigration.[31]

Word of the devastating loss at Hispaniola reached England in July 1655. Upon learning of the failure of his design, Cromwell fell into despair. Like Sedgwick, he felt that God was angry with the English and specifically with him.[32] When Penn and Venables arrived in England in September, they were called before Cromwell and the Council of State to answer for their apparent failures. In his frustration, Cromwell threw the generals into the Tower of London for abandoning their forces and for failing to capture the Spanish plate fleet on their return voyages. But despite his deep disappointment and spiritual self-doubt, the Protector chose to hold on to Jamaica rather than abandon it. In fact he proceeded to declare war against Spain officially, as planned in October, claiming the Western Design was not a new war but a continuation of old wars against Spain in the New World. Perhaps he agreed with Thomas Modyford's assertion: "I am most confident, that if this place be fully planted, which in three or four years may with ease be done, his highness may do what he will in the Indies."[33]

Cromwell and others decided that the problem was not in the imperial designs of his ministers and merchant allies, but rather the men recruited to execute the plan. "If we look with an impartial eye," explained one pamphlet in late 1655, "upon the major part of those that came out of England to be (as indeed they were) raw Soldiers, Vagabonds, Robbers and runagate servants, certainly these Islands must be the very scum of scums, and mere dregs of corruption." Many of the commissioners blamed those recruited in Barbados and Saint Christopher in particular. "I believe they were a people much bound up in the thoughts of their own strength," wrote William Godfrey from Jamaica in April 1656, "not considering the power of God's ability in subverting their covetous expectations of Indian treasure into dust." As late as September 1656 a newsletter to William Clarke, secretary to the army in Scotland, reported that "there were not left of the land soldiers upon Jamaica above 1,500 . . . some dying before being over-run with a spirit of laziness that they have not wrought anything in a way of a plantation."[34]

Jamaica clearly needed a fresh supply of people. In order to succeed, the colony had to be perceived as friendly to nonmilitary interests, such as planters and merchants. There were many official plans to populate Jamaica with settlers from as early as two months after the initial conquest. In August 1655, Cromwell issued a proclamation to encourage the settlement of the island by offering "that every planter or adventurer to that island shall be exempt and free from paying any excise or custom for any manufactures, provisions, or any other goods or necessaries, which he or they shall transport to the said island of Jamaica." The proclamation also declared that it was the goal of the English state to transform Jamaica from a military outpost by "the constituting and settling of a civil government" as quickly as possible. In addition, Cromwell encouraged the governors of other English colonies to help settle the island. In a letter to the governor of Bermuda, Vice Admiral Goodson indicated that Jamaica would be happy to welcome settlers from that colony, and intimated that a number of settlers under the leadership of Governor Luke Stokes of Nevis planned to leave that colony for better prospects in Jamaica. Cromwell also sent Captain Daniel Gookin, an influential Puritan and occasional resident of Massachusetts, to New England in December 1655 with the purpose of recruiting settlers for Jamaica. To encourage Bostonians to move, Gookin arrived with a proclamation promising "Ships for transportation; a sufficient proportion of Land to them and their heirs for ever near some good harbour in the said Island; Protection (by Gods blessing) from the enemies; a share of all the Horses, Cattle and other beasts, wild and tame upon the place freely, Together with other Priviledges and Immunities." Officers in Jamaica promised to assist Gookin to send the settlers to the new colony.[35]

Plantation and migration, forced or otherwise, characterized Cromwellian imperialism, and plans to populate Jamaica with hardy laborers and godly servants coincided with similar efforts in Ireland. Often these endeavors involved the same people and families; Daniel Gookin's brother Vincent, for example, was instrumental in promoting English settlement in Ireland. As in the case of Ireland, promoting migration to Jamaica often involved the Scots. Sending people from Scotland to the New World had been part of the original discussions of the Western Design in the spring of 1654. In a letter to Thurloe in September 1655, Lord Broghill, Lord President of the Council of Scotland in Edinburgh, indicated that there was a proposal to send people from Scotland to Jamaica. "If I doe not mistake," Broghill noted, "there are three sorts of persons to be exported, viz. such men, as are to be recruits; such as are to be planters; and such women, as will go over with their husbands, or will adventure to seek husbands there." In addition, in the spring of 1656, Cromwell established a "committee for managing the affairs of Jamaica" that included Martin Noell and Thomas Povey, the merchants and army officers Captains Thomas Alderne and Stephen Winthrop, and Colonel Tobias Bridges. In June 1656 they issued a report to Cromwell urging him "to support Jamaica as your principal fort and settlement in the West Indias." They suggested that Scottish Highlanders be sent to the island by contracted merchants, presumably Noell and Povey themselves. The English were also encouraged to migrate, and by 1657 pamphlets promoted the commercial potential of planting in Jamaica and argued that the settlement of the colony was in the "Public Interest."[36]

The Protectorate seemed committed to promoting Jamaica's development into a successful plantation colony. The only plan that came to fruition, however, was the scheme to transplant fourteen hundred people with Governor Stokes from Nevis. Although it was clear to the Western Design's commissioners and planners that the permanent settlement of the island was of the utmost importance, Jamaica's transition from military conquest to plantation colony was by no means certain. Despite official encouragements and proclamations, few people were willing to risk death from war or disease to settle on Jamaica. Without serious financial and administrative support from England, Jamaica could never develop into a viable colony for soldiers, merchants, or planters. The men of the Jamaica committee grew increasingly impatient with the Protector. The tone of a report issued by Noell, Povey, Winthrop, and Bridges in June 1656 betrayed a growing frustration, "for as yet Jamaica looks only like a garrison, and rather as an Army then a colony." They perceived a lack of serious interest on the part of the Protectorate with the development of Jamaica and with the management of imperial affairs generally. Colonel Edward D'Oyley, who arrived in Jamaica to help fortify the island in late 1655, lamented to Thurloe that "wee are a desolate, and almoste an abandoned people."[37]

There were, of course, good reasons for this apparent neglect. By the spring of 1656, the government lacked the necessary funds to continue carrying out the war with Spain. Constant fears of further Spanish attacks made diminishing the military presence on the island impossible. In 1657 and 1658, in fact, the Spanish attempted to reconquer the island but were thwarted by successful campaigns led by D'Oyley. D'Oyley, a close friend of Thomas Povey, was a staunch Parliamentarian and New Model Army officer who was sent to Barbados in March 1655 to raise a regiment for the design and arrived in Jamaica later that year. He quickly rose through the army ranks and by 1657, due in part to the deaths of so many of the other officers, was in charge of the colony. D'Oyley became one of the most vocal proponents of Jamaica's need for civilians, especially planters and merchants, to settle on the island. In October 1656, as commander in chief, he convened a council of war to decide "the disposal of ye several regiments of ye Army in places convenient within this island for and towards their settlement by way of planting." Other remaining officers also actively tried to promote planting. Lt. Col. Francis Barrington, for example, had hopes of building a "sugar work" as early as 1657. The situation on the ground was slow to improve, however, and D'Oyley continued to send letters describing a desperate want of provisions, arms, ammunition, and, most of all, people on the island.[38]

The situation in Jamaica was well known in England. One pamphlet from September 1655 claimed that the Western Design "is now indeed the discourse of the Nation." There were plenty of people who were skeptical of the execution of the entire plan, which became a focus for critics of the Protectorate throughout 1655–1656. Many argued that Cromwell's imperial plans smacked of monarchical aspirations. Others felt that Jamaica was a distraction from more important domestic political and economic concerns. One observer maintained that the entire Western Design was part of an imperial scheme orchestrated by Cromwell and his cronies to crown him emperor of a vast British dominion, which included Scotland, Ireland, and the American colonies. "It remained only," the author concluded, "that he should make himself Lord Paramount, King or Emperor over the whole, and the succession of his heirs."[39]

The exorbitant costs of the war, the poor execution of the design, and the militaristic direction of the government were the primary topics of debate when Cromwell was forced to order the election of a new Parliament to fund the war in the summer of 1656. There was a proliferation of pamphlets on the Spanish war and its consequences. One urged people not to be afraid to vote their consciences against Cromwell's candidates, and appealed to the popular memory of the tragedy that befell the army and navy in Hispaniola and Jamaica. It urged people to remember "the cries of your poor brethren the honest Sea men, the wall and bulwark of our Nation against foreigners, who have so freely ventured their lives upon all accounts and calls, and are now barbarously forced from their wives and children to serve the ambitious, and fruitless designs of one man?" Others embraced Cromwell's imperialist stance in the West Indies. "It is true, He is a Great Conqueror," one sycophantic sympathizer wrote, "yet his Mercy and Goodness are his best Arms and strongest Forces; for no bounds can be set to a *Royal* Gentlenesse, and the Jurisdiction of a Prince's love is unlimited." In the event, many of the MPs elected to the Second Protectorate Parliament in 1656 were deemed too hostile to the regime, and at least one hundred members were blocked from attending. One purged MP condemned Cromwell's "Kingly" aspirations, and warned people to "recollect at what vast charge he hath maintained those fleets and Armies for these two last years against the Spaniard." The fact that the Western Design played such an important role in the 1656 elections illustrates that the regime's imperial plans and the execution of the war against Spain concerned many in England. Not only were people troubled with the conduct and costs of the war and the terrible state of English forces, but some were also apprehensive of what the conquest of Jamaica and its development into a plantation colony meant for the Protectorate and the fragile English republic.[40]

Considering the desperate situation on the ground in Jamaica, the mounting opposition at home for the design, as well as the difficulties promoting the colony, it seems reasonable to ask why Cromwell and his ministers decided to keep Jamaica. It clearly would have been much simpler and cheaper to have abandoned the design altogether. Traditionally, historians have focused on Cromwell's religious convictions and anti-Catholic prejudices; to have given up Jamaica and the entire design would have been an admission of Protestant defeat, which he was unwilling to make. As evidence, they turn to Cromwell's opening speech to Parliament in September 1656, in which he described Spain as England's "natural enemy," and "a State that you can neither have peace with, nor reason from," that supported the interests of the exiled Stuarts at home and abroad. For example, Karen Ordahl Kuperman has emphasized the providential nature of Cromwell's Puritanism on his imperial decisions in the Caribbean. She places the Western Design and the ultimate decision to stay and settle Jamaica as part of a larger Puritan transatlantic imperial mission. The New England colonies were always considered a temporary stopping point in this mission, she claims, for the real goal of the Puritans was the establishment of a permanent colony in the West Indies.[41] After the loss of Providence Island to the Spanish in 1641, the decision to stay and settle Jamaica was a culmination of this godly obligation.

Cromwell's religious convictions and sense of providentialism, as well as his deep disappointment over the humiliating failure to capture Hispaniola, were certainly important factors that contributed to the decision to keep Jamaica. But the continued influence of colonial merchants over Protectorate imperial affairs should not be discounted. Seizing territory and trade routes from the Spanish and creating new plantation colonies as markets for servants and slaves had been their goal all along, and abandoning what the army and navy had managed to capture was not an option, as far as they were concerned. Those who had orchestrated the Western Design, however, grew increasingly disillusioned with its execution and what they perceived as a lack of serious interest in promoting Jamaica on the part of the Protectorate. In 1657, Martin Noell, Thomas Povey, and their associates attempted to make serious changes to the Protectorate's imperial administration by proposing the formation of a joint-stock West India Company. The company was envisioned for the "checking ye pride of the Spaniards" and "ye improvement of [England's] distant Dominions" in the West Indies. They proposed creating a company with Parliament's approval, designed with the purpose of promoting English commercial interests as well as settlement of more colonies. At first, the English navy would provide the necessary ships and ammunition, but once the company was established, it would be able to maintain itself through privateering raids on the Spanish plate fleet. According to the plan, the Protectorate would encourage the manning of such ships, but it would not incur any additional expenses by paying the recruits, as the seamen would be hired on the privateering standard of "no purchase, no pay," meaning that all income would come from plunder, "which is the greatest encouragement and temptation that can be applied on such occasions." Privateering, although seemingly at odds with commercial interests, was in reality another component of the merchants' understanding of empire as a fierce game of international competition. In fact, Noell and Povey's associates had been involved in privateering raids against the Spanish in the Caribbean decades earlier.[42]

According to the company's designers, the benefits to England would be manifold. First, it would ease the cost of maintaining and defending overseas colonies, especially "carrying on ye settlement of Jamaica." It would disrupt Spanish trade and force a commercial settlement between the two nations that would benefit England. In addition, the English state would profit from the prizes taken, as legally one-fifth of all condemned cargoes went into the Protectorate's coffers. The company would also send servants "collected of vagabonds, beggars or condemned persons, & proceed with them to Jamaica." These merchants continued to exploit the idea that England was overpopulated and popular fears of social disorder that went along with it. The major justification for the company, however, was that it would provide the cash necessary for maintaining Jamaica, which "must certainly be of vast expense to the State."[43]

This scheme for a joint-stock privateering company, licensed by Parliament, established to provide the financial support necessary for Jamaica's development, is a revealing example of mid-century imperialist ideology espoused by the Western Design's chief architects. They were not alone in believing that empire building, through colonial settlement and joint-stock company sponsorship, should be a primary concern of the state. John Bland, who later became governor of the English colony in Tangier, wrote in 1659 that a good way "to nourish and increase Trade and Commerce in this Nation, is, the carrying on, and settling by publicke hand all Forain plantations." According to Bland, the best way for the state to go about this was to promote trading "Companies and Corporations, the only Foundation and Pillar upon which a lasting Monument of Trade and Manufactories is to be built and preserved." By encouraging colonization and trade, "this Nation will find an admirable remedy for the disburdening it self of our supernumerary people which increase among us, without fomenting wars to be rid of them." Similarly, Samuel Lambe wrote in his 1657 pamphlet, "The people of England increasing so much notwithstanding the late wars, and the Land (though full of plenty) not increasing with them being an island, witness the many . . . daily going for Ireland and the Plantations, and yet there is no miss of them."[44] This imperial ideal of state-sponsored trading companies moving England's superfluous populations across the Atlantic matched the goals of men like Noell and Povey and their proposed West India Company.

After they presented this proposal to the Council of State in 1659, however, it appears to have been lost in the political chaos of the time. With the death of

Oliver Cromwell in 1658 and the political upheavals of the last Protectorate governments, Noell and Povey grew more discouraged over the state's failure to support Jamaica. Povey wrote to his friend Colonel D'Oyley in Jamaica, explaining his deep disappointment. "It must be sadly observed that no affaire of consequence was ever in any age engaged in by this nation undertaken with less controle, conducted with less prudence, attempted with less courage, prosecuted with less success, and attended from time to time with less care and assistance from the state, then this Expedition, which was entered into with soe much noise and braverie that it startled almost all the known world." Povey continued, "The old Protector and his Council were so much ashamed of the miscarriages of the first enterprize and were soe vexed and busyed in encountering those numerous ill consequences which have arised out of it, that they almost wholy did cast of[f] the thoughts of it, and as it were diserted it as unprofitable and remote and hopeless consideration." Noell and Povey both hoped that a new regime would help them realize their imperial vision, "as it was never the interest of the State to ingage in soe vast and important a designe."[45]

CONCLUSION

For all of its contemporary uncertainty, the conquest of Jamaica in 1655 was a key component of the imperial direction of the Commonwealth and Protectorate governments. The conquest of Jamaica galvanized an imperial vision in which the acquisition of overseas territory and its economic exploitation with servile labor explicitly characterized England's imperial policies and became the direct concern of the burgeoning imperial state. It fundamentally changed England's imperial outlook. The men who had orchestrated and financed the Western Design, including Martin Noell, Thomas Povey, Thomas Modyford, and Edward D'Oyley, wanted to capture territory from Spain in order to expand their markets in sugar, servants, and slaves. They also wished to assert imperial and commercial authority over existing colonies. In doing so they brought Barbados planters, who were developing their own imperial ideology, into conflict with the metropolis and the imperialism that the Western Design represented. Initially, the colonial merchants and their political allies found their plans of conquest and commercial control meshed with those of the Protector and hoped to develop Jamaica into a plantation colony as well as a base for privateering operations. They were deeply disappointed, however, with what they perceived as the government's failure to cultivate the island's full economic potential. These men could only hope that the imperial aspirations of the restored monarchy would better coincide with theirs.

3

RESTORATION IMPERIALISM: THE SHAPING OF IMPERIAL ADMINISTRATION, 1660–1671

With the death of Oliver Cromwell in late 1658 and the uncertain political situation in Britain, Governor Edward D'Oyley of Jamaica became extremely concerned for his colony and his position. "Your honours may now easily imagine," he wrote to the commissioners of the Admiralty in July 1660, "with what sorrow and unwillingness I part with this frigate, whose departure not only fills me with apprehension of our future condition but imprints into ye sense of being disserted by our Country." D'Oyley concluded, "All our hope rests in this, that when God shall give a settlement to ye nation, and put a period to those unnatural divisions, this unjust & useless war with Spain will either be owned or disowned, and accordingly retain either a vigorous resolution with a hearty concurrence of ye nation, or an absolute dissertion." D'Oyley had good reason to be concerned, because in fact it was not clear what Charles II would do with Jamaica. In 1656, Charles had promised Spain he would return the island when he recovered the throne, but by 1660 he felt no obligation to fulfill this promise. Rumors even circulated in the West Indies that the colony would be abandoned.[1]

In 1660 Jamaica was at a crossroads. It could be deserted with certain embarrassment, left as a military outpost to plunder the Spanish fleet, or developed into a plantation colony with full support from England.[2] For five years, the officers in charge of the island and the merchants and planters who had orchestrated the Western Design had urged the government to transform the military garrison into a settled colony for the benefit of traders and plantation owners. Despite proclamations and official encouragement, without considerable financial investment, administrative support, and a steady supply of people, this vision could never be realized. The merchants and army officers who had encouraged Cromwell to hold on to his conquest now had to convince the restored king to do the same and get him to promise a serious commitment to the colony.

Traditionally, historians have argued that the Restoration government, especially during its early years, lacked a coherent imperial agenda. Jack Sosin, for example, emphasizes the seemingly chaotic and unsystematic nature of Restoration imperial administration. Sosin and others have also argued that efforts by the restored monarchy to profit from colonial trade simply reflected the mercantilist outlook of a perpetually cash-poor Crown and not any underlying or consistent imperial agenda. Robert Bliss has rightfully placed the formation of the restored monarchy's imperial plans in the context of the political settlement at home. Rather than focusing on the Navigation Acts and other pieces of commercial legislation as essential to Restoration imperialism, Bliss argues that such laws and imperial policies more generally need to be understood as part of the regime's desire "to secure and then sustain its power." But in doing so he misunderstands some of the key political and social developments in the Caribbean colonies and dismisses the significance of monopoly trading companies to the English government, such as the African Companies, and the growing importance of slavery to Restoration imperial designs.[3]

This chapter investigates the competing imperial visions that evolved during the first decade of the Restoration. It focuses on the first two African Companies and the ways that different groups with colonial interests were forced to confront them and the political authority they represented. These companies, which were granted royal charters in 1660 and 1663, respectively, held monopolies on all trade to and from West Africa. Their monopoly was enforced by a joint-stock structure; only those subscribing could participate in the African trade, and planters could only purchase slaves from company agents in the colonies. Monopoly was considered essential to defeat international competition and represented a view of political economy in which wealth was necessarily limited. This did not merely reflect a traditional mercantilist economic perspective, however, because the imperialism embodied by the company had an explicitly political component, as well. The company's monopoly rested firmly in the authority of the king's prerogative through its royally granted charter. Belief in the definitive authority of the royal prerogative was one of the most consistent ideologies held by the later Stuarts. According to this position, the king had ultimate control over all political, economic, diplomatic, and military concerns. For Charles II and his brother the Duke of York, the administration of the colonies was the king's exclusive domain, and the royal prerogative allowed them to govern their entire empire as they saw fit.[4]

The African Company's monopoly was central to the overall imperial outlook of the restored monarchy and served as a commercial arm of the royal prerogative in the colonies. This brought the company into conflict with a variety of constituencies, including planters, privateers, merchants, and even colonial officials sent with orders to enforce its monopoly. It was in these confrontations that competing visions of empire emerged and evolved among these different (although frequently overlapping) interests. This, in turn, influenced the shaping of Restoration imperial policy. As this and the following two chapters will illustrate, the administration of the overseas empire by the later Stuarts was admittedly haphazard and uneven, and examining confrontations with the African Company provides a sense of the waxing and waning quality of early modern imperial administration. But disorganized implementation and the actions or inactions of unreliable servants did not betray a lack of imperial intent on the part of the Crown. Later Stuart imperialism needs to be understood as a trajectory of policies, laws, and customs over the course of nearly thirty years. Looking for "coherence" at one particular stage misses the point because it is necessary to understand adaptations to changing situations as part of an entire process of imperialism.

The imperial agenda of the restored monarchy was based on reaping the benefits of colonial servile labor through the use of monopolistic merchant/state enterprises, such as the African Companies. As the King-in-Council proclaimed in August 1663, these policies were crucial "for the keeping our plantations in a constant dependence on us & [to] maintaineth a thorough correspondence betwixt our subjects here & there, which in process of time otherwise would decay."[5] But this was more than simple mercantilism. Over the course of the 1660s, this vision evolved into an imperialism in which colonies were to be not only economically subordinate to the home country, but explicitly politically subordinate as well. Those with interests in the colonies, on the other hand, tended to emphasize the fact that they had enjoyed relative autonomy in the past and, as Englishmen, would like to keep enjoying such "liberties," especially that of "free trade." In doing so they developed a concept of a mutually dependent empire, in which colonies were understood to be economic and political extensions of England. Central to the development of both ideals was the expansion of African slavery and England's involvement in the transatlantic slave trade. As this and the subsequent two chapters will show, there were vigorous disagreements over how the slave trade and the empire should be managed. These confrontations revealed how slavery emerged as a key element of English imperialism both for colonists and for the Crown.

EARLY RESTORATION IMPERIALISM AND
THE AFRICAN COMPANIES

Those who had orchestrated the Western Design lost no time in 1660 trying to convince the new regime to keep Jamaica. Although many had been steadfast Parliamentarians, they were more than prepared to cooperate with the restored monarchy to promote their imperial and commercial interests. Charles II and his brother the Duke of York were equally willing to work with former Parliamentarians, many of whom were instrumental in bringing the Stuarts back to England, most notably General George Monck, who became the first Duke of Albemarle. In addition, many of the colonial merchants who had orchestrated the Western Design retained or resumed influence over commercial and imperial affairs. In 1660, the Privy Council established a Council of Trade and a Council of Foreign Plantations, both of which were designed by the new Lord Chancellor Edward Hyde, Earl of Clarendon. The councils shared twenty-eight members, including the merchants Thomas Kendall (Thomas Modyford's brother-in-law), Sir Andrew Riccard, and Sir Nicholas Crispe (a longtime trader to Africa), and the ubiquitous Martin Noell and Thomas Povey.[6] Historians have tended to dismiss the influence that merchants and colonial officials ultimately had over these councils, not to mention the overall importance of the councils themselves. But Clarendon's reliance on those with strong kinship and business ties to the American colonies should not be underestimated. Noell, Povey, and others had been intimately involved in the planning and implementation of the Western Design, and their access to information on the West Indies must have seemed invaluable.[7] Many of these merchants and experts on colonial affairs played an essential role in laying some of the key foundations of Restoration imperialism: the formation of the first African Companies, and the decision to retain Jamaica.

Charles II's government attempted to profit from its overseas empire by establishing joint-stock corporations that had trading monopolies granted by the king. In December 1660 the Company of Royal Adventurers into Africa was organized and given a charter by Charles II. It was founded by the Duke of York and his cousin Prince Rupert, with the support of a long list of courtiers and a number of men with colonial interests and close connections to Stuart households. Eight men who served on both the Council of Trade and the Council of Foreign Plantations were original subscribers to the company. They were mostly merchants, all had colonial connections, and some had been involved in planning and promoting the Western Design, including Crispe, Riccard, Sir John Shaw (a commissioner of the customs), John Colleton (whose brother Peter ran a large sugar plantation on Barbados), and, of course, Martin Noell and Thomas Povey. The company was given a monopoly on trade from the west coast of Africa for "discovering the golden mines and settling of plantations there." The Crown claimed two-thirds of all gold extracted by the company, which would retain the remaining third. To achieve these goals the company had extraordinary power to act with full military authority over all territory it conquered and settled in Africa.[8]

Cromwell's merchant allies found the restored monarchy sympathetic to their imperial ideals and commercial designs. Their next task was to convince the king to hold on to Jamaica and promote its development as a plantation colony, one where demand for African slaves would rival Barbados. In the first instance, the Privy Council solicited suggestions from Thomas Povey, who as secretary to the Council for Foreign Plantations was asked to gather information about Jamaica from merchants and army officers. Povey looked upon the Restoration as a fresh opportunity for investment and profit in Jamaica. In April 1660 he issued his report, which contained suggestions for providing the island with soldiers and provisions. But he also advised that the army be reduced in size and that prisoners from England be sent to the colony for its speedy settlement. The following month he issued a further report that provided twenty-five reasons why England should retain Jamaica, which included supporting those colonists who had already transported themselves at "vast charge." Povey also argued that Jamaica offered opportunities for people who "are forced to desert the [other] Carribbee Islands, their plantations being worn out, and their woods waste." He claimed that settling Jamaica "would be so obnoxious to ye Spaniard that probably he will rather permit a trade then prosecute so disadvantageous a warre." He concluded, "If the King doth owne and supply this people and place, hee may enable them to make a full compensation for the dishonour and miscarriage of the first Grand Design, but if they should be diserted or otherwise enforced to surrender the island on disadvantageous tearmes, the English honour will thereby receive new and irreparable wounds."[9]

The Privy Council also heard from Captain Thomas Lynch, who had served under General Venables in the 1650s. Lynch, who eventually became a governor of Jamaica and a major plantation owner, suggested that "a person of Honour & Reputation [must] be commissioned" governor of the colony. Lynch also urged that the army be disbanded, not only because the soldiers had proven themselves unwilling to plant, but because "the very name of soldier is generally so much dreaded that persons of quality have alleged, that they removed not to Jamaica, because they would not live under the discipline of any martial law." But the army had to be paid before it could be disbanded. Lynch suggested that the state pay soldiers in the form of indentured servants taken from "vaga-bonds, beggars and petty felons" in England, which "would likewise rid this Kingdom of abundance of idle and burdensome people." In order to encourage merchants to come to Jamaica, Lynch recommended that the island's fortifica-tions be strengthened. He also proposed that no other colony be established in the region, and that the king purchase a plantation on the island.[10]

Further suggestions for Jamaica came from James Ley, third Earl of Marlborough, a royalist naval officer with interests in the West Indies, who also served on the Council of Trade. To promote Jamaica as a plantation colony, he emphasized the overall need for labor on the island and suggested that the new Company of Royal Adventurers into Africa take advantage of the situation. Although the slave trade was not mentioned in the company's charter in 1660, Marlborough urged "the R[oyal] Company be persuaded to make Jamaica the staple for the trade of Blacks as they shall think fit to be sold to the inhabitants for goods." He also suggested that the king purchase one hundred slaves to be sold on the island. In addition, Marlborough recommended "that care be taken for ye sending over women for planters wives; and that Newgate and Bridewell may be spared as much as may be; and instead of such, that poor maids (with which few parishes in England are unburdened) be sent over."[11]

Here were three plans for Jamaica that those who had sponsored the Western Design had hoped to see. For years they had urged Cromwell to promote similar schemes to populate the island with settlers, convicts, servants, and slaves but had been disappointed by the Protectorate's unwillingness to promote Jamaica's economic development. But in December 1660, the same month the Company of Royal Adventurers was founded, the restored monarchy officially chose to hold on to Jamaica. These resolutions must be understood as interrelated. The decision by Charles II, Lord Chancellor Clarendon, and the Privy Council to retain Jamaica was influenced by the men who had supported the Western Design and were now in positions of power on the Councils of Trade and Foreign Plantations, as well as in the African Company. The decision to keep Jamaica, however, did not represent a mere continuation of Cromwellian mili-tary and commercial policies on the part of the Restoration government. It is imperative to consider the decision to maintain Jamaica in 1660 as part of the Restoration's own imperial agenda and to understand that the hopes of the merchants and officers who had conquered the colony were met with the impe-rial aspirations of the new regime.[12] It demonstrated a broad agreement on the part of Protectorate advisers like Noell and Povey with Restoration imperial designs. They shared a desire to develop plantation colonies to expand the servant and slave trades for the benefit of English merchants and the state.

Although there was no mention in the 1660 charter of the slave trade, as Marlborough's plans indicated, there was hope that the African Company would be involved in the trade. However, there is little indication the company did much besides capture a few islands in the Gambia River from the Dutch and send some ivory, wax, and hides back to England. It never received the full amount of funding from its original subscription, and in late 1662, the company's directors asked the king to grant a new license. The charter for the Company of Royal Adventurers of England trading into Africa was issued in January 1663. This new company had a different governing structure, made up of a governor, subgovernors, and deputy governors, as well as a large court of assistants with rotating membership. In addition to many of the same courtiers who had founded the previous company, this one also included numerous merchants and others with colonial interests as its founding members. For example, Sir James Modyford and Sir John Colleton came from families who owned large sugar plantations in Barbados; their brothers Thomas and Peter, respectively, became the company's agents in the colony in 1663. Other founding members included Sir Martin Noell, knighted in 1662; his sons Martin, Edward, and James; and the ubiquitous Thomas Povey. The presence of these men as founding members of the Royal Adventurers not only underscored their ascent to positions of influence over imperial affairs during the early years of the Restoration, but also illustrated the centrality of the slave trade to their personal interests and to the interests of the state's evolving imperial policies.[13]

The Company of Royal Adventurers was founded with the explicit purpose of selling African slaves to English planters and Spanish merchants to divert the trade away from the Dutch, who dominated the slave trade by the middle of the seventeenth century. The company's "Publique Declaration and Invitation" in January 1663 stated that its monopoly was necessary "by reason of the universal intestine Confusion of the Times; by the advantage whereof, other Nations have taken confidence so far to invade and disturb His Majesty's Subjects in the said Trade, that it is in danger utterly to be lost to this Nation." In other words, whatever trade another nation gained, England necessarily lost. The African Company's monopoly represented a major component of later Stuart political and imperial ideology. As the company itself declared in early 1663, "his Majestie['s] granting of any such license, is a Prerogative of the Crown, as being the suspension of a law, and soe, a meere act of Royal Grace and therefore is free to be placed where his Majestie shall please, without giving any just cause of complaint to any others, that share not in it."[14] In other words, the company was an extension of the royal prerogative and subject to no other legal limitations.

In order to maintain its monopoly and ensure profits, the African Company needed colonial officials to help enforce its charter, an expectation that was usually incorporated into governors' instructions.[15] Governors were required to make sure "interlopers," or illegal private traders, were unable to land or sell cargoes in the colonies. They were also expected to seize interloping ships, or allow the company the freedom to do so, and to prosecute those caught trading illegally. In addition, colonial officials were required to help the company collect debts from planters who generally lacked hard currency and relied heavily on credit as well as in-kind payments of sugar and other commodities. Unable to collect cash for the slaves they sold to English planters, the African Company turned to the Spanish, who could pay for slaves with hard currency. The *asiento*, or exclusive contract to provide the Spanish with slaves, was highly coveted by the English, and profiting from the slave trade to the Spanish was a central goal of the reorganized African Company. In an arrangement established at the formation of the new company in 1663, the Spanish agreed to pay a duty of 5 percent for all cargoes purchased in English plantations, intended to go directly into the Crown's coffers.[16] Unlike the Cromwellians, rather than fight the Spanish in the New World, the restored monarchy hoped to profit from Spanish wealth through plunder and trade.

By seeking access to the Spanish American market for African slaves, the company hoped not only to eliminate English interlopers, but to further undermine the Dutch. In a petition to Charles II in February 1663, soon after receiving its new charter, the company indicated its desire to control this trade exclusively because "it's thought reasonable that the Company should injoy all those benefits, which are ye necessary consequences of his Majesties charter." The company claimed that if the trade remained open "it will be impossible to reserve the benefit to the English only. For avaritious or necessitous persons will without doubt lend their names to disguise the good of the French, Hollander & other strangers, who will not only draine the advantage from his Majesty's subjects, but find meanes also to cheat the King of his due, by conveying the Spaniards' commodities from our plantations directly to foreign parts." The same day Charles II received this petition, he issued orders to the governor of Barbados to allow the Spanish to trade freely in his colony, "the Act of Navigation or any other law, statute or ordinance or any letters of mart or reprisal given or to be given to the contrary notwithstanding." A few weeks later, he issued a similar order to the governor of Jamaica.[17] The willingness of the king to agree to these demands illustrated the central role the company played in Restoration imperial and commercial designs. This intention to cultivate a lucrative slave trade with the Spanish set the tone for Stuart imperial policy for the next two decades.

COMPETING IMPERIAL IDEALS: PLANTERS
VERSUS THE CROWN AND COMPANY

The African Company's desire to profit from selling slaves to the Spanish put it at odds with a variety of different colonial constituencies, most notably planters. This was especially true in Barbados, where by the 1660s the elected assembly was made up of the richest and most powerful planters in the colony. They felt that selling slaves to Spanish merchants diminished the availability of much-needed labor in the colony and made those slaves that did enter the Barbados market unaffordable. And by 1660, Barbados was well on its way to becoming a sugar plantation colony totally dependent on slavery. Russell Menard has estimated that by 1660 Barbados had approximately twenty-six thousand white inhabitants and twenty-seven thousand black slaves.[18] The African Company wanted to harness this demand for slave labor in the English colonies, while at the same time profit from the Spanish American slave market.

In early 1660, the planter and promoter of the Western Design, Colonel Thomas Modyford, had been named governor of Barbados by the Protectorate Council of State but lost that position after the Restoration, and the governorship returned to Francis, Lord Willoughby of Parham. The idea of a proprietary governor returning to Barbados was deeply troubling for many planters, who had hoped that political confusion in England would allow them once again to enjoy relative autonomy. Issues of land ownership and dubious tenure practices could be called into question with a new proprietor making claims for control of land and revenue. In the event, Willoughby was willing to strike a deal with both planters and the Crown in order to take up his position. The Crown, anxious to avoid any question about its legal authority in the colonies, would assume the proprietary over "the Caribbees," and planters' questionable property holdings would be secured. The Privy Council ordered that in exchange for these concessions, Barbados would pay a set customs duty. After arriving in August 1663, Willoughby convinced members of the assembly already in session to grant a permanent revenue to the Crown in the form of a 4.5 percent tax on all "dead" commodities produced and exported. After much wrangling the assembly agreed to the tax with the understanding that a good portion of the revenue would remain in Barbados to maintain the colony's defenses.[19]

In addition to securing revenue, Willoughby had been instructed to allow the African Company to sell slaves to Spanish traders. But in November 1663, the company petitioned the king that Willoughby had obstructed its agents' attempts to establish such a trade in Barbados. The company reported that its agents on the island, Thomas Modyford and the merchant-planter Sir Peter

Colleton, "having more Negroes for your petitioners accompts then the planters of that island had occasion to buy, did resolve and accordingly dispatch one hundred & sixty of them (which were never landed upon the island) to be sent upon your petitioners' ship the *Blackmore* to the Terra Firma." Instead of allowing the agents to send the slaves to South America freely, Modyford and Colleton claimed Willoughby collected an export duty of 5 percent because the cargo was being sent to a foreign port. The company asked the king "to give your express order and command to the said Lord Willoughby to make immediate restitution to your petitioners said factors of the said three hundred and twenty pounds," and to cease collecting the tax in the future. Within weeks Charles II dispatched a letter to Willoughby stating almost exactly the requests of the Royal Adventurers, and in December, the king issued licenses to Spanish merchants allowing them to trade in Tangier and Barbados.[20] The willingness of Charles II and his Privy Council to agree to the African Company's demands illustrated the important role the company played in Restoration imperial plans.

As governor of the Caribbees, Willoughby was in charge of both Barbados and the Leeward Islands. These colonies were financially and militarily stretched to the limit as European allegiances and diplomatic arrangements shifted throughout the 1660s. Willoughby regularly criticized imperial policies that to him seemed to weaken colonies, such as the Navigation Acts, which had been renewed in 1660. In 1664 he claimed that trade in Barbados and Nevis had ground to a halt because ships "were tyed up by these Acts," which he argued diminished the Crown's revenues. War with the Dutch and later the French devastated the Leeward Islands and seriously threatened Barbados during the mid-1660s, draining the islands of stores, money, and men. Although the Council of Trade considered altering the Navigation Acts during war, this plan never came to fruition.[21] After thwarting an attempt by the Dutch to take Barbados in April 1665, Willoughby complained that the colony lacked basic necessities for self-defense, such as gunpowder and arms. He was especially frustrated over the issue of revenue, and claimed that because the king had ordered that the 5 percent imposition for slaves sold to the Spanish should be reserved for the African Company, Barbados lacked a major source of income. He turned to the colony's assembly, but its members were outraged that the 4.5 percent duty, instead of being used for the island's defenses, appeared to be going straight into the Crown's coffers. Under the leadership of its new speaker, Samuel Farmer, the assembly blocked Willoughby's efforts to build up the island's defenses. "My back is at the wall," he later wrote, "and I find good words & meek carriage begets little but contempt, where no other can be used amongst a people who have been rough bred, & not used to the yoak; no money to be raised, without their own consents, therefore nothing to be done but what they please."[22] In his frustration, Willoughby revealed the extreme lengths colonial planters seemed to be willing to go to in order to avoid paying taxes or submitting to imperial regulations. He felt he had little choice but to dissolve this assembly.

This conflict over the use of the 4.5 percent duty and the rights of colonial assemblies provides a sense of how various interests began to articulate and refine their own imperial agendas. It demonstrated the difficulties governors like Willoughby had in acting on behalf of the Crown, while at the same time feeling hamstrung by the Crown's policies. On the one hand, as governor, he wanted to ensure that Barbados and the Leeward Islands prospered, and he clearly felt it was his duty to tell imperial authorities when he thought certain policies or regulations hindered that development. On the other hand, Willoughby knew he had to keep planters and their potentially seditious ideas in check; it was one thing to plead or petition, but it was another thing to demand rights and privileges. The following year, in January 1666, Saint Christopher in the Leeward Islands fell to the French. Willoughby feared for the safety of Barbados and called a new assembly early that year, which ultimately proved more inclined to raise funds for the island's protection. In July, Willoughby left Barbados with a small militia to try to recover Saint Christopher on the king's orders. Before leaving, he once again urged Charles II to grant English colonists the liberty to trade freely "with all places & people in amity with your Majesty," especially "to Guinea for Negroes." Willoughby and his ship were lost in a hurricane before reaching the Leeward Islands. In the meantime Saint Christopher and Antigua were utterly destroyed by the French, who confiscated land and slaves and left the English colonists to starve.[23]

ENGLISH CARIBBEAN SOCIETY AND THE EMERGENCE OF THE PLANTERS' VISION OF EMPIRE

When Francis Willoughby departed Barbados, he left his nephew William in charge as deputy governor. William faced many of the same problems his uncle had, including the multiple ways that the colony's growing dependence on slavery transformed Barbados into a dangerously racially polarized society. He was especially concerned about his inability to muster a sufficiently large or dependable militia during the threat of foreign invasion. In December 1666, he claimed that of the seven thousand white men eligible to serve in the colony's militia, only two thousand could be counted on to provide loyal service. In a particularly insightful letter to the king, he described why the bulk of the white population could not be trusted during an emergency. "Smalle planters" he wrote, "who formerly have bin accompted the strength of this island but at present through want of Negroes and scarcity of all things needefull, are so impoverished & disheartened that theire interest and consequently the welfare of this place is but little esteemed by them." He noted that landless day laborers were equally unreliable, "haveing passed a sharpe servitude in this country & findeing no meanes heere to mend theire condition, will without difficultie stoope to any alteration." Finally, indentured servants, because they were treated so harshly, would willingly abandon Barbados altogether and were "ready to serve new Masters." Willoughby warned that these people "being without interest or hopes of benefit heere, 'tis much doubted whether they will expose themselves to danger for the preservation of it."[24] In other words, such people could not be counted on to defend Barbados because they felt they no longer had a stake in the colony's society.

William Willoughby eloquently described the precarious social and political situation that had developed in Barbados as a result of the colony's growing reliance on slave labor. Maintaining stable populations of servants and small planters had become increasingly difficult because by the 1660s most arable land had been claimed by powerful and wealthy plantation owners. Smaller planters who could not turn a profit were often forced to sell their land, and indentured servants who had completed their terms could not look forward to owning land if they remained in the colony. These were the very men who would have made up the bulk of the colonial militia. The consolidation of land into larger and larger sugar plantations benefited those few wealthy men who often served on the island's council and assembly and proved so vexing to the Crown. According to colonial officials like Willoughby, it was therefore in the interest of the English government to try to hinder their progress by helping small planters to acquire land, servants, and slaves. Whether or not this would have been the case is debatable, but Willoughby's analysis highlighted some of the complex ways slavery had transformed Barbados society by the 1660s. These changes also seem to have contributed to changing migration patterns to and from the colony. Richard Dunn has estimated that perhaps ten thousand people left Barbados during the second half of the seventeenth century. Most well known were migrants to South Carolina, but Barbadians also settled in places like Virginia, New York, Jamaica, and New England. As a result of this emigration, combined with high mortality and low birth rates, the white population in Barbados peaked at thirty thousand around 1650 and declined steadily for the rest of the century. In stark contrast, the slave population increased dramatically. In 1650, blacks, the great majority of whom would have been slaves, made up approximately 30 percent of the population; by 1660, the proportion was about 51 percent and by 1670, 64 percent.[25]

The ways that colonial officials and powerful planters chose to interpret and attempted to address these social changes are especially revealing. The men of the Barbados Council, for example, argued that one of the main causes of depopulation by whites was the lack of availability of African slaves. They claimed this resulted in rich planters producing less sugar than they otherwise would, which forced poorer planters "daily to forsake these countries." This "hath been a greater loss in the revenue of the customs to your Majesty, than the Spanish trade which [can in] any ways recompense." In his report William Willoughby agreed, and urged the king to send supplies and "Negroes on reasonable termes." Other officials expressed similar concerns and proposed comparable solutions. When William Willoughby's father, also named William, became governor in 1667, he was instructed to "prevent ye departure of freemen out of your several colonies," but like his predecessors, he felt that England's imperial policies hindered rather than helped the colonies under his jurisdiction. "Two things there are," Willoughby urged Charles II, "which except speedily remedied whither peace or war will ruin these plantations." He continued, "First, the want of free trade with Scotland by which formerly this and the rest of the islands was supplyed with brave servants & faithful subjects . . . The second a free trade to Guinney for Negroes . . . So excessive scarce & dear are they now here that the poor planters (on whom I must rely for ye justifying ye Majesty's right) will be forced to go to foreign plantations for a livelihood."[26] Even in times of dire emergency, such as war or slave uprisings, and despite heavily skewed population ratios, West Indies planters continued to clamor for more slaves.

In a place like Barbados, it was this dangerous reliance on slave labor that contributed to the emergence of a particular imperial ideal among West Indies planters. Constructing brutal social and legal systems to maintain white mastery became central to this vision of empire. In addition, demands for free trade to Africa, or at least a trade free from the control of a monopoly company, and for increasing numbers of slaves on "reasonable terms," became its complementary theme. It is interesting to note that this ideal developed not only from demand for slave labor but that it came to be understood as a solution to the problem of white depopulation in the English Caribbean colonies. Although petitions from the colonies still requested more servants from places like England and Scotland, a common feature became requests for more slaves. In the long run, of course, this intensified existing social, economic, and political tensions in Barbados.[27]

Restoration imperial policies also seemed to exacerbate the problem of maintaining the white population in Barbados. For example, throughout the 1660s, each new governor of Jamaica was ordered to encourage migrants from Barbados and the Leeward Islands to seek their fortunes in the new colony. Moving people from one colony to another reinforced a system in which colonies competed with each other for scarce resources, and, not surprisingly, it put the Barbados planters on the defensive. In 1661, Governor D'Oyley of Jamaica was ordered to send Captain Richard Whiting to Barbados "to fetch passengers," but he was "met with great obstructions in that designe, . . . the chief men here being very averse from acting any thing to the good of Jamaica." After appointing Thomas, Lord Windsor, governor of Jamaica in 1662, the king and Council of Trade ordered him to issue proclamations "in our neighbour colonies and plantations, for the transplanting of all such persons, goods, and families as are willing to transport themselves to our island of Jamaica." In June 1662, Windsor stopped at Barbados, where he declared that all those willing to go to Jamaica could depart with his fleet, regardless of profession or religious persuasion. Not surprisingly, this blanket freedom to leave caused anxiety among the island's planter oligarchs, who were afraid that indentured servants and debtors would quit the island as they had in the Western Design in 1655. In an attempt to prevent people from departing, the Barbados Assembly and Council passed an act ordering that all those wishing to leave should sign a registry with the island's secretary general. Rather than registering with the colony's secretary, however, those wishing to leave apparently signed with Windsor and his commissioners. The assembly complained that "there was no care taken by those Commissioners to discover whether they entred their right names, or whether they were free men, or persons indebted." Governor Willoughby later offered his own opinion that promoting Jamaica's development "hath robbed your other colonies of people."[28]

Despite these pleas, such policies of transplantation continued. When Thomas Modyford was appointed governor of Jamaica in 1664, he received similar orders to encourage people to move with him from Barbados and the Leeward Islands. All those wishing to leave would have free passage to Jamaica, where they were guaranteed land, freedom from customs for twenty years, and "free trade with all nations in amity with England except for Negroes which are to be furnished by the Royal Company." Modyford optimistically hoped that Barbados would provide Jamaica a "yearly supply of 1000 persons," and according to his own records, 987 people came from Barbados in June 1664. It did not take long for Governor Willoughby to protest politely to Secretary of State Sir Henry Bennet. "I shall make it my humble request to you that you will be pleased to divert the King from giving me any more such orders," the governor implored, "for it is not beginning at the right end to improve his Majesty's interest in these parts for he doth but take out of his right pocket, to put into his left." Willoughby continued, "Europe is the magazine of people, & from thence his Majesty might to send them a constant supply every year into all these parts."[29]

Transplanting people from one colony to another was nothing new; Cromwell had encouraged moving settlers from the Leeward Islands and New England to Jamaica and Ireland. And despite the restored monarchy's desire to promote Jamaica, it wanted to do so as cheaply as possible, and therefore turned first to existing colonies. There were a variety of reasons for this. First, it was thought that these settlers, especially from the other West Indies colonies, would have the experience and physical disposition necessary for survival. Chances were they had already gone through the "seasoning" process of moving to the tropics, and they might have had some experience working on a sugar, indigo, cotton, or tobacco plantation. According to one promotional pamphlet for Jamaica circulating in England in 1661, "the Major part of the Inhabitants being old West Indians, who now naturalized to the country, grow the better by their transplantation." Even more important, there were fewer people in England who were willing to go overseas by the mid-seventeenth century, as discussed in chapter 2. This was the consequence of many factors, not the least of which was a slight population decline in England during the middle of the 1600s, which resulted in higher wages at home that might have made it less likely for people to migrate. In addition, popular pamphlets in England had depicted Barbados as a colony with little land or opportunity since at least the time of the Western Design. One pamphlet from 1655 warned that "Barbados, (with the rest of those small islands, Subject to this Dominion, who were wont to be a receptacle for such vermin) are now so filled, that they vomit forth of their superfluities into other places." The 1661 pamphlet promoting Jamaica similarly claimed "in St. Kitts, Barbados, &c. you cannot turn a Horse out but he presently trespasseth upon his neighbour, if not upon your own [sugar] canes: the most barren Rocks (even in the Scotland of Barbados) owning a Proprietor, and the whole Island pestered with a super-numerary *glut* of Inhabitants; too small a Hive for such a swarm of people."[30] These images of colonies filled with "swarms of people" were remarkably similar to those describing England during the late sixteenth and early seventeenth centuries to promote transatlantic colonization. These perceptions, combined with the dramatic increases in the slave population, made Barbados a much less desirable destination for would-be servants and free migrants.

The African Company played an important role in shaping these perceptions, and grievances about the company poured out of Barbados during the mid-1660s. In September 1667, the assembly issued a petition to Charles II reiterating Willoughby's requests for freer trade. They claimed the remedy to Barbados's hardship was simple: the king should grant the colony the freedom to trade "to any place in amity with England." As for the African Company's monopoly, the Barbadians "humbly pray that we may be permitted free trade on the Coast of Guinney, for Negro servants." According to the colonists, if the Crown was reluctant to provide enough stores and arms for Barbados, the least it could do was provide the colony with the means necessary to supply itself with slaves. The assembly's demands for "free trade" did not signify a simple economic disagreement with "mercantilist" imperial policies, however.[31] Such conflicts represented a much larger struggle between competing imperial ideals over the political and economic relationship of the colonies to the metropolis.

Demands for freer trade to Africa, even in the context of war and economic hardship, prompted the Company of Royal Adventurers to defend its position. In 1667, the company published a pamphlet that seemed to answer many of the charges made by the Barbados Assembly, declaring that the company "supplied the Plantations more plentifully and cheaper, and given as much credit or more for Negroes, than ever the private Traders did or could give." It defended selling slaves to Spanish merchants and claimed the company did so "for preventing of that Bargain to Hollanders." In a direct response to the Barbados petition, the company's secretary, Sir Ellis Leighton, argued that free trade would only benefit Barbados, rather than "preserve the trade of the nation." For the company, it was an either/or proposition: if Barbados prospered because of free trade, England would necessarily suffer. There was unwillingness or inability to think of colonies as economic or political extensions of England, which was exactly how Barbadians viewed themselves and their colony. "We think their desire of a free trade will prove as unpracticable and pernicious to themselves as it would be destructive to all other publique interests as well as ours," Leighton wrote.[32]

In the meantime, things went from bad to worse in Barbados. In April 1668, a fire devastated a good portion of the main port of Bridgetown, destroying the supply magazine. Some "Merchants and Planters of Barbados" used the occasion to once again ask for "free trade for Negroes and for servants from Scotland." In a petition that August, the assembly complained about what they saw as flagrant misuse of the 4.5 percent revenue by the Crown. In addition to repeating requests for free trade, especially for slaves, this petition went further and asked the king to consider "granting us a charter including the benefits hereby requested, and such other immunities as we shall propose to your Majesty which shall not be derogatory to your Majesty's Honour." This request for a "charter" to help the colonists ensure their perceived rights and privileges was remarkable and indicated that their concerns about the reach of imperial authority went beyond commercial policies and extended to the nature of the political relationship between colony and Crown. It was a shocking proposal that aimed to preserve local autonomy at the expense of imperial authority, which stemmed in no small part from the colony's transformation into a slave society and from experiences and problems with the African Company. Barbados planters desperately wanted to stake a claim to their own freedom in order to distinguish themselves from the situation of their slaves. In order to do this, West Indies colonists hoped to codify a negotiated, integrated empire, in which colonies were seen as political as well as economic extensions of England. For his part, Willoughby fully understood the implications of the assembly's request and was quick to distance himself from this "impudent address" by which the assembly "fully declared what they aime at."[33]

Facing increased pressures from the confused implementation of the 4.5 percent duty and accusations by the assembly of mismanagement, Willoughby was granted permission to return to England in early 1669. Once in London, Willoughby took up his seat in the House of Lords and attended meetings of the Council of Trade. In the meantime, the Barbados Assembly organized a lobbying group of "Gentlemen Planters," made up of absentee planters resident in England, who were paid by the island's assembly to serve as their advocates in London and to attend meetings of the Council of Trade. In early 1671 Willoughby and the Gentlemen Planters worked to defeat an effort led by English sugar refiners to increase duties on sugars refined in the colonies. According to the Gentlemen Planters, English refiners had formed an alliance with merchants with interests in the Portuguese trade who imported Brazilian sugar into England. This coalition had convinced the Commons to pass a bill that increased taxes on imported refined sugar by four times.[34]

Before the House of Lords took up the bill, the refiners and planters each presented their cases to a special committee of the Lords, each side offering doomsday scenarios should the legislation pass or not. Members of the committee hearing the testimony included Willoughby, the Earl of Sandwich, and Sir Anthony Ashley Cooper, who led a newly reformed Council of Plantations. The positions of the refiners and planters represented two fundamentally different understandings of political economy and, ultimately, competing imperial agendas. According to the English refiners, it was "undeniable" that as more refineries opened in England, "soe it must Decrease in other Countreys." They argued that the new legislation "will be an Advantage to our English Planters that they may have a markett for theire [unrefined] sugars in England without running a second Risque to seeke a foraigne market." For the refiners, it had to be one way or the other: either refining prospered in England or it prospered in the colonies and foreign countries. This underscored a reluctance to envision the colonies as fundamental parts of the realm in political or economic terms. In contrast, the planters viewed the colonies as integral to the empire and argued that colonial production, because it was actually English, should not be subject to import duties. They maintained that manufacturing in the colonies was bene-ficial for the imperial economy and did not necessarily compete with English sugar refiners. They accused the refiners of planning to "engross" the sugar market.[35]

The Lords committee, after hearing these appeals and greatly influenced by the presence of the governor of Barbados as a member, reported in April 1671 to the entire House of Lords that if the bill took effect as the Commons had designed it, "the Planters being so discouraged, it would produce the evil Consequences of the Loss of our Navigation, and the Consumption of our Home Manufactures, destroying the *English* Refiners, losing a Million in the Balance of our Trade." They proposed that the House of Lords alter the bill by "lessening the Impost upon White Sugar One Farthing and Half a Farthing in the Pound." The Lords committee went further and argued "That, by encour-aging the *English* Sugar Plantations, and making it a Matter of State so to do, we might in short Space of Time engross that Manufacture to ourselves" at the expense of other nations. In other words, the government should do its utmost to promote the sugar plantations for the benefit of the entire imperial economy. The colonies were integral parts of the realm, and therefore any manufacturing occurring in the colonies benefited the whole empire. The House of Lords followed the committee's suggestions and voted to lower the duty on refined sugar. These actions, however, triggered a constitutional crisis, as the Commons claimed the Lords had no right to alter a bill concerning taxation. In frustration the king prorogued Parliament on April 22, 1671, and with more than a little relief, the Gentlemen Planters informed the Barbados Assembly "we are eased of this tax for the present."[36]

This conflict between English sugar refiners and colonial planters repre-sented more than a simple conflict over commercial regulations. On the one hand, refiners in England argued that manufacturing should be confined to the home country and that sending brown sugars from Barbados to be finished in England was best for the nation's economy and balance of trade. On the other hand, planters felt that the development of manufacturing in the colonies was in their economic interest, because they could charge higher prices for refined white sugar than for unfinished brown. And as far as they were concerned, manufacturing in either the metropolis or the colonies was economically bene-ficial to the entire empire. It made little difference where the manufacturing took place, because colonies were not in competition with the home country. What was only occasionally mentioned in the debate, however, was the fact that both the planters' and the refiners' imperial visions depended so heavily on African slavery.

The Barbadians' clamoring for an open slave trade, their unwillingness to deal with land consolidation, issues of population and security, and the quarrel over sugar refining raised the concerns of imperial authorities. But the conflicts between Barbados and London during the 1660s did not represent a simple economic division between mercantilist commercial policies and colonial demands for free trade. By requesting a more-open slave trade, not to mention charters codifying local autonomy, Barbados planters were asking the Crown to eliminate key components of the Restoration imperial agenda, which centered on monopoly and increasingly on the use of royal prerogative. As a result, as far as imperial authorities were concerned, planters were guilty of questioning the very foundations of the empire and the royal prerogative upon which it was based.

JAMAICA AND PRIVATEERING

Other groups with colonial interests confronted Restoration imperial designs and the policies of the African Companies, including privateers who made Jamaica their home base. During the 1660s, the colony took center stage for English imperial administration, as Charles II hoped to transform the island into a profitable plantation colony.[37] To promote the development of Jamaica as "the most eminent plantation of all his Majesty's distant dominions," Charles II issued a proclamation in December 1661 encouraging people to move to the island. It promised each free person over the age of twelve the right to claim thirty acres of land, and allowed for the unobstructed passage of people and their possessions (except for gold and bullion) from England. In order to ease the transition to planting, the king also declared his intention to provide disbanded soldiers in Jamaica with a "Royal Gift," which included a supply of three hundred African slaves from the Royal Company. Jamaica seemed an ideal place for the company to establish itself in the slave trade, especially to the Spanish colonies. But the company's desire to develop a peaceful trade with the Spanish was obstructed by the activities of Jamaica's infamous privateers. Governor Edward D'Oyley had invited buccaneers from the island of Tortuga to help protect the island in 1657, and in the subsequent years, many of the English soldiers sent during the Western Design had joined their ranks.[38] Although England and Spain agreed to a peace treaty at the Restoration, D'Oyley and the next three royal governors of Jamaica all actively promoted privateering raids against Spanish ships and ports as a means to raise revenue for themselves and the island and to help protect the colony from foreign attacks. Eventually these activities brought Jamaica into conflict with the African Company and the Crown.

D'Oyley was reappointed governor by the restored monarchy in the autumn of 1660. He was granted total authority over land distribution and military affairs. Reflecting the Restoration government's desire to develop Jamaica as a plantation colony, one of the first things he set about doing was establishing laws to regulate servants and slaves on the island. In July 1661 D'Oyley and the council adopted their own version of Barbados's rigid slave and servant code, which had been implemented in 1660. It established a strict system of punishment for servants and slaves who assaulted or killed their masters, married without their masters' permission, or otherwise deserted their obligations. In addition, the Jamaica Council ordered all servants under the age of eighteen arriving without a contract to serve masters for seven years, and those over eighteen for five years. Although in 1661 the colony had only approximately three thousand white inhabitants and about five hundred slaves, D'Oyley and imperial authorities were determined to transform Jamaica into a plantation society dependent upon servile labor.[39]

By the early 1660s there was already demand for slaves in Jamaica. Dutch merchants had started to take advantage of this emerging market, and D'Oyley even tried to profit from the trade. In June 1661, the governor seized a Dutch ship with 180 slaves off Cagway Bay and tried to convince the island's council to allow him to purchase the slaves for resale despite the Navigation Acts. He argued that the king had promised "to make yt island a glorious place; & yt ye way to do it, was by supplying ye island with slaves & servants." The council refused to go along, but D'Oyley, "inraged," went ahead and purchased the slaves the same day. Captain Richard Whiting managed to seize the ship from the governor, but not before D'Oyley had sold at least 40 of the slaves. The council demanded an explanation, but D'Oyley simply responded that he was not answerable to them, only to the king. Whiting reported a similar incident in March 1662, in which D'Oyley again seized a Dutch slave ship and sold 45 slaves for his own profit.[40]

Despite the growing demand for slaves, Jamaica's transition to a plantation colony was too slow for many on the island. D'Oyley himself understood that quick profits could not be made from planting, and he continued to license former Cromwellian soldiers as privateers against the Spanish. But D'Oyley's tenure was to be short-lived. Charles II announced the appointment of Thomas, Lord Windsor, as the new governor in late spring 1661, and unofficial word reached Jamaica that fall. Windsor had been a royalist army officer and was serving as Lord Lieutenant of Worcester, where he had a reputation of cracking down on republican radicals. Significantly, Windsor was given permission "to entertain any commerce with the Spanish Plantations . . . if you find it to be advantageous for the prosperity of our island." If Spanish governors were unwilling to trade, an additional instruction gave Windsor permission to "endeavour to procure and settle a trade with his subjects in those parts by force." In Jamaica, this meant enlisting privateers. After arriving in August 1662, Windsor declared war on the Spanish colonies and commanded an experienced privateer named Christopher Myngs with thirteen hundred privateers to raid Campeche (in southern Mexico) and Cuba. When Myngs's fleet returned from Santiago, Cuba, in October 1662, Windsor took his share of the plunder and returned to England after spending just ten weeks on the island.[41]

Windsor's official sanction to use privateers illustrated the government's ambivalence regarding privateering. Raiding Spanish ships and ports and the financial and military benefits it provided Jamaica placed the restored monarchy in an awkward position throughout the 1660s. On the one hand, the Crown was happy to reap the rewards of privateering and enjoyed the protection and financial independence it gave the fledgling colony. Although the Stuarts promoted peace with Spain officially in Europe, as Windsor's instructions indicate, they were more than willing to allow that peace to lapse "beyond the line." Plundering from other European powers was hardly antithetical to the vision at the heart of Restoration imperial designs, which understood international competition to be fierce and resources to be finite. Such a policy, however, seemed to be at odds with the regime's imperial and commercial aspirations. When the Royal Company of Adventurers of England trading into Africa was reorganized in 1663 it became a top priority for its investors and governors to cultivate a peaceful trade with Spanish merchants in the West Indies.[42] The threat of attack by English-sponsored privateers would diminish the company's ability to gain the trust of the Spaniards in the New World. Influenced by the African Company, restraining privateers became official imperial policy by 1663.

The English government's official desire to rein in privateers was slow to reach Jamaica, however. Upon his departure, Windsor left his deputy governor, Sir Charles Lyttleton, in charge of the island's affairs, and he authorized another attack on the Spanish Main in November 1662. In April 1663, the King-in-Council ordered Lyttleton to cease all such raids because they distracted inhabitants from planting, which was described by the king as "that industry which alone can render ye Island considerable." The order did not reach the deputy governor until October, however, after he had orchestrated further raids on Campeche and the Yucatan Peninsula in Mexico. Lyttleton admitted he had been informed of the desire for peace but claimed he had been told "the warr with the privateers was not intended to be taken off by the king's instructions." This apparent confusion over where exactly privateering, and colonial policy as a whole, fit into Charles II's diplomatic agenda illustrated the Crown's ambivalence regarding the practice.[43]

Privateering faced an uncertain future in Jamaica, however, in large part because of the interests of the African Company. In order for the company to profit from trading with Spanish merchants, colonial officials had to discourage privateering. It was therefore necessary for colonial governors to be sympathetic to the company and its aspirations. The company's earliest influence over administration in Jamaica occurred in 1664 when Charles II appointed the Barbados planter, politician, and former promoter of the Western Design, Sir Thomas Modyford, governor of Jamaica. Modyford had been serving as one of the African Company's factors in Barbados and had promoted the idea that the best way to turn a profit was to encourage trade with the Spanish. Modyford had numerous connections with London's colonial merchant community, many of whom were active in the new Royal Company as well as on the Council of Foreign Plantations. His brother, Sir James Modyford, was a founding member of the company in 1663, and his brother-in-law, Thomas Kendall, served on the Councils of Trade and Foreign Plantations. He had long since been connected to the powerful colonial merchants Martin Noell and Thomas Povey, who had worked with Modyford in promoting the Western Design. In addition, Modyford was a cousin of the Duke of Albemarle, and this connection almost certainly influenced his appointment.[44] Considering these credentials, Modyford probably seemed to be an ideal candidate as far as the government and the African Company were concerned.

Most of Modyford's instructions were similar to those of his two predecessors, with some important differences. Unlike Windsor's carte blanche to use force against the Spanish if they refused to trade, Modyford was ordered to restrain privateers "for the future persuading and encouraging the inhabitants rather to turn their labour and industry to the manuring [of land] and benefit of ye plantation." In addition, Modyford was urged to promote the interests of the African Company, "since you have had it in your care whilst you resided in our island of Barbados." In order for the company to benefit from selling slaves to the Spanish, the Spanish had to feel that it was safe to trade in Jamaica in the first place. Significantly, however, Modyford was granted permission to act as he saw fit "with the Advice of the Councill" in "extraordinary cases . . . for which it is not easy for us to prescribe such rules and directions for you."[45] This discretionary clause would soon put Modyford into direct conflict with the interests of the African Company and imperial authorities.

Upon arriving as governor, Modyford declared that "all acts of hostility against the Spaniards should cease." He soon learned, however, that there were

"noe lesse than 1500 lusty fellows now abroad" serving as privateers on Lyttleton's
commissions. He feared that "if made desperate by any act of injustice or oppression, [the privateers] may miserably infest this place" and endanger Jamaica's
well-being. He supported a scheme for the English to invade Tortuga, the island
haven for pirates ostensibly controlled by France, but nothing came of this plan.
In the meantime, England's relations with its European rivals underwent significant change. By 1664, a group of influential courtiers and naval officers, led by
the Duke of York, began to argue that it was in England's national interest once
again to fight the Dutch for imperial and commercial dominance. York's coalition included many politically powerful African Company merchants who
argued that the Dutch intended to monopolize global trade through unfair
practices and violence. The duke needed little convincing that the republican
Dutch threatened the restored monarchy and England's economic prosperity.
Ideological hostility toward the Dutch became another main feature of the
Stuarts' overall imperial and diplomatic agenda.[46]

In the Caribbean, the English sought to conquer small islands held by
the Dutch to remove them as an economic force in the region. It was hoped the
privateers would aim for Curaçao, the center of the Dutch slave trade near
the northern coast of South America. In November 1664, six months before the
official declaration of war, the King-in-Council ordered that although Jamaica's
privateers should cease hostilities against the Spanish, they were free to attack
Dutch ships and settlements. Modyford, however, was more concerned with
the maneuverings of the French than the Dutch in the Caribbean. He offered
his own proposal for war, which included sacking a series of smaller Dutch
islands, starting with Saint Eustatius and Saba, near Saint Christopher. From
there, forces would move on to Curaçao and eventually take Tortuga and
Hispaniola from the French. Modyford argued that by removing the French as
well as the Dutch from the West Indies, the English and Spanish could be left
to develop peaceful trade. This was a plan designed to win the endorsement of
Secretary of State Henry Bennet (now Lord Arlington), the former ambassador
to Spain and a strong proponent of curbing privateering. In April 1665, Modyford
commissioned his lieutenant governor, Colonel Edward Morgan, and sent him
with a fleet of ten ships and nearly five hundred privateers to Saint Eustatius.
Anticipating criticism that this scheme diverted men from planting, Modyford
claimed that there was "scarce a Planter amongst them brave Resolute fellowes"
sent out with Morgan. Upon landing on Saint Eustatius, Morgan collapsed and
died, but the English were able to capture it and the neighboring island of Saba
under the command of Colonel Theodore Cary. Although the islands were
small, the plunder was significant. Modyford reported that at least nine hundred

slaves were seized, "about 500 of which" were brought to Jamaica "with many coppers & stills & much mill works to ye great furtherance of this collony."[47]

According to Modyford, the campaign to capture Curaçao was "frustrated," however, because of Cary's greed and ineptitude. Modyford planned to have the remaining privateers in Jamaica carry out his plans for Curaçao, but he grew anxious about what they would do after the Dutch campaign ended. In February 1666, he easily convinced Jamaica's council that privateering against the Spanish as a means to maintain the loyalty of the buccaneers was "a matter of great security to this island." Modyford maintained such a policy "helps the poorer planters by selling his provision to the men of war," which "will enable many to buy slaves, and settle plantations." Modyford presumably felt that during war he was well within the limits of his discretionary instructions that referred to "extraordinary cases." As soon as he learned that Albemarle had granted him tacit permission to issue licenses to privateers against the Spanish, he declared war against Spain. Rather than attempting to take Curaçao, which was still part of Modyford's official plan, the privateers under the command of Captain Edward Mansfield in May 1666 recaptured Providence Island, which the Spanish had taken from the English in 1641.[48]

Although protected to a certain degree by his cousin Albemarle, Modyford still had to justify his actions to imperial authorities, especially Arlington. "My Lord you cannot imagine what a universal change," Modyford reported to Arlington in August 1666, "there was presently after this declaration in ye faces of men" in Port Royal. Without these commissions, Modyford claimed, "I could not have kept this place against French Buckaneers, who would have ruined all our sea side plantations at least & perhaps with our own men have put faire for ye Main." Modyford added, "There is no profitable employment for the privateers in the West Indies against the French or Dutch; & they being a sort of people which will not be brought to the humour of planting, [and] will continually prey on the Spaniards, whether they be countenanced in it at Jamaica or not."[49] Better the privateers had English commissions, Modyford maintained, so that the English king and his colony could reap the benefits of their marauding.

Despite his claims that revenue raised by privateers helped finance plantations, Modyford's decision to license attacks on the Spanish were at odds with his instructions to protect the interests of the African Company and the slave trade. But Charles II's ministers were willing to turn a blind eye to privateering against the Spanish in the West Indies, at least during war, so long as the privateers successfully protected Jamaica and brought in revenue. The Spanish, moreover, were perpetually wary of English intentions, especially in Jamaica. As the colony's provost marshal Thomas Lynch noted in 1664, few if any Spanish merchants had dared to enter Port Royal's harbor to trade for slaves or anything else and instead turned to "Genuese" traders for slaves. In addition, the Royal Company had not been able to supply Jamaica with many slaves to begin with, and once the war against the Dutch began, the company practically ceased operations.[50] Not only had trading become too dangerous, but the company also had to defend its fortifications in West Africa from the Dutch. The company had even been authorized by the Duke of York as Lord High Admiral to call its own council of war to plan attacks and reprisals against the Dutch West India Company. Under the command of Sir Robert Holmes, in late 1664 and early 1665 English and African mercenary forces captured many Dutch outposts in West Africa, including Gorée. This prompted a massive naval response by the Dutch, and in the spring of 1665 Admiral Michiel de Ruyter recaptured all that Holmes had taken and more, leaving only Cape Coast Castle (in modern-day Ghana) for the English.[51] The company had become an instrument of the Stuart war for imperial and commercial dominance over its chief political and economic rival. Wars against the Dutch and the French and toleration of privateering against the Spanish were military manifestations of the restored monarchy's imperial and economic agenda in the 1660s. While Modyford's actions clearly contradicted official policy, at the same time they fit together with the government's broader imperial and economic strategy, in which the only means to guarantee England's commercial and military supremacy was to eliminate, conquer, or steal from foreign competition.

For the remainder of the decade, Modyford continued his unofficial war against Spain. He actively encouraged privateering, despite the 1667 Treaty of Madrid, which called for a cessation of hostilities between the two countries.[52] From 1667 to 1669, Captain Henry Morgan, under orders from Modyford, led devastatingly successful campaigns against the Spanish in Panama, Cuba, Portobelo, Santo Domingo, and Maracaibo. The Spanish retaliated by attacking the northern shore of Jamaica and taking prisoners in early 1670. Later that year, Modyford and the Jamaica Council responded by declaring war against Spain, promoting Morgan to admiral of Jamaica, and authorizing him to raid the Spanish Main.[53] This led to Morgan's most infamous and spectacular raid, on the Isthmus of Panama in January 1671 with a fleet of thirty-eight ships and about two thousand men. Morgan's men burned the city of Panama to the ground and looted the surrounding area for a month. Meanwhile, England and Spain had formalized a new Treaty of Madrid in late 1670, once again setting terms of peace between the two nations. According to the new treaty, Spain formally recognized England's conquest of Jamaica. Despite the fact that direct trade between Spanish and English colonies remained illegal, it was widely expected that English merchants were free to cultivate peaceful contraband trade. But official toleration of privateering was over. Although word of the Panama raid did not reach London until the summer of 1671, Charles II and his advisers knew Modyford could not be trusted to enforce this new treaty and chose Sir Thomas Lynch to replace him in late 1670. Lynch was ordered to do what Modyford had dramatically failed to do: rein in the privateers for the good of imperial stability, relations with the Spanish, and the interests of the African Company. He was sent with instructions to arrest Modyford and send him to London for prosecution. The heyday of the officially sanctioned (or conveniently ignored) privateer was over, and never again would a colonial governor declare war on another European power without the direct order and consent of the metropolitan government.[54]

CONCLUSION

The 1660s ended with a renewed interest on the part of the Crown in centralizing imperial control, and more strongly confronting challenges to imperial authority. This stemmed from a realization on the part of the English government that changes had to occur to make colonies more obedient and reliably profitable. As a result, the late 1660s and early 1670s were a turning point in imperial administration, which occurred as a direct result of confrontations between the Crown and company on the one hand and planters, privateers, and colonial officials on the other. Amid these confrontations, different interests were forced to articulate, clarify, and in the case of the Crown, codify their own imperial visions. Establishing and expanding brutal slave regimes based on racial difference while at the same time demanding charters guaranteeing rights and liberties on the part of colonial assemblies were both manifestations of the planters' imperial ideal. The desire to ransack Spanish ships and settlements with impunity and even the protection of the Crown represented that of many privateers. The end of the 1660s marked a transitional moment to the second phase of Restoration imperialism, which witnessed an increasing willingness to emphasize colonial dependency and accentuate the reach of the royal prerogative. The main instruments of this control would be the re-formed Royal African Company and a more finely tuned sense of extending the authority of the royal prerogative on the part of the Crown.

4

POLITICIZED EMPIRE: THE CROWN, THE AFRICAN COMPANY, AND CENTRALIZATION, 1671–1678

In September 1670, before being removed from the governorship, Thomas Modyford informed Secretary of State Arlington of rumors circulating in Jamaica that "his Majesty as Lord of this island may impose wt taxes he pleaseth on ye native commodities of this place." He warned that colonists were afraid that soon "we shall be under an arbitrary government which your Lordship well knows how much Englishmen abhor." Modyford urged the king to declare that neither "he nor his successors will impose any tax, tallidge, ayde, subsidy, loane or any other charge upon them without ye consent of ye major part of ye representatives of ye freeholders of his island, according to their usual manner (by the Royal Writs) assembled." In the same batch of letters, Modyford also offered criticisms of the African Company and its monopoly. He pleaded, "for ye further encrease of his Majesty's subjects wee may have licence Gratis or at more moderate rates to trade for Negroes in Afrik, giving security to carry them to noe other market but this." He continued, presumably referring to the Duke of York and his allies, "Did those Honourable persons which make yt Royal Company so glorious, but fall into considerations, how much more it is his Majesty's interest to encrease ye number of his subjects yn bullion of gold or silver (which by law all nations may import) they would not only freely consent to this proposal for us, but for ye whole nation & forrayners also; Mankinde is ye principall, Gold ye accessory, encrease ye first considerably & ye other must follow."[1] It is unclear why Modyford issued these warnings. Calling for an open slave trade was certainly nothing new for a colonial governor. But Modyford claimed slavery was not only beneficial because it improved colonial production. In his estimation, remarkably, slaves became "subjects" of the Crown and were therefore a net increase in population to the entire realm. The fact that the African Company's backers and imperial authorities focused so much of their energy on accumulating bullion and monopolizing trade was misguided as far as Modyford was concerned. The supply of forced labor in the colonies was the key to imperial success.

Modyford's remarks about the African Company, coupled with his warnings about arbitrary taxation without representation, represented a good articulation of what had evolved as the colonial-planter imperial ideal during the 1660s, a vision that Modyford had helped mold. It turned out Modyford's thoughts offered a prescient foreshadowing of things to come. During the next decade, the Crown attempted to implement some of the "arbitrary" designs Modyford described. The second phase of Restoration Stuart imperialism was marked by serious attempts at increased centralization and control in terms of revenue extraction and the extension of executive authority. Noting this trend, scholars have offered a variety of explanations for this apparent shift in policy during the 1670s. Philip Haffenden argues that this development was primarily legal in origin and offered a "prelude" to the imperial designs of the Tory Reaction and the reign of James II of the next decade. Richard Dunn has posited that the imperial "crack down" of the 1670s was motivated primarily by concerns of "English mercantilists [who] were determined to gear [colonial production] to the needs of the home market." Offering another approach, Stephen Saunders Webb has emphasized that the government's central concern was maintaining control of the colonies by military force, and that all other considerations were secondary. Robert Bliss has suggested that increased attempts at imperial control merely reflected the desire for greater efficiency in government, and not any underlying political ideology.[2]

Although scholars are correct to mark the 1670s as a turning point in English imperial administration, none takes into consideration the prominent role that the African Company and England's participation in the slave trade played in shaping these new arrangements. During the 1670s, Restoration imperial designs underwent significant transformation in response to changing political, economic, and social circumstances at home and in the colonies. As many historians have noted, the 1670s were a particularly volatile decade. The emergence of vocal, although hardly cohesive, groups opposed to the Crown's diplomatic, military, economic, religious, and imperial positions contributed to the divisiveness of the age. Major events such as the Stop of the Exchequer (1672) and the Third Anglo-Dutch War (1672–1674) had a direct impact on imperial administration. In 1670 and again in 1672, the Council of Trade and Foreign

Plantations was transformed and in 1675 experienced further overhaul in light of political upheaval in the government. Most significantly, the African Company was reorganized in 1672. All of these events had implications for colonial governance and reflected the government's efforts to centralize imperial administration through a more-effective use of the king's prerogative authority in the colonies.

This chapter explores how the English government attempted to implement its imperial agenda in the West Indies during the early to mid-1670s. The Crown's vision of empire had commercial, legal, and military dimensions and led to continued confrontations over the power, influence, and authority of the African Company. As Stuart politics and imperialism became more politicized, so did the influence and underlying political-economic foundations of the African Company. Many planters, merchants, privateers, and colonial officials continued to be critical of the company's monopoly and its power to seize illegal slave cargoes. Such groups regularly sent petitions and complaints to London and occasionally obstructed the company's ability to function in the colonies by altering local laws or ignoring the company's authority. In doing so, these constituencies continued to refine their own imperial ideals that had emerged during the previous decade, which were based on maintaining oppressive slave regimes by opening the slave trade and maintaining a flexible political relationship with the English government. In response, imperial authorities tried to contain these dissenting voices at home and in the colonies. The conflicts that resulted did not merely reflect disagreement over commercial policies, however, but had political and ideological significance. By the end of the 1670s, the Crown responded more forcefully than ever to such perceived threats to the integrity of the empire.

CHANGES IN IMPERIAL ADMINISTRATION

The transition to the second phase of Restoration imperialism at the end of the 1660s involved alterations in colonial governance and imperial administration in London. The Second Anglo-Dutch War had ended with a humiliating naval defeat of the English on the river Medway, forcing peace negotiations in the summer of 1667. On top of these military disasters, the English government was stretched to its financial limit due to a devastating outbreak of plague in 1665–1666 and the Great Fire of London in September 1666. Some sought to blame the demoralizing outcome of the war and the perceived financial corruption that lay behind it on Lord Chancellor Clarendon. Clarendon's impeachment in 1667 led to the reorganization of Privy Council committees, including the Councils of Foreign Plantations and Trade. A new Council of Trade was created in 1668, which was ordered by the Privy Council's plantations committee to conduct an investigation into the state of the West Indies colonies. The council's subsequent report highlighted numerous problems with colonial administration, including the fact that governors did not swear the required oaths to uphold the Navigation Acts, allowed colonists to trade with foreigners, and evaded customs requirements. They suggested that customs farmers maintain one person in each colony to collect revenue and administer proper oaths to colonial officials.[3] Although nothing came of this plan, it indicated a new tendency toward centralized imperial control.

The Council of Trade was once again reorganized in 1670, and its directives also reflected an increased desire for information and more centralized control of colonial affairs. The new Council of Plantations, under the leadership of the Earl of Sandwich and Sir Anthony Ashley Cooper, was ordered "to enquire and inform yourselves by the best ways and means you can of ye state and condition of all and every our said respective colonies and plantations, what it is, by whom they are respectively governed, and what commissions, powers and instructions have been granted by us, or any way derived from us to that end, and how ye same have been duly executed and observed." Such information was necessary to determine the nature of the political and economic relationship between the colonies and the metropolitan government. It was understood that new levels of oversight were essential to keep colonial officials and assemblies from overstepping their authority and to keep colonial populations submissive to imperial policies. This occurred in large part as a reaction to the problems governing Barbados and Jamaica during the 1660s.[4]

The African Company also transformed during the early 1670s. The old company, already in dire financial straits before the Second Anglo-Dutch War, was in terrible shape by war's end. Although the Treaty of Breda restored most of the company's African holdings, it was unable to reestablish its trade to Africa with any seriousness. Since 1666, in fact, it had been granting licenses to private traders who could provide their own ships and capital. During 1668 and 1669, the company actively tried to collect remaining unpaid subscriptions to its stock, which met with little success. Devastation of its holdings in Africa during the war, coupled with the large debt owed to the company by shareholders and colonial planters, made the creation of a new company imperative.[5] A subscription was opened for a new corporation in late 1671, and in September 1672 Charles II issued a charter for the Royal African Company. A wide variety of courtiers, merchants, and others with colonial interests invested in the joint-stock company. The Duke of York served as governor from 1672 until his departure from England

in the Glorious Revolution of 1688. Sir Anthony Ashley Cooper, now Earl of
Shaftesbury, was among the founding members, and other subscribers included
Prince Rupert, the Earl of Arlington, the Duke of Buckingham, and Treasury
Secretary Lord Clifford. Other notable shareholders included Thomas Povey, the
colonial merchant who had helped orchestrate the Western Design and who had
recently served as York's personal treasurer; the future East India Company
governor Josiah Child; Sir Charles Lyttleton, the former deputy governor of
Jamaica; the future secretary of state for the northern department, Sir Joseph
Williamson; and Shaftesbury's close associate John Locke. In addition to its extensive monopoly powers, the company had the authority to establish a court of judicature in Africa, made up of one lawyer and two merchants to "have cognizance
and power to hear and determine all cases of forfeiture and seizures of any ship or
ships goods and merchandises trading and coming upon any the said coasts or
limits contrary to the true intents of these presents." These quasi-Admiralty powers
were extraordinary; not even the East India Company had this authority until
1683.[6] These powers were seen as a direct extension of the king's prerogative as
well as the Duke of York's authority as Lord High Admiral.

    In addition to reorganizing the African Company, in 1672 the King-in-
Council further restructured the Council of Trade. In September, the same
month the king granted the company its charter, he established another new
council. Many of the subscribers to the African Company also served on this
council, including Shaftesbury, York, Prince Rupert, and Locke, who served as
its secretary. Shaftesbury was especially influential on this new committee. He
had been involved in colonial affairs since the 1640s, when he became a part
owner of a plantation in Barbados. He had also served on Cromwell's advisory
committee that oversaw the Western Design. In addition, Shaftesbury was a
major investor and proprietor of the Carolina colony established in the 1660s.
His political career was in its ascendancy as a leading member of the so-called
"Cabal" alliance of the king's chief ministers after Clarendon's downfall, and in
November 1672 was named Lord Chancellor. In addition to his service on the
Council of Trade, he worked as the African Company's subgovernor from 1672
to 1673, and in 1674 he was elected to the company's court of assistants.[7]

    Political instability in England during the early 1670s had a direct impact on
imperial administration and the shaping of colonial policies. There were many
interconnected problems facing Charles II and his government, especially the
Crown's desperate need for money as well as deteriorating relations with the
Dutch. In late 1671, as the new African Company opened its subscription books,
the Treasury essentially ran out of funds. In January 1672, the king ceased
repaying the government's debts in an action known as the Stop of the

Exchequer. This threw the government's financial situation into turmoil, as the king and his closest advisers had secret plans to once again declare war on the Dutch. Historian K. G. Davies has suggested that owing to Dutch dominance of African trade, those who were aware of this arrangement, including York and his inner circle, took the opportunity to invest in the new African Company, hoping that war would distract the Dutch and its merchant marine from the African trade. Davies points out that a number of the king's ministers who would have known about the treaty purchased shares in the new company, including Arlington, Clifford, Shaftesbury, Buckingham, Prince Rupert, Sir William Coventry, and Sir Joseph Williamson. After raising money through private bankers, England declared war on the Dutch in March 1672. It is telling that the Royal African Company was reorganized at the same time that plans were under way to embroil England in yet another war with the Dutch.[8] The company's predecessor corporation had been used by the state as a tool of war during the 1660s. Although the Third Anglo-Dutch War was fought primarily in European waters and not in West Africa, the new company's main commercial purpose was to remove the Dutch from supplying slaves to English and Spanish colonies. It is not surprising that in the midst of imperial reorganization and centralization, as well as continued anti-Dutch sentiment on the part of the Stuart court, the new African Company would have a pivotal role.

The Royal African Company was commercially successful during the 1670s. In the West Indies, it increased its market share relative to both Dutch traders and English interlopers. Economic historians have in part attributed this success to the privileges granted by the company's charter, which gave it a kind of "patent protection." In addition, over the course of the 1670s, the African Company came to be seen as not only a staunch ally of the Crown but intertwined with Crown policies, politics, and interests. The company came to be closely associated with the Stuarts and their political ideologies, especially the belief shared by Charles II and his brother in the definitive authority of the royal prerogative.[9] In large part this had to do with York's influence over the company, which contributed to serious conflicts between the company and various interests, including planters, colonial governors, merchants, as well as politicians in England who distrusted York and his political and religious ideologies. Although many of these conflicts ostensibly had to do with differences of opinion regarding commercial policies, they were also deeply political, as the ways in which the company and Crown responded to these confrontations will reveal. These disagreements led all sides to attempt to better articulate their own imperial visions and ideals.

THE ROYAL AFRICAN COMPANY,
PLANTERS, AND PRIVATEERS

The African Company's monopoly and the royal prerogative on which it was based were put to the test in Barbados in the years immediately following the company's reorganization. The Council of Trade created a new structure of government for Barbados in late 1670, just as the sugar refining conflict described in the previous chapter gathered momentum in Parliament. William, Lord Willoughby, returned as royal governor with a new set of instructions that aimed to limit the power of the colony's assembly and council. First, the Leeward Islands, the residents of which had long since requested to be a separate colony, were administratively split from Barbados and given their own governor, Sir Charles Wheeler. Willoughby came to Barbados in 1672 with his new instructions, including limitations on his power to appoint or remove the colony's council members. He was specifically ordered to report to London on the political opinions of all council members in order to keep track of potential troublemakers. In addition, the island's laws were only to remain in force for two years unless approved by the king. Previously, laws were in force indefinitely unless explicitly vetoed. After Willoughby's return, Barbados bore the brunt of the Third Anglo-Dutch War in the Caribbean, and he was instrumental in organizing a successful raid on the Dutch island of Tobago.[10] But the governor died shortly thereafter, just as the new Council of Trade and the Royal African Company tried in earnest to get colonial governance and trade under their firm authority.

The King-in-Council appointed Sir Jonathan Atkins, a career army officer and former governor of Guernsey, to succeed Willoughby. Imperial authorities hoped his status as an outsider to Barbados would make him willing to confront the planters in the colony's assembly who had caused so many problems for imperial authorities. Atkins's instructions and commission reflected the Council of Trade's desire for greater control over imperial administration. Unlike his predecessors, Atkins no longer had the power to appoint the members of the colony's council; instead, he would come to Barbados with names preselected by the King-in-Council. But Atkins, who as governor of Guernsey had been allowed relative autonomy in such matters, resented the new restrictions. Before leaving England, he pointed out to the Council of Trade that the king would inevitably turn to Barbados merchants and planters residing in England for suggestions on who should be appointed to the council, thus ensuring that the planter interest in the colony would remain strong. This seemed strange to him because he understood that he had been appointed specifically because he was not "a Planter . . . which I am told the king refused being informed they were so much more inclined to Popular government." In response, the secretary of the Council of Trade, John Locke, scoured previous governors' instructions and commissions to justify the king's authority. "The Nomination of ye Councill [is] reserved in his Majesty here," Locke maintained, "Because ye Government would thereby more immediately depend upon his Majesty and so ye Island be better secured under his obedience."[11] Dependence on England and obedience to the royal prerogative explicitly dictated Restoration imperial designs by 1673.

By the time Atkins arrived in Barbados in 1674, the assembly had been at odds with the African Company and its agents for some time. For the company, the main issue was planters' outstanding debts. In 1673, the company's factors on the island, Robert Bevin and Edwin Stede, wrote to the Council of Trade complaining that the island's laws concerning debt collection favored debtors rather than creditors. "By the law of this island," the agents explained, "no freeholder . . . can be arrested or imprisoned notwithstanding his debt be of 100 times more value than his land, which is contrary to ye law & practice in England & breeds great delay here." What was worse, those in charge of assessing the value of a freeholder's property were usually other planters also in debt to the company, who therefore tended to undervalue the property of their fellow debtors. Eventually Atkins managed to get this law repealed, but the antagonistic relationship between Barbados planters and the African Company remained.[12]

Edwin Stede, the company's most vocal factor, was by no means friendly with most of the planters on the assembly. In addition to Stede's serving as the African Company's agent, in 1670 the king appointed him provost marshal, and in 1674 he became collector of the customs. This was a position created to gather the revenue raised by a new act regulating colonial trade. Passed in 1673, the Plantation Act placed customs duties on enumerated goods traded between England's colonies unless the ship's captain left a bond, or monetary promise, to return with the goods to England. Tobacco was to be taxed one penny per pound, and sugar five shillings for each one hundred pounds. Colonial governors were required to swear an oath to make sure the act would be enforced, and collection of the duty was charged to new commissioners of the customs to be assigned to each colony. The act was especially troubling for Barbados, which relied on trading sugar to New England and other northern colonies for basic supplies of timber and food. The act represented a desire to extract as much revenue from the colonies as possible and to force a dependence on the English government.[13] Therefore Stede, as African Company factor, provost marshal, and collector of the new customs, represented the encroachment of imperial authority and was especially distrusted in Barbados.

Although Atkins had been appointed because he was an outsider, he soon allied himself with the powerful planters of the assembly for his own political survival. In doing so he effectively declared his opposition to Stede and the African Company and embraced the imperial vision of the colony's big planters. In November 1675, an interloping ship with eighty slaves was seized by Stede and his new partner, Stephen Gascoigne, but shortly thereafter the slaves "were violently taken away from them, and they and those who assisted them beaten & wounded." The agents complained to Atkins, who arrested "the assaulters" and held them "in recognizance of 40s with two sureties of 20s a piece to appear at the next sessions." But Stede and Gascoigne decided not to prosecute the case because "it will be not easy matter for us to obtain a verdict against interlopers, especially since it is a maxime with many in this country that the King cannot grant any such Charter as yours is, to exclude the rest of the subjects from trading where they please without it were ratifyed by Act of Parliament in England." They placed the blame squarely on Atkins for allowing known interlopers to hold government offices and for perpetuating an atmosphere that was antagonistic to the company and the king's prerogative. In March 1676, Atkins's friend and ally Secretary of State Sir Henry Coventry wrote admonishing him for not being tough on interlopers and for the violence of the November incident, and "for taking so small and insignificant a recognizance in the case of so high an offence." The warning was the first in a long line of reprimands to Atkins issued at the insistence of the African Company. Such protests became so frequent that Atkins later complained that he felt "the merchants of the Guinea Company" had far too much influence over imperial affairs, and insinuated that "their several designs take upon them in some measure or other to be Governors of Barbados, so that having so many masters, I know not who to please."[14]

The ability of interlopers to find a market in Barbados reflected the colony's growing dependence on slavery. But the dangers inherent in this system continued to worry the white planter establishment. In the spring of 1675, these fears were nearly realized when an attempted slave revolt was discovered. According to an English pamphleteer who reported the incident, "this Conspiracy first broke out and was hatched by the Cormantee or Gold-Coast Negro's about three years since, and afterwards cunningly and clandestinely carried, and kept secret." A female domestic slave, upon learning of the plot, came forward to her master who in turn told Atkins. The governor swiftly rounded up the alleged ringleaders and was "forced to Execute 35 of them for example to the rest." The following year the Barbados government passed a number of laws that aimed to strengthen the 1660 slave code by imposing greater punishments on slaves caught trespassing or harming whites or their property, as well as limiting the movements of slaves between plantations in an attempt to prevent such plots in the first place. In addition, slaves were forbidden from performing work in "arts and trades." By making it a crime to allow slaves to perform skilled and semiskilled labor, it was hoped that white servants and former servants would be less likely to leave the island, which continued to be a significant problem. By 1670, Barbados had a population of approximately 22,400 whites and 40,400 blacks, and by the end of the decade, about 20,500 whites and 44,900 blacks, continuing the population trends described in the previous chapter.[15] The conspiracy, and the reaction to it, further heightened racial tensions in Barbados and was an indication of the colony's inherent vulnerability as it evolved into a slave society. Slave conspiracies and uprisings contributed to an atmosphere of fear among the colony's white planter elite, who incorporated the use of extreme violence as a means of social and economic control into their imperial ideal. This social reality also informed how planters responded to imperial directives from the metropolis.

Barbados was not the only colony to experience conflict with the Crown during the early 1670s. Jamaica had its own confrontations with the English government over the authority of the Royal African Company. In August 1671, the colony's governor, Sir Thomas Modyford, was arrested and sent back to London for disobeying instructions and allowing Jamaican privateers to attack Spanish ships and cities. His actions were in direct opposition not only to the king's and Council of Trade's orders, but also to the interests of the African Company. His replacement, Sir Thomas Lynch, was sent as lieutenant governor with explicit instructions to restrain privateers and promote peaceful trade with the Spanish. Like Willoughby in Barbados, he had orders to keep tabs on the political opinions and activities of the colony's council members.[16] After sending Modyford back to England as a prisoner, Lynch began in earnest to curtail the actions of privateers by announcing the king's intention to forgive their past offenses if they became planters or joined the navy. Many privateers soon realized they could not secure their interests with a governor intent on maintaining peaceful relations with the Spanish, and they left Jamaica to seek out French commissions on the island of Tortuga. Lynch then attempted to appease the growing class of planters on the island, many of whom served on the first assembly he called in February 1672. In addition to issuing significant grants of land to his friends and allies, Lynch allowed an act to pass "declaring the laws of England in force" in Jamaica.[17] Colonists wanted to be assured that their rights and liberties were secured against the encroachments of the Crown, but this action raised many questions. If the laws of England were in force in the colonies, what did that mean in terms of the political relationship with the metropolitan government? What did it mean relative to other laws specifically written in the colonies that did not agree with "English law," such as laws governing slaves? Did English common law have primacy in Jamaica at the expense of Admiralty or other jurisdictions? Did the colonists and their governor have the right to make this declaration in the first place? For the time being, however, Lynch wanted to oblige the assembly to ensure peace and help him cultivate trade with the Spanish.

As a sugar planter, Lynch was a strong advocate for the development of the slave trade to Jamaica. He even offered to serve as the African Company's agent in the colony, probably with as much desire to profit from selling slaves to the Spanish himself as to promote the company's interests. He conceded that this was an uphill battle, as Spanish governors were "so fearful" of the English because of their history of privateering. In 1673 Lynch urged the Council of Trade to persuade the company to take advantage of the imminent expiration of the *asiento* treaty, but the Spanish proved unwilling to consider the possibility of an English proprietor of the contract. The Spanish continued to be wary of the English because many former buccaneers from Jamaica had turned to another enterprise, the cutting of logwood along the Bay of Campeche and the Mosquito Coast of Central America, territories claimed by Spain. Logwood was used as a dye, and the English found the trade to be extremely profitable. But the Spanish considered the cutters to be nothing better than pirates illegally squatting on their land and stealing resources. Caught between antagonizing Spain and reaping logwood's financial benefits, the English government treated the issue of logwood cutting, as it did privateering, with a fair amount of ambivalence. In the summer of 1672, the Queen Regent of Spain authorized her privateers to attack English ships carrying logwood, and by July 1673 Lynch claimed that at least forty Jamaican ships had been taken by Spanish privateers.[18]

Despite the logwood controversy, however, a robust contraband slave trade to the Spanish flourished during Lynch's governorship. Frequently individual merchants based in Port Royal bought slaves from African Company factors and would then sell them to Spanish traders who came to the colony. Although it was technically illegal, English and Spanish authorities, colonial servants, and company agents condoned and often personally profited from such trade.[19] Lynch's efforts to gain the *asiento* for the African Company never came to fruition, however, in large part because of the changing political climate in Europe. The Third Anglo-Dutch War, which broke out in March 1672, was hardly good news for Lynch, who reported that summer, "we have noe ships, [and] our forts not finish'd." Rumors circulated in London that the Dutch, in an alliance with the Spanish, aimed to take Jamaica, and frigates were sent to protect the island

and to organize a possible English invasion of Curaçao. In the spring of 1673, Lynch declared martial law and conscripted the labor of hundreds of slaves, many owned by members of the assembly, to build up the colony's forts and fortifications. Unhappy that the governor and council had drafted their servants and slaves, the assembly refused to allocate any funds to fortify Port Royal, despite the king's orders that the colony pay for such defenses itself. Lynch's frustration with the assembly was palpable when he later concluded that "Assemblyes are apt to be refractory, when they are not restrayned by an absolute character & power such as (I suppose) ye King will conferre on that noble man he sends Governour that his Majesty's authority & interest be here establish't betymes."[20]

The war continued poorly for the English in Europe and the West Indies. During the summer of 1673, wary of Dutch, French, and Spanish intentions in the Caribbean, Charles II and his Privy Council turned to the one man in London who knew the most about the region, Captain Henry Morgan. After his arrest for unauthorized privateering, Morgan proved he had no knowledge of the Treaty of Madrid and managed to win a reprieve. Now he wanted to get back to Jamaica. In August 1673, Morgan issued a report suggesting that the king "order one fifth Rate Frigett for my transportation & give the merchants of [Jamaica] leave to send a ship of 26 guns," for their protection. The following year, Morgan and Sir Thomas Modyford, who had also been released from the Tower of London, met with John Evelyn, who claimed the men "told me 10,000 men would easily conquer all the Spanish Indies, they were so secure." Although the Crown never seriously considered trying to conquer more Spanish territory, Morgan and Modyford were still set on disrupting Spanish trade and settlement in the New World and seemed to find a receptive audience with Charles II. In the meantime, England had broken its alliance with France and signed a separate peace with the Dutch in February 1674. But English fears of French and Spanish intentions in the Caribbean remained strong, especially while logwood cutting remained a significant issue. Who better to keep enemies in check than the most notorious privateer of the age? Both Morgan and Modyford would be sent back to Jamaica with the blessing and encouragement of the imperial administration. Although Morgan would not be officially sanctioned to coordinate privateering raids, there was some expectation that his presence in the region might instill fear with England's enemies.[21]

The return of Morgan and Modyford to Jamaica seems puzzling, however, considering the African Company's anti-privateering position, as well as the Crown's desire to promote peaceful trade with Spain in the West Indies. Lynch, after all, had been sent to Jamaica in 1671 with explicit instructions to discourage buccaneers. But tacit approval of privateering did not necessarily represent the abandonment of the underlying interests of the company and its political-economic position. Raiding Spanish, Dutch, or French ships and ports for gold, silver, slaves, and other goods meant that the enemy would necessarily have fewer resources. And importantly for Jamaica, privateers provided relatively cheap protection against foreign invasion. At the same time, however, the Spanish had to be appeased for the continued problem of logwood cutting. At the request of the Spanish envoy in London, Lynch was removed as lieutenant governor of Jamaica for allowing logwood cutting to continue. In January 1674, the Earl of Carlisle was named the new governor, with Henry Morgan as his deputy. Carlisle refused the commission, however, and the third Earl of Carbery, John, Lord Vaughan, was appointed in his place.[22] Vaughan and Sir Henry Morgan, who was knighted just before Christmas 1674, left in separate ships for Jamaica in January 1675.

Vaughan, another outsider who had been a reliable servant to Charles II in Parliament, was sent with orders to promote the interests of the African Company and to maintain peace with Spain. But the arrival of Vaughan, Morgan, and Modyford threw Jamaica's politics into turmoil. At first, Vaughan seemed to take his instructions seriously, especially in terms of enforcing the African Company's monopoly. But the logwood issue remained unresolved, much to Vaughan's consternation.[23] In addition, Vaughan's willingness to support the African Company and his order to restrain privateers alienated him from most of the political groupings on the island. Traditionally, historians have portrayed colonial Jamaican society and politics as deeply divisive and dysfunctional, with planters and privateers at odds over a variety of issues regarding the economic development of the colony. But distrust of the African Company and its power often provided a way for these seemingly disparate groups to find some common ground. The last thing either privateers or planters wanted was the company monopolizing the slave trade or a governor undermining efforts to continue raiding Spanish ships and ports. This indicates there were more overlapping interests between the planters and privateers than we might at first expect. Morgan's arrival in Jamaica as deputy governor, council member, and Admiralty Court judge, however, acted as a counterbalance to Vaughan's official orders to discourage the privateers. Although he could no longer issue commissions or act the pirate himself, Morgan profited immensely from his connections to the French buccaneers who had helped him in the Panama raid of 1671.[24]

As an outsider to the island, Vaughan had an extremely difficult time making allies of either Morgan's privateering party or Lynch's planter cronies in the assembly. Instead, he relied on Modyford, now chief justice for the colony, for political support and survival, a move that triggered jealousy and animosity from other political factions. The meeting of Vaughan's first assembly in the spring of 1675 did not go well for the governor. The speaker of the assembly, Samuel Long, was an old ally of Lynch's who obstructed Vaughan's attempts to exercise executive authority and went so far as to remove the king's name from the 1675 revenue bill to ensure that money raised would remain in Jamaica. Upon learning of this incident, the English government launched an investigation into Jamaica's laws. In addition, Vaughan had significant problems with Morgan, whose actions helping the French buccaneers placed the governor in an extremely difficult position. Once Morgan's profiteering became intolerable, Vaughan sent evidence of Morgan's actions to London and was then ordered to investigate Morgan's conduct and report his findings to the colony's council. By alerting imperial authorities, however, Vaughan raised suspicions about his own conduct and failures in office, and the English government began to take a particular interest in Jamaica.[25]

THE LORDS OF TRADE AND COMPETING VISIONS OF EMPIRE

Governors Atkins and Vaughan had both been selected because they had no apparent ties or obligations in the colonies, but both proved to be disappointing imperial servants. In large part this dissatisfaction stemmed from highly politicized changes in imperial administration that occurred soon after both men left England. By 1675, a new administrative body charged with imperial administration, the Lords of Trade, enforced the Crown's political and economic agenda in the colonies more forcefully than any previous committee. The origins of the Lords of Trade reflected the contentious environment that had come to characterize Restoration political culture and occurred as a direct result of the Earl of Shaftesbury's fall from political power. Since 1672, Shaftesbury had served as president of the Council of Trade and as Charles II's Lord Chancellor, and both Atkins's and Vaughan's instructions had been crafted by Shaftesbury's council. But within a year, Shaftesbury became politically isolated. England's poor showing in the Third Anglo-Dutch War contributed to Shaftesbury's situation. Although he had strongly supported the war initially, by the spring of 1673 he began to voice concerns about England's alliance with France. He also became an outspoken opponent to the Duke of York's marriage to the Catholic Italian duchess Mary of Modena, and in late 1673 he was removed as Lord Chancellor. Throughout 1674 in the House of Lords, Shaftesbury repeatedly called for stricter enforcement of laws depriving Catholics of political power, and even supported talk of excluding York from the succession.[26]

Despite Shaftesbury's removal from the Privy Council, he continued to attend Council of Trade meetings until March 1674. His presence at these meetings has led historians to minimize the significance of his fall from royal favor in terms of imperial administration. But by 1674, Shaftesbury's political influence was greatly imperiled by his strong anti-Catholic, anti-York position, which made him especially dangerous to the Stuart court. Therefore his removal from royal favor should not be minimized. When his Council of Trade was dissolved by the king and the new Lords of Trade created in 1675, it was under the direct influence of York and in opposition to men like Shaftesbury, who was eventually considered so dangerous to the regime that he was sent to the Tower two years later. Shaftesbury's removal from power and influence was underscored by his decision between 1675 and 1677 to sell his shares in the Royal African Company, which by the mid-1670s had become a bastion of ultra-Royalists who had no sympathy for any opposition to York or the Crown's imperial and commercial policies. Shaftesbury was joined by his protégé John Locke, who also sold his shares at this time.[27]

The creation of the Lords of Trade, so deeply implicated in metropolitan political maneuverings, marked a significant turning point in imperial administration. Over the course of its thirteen-year existence this committee embarked on an ambitious plan of imperial centralization and increased metropolitan control of imperial affairs. The new Lords of Trade was a committee of the Privy Council, and as such it was under greater control and influence of the Crown than had been previous colonial committees. It was dominated by York and the new Lord Treasurer, Thomas Osborne (soon to be the Earl of Danby), a politician with strong loyalties to the king and the idea of monarchical privilege. The committee was packed with men loyal to the Stuarts and their imperial ideology of extending the reach of the royal prerogative in the colonies and continued hostility toward the Dutch.[28] Members included the future governor of Jamaica and career military officer Charles Howard, Earl of Carlisle; the Anglican Royalist, Royal African Company founder, and longtime servant to the Stuarts, William, Earl of Craven; and Thomas Belasyse, Viscount Fauconberg, who would later become a fervent anti-Exclusionist. Many owned stock in the African Company, including Vice Chamberlain Sir George Carteret and Secretary of State Sir Joseph Williamson.[29] The Lords of Trade and the imperial policies it generated were deeply connected to metropolitan political events, imperial institutions, and ideological conflicts. The men on the committee were in no mood to deal with recalcitrant governors and assemblies or to entertain any ideas emanating from the colonies about opening up the slave trade.

In November 1675, in the wake of the attempted slave uprising and a hurricane that devastated parts of the island in August, Governor Atkins authorized the Barbados Assembly and Council to petition Charles II with three grievances. The first concerned the long-hated 4.5 percent duty on raw materials exported from the island. The second requested an end to the African Company's monopoly and a suspension of the Acts of Trade and Navigation in order to enable trade with Scotland for servants. The third had to do with properly measuring casks of sugar for export. On the second grievance the petition read, "whereas the produce of your Majesty's island depends upon the labour of Negro slaves (of whom we need a great continual supply & without whom we cannot subsist), The Royal African Company . . . doe supply us very scantly with them and their price is become excessive; wee are well assured that your Majesty established that Company to enable them to buy cheaper of the African Infidels, & not to enable them to sell dearer to yr own subjects: And doubtlesse they might afford them much cheaper then can be done in open trade." The assembly's complaints were not new; during the governorships of both Francis and William Willoughby, its members had requested an open trade with Africa for slaves. This was the most important component of the colonial-planter imperial ideal. But this was something Atkins had been ordered to control. As an outsider to the island and its politics, it was hoped he would have more sympathy with Crown and company policies than with those he was sent to govern. Atkins explained to Coventry that he had allowed the petition because he "esteemed it my duty to join with their interest while seeing the contents are true." He even asserted in direct opposition to imperial policies that "whensoever you intend to plant a new colony, you must make their port a free port for all people to trade with them that will come."[30]

Upon reading the petition and letters, the members of the Lords of Trade were appalled. Atkins had to be reprimanded "for using these expressions without giving any reason for them, and where he proposes a liberty of trade as necessary for settling a new plantation, the Lords take notice of this notion as dangerous in regard of the old ones," they continued, "and prejudicial to England itself, and resolve to give him a cheque for upholding this maxime of a free trade." A colonial governor suggesting the possibility of free trade almost amounted to treason as far as the Lords of Trade were concerned. This was not simply an example of colonists disagreeing with mercantilist commercial policies. It represented a much more serious ideological divide that had to be contained, because it threatened the authority of the African Company, existing English laws, and the royal prerogative. In the fall of 1676 the Lords of Trade held hearings to investigate the claims made by the governor and assembly.

They invited Sir George Downing, the former ambassador to the Netherlands and one of the chief architects of Restoration finance; Sir Peter Colleton, the absentee sugar planter and African Company investor; and Colonel Edward Thornburgh, the colony's agent in London, to attend. At one meeting Thornburgh "confessed that Barbados is at present well enough supplied with Negroes, and that the complaint was made at a time when the Dutch war had occasioned a great scarcity of them, and therefore disowns the instance which is now made by Sir Jonathan Atkins in this behalf."[31] The effect of the investigation was to present the planters' complaints as baseless and make the governor out to be a troublemaker.

In November the Lords of Trade issued a report to the king, stating clearly that the opinions expressed by the Barbados planters and governor were at best dangerous and at worst treasonous. "We need not lay before your Majesty," the report warned, "of what evil consequence it is that any of your subjects should presume to petition your Majesty against Acts of Parliament (which are ye laws they must live under) and call them grievances." The "whole frame of the trade and navigation of this Kingdom doth turn" on these laws, it continued. Granting a "dispensation" to the colonists in Barbados would undermine the very foundation of the empire. In any event, such an action would be "only fit to be done by your Majesty in Parliament, the whole nation being concerned in it." The Lords of Trade had especially harsh words for Atkins. "We humbly conceive that your subjects of ye plantations would hardly presume to make any address of this kind to your Majesty were they not connived at therein by your Majesty's governor." Atkins, they maintained, was at the root of this discontent and was essentially instigating potential rebellion in Barbados. "We find him, if not ye prompter, yet ye consenter with ye inhabitants of the island for suspending ye Acts of Navigation and Trade, and that he doth labour with more arguments for it than ye inhabitants themselves in their said paper of grievances." This showed a blatant disregard for his duties and instructions. "It was ye duty of your Majesty's governor," the report reminded the king, "to have suppressed any such address from the inhabitants. We are therefore humbly of opinion that it is very necessary for your Majesty's service that Sir Jonathan Atkins should by letter from your Majesty be severely reprehended for his error and mistake, and by his concurrence encouraging ye people therein." Charles II did send a reprimand to the governor in December, but interpreted Atkins's potential insubordination as "zeal" for the welfare of Barbados, and stated "we chose rather to caution you upon this occasion to be more careful and circumspect in your proceedings for the time to come." The Lords of Trade issued its own order to Atkins, "commanding him to secure the Royal Company, and their agents in their quiet enjoyment of their privileges, and to take care that no vexatious actions be brought, and encouraged there against them, contrary to law and his Majesty's Charter."[32]

According to the king, the Lords of Trade, and the African Company, to criticize the Navigation Acts or the company's charter was an attack on the royal prerogative that would subvert the ideological framework upon which the entire empire depended. Although English people in the colonies had the right to petition the king, according to the Crown's emerging imperial ideal, they did not have the right to be critical of laws deemed essential for the functioning of the empire. As the Lords of Trade wrote to Atkins, "we do not so much wonder at these representations from the body of a people, who may by malicious or unadvised suggestions be perswaded into misapprehensions of their own interest and welfare," but a colonial governor should know better. Atkins continued to question the authority of the Crown over colonial affairs, however, and even went so far as to claim that the king lacked the power to make appointments to important offices in Barbados. To imperial authorities, this was absurd; the king had the absolute authority to make the appointments he wished anywhere in the realm. Coventry warned the governor, "The advice that I should give you is this, if you are at any time aggrieved at any commands of his Majesty's, seek the remedy by way of address and not by disputing his power especially where the law is on his side." The position of the king and the Lords of Trade was clear: no colonial assembly or governor had the right to undermine or question the authority of the royal prerogative.[33]

These disagreements were emblematic of the widespread problems with English colonial governance in the late seventeenth century. Stuart imperial policies, embodied in the African Company's monopoly, frequently led to significant conflicts between the Lords of Trade and colonial administrators, planters, and merchants. These confrontations forced all sides to refine their own concepts of how the empire should function and be governed, and made the business of governing colonies increasingly political and divisive. By attempting to silence dangerous opinions in the colonies, the Lords of Trade hoped to limit the growth of similar ideas at home. This was especially important in 1676, a year that was proving to be extraordinarily difficult in terms of imperial administration. News of a violent rebellion in Virginia reached London early that year, and in the following months, nearly all other imperial affairs were put on hold while the King-in-Council organized an expedition of one thousand soldiers to be sent to suppress Bacon's Rebellion. In addition, a bloody war broke out in New England with the Algonquin tribes of eastern Rhode Island and Massachusetts Bay, known as King Philip's War.[34] The combination of these events led the Lords of Trade to be even more rigorous in their

attempts at increasing imperial control over transatlantic colonies during the
next decade.

The Lords of Trade in 1676 also had to deal with encroachments on the
African Company's authority in Jamaica, which would shape how they viewed
governance in that colony. In early 1676, an interloping slave ship, the *St. George*,
was seized outside Port Royal on Governor Vaughan's orders. Traditionally such
cases were heard at the colony's Admiralty Court, but the ship's captain and his
lawyer argued that the Admiralty lacked jurisdiction in the case. This was
because of an act passed during the previous year's session of the assembly that
made the waters where the ship was captured "within the Parish of St. Dorothy's,
within the body of the island." Therefore the ship had been captured beyond the
Admiralty's jurisdiction, which "reacheth not within the body of any county, but
on the high sea onely." The ship's captain and his lawyer maintained the case
should instead be heard at the colony's Court of Common Pleas and therefore
subject to a jury trial. The three Admiralty judges, including Sir Henry Morgan
and his brother-in-law Robert Byndloss, agreed with this argument and ordered
the ship's cargo released. Outraged, Vaughan immediately dismissed Morgan
and Byndloss. Morgan, who also served as the colony's deputy governor, revealed
in a letter to Secretary of State Henry Coventry the true purpose of the law when
he admitted that transferring cases from Admiralty to Common Pleas made it
impossible for the African Company to win a conviction against illegal traders.[35]
No jury made up of planters and privateers, the company's traditional enemies
in the colony, would ever find in favor of the company. The law not only
appeared to be designed to challenge the authority of the Admiralty but also was
specifically aimed at weakening the African Company's ability to prosecute
illegal slave traders in Jamaica.

Not surprisingly, the case did not sit well with the Lords of Trade, who sought
the legal opinion of Richard Lloyd, Advocate of the Admiralty Court in England,
as well as Attorney General William Jones. Lloyd reported that the English
court "would not have dismissed a case of this nature," and that the Jamaican
assembly did not have the authority "to make the high sea part of a parish, much
less to deprive the Lord Admiral of his jurisdiction." Not only did the law obstruct
the African Company's right to pursue interlopers, it directly challenged the
authority of the Lord High Admiral, the Duke of York. It seemed to be a double-
edged attack on the prerogative. Attorney General Jones agreed and went further
than Lloyd in his conclusions. It was not clear to Jones whether or not the laws
of England were in force in Jamaica, something colonists had been claiming
since Lynch's governorship. "But this I conceive is playne," Jones asserted, "that
by his Majesty's acquisition of that country he is absolute sovereigne thereof,

And may impose what forme of constitution both of Government and Lawes he pleaseth. And the Inhabitants are in no sort intitled to ye Lawes of England or to be governed thereby, but by ye mere Grace and Grant of ye King."[36] In other words, the king's authority over imperial governance was absolute, and legally he could do with his colonies what he pleased. In response, Secretary of State Williamson drafted a memorandum to be sent to Jamaica, whereby "his Majesty will not have his prerogative questioned at Jamaica (which is and ought to be governed by his prerogative); His Royal Highness's jurisdiction as Lord High Admiral trampled on nor the Royal Charter granted to the Royal African Company of England to be there questioned as a monopoly." The Lords of Trade ordered Vaughan to "take care to preserve the jurisdiction of the Admiralty, and that the King's Prerogative be not called in question concerning forfeitures."[37] Prerogative, above all else, had to be preserved.

By late 1676, the Lords of Trade, already suspicious of Jamaica's assembly, laws, and government, were in no mood to entertain any ideas altering Admiralty jurisdiction or limiting the prerogative of the African Company and, by extension, the king. Vaughan became the focus of much of the criticism for the incident. Coventry reprimanded the governor for the "dexterous disappointing not only the Duke of York's jurisdiction of the Admiralty, but in effect annulling his Majesties charter to the African Company, and encouraging other plantations to do the like." For the time being Vaughan remained in Jamaica, but his relationship with the assembly and council became strained, which Deputy Governor Morgan attributed to "some Commonwealth Spirits that do what they can to lessen his Majesty's prerogative & ye honour of his government & governour." In May 1677, Vaughan offered his own thoughts on Jamaica's government. Leaving political control in the hands of the assembly, which had proven itself "obstinate as much as illiterate & so factiously bent," results in getting little if anything done. "The title being called representatives makes them swell into very high conceits." Vaughan concluded the problem lay in Jamaica's constitution, which provided "so little power in the governour, & so much given the people." Ultimately, Vaughan's opinions were not enough to save his job. The day the governor dissolved the assembly in July 1677, word reached Jamaica that he would be replaced by a member of the Lords of Trade, Charles Howard, Earl of Carlisle.[38] But interestingly, many of his suggestions were contained in the new governor's instructions.

Like many political and military servants of the Restoration era, Carlisle had a mixed political background with both royalist and parliamentarian sympathies during the Civil War and Interregnum periods. Carlisle was in some ways a surprising choice. He was known to be close to Shaftesbury, and had even supported the idea of excluding York from the succession in early 1674. But Carlisle added a noble title to the office and served on the Lords of Trade and in other ways probably seemed a good choice. He came from the prominent Howard family; had served as England's ambassador to Russia, Sweden, and Denmark; and had acted as Lord Lieutenant of Durham, Cumberland, and Westmorland. Carlisle's family connections and military and diplomatic experience made him an ideal candidate to restrain the troublemakers on the Jamaican council and assembly, especially as war with France seemed imminent in 1678.[39]

In addition to choosing Carlisle as the new governor, the Lords of Trade took the opportunity to attempt to transform the constitutional relationship between Jamaica and London. Imperial authorities wanted to be sure that Jamaica, where the assembly consistently obstructed the interests of the Crown and the African Company, was brought into line. Carlisle arrived in July 1678 armed with orders to force the council and assembly to accept forty laws imperial authorities wanted to be made permanent. This included a revenue bill and a militia bill that granted the governor supreme authority to declare martial law and impress men into service during military emergencies. Carlisle's commission also included instructions to overhaul Jamaica's government. Assemblies would in future only meet at the behest of the king, not the governor. Acts that originated in the assembly and signed by the governor now explicitly had to be sent to the King-in-Council for amendment and approval. The laws would then be sent back to the assembly for final acceptance or refusal, but the assembly would not be able to amend any bills approved by the king. This arrangement was a version of "Poynings' Law," which had been in place in Ireland since the late fifteenth century. In addition, members of the colony's council would henceforth be preselected by the Crown, and the governor would have the authority to remove council members as he wished. The laws were intended to concentrate political power in the hands of the governor at the expense of the assembly. In order to emphasize the king's authority over colonial lawmakers, it was ordered that "the present style of enacting laws [with the preamble] *By the Governor, Council, and Representatives* be converted to, *By the King's most excellent Majesty by and with the consent of the General Assembly*." The new constitution aimed to assert the authority of the governor, who became the king's viceroy in all but name.[40]

Attempting to impose a new structure of government in Jamaica was part and parcel of the imperial agenda of Charles II and the Lords of Trade, under the direct influence of men like York and Danby. It stemmed from a long history of political conflict between the colony and the Crown, which often had to do with the power and influence of the African Company in Jamaica. This decision in 1678 was likely related to the controversy surrounding the interloping ship the *St. George* and the contested jurisdictions of the African Company and Admiralty. In addition to attempting to alter Jamaica's relationship to the Crown, the Lords of Trade attempted similar transformations in other colonies during the late 1670s. A new governor of Virginia, Lord Culpepper, was sent in late 1679 with orders to transform that colony's government along similar lines in the wake of Bacon's Rebellion three years earlier. Around the same time, the King-in-Council also began legal proceedings to recall the charters of Massachusetts Bay, Rhode Island, Connecticut, Maryland, and the Bermuda Company in order to restructure those governments more favorably for the Crown.[41] These were all attempts to centralize authority, limit local autonomy, and create a clearer political relationship between the colonies and imperial authorities. This indicated a desire to eliminate the ambiguity that seemed to plague English imperial governance, which had promoted confusion and allowed colonists too much flexibility and independence. With these directives, colonists would be reminded of their foremost obligation to be obedient to Crown commands.

The new constitutional arrangement had legal, economic, and military objectives all aimed at extending and strengthening the authority of the royal prerogative in the colonies. In settling the issue of revenue permanently, it was hoped Jamaica would provide a steady flow of money without the nuisance of regular assemblies and their "Commonwealth Spirits." With the militia bill, governors would be able to declare emergency powers without obstructions from planters on the council, who might object to the conscription of their servants and slaves to build fortifications, not to mention the suspension of civil law. By seizing control over when and how often the colony's assembly would meet, imperial authorities attempted to strip lawmaking power from the legislature, whose "resolutions," according to the King-in-Council, had proven "less agreeable to His Majesty's intentions." Underlying the entire plan was a firm commitment to promoting England's imperial interests, removing ambiguity in governance, and more powerfully extending the authority of the royal prerogative.[42]

It is important to underscore that this attempt to overhaul Jamaica's constitution came in the aftermath not only of Vaughan's troubles with the colony's legislature, but also the problems with Atkins in Barbados, King Philip's War in New England, and Bacon's Rebellion in Virginia. Bacon's Rebellion was especially troubling to the Crown and contributed to the idea growing popular in London that colonies, if given too much autonomy, could disintegrate into anarchy. Not only was rebellion in and of itself deeply troubling, but the Crown had expended significant resources to suppress the revolt in Virginia. By openly flouting laws and the jurisdiction of the Crown and the African Company,

Jamaica seemed headed in the same direction. The fact that the new arrangement apparently needed the consent of the colony's council and assembly, however, was a fascinating recognition on the part of the English government that its powers were uncertain in this matter. Despite Attorney General Jones's assertion in the case of the *St. George*, it remained unclear which laws were in force in Jamaica, either by the grace of the king or otherwise.[43] This uncertainty was exactly what the Crown and the Lords of Trade hoped to do away with. Carlisle would soon meet stiff resistance from the colonists to these new plans, but for the time being, it appeared that imperial authorities intended to do away with such ambiguity.

CONTEMPORARY DEBATES ON POLITICAL ECONOMY AND EMPIRE

Conflicts with governors, assemblies, and colonial constituencies exposed significant differences of opinion in terms of imperial outlooks and ideals. But colonial officials and planters were not alone in criticizing England's commercial and imperial policies during the 1670s. Throughout the period, a number of economic writers took direct aim at England's imperial policies, especially the Navigation Acts and chartered monopolies, indicating that the "mercantilist mind" had its share of detractors. The overwhelming historiographical focus on the hegemony of mercantilism has led scholars to misidentify the parameters of imperial and economic debates in early modern England as well as their impact on the developing empire. A number of economic writers were highly critical of the government's mercantilist policies. For example, Roger Coke in 1670 argued for an end to the "law of Navigation [that] excludes much the greater trading part of the world from Trading with us from abroad" as well as the dismantling of monopoly "corporations [that] restrain our Trade to as few at home: so as Trade, which ever flourishes in multitude and freedom, is by us, by all imaginable ways circumscribed, taxed, and reduced to a few." The political writer William Petyt claimed, "Nor can the like Expedient be found in any Nation on the Earth, who have or aspire to a great Navigation or Trade." In 1671 the merchant and republican Slingsby Bethel argued that monopolistic "Societies, in restraining the number, both of Buyers of the Native, and Sellers of the Foreign Commodities, must consequently tend to the abating the price of the first, and enhancing the rate of the latter." In addition, Bethel maintained that liberty of conscience should be granted to all Protestant Dissenters to encourage trade, but that Catholics, "because they own a foreign head upon the accounting of their Religion" should be actively discriminated against, rhetoric clearly aimed at the Duke of York. Rather than fight the Dutch as a commercial and ideological rival, Bethel called for a trading alliance and "union" with the Netherlands to improve England's trade and technological development. Many of these writers saw the French as the real threat to England's security and economic well-being. Carew Reynell in 1674 not only insisted that "the Guiny Trade would be much advanced by being freer," but also urged Charles II to be wary of emulating the absolutist style of the French king. "If his Majesty desires to advance his Empire, it is but granting more privileges to Trade, and security to mens persons and properties from Arbitrary power."[44]

Many of these writers not only took aim at England's imperial and commercial policies; remarkably, as demonstrated in chapter 2, some also took issue with the existence of an overseas empire. Rather than relieving England of its dangerous overabundant population, colonies actually appeared to drain England of its potential wealth. By the 1670s, this idea had even entered popular political discourse. In November 1675, Sir William Coventry, who was hardly afraid to shy away from criticizing the court and its policies, claimed in a Commons debate regarding a bill that would have banned the export of wool that "we have fewer people than ever we had, and more product, by the plantations, *Ireland*, (and speaks not of the plague and war) which continually drain from us."[45] According to this position, migration to the colonies would ultimately leave the nation poor and defenseless. Instead of focusing on imperial expansion, England should turn its attention to promoting the growth of its most important economic resource, its population.

Contrary to the supposedly hegemonic mercantilist mentality, these thinkers viewed the establishment of colonies as detrimental to the national interest because they drained England of its own valuable workforce. According to these critics, by focusing on empire building instead of maintaining population, England had lost out on trades it had traditionally dominated, because other nations had taken advantage of England's imperial distractions. "After our American Plantations became peopled by us," complained Roger Coke, "the Dutch began to partake with us in the Turkey and Muscovy Trades; our Stable at Antwerp diminished in a very great measure . . . we neglected the Fishing Trade, whereby . . . the Dutch in a manner became solely in a short time possessed of it." One author in 1686 wrote, "That people that can get the Trade of the World may quickly, without pursuing the toils of the Caesars and the Alexanders, be, (in effect) Lords of their Neighbours." These writers were concerned with international competition, but not because they viewed the possibility of unlimited economic growth as unattainable. According to these commentators, in order for England to compete successfully with its economic rivals, it should focus on the proper management of labor and population, not on territorial acquisition and conquest. "These Plantations may be Considered as the true Grounds and Causes of all our present Mischiefs," bemoaned Petyt, "for, had our Fishers been put on no other Employment, had those Millions of People which we have lost or been prevented of by the Plantations, continued in England, the Government would long since have been under a necessity of Easing and regulating our Trade." Although some felt that certain colonies were worth holding on to, many agreed that new colonial endeavors should be abandoned. "Most of our Plantations in the West-Indies," warned Carew Reynell in 1674, "except Barbados and Jamaica, are but unprofitable." Coke admonished, "In this condition I leave to thee, Reader, to judg whether it will not be yet much more pernicious to the Trade of this Nation to endeavour a further discovery of new Plantations."[46]

These ideas contributed to the volatile political atmosphere of the day and indicated that English imperialism, like English politics, did not develop without conflict and controversy. Such sympathies and the people who supported them were increasingly seen as dangerous to the integrity of the empire and as maliciously contributing to political instability. Charles II's government felt so strongly about this that it issued a proclamation on January 1, 1676, suppressing coffeehouses and other public spaces where such pamphlets and their dangerous ideas circulated. Although this proclamation proved politically disastrous and was abandoned in a matter of weeks, it was a strong indication of lengths the government went to in trying to control public debate.[47]

These critics of empire demonstrated the intimate connection between domestic political divisiveness and imperial policies and designs. For example, in the 1680s Coke became a well-known Whig pamphleteer and opponent of James II's political and commercial designs. Not much is known about Reynell's political leanings, but Bethel was eventually considered a serious threat to the Stuart regime. He was openly critical of many of Charles II's policies, especially regarding religion and trade. He was later a radical Whig and served as a sheriff of the City of London during the Exclusion Crisis and was known to be associated with Algernon Sidney.[48] In addition, he was related by marriage to Buckingham and was also said to be close to Shaftesbury, neither of whom were held in the court's esteem by the mid-1670s. The anti-imperial rhetoric of men like Coke and Bethel was especially dangerous to the Duke of York and the Lords of Trade, as it aimed directly at the heart of their imperial aspirations, not to mention York specifically for his anti-Dutch position as well as his Catholicism. Such ideas also indicate that notions of "free trade" did not develop in colonial isolation, but were part of a transatlantic economic discourse.[49] In the highly charged political atmosphere of the mid-1670s, such sympathies and the people who supported them were increasingly seen as dangerous to the African Company's monopoly, the integrity of the English empire, and the royal prerogative on which they both relied for legitimacy.

CONCLUSION

The imperial policies of the second decade of the Restoration were characterized by efforts at imperial centralization and control and were implemented as a result of the perceived failures of the 1660s. Beginning with the creation of a new Royal African Company and Council of Trade in 1672, to the politically charged atmosphere surrounding the creation of the Lords of Trade in 1675, the 1670s were a transformative decade. On the eve of the Exclusion Crisis, imperial authorities had been dealing with troublemaking assemblies in Barbados and Jamaica for years. Confrontations over the power and jurisdictional authority of the Royal African Company framed many of these debates. But conflicts over commercial regulations and the company's monopoly went beyond purely economic disagreements. They were frequently as much political and ideological as they were economic. The Barbados grievances authorized by Atkins in 1676 and the law altering Admiralty jurisdiction in Jamaica in 1675 were especially dangerous in this tense political environment. Responses by English imperial authorities to these actions and ideas indicated that the Crown viewed complaints about the Navigation Laws and the African Company's monopoly as potential threats to the stability of the government at home and in the colonies. In order for the goals of Restoration imperialism to be realized, colonies had to be brought under firmer control. The coming of the Exclusion Crisis, however, would test the government's ability to implement these transformations.

5

EXCLUSION, THE TORY ASCENDANCY, AND THE ENGLISH EMPIRE, 1678–1688

On the eve of the Exclusion Crisis, the Lords of Trade and Plantations were on high alert. Consistent problems governing Barbados and Jamaica, not to mention Virginia, New York, and New England, heightened imperial tensions throughout the 1670s. Some colonial governors, like Sir Jonathan Atkins of Barbados, seemed to thrive on repeatedly angering imperial authorities. In early 1678, William Blathwayt, the principal secretary to the Lords of Trade, ordered Atkins to send a complete survey of the colony's laws for the lords to investigate. The committee's desire to "acquaint themselves with the true constitution of each [colonial] government" was a reflection of their wish for greater control over colonial administration. Atkins had sent some laws to London in 1677, but Blathwayt and the committee grew increasingly dissatisfied. In April 1679 Atkins finally sent the laws, but he argued that "there was never any laws sent home before by any of the preceding Governors."[1]

The conflict did not end there. In the meantime, the man in charge of collecting the 4.5 percent duty on all goods exported from Barbados, Colonel John Strode, petitioned the Lords of Trade complaining of two laws in effect in the colony. The acts, passed in 1675 and renewed in 1678, allowed merchants to reclaim duties collected on goods that were subsequently "lost or taken at sea." Strode protested that the laws were "repugnant to law & equity, and are made solely for lessening ye King's revenue." Upon investigating this claim, the Lords of Trade discovered they had no record of either law among the papers received from Atkins that summer. The acts themselves were bad enough, but it was far worse that Atkins had apparently tried to prevent the Lords of Trade from finding out about them. The Lords nullified the laws and informed the king that "Sir

Jonathan Atkins has failed to be accomptable unto us of divers particulars relating to his Government, without a true and constant knowledge whereof, we shall find ourselves unable to perform that service towards your Majesty which is incumbent on us." The King-in-Council ordered Atkins to "not intermeddle with our revenue so that any part of it may be thereby lessened or interrupted," and warned him that if he failed to follow orders, he would lose his job. The king soon issued orders to all colonial governors warning them that neglecting to send home laws for inspection "had not better effects than a rebellion."[2]

The use of the word "rebellion" in December 1679 was telling and deliberate. In the summer of 1678, Titus Oates made allegations of an extensive Popish Plot to assassinate the king and slaughter untold numbers of English Protestants. Although his claims eventually proved to be entirely fabricated, Oates's revelations triggered widespread political uncertainty and implicated many Catholics and Catholic sympathizers with close ties to the government. The Duke of York was especially vulnerable. Those who had been wary of what they felt to be the arbitrary and popish tendencies of Charles II's government saw their opportunity and began a movement to exclude York from the succession. From 1679 to 1681, the House of Commons tried on three occasions to pass a bill that would have excluded York or any Catholic from taking the throne. Exclusionists, who generally became known as Whigs, were unsuccessful in their efforts. But the unstable political environment generated by Exclusionist Whigs and their anti-Exclusionist Tory opponents had far-reaching consequences.[3] Many scholars have maintained that the Exclusion Crisis was not simply about removing York from the succession, but that it was a divisive ideological crisis of confidence in Charles II and his government.[4] Most important, the crisis was understood as a serious threat to the regime by the Stuarts and their allies. Therefore in 1679 fear of rebellion at home and in the colonies on the part of the Crown was very real. Colonial governors failing to follow orders threatened to undermine the integrity of the empire and the prerogative authority upon which it was based.

This chapter explores the imperial implications of the Exclusion Crisis and its aftermath. The period began with the Crown on the offensive, continuing its assault on colonial autonomy that had been initiated by the Lords of Trade in 1675. But the Exclusion Crisis greatly weakened the government's ability to govern the colonies effectively. This reflected the inherent connections between domestic and imperial affairs as the crisis reverberated across the Atlantic. The Royal African Company's authority and influence was significantly undermined by the unpleasant focus on its governor the Duke of York, who spent much of the crisis in exile. But the Crown and company also learned from this moment of weakness, and in the aftermath of Exclusion both emerged stronger than ever. Charles II and York felt that in order to ensure stability at home and in the colonies, utmost care had to be taken to control and even remove potential troublemakers from power, especially those with Exclusionist or Whiggish sympathies.

The final years of Charles's reign, 1681–1685, have traditionally been called a period of "Tory Reaction." Tory political ideals were dominant, and anti-Exclusionists were firmly in control of key political offices, both nationally and in municipal governments. Exclusionist Whigs were silenced or fled the country. In terms of imperial administration, the Tory Reaction is more accurately described as a Tory Ascendancy, which continued through James II's reign (1685–1688). This final phase of Stuart imperialism was marked by the reemergence of the African Company at the center of English imperial and commercial designs. For York and the African Company, the accumulated lessons of the previous two decades underscored the need for strong policies but also a willingness to adapt to changing military, diplomatic, political, and economic circumstances. The company also became more successful commercially, as its monopoly was better enforced and interlopers lost market share in the West Indies.[5] This inevitably brought further confrontations with big planters, independent merchants, and colonial governors. By the time of James II's reign, all three of the West Indies colonies had governors or lieutenant governors handpicked by the king because of their unwavering support of extending prerogative control in the colonies, armed with new instructions to promote the commercial and diplomatic interests of the African Company. Central to the evolving imperial agendas of both colonists and the Crown was a growing reliance on slavery and the transatlantic slave trade.

THE EXCLUSION CRISIS AND
IMPERIAL ADMINISTRATION

The Exclusion Crisis has often been treated by historians as a moment when imperial affairs took a back seat to more pressing domestic concerns. But political upheaval in England informed almost all major policy decisions regarding imperial administration. In the wake of the investigation into the Popish Plot in the fall of 1678, the Catholic Duke of York became the focus of intense suspicion and mistrust. In addition, the House of Commons began impeachment proceedings against Lord Treasurer Thomas Osborne, the Earl of Danby, who was removed from the Privy Council and Lords of Trade. He faced charges of maintaining a standing army in England on the pretense that war against France was imminent, but that war never materialized. According to Danby's enemies, this army was meant to be used to promote the interests of "popery and arbitrary government," which became the rallying cry of the Exclusionist movement. In response, Charles II dissolved the Cavalier Parliament and called the first election since 1661. The new Parliament that met in March 1679 contained significant numbers of MPs opposed to York, Danby, and the continued succession. In response to this volatile situation, the king sent York to Brussels until the political atmosphere calmed.[6]

The removal of both Danby and York from the center of government meant that two of the strongest advocates of the royal prerogative and the African Company were unable to influence imperial policy. They were also no longer in a position to protect their allies in the colonies. For example, Governor Sir William Stapleton of the Leeward Islands, a Catholic, became the subject of a witch hunt in the wake of the Popish Plot revelations. The merchant William Freeman, Stapleton's friend and agent in London, warned the governor of a campaign instigated by Sir Charles Wheeler, Stapleton's disgraced predecessor, to have him removed from office by taking advantage of popular anti-Catholic sentiment. After York departed for Brussels, Freeman feared for Stapleton's position because "The mindes of the peaple generally [are] disturbed, and extreamly vigorous in prosecution of all Roman Catholicks." Although Stapleton, like his patron, ultimately survived the crisis, Exclusion had exposed underlying vulnerabilities in imperial governance and administration.[7]

The Exclusion Crisis affected imperial administration in other ways. In April 1679, the king created a new Privy Council and Lords of Trade, and in an attempt to neutralize the opposition he reappointed Shaftesbury to the Lords of Trade and as Lord President of the Privy Council. Shaftesbury remained an outspoken opponent of the court, however, and ultimately his appointment lasted only seven months. But in the wake of heightened political anxiety triggered by the crisis, colonial governors were under intense pressure to provide imperial authorities with the information they demanded. In early 1680, the Lords of Trade issued orders to the governors and councils of Barbados, Jamaica, the Leeward Islands, and Virginia to "transmit unto us quarterly . . . a particular account and Journal of all matters of Importance," including transcriptions of debates in colonial councils and assemblies "upon the framing and Passing of Laws."[8] In addition to reprimanding Governor Atkins, they ordered the governor to conduct a census to learn about not only the colony's population, but property holding, tax rates, and trade. Information was deemed necessary to head off potential rebellion at a time of massive political unrest.

York's exile and the regular attacks on the prerogative also significantly weakened the African Company. In April 1679, the House of Commons created a

committee to investigate "miscarriages" on the part of ships leased from the Royal
Navy by the Company in pursuit of interlopers off the coast of Africa. In May, this
committee received orders to investigate the company's books and charter, and in
response the company drew up a petition defending its monopoly. The petition
was read in the Commons on May 27, but later that day the king prorogued
Parliament, which was eventually dissolved. Although the company was safe for the
time being, its directors maintained the committee should this campaign resume.
In fact, during the Exclusion Crisis many worried for the African Company's existence. In late October 1680, William Blathwayt admitted that the company was
"never in a worse condition to defend themselves than at present. The D. [of York]
being absent, the Parliament sitting where the patent is like to be questioned, and
there being petitions against [the company] from other plantations."9

In response to this hostile environment, the African Company published a
pamphlet entitled *Certain Considerations Relating to the Royal African
Company of England.* This was the first publication directly commissioned by
the company since 1667. It asserted that its monopoly and joint-stock structure
were essential to make sure profits made it to England. "Trade and Commerce
cannot be maintained or increased without Government, Order, and regular
Discipline;" the author(s) maintained, "for in all confused Traffique it must
necessarily happen, that while every single Person pursues his own particular
Interest, the Publique is deserted by All, and consequently must fall to Ruine."
The position of the African Company had not changed since its inception.
Monopoly was essential to protect English interests against those of other
nations. A joint-stock structure was necessary to help pay for the "constant
maintaining of Forts upon the place [Africa], and Ships of warre to protect the
ships of Trade." And because of the company's trade, "A great increase is made
to His Majesties Revenue, and to the Wealth of this Nation." By promoting the
slave trade to the colonies, the pamphlet continued, the company "hinders the
exhausting this Nation of its natural born subjects."10 With this remarkable
statement, this pamphlet directly answered concerns raised by the critics of
empire outlined in previous chapters. Because of the slave trade, English colonies did not drain the home country of much-needed laborers. Like colonial
planters, the African Company promoted the idea that slavery and the slave
trade contributed to the economic well-being of the entire realm. But the
company's vision of a commercial, exploitative empire was driven by monopoly
and the royal prerogative. During the Exclusion Crisis, however, publishing
pamphlets seemed the only method the company had to assert its authority.

Relations with the Caribbean colonies were also affected by Exclusion.
Governors like Atkins, who appeared to be losing control over those they had

been sent to govern, were especially worrisome at this time of political uncertainty. While Atkins initially had the support of the planters and assembly, he found himself politically isolated after he began seizing interloping ships on behalf of the African Company. In retaliation, the assembly refused to pass an excise tax on "strong liquors" in 1680. Deputy Governor John Witham, a staunch Royalist and supporter of the African Company, offered William Blathwayt his opinion that the men of the assembly were "of phanatick principles, many of them are become interested in the interloping trade against ye Royal Company's charter."[11] As far as Witham was concerned, these "phanatick principles" went beyond simply ignoring the Crown's commercial laws and regulations. Such language was deliberately provocative in the summer of 1680. Witham would have been well aware of the political upheaval in Britain and probably knew that describing the recalcitrant assembly as "phanatick" would be alarming to imperial authorities. During the Exclusion Crisis, such principles represented the severest contempt of the king's prerogative authority.

Eventually, Atkins ordered his officers to begin collecting information for the census as he had been commanded, but by the time the information arrived in London in the summer of 1680, it was too late. Already suspicious of any information conveyed by the governor, the Lords of Trade refused to believe the data was reliable, and that summer Atkins was recalled. In a letter to the governor of Jamaica in July 1680, Blathwayt provided some indication as to what led to Atkins's dismissal. "There is no reason given why Sir J. Atkins is recalled, more than that he has been in the government six years. But the dissatisfaction of the committee have always expressed at his returns and manner of correspondency [and] the continual complaints of the African Company against him may be considered as ingredients to this resolution." Blathwayt concluded, "This I mention in the greatest confidence to your Lordship, and not as reasons publicly alleged against him."[12] Although by 1680 the African Company lacked the political influence it had once enjoyed, Atkins had clearly taken a step too far. Imperial authorities had to be sure that those sent to govern the colonies did all they could to defend the Crown against attacks on the prerogative, especially during a serious political crisis.

The trouble Atkins caused the African Company was clearly a factor in the governor's recall. One might ask why it took so long for Atkins to lose his appointment, considering the serious nature of the complaints against him over the course of six years. It has been suggested that Atkins remained in office as long as he did because the members of the Lords of Trade were preoccupied with the upheavals of the Popish Plot and Exclusion Crisis.[13] The problem with this analysis is that it interprets the Exclusion Crisis as solely a domestic problem, in isolation from larger imperial concerns and conflicts. But to understand colonial administration as separate from domestic affairs, especially during times of political crisis, is a fundamental misreading of the political climate of late-seventeenth-century England. Attacks on the king's prerogative and sovereignty were serious threats to the entire foundation of the monarchy, whether they came from Westminster or Barbados. This still begs the question of why Atkins lasted as long as he did as governor. His close relationship with Secretary of State Henry Coventry no doubt helped his longevity of tenure. But by early 1680 Coventry had retired and was no longer in a position to protect or defend Atkins. Shortly after Coventry's departure, Atkins's removal, already long suspected, became a certainty.

JAMAICA'S CONSTITUTIONAL EMERGENCY AND THE ROYAL AFRICAN COMPANY

The new governor of Jamaica, the Earl of Carlisle, left England in the spring of 1678, a few short months before the revelations of the Popish Plot rocked the country. As soon as he arrived in Jamaica that summer, Carlisle confronted significant opposition from the council and assembly to the new plans for the colony's constitution, outlined in the previous chapter. Carlisle blamed notions of popular sovereignty and consent that seemed to plague the colonists' minds. "Popular discourse prevails here as well as in England," Carlisle tellingly reported to Coventry, "and I find a few men's notions have taken such place that the leading men of the Assembly rather set themselves to frame arguments against the present constitution, then to accommodate things under it."[14] The assembly urged the governor to explain to the king that the new arrangement was "absolutely impracticable" and would "not onely tend to the great discouragement of the present planters, but likewise put a very fatal stop to any further prosecution of the improvement of this place." They continued, "There being nothing that invites people more to settle and remove their families & stockes into this remote place of the world" than "the assurance they have always had of being Governed in the same manner, soe that none of their natural rights should be lost, as long as they were within the dominions of the Kingdome of England." In defending their position, the Jamaican colonists emphasized their Englishness and right to be governed by English laws, a refrain familiar to scholars of colonial American history. The planters saw themselves as contributing to the economic, political, and military well-being of the entire realm and understood Jamaica to be an integral part of the empire, if not an extension of England itself. They believed the new constitution interfered with those rights and inserted an arbitrary and unnatural divide between the colony and metropolis.[15]

Unstated in this assertion of "English liberties," of course, was the fact that Jamaica's prosperity increasingly depended upon the forced labor of enslaved Africans. The colonists' role as good Englishmen who created revenue for the imperial economy, with all of the liberties and privileges that implied, depended upon a brutal slave regime built on racial difference. Slavery and the slave trade, as both the colonists and the Crown realized, were in the process of becoming defining features of Jamaica's society and of England's transatlantic empire. Jamaicans had adopted Barbados's oppressive slave code in the 1660s, and in 1684 would develop their own slave law, which was instrumental in contributing to the development of equating blackness with slavery throughout the colonies. Large plantations were becoming important elements of Jamaican society, and planters demanded ever-increasing numbers of slaves. Richard Dunn has calculated that from 1671 to 1684, the number of plantations on Jamaica increased from 146 to 690. He has also estimated that between 1660 and 1680, the slave population in Jamaica grew from approximately 500 to about 15,000, an increase of thirty times. The demand was practically insatiable.[16]

In the debate over the new constitutional arrangement for Jamaica, it became clear that both colonists and the English government recognized the importance of slavery to their local and transatlantic economies. What remained a matter of debate was whether or not English laws and liberties extended to the colonies and whether the slave trade should be controlled by a state-sponsored monopoly. The conflict revealed competing opinions regarding how the empire should function. For the company and Crown, the empire could only serve its real purpose through colonial subordination and reliance on the home country. In contrast, those with colonial interests articulated a vision of empire based on mutual dependence and benefit and saw colonies as political as well as economic and cultural extensions of England.

Carlisle, realizing he was fighting a losing battle, chose to strike a deal with the colonists: if the assembly passed a temporary revenue bill, he would make sure their case was heard in England. The assembly and council agreed. Anticipating a cool reception in London, Carlisle attempted to justify the assembly's objections, or rather his failure to contain them. "My Lords, I find that the present form appointed for the making and passing of laws considering the distance of the place is very impracticable, besides very distasteful to the sense of the people here." After dissolving the assembly, Carlisle asked for orders to call a new one, "to re-enact and make what laws are fit for this place."[17]

In spite of the apparent distractions of the Popish Plot and the growing movement for Exclusion, the Lords of Trade began an investigation into Jamaican
affairs as soon as they learned of Jamaica's recalcitrance in the spring of 1679.[18]
In May they issued a report outlining the "unreasonableness" of the assembly's
objections. "It is not to be doubted but the Assembly have endeavour'd to grasp
all power as well as that of a deliberative voice in making laws," it continued,
"but how far they have thereby entrenched upon your Majesty's prerogative &
exceeded the bounds of duty & loyalty." The king's authority over militias,
revenue extraction, not to mention all constitutional and legal matters in the
colonies, was absolute and unquestionable. The Lords of Trade understood
that the Jamaican case had broader implications, as they informed the king that
"your Majesty's resolutions in this are like to be the measures of respect &
obedience to your Royal Commands in other colonies."[19] After all, as Blathwayt
informed Carlisle, "the rebellion of Virginia was occasioned by the excessive
power of the Assembly." The Lords of Trade were determined not to have
another Bacon's Rebellion on their hands and felt the new laws were necessary
to prevent further colonial recalcitrance. They ordered Carlisle to call a new
assembly, and if he failed to persuade its members to accept the new constitution, the government would revert to martial law.[20]

Throughout 1679, the Jamaican assembly continued to block the new
constitution. Leaders of the assembly, according to Carlisle, were influenced by
events in England. "Now I heare they have purposes in this affaire to address
the Commons of England," he informed Coventry, "who, 'tis reported here,
were about making an act to punish any levying of money but by consent of
Parliament, whether they may include the Plantations I know not." For a colonial assembly to petition Parliament rather than the king or the Lords of Trade
in such a serious matter of imperial governance, as Carlisle had suggested might
happen, would have been interpreted as dangerously novel. News of the political turmoil in England had reached Jamaica at least as early as February 1679,
and it appeared to Carlisle that the assembly's leaders hoped to take advantage
of the perceived weakness of the royal prerogative at home.[21] With Parliament
asserting itself in England, the Jamaican assembly felt it could do the same.

But the assembly never petitioned Parliament about the new laws. Instead,
the colonists took aim at the commercial embodiment of the prerogative in the
colony, the Royal African Company. Led by Chief Justice Samuel Long and
Speaker of the Assembly William Beeston, the assembly and council petitioned
the Duke of York in October 1679.[22] They asked him to persuade the company
"to furnish this island annually with a plentiful supply of Negroes at moderate
rates, whereby his Majesty's customs will be considerably encreased, and

accordingly the country exceedingly strengthened and improved." Petitions like this were not unusual; the duke and the company were regularly lobbied by planters for better supplies and lower prices. But the issuance of such a petition at the height of a crisis that ostensibly had to do with the political relationship between Jamaica and England underscored the central place the company had in Jamaican society and that slavery had in the imperial economy. For the planters, a steady supply of African slaves made their plantations function and made Jamaica valuable to the empire. It was therefore in the Crown's interest, they argued, to enable them to have access to large numbers of slaves at low prices. According to the petitioners, through its monopoly, the African Company hindered the colony's prosperity and threatened to obstruct the economic health of the empire. This point was driven home by this and numerous other petitions that asked for opening access to the slave trade.[23]

It made sense that this petition would come from the principal politicians and planters of the island during the constitutional crisis. During the 1670s and 1680s, the majority of those purchasing slaves were Jamaica's "leading men," such as assembly and council members and other office holders. The assembly's complaints against the African Company amid the constitutional crisis demonstrated that for the colonists, economic concerns were intimately tied to legal, political, and military ones. In fact, the Jamaican assembly did not consider the new constitution or the new militia or revenue bills during the fall 1679 session until after this petition had been issued.[24] The new laws codifying a more clearly delineated relationship to the Crown, alongside the company's monopoly and political influence, were understood by the planters as creating an artificial divide between colony and metropolis. For the colonists, this resulted in hindering their liberties and Jamaica's economic prosperity. With the prerogative under attack in England, the time probably seemed appropriate to go after the commercial arm of the prerogative in the Caribbean. The petition to York at this particular moment illustrates the important role the African Company played in the commercial, political, and military life of the colony.

This appeal from Jamaica, and the entire constitutional crisis, came at a particularly anxious time for the company and the English government, with York in exile and much of the country in political turmoil. As Exclusion came to a head in late 1679, Blathwayt fired off a letter to Carlisle asking why the assembly had "left His Majesty but a small share of the sovereignty and may as well question that which remaines." This language was reminiscent of Tory anti-Exclusionist propaganda used to defend the succession and the king's prerogative. In other words, the Jamaican situation, which certainly would have been troubling to the government at any time, had particular resonance because of when it occurred. The Lords of Trade, and especially its secretary, took the case extremely seriously. In the short term, Carlisle had Long and Beeston, the men who had orchestrated the petition, arrested and sent to England to face charges of treason. The following spring, worried for his reputation, Carlisle left for London to explain his position and failure to follow orders.[25]

The constitutional standoff between Crown and colony continued throughout 1680. The Privy Council and Lords of Trade, in the midst of Exclusion turmoil, wanted to be reassured of the legality of the king's actions in Jamaica. They asked the opinion of the attorney and solicitor generals, who in turn asked the opinion of the chief justices. Unfortunately the justices' legal opinions do not survive. What is known is that over the course of the summer and fall of 1680, the Lords of Trade seemed increasingly unsure of themselves. In a series of hearings held in September and October, in the presence of Carlisle, Long, and Beeston, the Lords of Trade made it clear they were willing to drop the new constitution so long as the assembly passed a revenue bill for at least seven years. Historians have interpreted this willingness to abandon the new laws as possible proof that the opinion of the chief justices was not favorable to the Crown.[26] This is certainly a plausible explanation. What makes this turn of events all the more interesting, however, is that in addition to discarding the new constitution, the Lords of Trade were willing to go further and respond to new demands on the part of Jamaica's planters present in London.

Despite the emerging constitutional compromise, on November 4 the "gentlemen of Jamaica," including Long and Beeston, issued another petition to the Lords of Trade. It asked for three things: "An assurance to continue [the government] under what is now settled," increased support for "discouraging privateers and pirates," and finally, improved "regulation of the negro trade." The bulk of the petition concerned the third issue. The petition criticized how the African Company's managers conducted business, accused the company of "unreasonable and unconscionable dealing," and condemned the company as a tool of the imperial government. "The authority, interest and power the said Company hath," the petition read, "is a general oppression and grievance unto his Majesty's subjects at home and abroad." The company's monopoly, it claimed, was "a hindrance of the increase of his Majesty's dominions and of shipping and navigation and lessen[s] his customs and revenues." In contrast, "the planters of Jamaica have laid out six times more than the said Company's stock in settling the said island, and that it is by their industry, labour, and pains, brought to what it now is." It concluded, "we humbly offer this expedient to your Lordships that the trade of Guiney may be left open and free or under such a regulation in a national joint stock whereunto any of his Majesty's subjects may at any time be admitted to trade." The company "neither by their valour, counsel, nor estates have added anything to the increase, support and maintenance of any of his Majesty's Dominions."[27]

The language of this petition, like that of the assembly's plea to Carlisle in October 1678, revealed more than a simple disagreement over commercial policies. It illustrated how planters in Jamaica viewed the empire and their place within it. According to their position, the colonies were integral parts of England's imperial economy and as such should be allowed to flourish. To the planters, a more-open slave trade was essential for promoting Jamaica's prosperity and therefore the economic well-being of the entire realm. The company's monopoly, on the other hand, "put[s] his Majesty to great expences by frigats to protect their trade to the ruine and diminishing his Customs, trade and navigation." But "each Negro at work in the colonies produceth to his Majesty 10s (and most affirm 15s) per ann custom."[28] What emerges from this petition is not only the continued rhetoric of "English liberties" by the colonists, but the striking paradox of the increasing importance of African slavery to the early English empire. Planters argued they were good subjects because their plantations added revenue to the Crown. That revenue, however, was totally dependent on imported forced labor that the African Company's monopoly seemed to hinder rather than promote. The planters and their allies, including privateers and independent merchants, wanted to preserve the flexible relationship between Crown and colony while at the same time loosen restrictions on the slave trade. This remained central to their vision of a mutually dependent empire subject to English laws and legal traditions.

In late 1680, the Lords of Trade never seriously considered abolishing the African Company's joint-stock structure or monopoly. But, as the petitioners had hoped, the committee did use the opportunity to speed up negotiations by appealing to what the planters seemed to care the most about, the company's place in the slave trade. The Crown had already agreed to drop the new constitutional arrangement in exchange for a revenue bill. On November 11, a week after this petition was issued and the same day the second Exclusion Bill passed the Commons, the Lords of Trade ordered the company to "take care to send 3000 merchantable Negroes yearly to Jamaica, provided they have good payments of their debts collected there, and that they do afford merchantable Negroes to the inhabitants of that island at £18 p head." The company was later ordered "that they be not overhasty in calling in their debts, especially from such as are not in a present capacity of paying them without breaking up their plantations."[29] After years of expensive and potentially dangerous transatlantic conflict, the Lords of Trade were not only prepared for political compromise but were willing to use the African Company, the commercial arm of the royal prerogative in the West Indies, as a bargaining chip in the process.

After nearly two decades of almost constant confrontation, and with the very real threat of civil war and rebellion at home and in the colonies, the government capitulated on what the planters seemed to care about the most: the steady supply of African slaves. By giving the planters what they wanted, it was hoped that Jamaica would once again peacefully send revenue to the Crown. And the African Company was hardly in a position to block the compromise in 1680. In fact the most important factor influencing the shape of the compromise was how the Exclusion Crisis had damaged both York and the company. York was not only its governor and principal financial and political advocate, but the company's entire existence was based on its royally granted charter. Royal charters were steeped in the politics of the prerogative, a concept under sustained attack by a significant portion of the political nation for the better part of three years. The fall of 1680 session of Parliament, which occurred while the hearings on Jamaica took place, was particularly traumatic for the king, his brother, and the company. Throughout the session, the Commons regularly held heated debates over issues of sovereignty, the royal prerogative, and York's religion and, according to one man's opinion, generally ran "high against the Duke of Yorke." The king once again sent York to Scotland, leaving the company vulnerable during its governor's noticeable absence.[30]

In late 1680, the king and the Lords of Trade were wary of fanning the flames of anti-prerogative politics and were unwilling to risk rebellion or civil war anywhere in the empire.[31] During the Exclusion Crisis, the government simply did not have the manpower, money, or overall legal support to compel sweeping constitutional changes in Jamaica, and it offered the African Company as part of the sacrifice in order to maintain stability and a cash flow at a time of crisis. It also indicated a major recognition on the part of the Crown of the importance of slavery in Jamaica, and an embracing of a plantation future for the colony. It provided an indication that the Crown could use access to slaves as a means to manage colonial governance. By backing away from the new constitution and keeping planters happy with a guaranteed price for slaves, it was hoped that the African Company could cultivate its business with fewer interruptions, that the assembly would be more compliant, and that the Crown could peacefully collect the colony's revenue. The compromise not only indicated a realization that extending prerogative authority at a time of grave political instability was unwise, if not impossible, but was a recognition that promoting access to slaves could ease colonial reluctance to accept imperial directives. The deal with Jamaica in 1680, while not eliminating the company's monopoly, indicated a growing awareness on the part of the government that the prime way to keep West Indies planters content, and therefore loyal and quiet, was to provide them easier access to the market in slaves. Although the Crown retreated on a central tenet of its imperial policy, it did not represent an abandonment of the underlying ideologies that supported such a policy, as the coming decade would prove.

THE TORY ASCENDANCY AND THE YORKIST IMPERIAL AGENDA

The final years of Charles's reign have traditionally been labeled the "Tory Reaction," when Whigs were purged from political office and Crown policies became inextricably linked to Tory political ideology. Although there was hardly a "Tory consensus," in terms of imperial administration, the Tory Reaction is better described as a Tory Ascendancy, which lasted through the reign of James II (1685–1688). After the prorogation of the final Exclusion Parliament in March 1681, Charles II and his closest advisers wanted to reassert royal authority and emphasize the importance of obedience to the Crown. This meant removing Whigs from positions of power in order to make sure their ideas about popular sovereignty and limiting the prerogative never again became ascendant.[32] The most ambitious design that aimed to undermine the perceived Whig threat to stability was the *quo warranto* campaign, which began in earnest in 1683. This initiative forced corporate bodies, including a number of cities and towns, to prove "by what warrant" they existed, and in doing so, were forced to surrender their charters to the king. He was then able to issue a new charter, with new and more politically compliant corporate members. The *quo warranto* campaign extended to colonial charters, including a successful movement against the charter of Massachusetts Bay in 1684 and all colonial charters by 1686. In addition, the king and his council decided that calling another Parliament in England would be counterproductive to maintaining order and stability. Improvements in the collection of customs revenue, including from colonial trade, enabled Charles to maintain financial independence and rule without Parliament for the remainder of his reign.[33]

After the Exclusion Crisis passed, the Crown once again enjoyed the unfettered ability to attempt to reap the economic and diplomatic benefits of its empire. The Lords of Trade and the Privy Council, for example, continued to gather as much information as they could about the colonies and their laws by requiring governors to report regularly on all aspects of colonial government. The Lords of Trade experienced many personnel changes in the wake of the Exclusion Crisis, as a number of members passed away, retired, or were dismissed. By the time of James II's reign, the Lords of Trade was made up almost entirely of reliable Tory servants to the Crown. In 1686, the committee included such men as Lord Chief Justice George Jeffreys; Robert Spencer, Earl of Sunderland, a close associate of James's and a strong advocate of prerogative politics; James Butler, Duke of Ormonde, the Lord Lieutenant of Ireland; John Sheffield, Earl of Mulgrave, a loyal Tory servant on the Privy Council; John Ernle, a treasury commissioner who would later refuse to recognize the removal of James II from the throne in the Glorious Revolution; and Sir Edward Herbert, Earl of Portland, who was exiled with James after the Glorious Revolution.[34] All were firmly committed to James and his imperial program of consolidation and centralization.

Despite this membership, the Lords of Trade's overall importance as an administrative body diminished over the course of the 1680s. Instead, partisan bureaucrats assumed greater influence and power. The career of the committee's chief secretary, William Blathwayt, exemplified this transformation. Significantly, Blathwayt was given a patent in May 1680 to act as auditor general of the colonies with the power to collect and review all colonial revenue. Customs collectors in the colonies, created through the 1673 Plantations Act, sent revenue directly to Blathwayt, some of which served as his salary. The patent granted him the authority to appoint his own deputies to collect revenue on his behalf. This gave Blathwayt a tremendous amount of power as governors, officers, and customs collectors deferred to his judgment in important affairs and depended upon his assistance when problems arose. Traditionally, Blathwayt has been described as a Royalist motivated by self-interest and greed and a desire to promote the authority of the Crown over colonial affairs. There is no doubt of Blathwayt's aspiration to accumulate personal wealth by serving in as many administrative offices as possible, as well as his royalist (and eventually Tory) political affinities during the 1680s.[35] It is significant that Blathwayt's rise to prominence coincided with the Tory Ascendancy, as partisan administrators became reliable servants to the Stuart government. Others such as Sir Edmund Andros, governor of the new Dominion of New England, and Lord Howard of Effingham, governor of Virginia, would also rise to the occasion as loyal servants during James II's reign.

The extent and direction of James II's "imperial vision" has been hotly debated by scholars. Did James, who was removed from the throne during the Glorious Revolution because of his "absolutist" tendencies, apply his autocratic inclinations to imperial affairs? Some historians have argued that James had always been an imperialist, emphasizing that he played a central role since at least the mid-1670s in shaping imperial designs and policies as governor of the African Company, an active member of the Lords of Trade, and a strong promoter of imperial interests. Others have taken a more cautious approach. While acknowledging James's interest in the African Companies and colonial

expansion, they have downplayed his role in formulating any centralized imperial policy, noting his frequent absences from Lords of Trade meetings and
apparent lack of interest in governing his own proprietary colony of New York.
But James, especially by the 1680s, played a significant role in shaping a variety
of imperial designs. Through his unwavering belief in the royal prerogative,
James had a clear imperial agenda, even if its implementation was haphazard
and in many ways incomplete. Nevertheless, the overall thrust of his designs
indicated a pattern of centralization and control and ran parallel to his plans to
consolidate government in Britain.[36]

The creation of the Dominion of New England is perhaps the most concrete
example of how James hoped the empire would be governed. In late 1684, in the
wake of the *quo warranto* campaign against the charter of Massachusetts Bay, York
was instrumental in creating the Dominion, which consolidated Massachusetts Bay,
Maine, and New Hampshire into one administrative unit. Plymouth, Rhode Island,
and Connecticut were added the following year, and in 1688 the royal colonies of
New York and New Jersey joined. But before the structure of the Dominion could
be implemented, the Privy Council, including James, held a number of discussions
on how colonies ought to be governed. As scholars have noted, the contours of this
debate and the origins of the Dominion were deeply rooted in the politics of the
Tory Reaction. The primary question under consideration was whether or not the
Dominion should have a representative assembly. The Privy Council, and especially James, felt it should not, and wanted the governor to rule in consultation with
a governing council but no elected assembly. In addition to refusing to allow an
assembly in the Dominion at this time, James rejected the continuation of New
York's infant legislative body. This distrust of representative institutions as hindering
the power of the royal prerogative guided James's imperial designs.[37]

In addition to limiting colonial autonomy, James II and his allies on the Lords
of Trade set about overhauling the duties on colonial agricultural goods. In the
spring of 1685, the House of Commons confirmed the new king's plans for
increasing the export duties on colonial produce, especially on tobacco and sugar,
duties that were notoriously hated by colonial planters.[38] James II and his advisers
also discussed the possibility of creating a Dominion of the West Indies. In addition, in early 1688, a group of promoters urged the creation of a West Indies or
"South Sea" Company, created by the king's prerogative as a means to consolidate
the sugar trade. A formal proposal was made in March 1688 for a company with
£500,000 of stock that would establish a "Common Factory" in each of the West
Indies colonies, to which planters would have to deliver all colonial produce. In
exchange for the exclusive right to purchase sugar, the company would grant
planters "credit for three quarters of the valew of all Goods coming into ye Hands

of a Common Factory" in order for the planters to purchase the goods they needed. All sugar delivered to the common factories would then be sent to England for refining and resale, thus eliminating the need for export duties or enforcing the cumbersome Navigation Acts. This would also guarantee permanent revenue for the Crown because the company would take responsibility for all customs duties. One anonymous promoter of the scheme appealed to James's anti-Dutch sentiments and argued that it would greatly undermine the Dutch sugar-refining industry. Most important, the company would limit the possibility of a revolt among colonial planters because it would "unite the militia of each several island for the assistance & defence of the whole, [and] will make a descent upon any troublesome neighbour in those parts, secret, speedy, & successful without any charge to the Crown." Significantly, this promoter suggested that the entire scheme could be enacted "without any reach of law or assistance of Act of Parliament." Like the Dominion of the West Indies, the scheme for a West Indies Company never came to fruition. But the plan and the serious consideration it received reflected the imperial outlook of the king through its anti-Dutch, monopolistic, and militaristic approach to imperial governance and trade.[39]

Although James and his allies supported an anti-Dutch agenda, they remained relatively neutral when it came to the Spanish in the New World. James did not consider the Spanish to be a serious threat to English interests in the Caribbean. If anything, the Spanish were to be exploited and taken advantage of because of their perceived wealth, not to mention their military and political weaknesses. The anonymous promoter of the West Indies Company described the Spanish as having "laid aside all thoughts of enlarging dominion, or aggrandizing their monarchy." Similarly, William Blathwayt indicated in some private notes in 1685 that it was in "His Majesty's interest to hinder any other nation but the Spaniards to thrive or plant in the West Indies, especially in such places where they may be able to annoy either us or them." The Spanish, unlike the Dutch or the French, were acceptable because "they being already subservient to the court of Trade to the English Nation who reap the profit of their hazards & labour, without any expence to the Crown."[40] In other words, because of privateering, smuggling, and the African Company's efforts to sell slaves to Spanish merchants, England was able to siphon wealth away from Spain with little effort.

THE AFRICAN COMPANY AND THE TORY ASCENDANCY

Not surprisingly, the African Company's influence also transformed during the Tory Ascendancy. The company was once more at the center of imperial affairs, especially after York returned to England in the spring of 1682. It became increasingly commercially successful by continuing to improve its market share relative to both Dutch traders and English interlopers. During the 1680s, the company doubled its capacity to deliver slaves to the English West Indies. According to David Eltis, from 1672 to 1679 the company delivered approximately 22,012 slaves to Jamaica, Barbados, and the Leeward Islands, or about 56 percent of the overall total of 39,289. From 1680 to 1688, the company delivered about 53,663 slaves, or roughly 66 percent of the overall total of 81,039. The company was also an extremely profitable investment opportunity and regularly paid high dividends to its investors during the 1680s.[41]

Significantly, the African Company's power to seize slaves purchased from interlopers increased dramatically during the 1680s. As we have already seen, colonial governors were usually given clear instructions that it was within the company's power to seize interloping ships and cargoes after they had landed. What remained unclear, however, was whether or not it was legal to confiscate slaves acquired from interlopers after they had already been purchased. To many planters, because slaves were considered chattel, this seemed to be a violation of property rights. Governor William Stapleton of the Leeward Islands asked for advice with one such case in 1680, in which swords were drawn to prevent colonial officers from seizing slaves that had already been purchased from interlopers. Two years later the governor of Jamaica, Sir Thomas Lynch, wrote about an interloping ship that had landed and within twenty-four hours sold its cargo of slaves. The African Company's factors refused to try to seize the slaves, because they "fear Judges and Jurys will not allow seisures after they are put on shore, marked and property changed." Blathwayt referred this case to the attorney general, Sir Robert Sawyer, who gave his opinion that illegal property "may be seized wherever found whilst they remain in specie. Negros, being admitted as Merchandise, will fall within the same Law."[42] Not only did this confirm and expand the African Company's power to seize slaves purchased illegally, but it illustrated how the law had transformed regarding the status of slaves. Now according to English law, and not just colonial laws, slaves officially became movable property.

The African Company's ability to seize and prosecute interloping cargoes was also helped tremendously by a decision issued by the justices of the King's Bench in January 1685. The case of *East India Company v. Sandys* involved a private merchant, Thomas Sandys, whose ship had been confiscated by the East India Company while still in the Thames in late 1682.[43] The company's lawyers claimed that Sandys's attempt to trade in India without a license not only was a violation of its charter but that it threatened the public service performed by the company in conducting trade to the East Indies. Lord Chief Justice Jeffreys and a unanimous court agreed and firmly established the supreme authority of the royal prerogative over foreign trade, discovery, and conquest. "The kings of England have exercised this their prerogative in all ages," Jeffreys concluded, "and as the king has the power of restraint of the foreign trade, so he is only judge when it is proper to use that power." Jeffreys's opinion codified the king's right to use his prerogative authority over all imperial, commercial, and military affairs. This decision provided legal justification for both the East India and the Royal African Companies to pursue interlopers with impunity, and in light of the decision the African Company requested that colonial governors be reminded of their duty to prosecute interlopers to the fullest extent of the law. The governors of Barbados, the Leeward Islands, and Jamaica shortly received orders that interlopers, or those abetting interlopers, should "bee severely punished by Fine, Imprisonment & such other penaltys as the quality of their offence may require."[44]

In the aftermath of Exclusion, the African Company tried to chip away at the terms of the compromise over the price of slaves sold in Jamaica. This was a delicate issue for Sir Thomas Lynch, who had been reappointed governor in 1681. He found himself once again having to negotiate with the powerful planters in the assembly as well as the company and its interests. At first, because he had been sent with strict orders to settle the issue of revenue once and for all, he attempted to curry favor with the men of the assembly.[45] In his opening speech in September 1682, he assured them, "I know of no designe to injure you, or invade your just liberties," and presented himself as a peacemaker sent to calm "those passions that have soe long agitated you." In return for such reassurances, the assembly passed a seven-year revenue bill. It helped Lynch that he was not an outsider to the island, and the planters and privateers of the assembly, however much they disliked the imperial government's intentions, trusted him as a known quantity. It also helped that by the time Lynch arrived, the compromise on the price and number of slaves sent by the African Company had been in place for over a year.[46] Underscoring the act's importance to Jamaican planters, after passing the revenue bill, the assembly and council thanked the king for his "Grace and Justice in Assimulating our Government to that of our Native Country of England, [and] for your Majesties favour in ordering us supplies of Negroes at reasonable rates." This letter illustrated how the colonists understood the quid pro quo of empire: in order for the Crown to secure steady revenue, it had to be willing to compromise on certain issues. As Lynch told the assembly, it was in the king's interest to make sure Jamaica prospered, "for Colonyes that doe not thrive, are like scabs, they render nothing to, But draw Nourishment from the Body." With the most powerful planters happy on the

issue of the slave trade, the greater the chances were that they would not interfere with imperial governance or revenue collection.[47]

During the Tory Ascendancy, however, the company lost no time trying to
dismantle the compromise. In January 1683 the company requested the revocation of the original order. Considering the amount of debt owed by the colony's
planters, the diminishing value of Spanish currency used in the West Indies, the
falling price of sugar, and the persistence of interlopers off the West African
coast, no one could expect the company to sell slaves at such low prices. The
company's directors also pressed the Lords of Trade to "set aside" the law. The
resurgence of the African Company at the center of imperial affairs was underscored when Blathwayt warned Lynch "my opinion upon all these proceedings
[is] that the islanders should keep themselves well in ye opinion of the Council
in reference to the Company and live upon terms of moderation and civility."[48]
Blathwayt's letter indicated that political rhetoric attacking the company and its
interests that characterized the Exclusion era would no longer be tolerated.

Lynch thought the "Negro Act" would be settled relatively quickly, but the
issue dragged on for years. The African Company even appeared to be deliberately siphoning its trade away from Jamaica, "thinking that price [of £18] be too
small." This frustrated Lynch, who wondered why the company disregarded
Jamaica when he did everything he could to promote its interests.[49] "This sufficiently amazes me, since I have done (and you know it) all in my power to oblige
them," he wrote to Blathwayt in the summer of 1683. "I cannot bet what this
means, unless they would set up a commonwealth in a monarchy." Indeed, the
company's influence seemed stronger than ever. After another round of petitions, the Lords of Trade suggested that the price of £18 be abandoned, but
ordered the company "to furnish the island with five thousand Negroes within
the first year and with three thousand yearly afterwards." Included in the new
concession was language allowing company officials to impose a £5 fine for each
slave purchased illegally, confirming the powers outlined by Attorney General
Sawyer in early 1683. The following spring, the company managed to do away
with some of the new requirements and reduced its obligations from five thousand slaves in the first year to three thousand slaves per year. A draft of an act
containing this new compromise was sent to the Jamaican assembly and council
for passage in the summer of 1684.[50]

Lynch strongly supported the new proposal because he felt that such large
numbers of slaves would allow the *asiento* trade to flourish in Jamaica. Despite
the company's desire to cultivate this trade, Lynch's position brought him and
his colony into further conflict with the company, because Lynch was willing to
utilize slaves purchased from either the company or private traders to keep the

trade afloat. When he first returned to Jamaica in 1682, he noted that although interlopers "may choque the charter or hurt the Royal Company," their actions did not hurt "the King's Customs or Nation's trade, for every Negro's labour that produces cotton, sugar, or indigo is worth £20 p ann to the customs, [and] four times as much in cocoa if it stands and keeps its value. Nor is it possible to hinder the Importation [from interlopers], for the Island is large and slaves are as needfull to a Plantation as money to a Courtier, and as much coveted." But the company seemed unable or unwilling to tap into this growing market.[51] Not everyone in Jamaica wished to promote the *asiento*, however. Sir Henry Morgan and his privateering friends, who had long been wary of maintaining peaceful trade with the Spanish, actively tried to obstruct the trade. Although Morgan had been the darling of the Stuart court when he returned to Jamaica in 1675, he was removed from office in 1681 for continuing his anti-Spanish policies. In 1684, Morgan and his lawyer Roger Elletson persuaded two men to seize a Dutch-Spanish ship that had acquired a cargo of slaves at Jamaica. Lynch intervened and ordered the royal frigate assigned to the colony to help escort the foreign ship out of Port Royal's harbor. As a result of the vigilante justice by these "beggarly vagabonds," Lynch claimed the Spanish captain was now reluctant to return and the colony would lose out on this lucrative trade.[52]

Lynch died shortly after this incident, leaving his lieutenant governor, Sir Hender Molesworth, to deal with the consequences. Lynch had named Molesworth to office in 1683 as a way to counterbalance the "privateer interest" on the island. Molesworth had been the African Company's agent in Jamaica for many years and, like Lynch, was personally invested in the *asiento*, which he called "so considerable a trade" that benefited "the whole Kingdom of England." He did his best to suppress pirates and privateers who continued to plunder Spanish ships and ports and had to deal with further incidents of Jamaicans seizing Spanish ships without authorization.[53] According to Molesworth, English colonists were sometimes assisted in their efforts to thwart the trade by a former proprietor of the *asiento* who refused to recognize the new holder of the contract. According to Molesworth, this factor, named Santiago de Castillo, was "ye greatest enemy ye Assiento hath, [and] joynes with the disaffected to that trade (who are ye same in ye Gov't), discovering ye very secrets of it to give them ye better opportunityes of throwing all ye discouragements they can upon it." Although Molesworth did not directly accuse Morgan and his cronies of conspiring with Castillo, the implication became clear when in the same letter he reminded imperial authorities that Morgan and his allies were "great enemyes to ye Spanish Trade."[54]

Molesworth also had to deal with the significant social and political consequences of Jamaica's ongoing transition to a slave society. He had avoided calling an assembly for two years after Lynch's death and only called one to meet in June 1686 in the wake of a slave revolt that had broken out the previous summer. Immediately after the uprising began, Molesworth declared martial law and organized militias to suppress the rebellion, but this policy failed, as the slaves escaped into the island's dense interior and joined with communities of former slaves, known as Maroons. The militias had to be paid, and Molesworth asked the legislators to approve compensation. But the assembly refused to vote for any new taxes. "They must be willfully blind," Molesworth raged, "if they can be led away by false pretences against the common good."⁵⁵ This refusal to tax themselves represented the planters' imperial agenda at its most extreme: despite an ongoing slave uprising and the deaths of dozens of people, they were unwilling to pay to suppress the rebellion. The implication was that the Crown should pay for the colony's safety and security. The men of the Jamaica Assembly, both planters and privateers (and many of course were both), wanted all of the benefits of slave owning and maintaining mastery over slaves without paying for any of the consequences. They were willing to put their own lives in danger for the sake of profit. The episode revealed the vulnerability inherent for planters in a slave society and their need for assistance from the government to support white supremacy. Eventually, the assembly agreed in principle that the hired soldiers needed to be paid, and it proposed "an Imposition upon Negros exported" from the colony to pay the charges. What this effectively meant was a tax on the *asiento* trade. Molesworth knew the Crown and the African Company would never support such a move, and neither could he. He thought the tax was designed by "a party made of ye discontented" to bring the *asiento* "under such discouragement, as must necessarily have driven it from us." After a scathing speech in which he described the actions of the legislature as a "confused medly of Contradictions," Molesworth dissolved the assembly. In the meantime, word reached Jamaica that the new king had appointed Christopher Monck, the second Duke of Albemarle, to be the new governor-general of Jamaica.⁵⁶

POLITICAL DIVISIVENESS DURING THE TORY ASCENDANCY

Although the end of the Exclusion Crisis signaled a triumph of Tory ideology and the political strengthening of the Crown, it did not mean the end of political division and partisanship. A divisive atmosphere continued to shape political debate throughout the 1680s. This was true both in the colonies and the metropolis, as governors, planters, military officers, merchants, and privateers utilized highly politicized categories and labels to describe themselves and their enemies.

Although the African Company enjoyed significant power and influence over imperial affairs in London, it continued to be subject to criticism and ridicule from many colonial constituencies. Such politically charged language had real meaning at a time when many felt that another civil war had only just been narrowly averted. In 1681 the new governor of Barbados quickly became involved in a war of words with those he had been sent to govern. Sir Richard Dutton, another outsider governor, was handpicked by the Duke of York in an attempt to break the "plantocracy's" hold on power in the aftermath of Atkin's tenure. He attempted to govern with a heavy hand and to impose the resurgent Stuart imperial agenda of centralized control and colonial obedience. He quickly established himself in opposition to the island's powerful planters in the council and assembly. Upon Dutton's arrival, the assembly refused to pass a tax on liquor imported into the island, leaving the colony without funds to pay its debts or operate law courts or jails. This had serious consequences not only in terms of public safety but politically as well. In a letter to Sir Leoline Jenkins (a staunch Tory who replaced Coventry as secretary of state for the southern department in 1680), Dutton reported that the men of the assembly "thought Monarchy was upon its last legs in England, and I am confident they were preparing to set up here for a Commonwealth as early as any of the plantations should do, and it is my great unhappiness that I am here but a single person to resist such traitorous designes." Dutton further lamented to Blathwayt that "Rebellious Spirits in England and their traitorous libels influence the people here to be too inquisitive and busying themselves too much in state affairs."[57]

Dutton's rhetoric in describing his political adversaries was significant. In characterizing the Barbados Assembly with such loaded terms as "Commonwealth" and "traitorous designes," Dutton positioned himself as a defender of the Crown and the royal prerogative. Such words and their connotations were especially resonant in the aftermath of the Exclusion Crisis, when "Rebellious Spirits" and "traitorous libels" had threatened to throw the country into civil war. These words were an ideological code that created an "other," in this case, a dangerous political enemy. As Tim Harris has argued, the use of such political language reflected the partisanship of the age and "became everyday currency to describe the competing factions that existed in both the metropolis and in the localities." This ideological code extended to the colonies. Dutton's use of exaggerated terminology was intended to draw a stark contrast between himself and the disloyal colonists. Such insinuations about the political atmosphere in Barbados were indeed alarming back in England. Atkins, after all, had been removed not only for his administrative negligence, but for encouraging such "Commonwealth" principles among the planters in the assembly. Similarly, Dutton's deputy governor, Sir John Witham, complained about the political orientation of those he had been sent to govern. Witham wrote that "there be in this Colony many factious, seditious & ill affected persons, who are tainted with the old leaven and humours of '41, these, as well as many of ye Fanaticks, have at times, been very troublesom in this Government." The only way he could keep the "Fanaticks" under control, Witham claimed, was with the threat of legal action. In part because of his adept use of this political vocabulary, imperial authorities were confident in Dutton's ability to keep the planters of Barbados under control. Blathwayt urged Dutton to explain to the assembly that its obstinacy was not appreciated in light of the failure of Exclusion. "Those of Barbados shall be informed," Blathwayt noted, "of the great change in affairs here, that loyalty receives its due countenance, and sedition its punishment." The king, he continued, "resolves to govern by law so he will lose no part of his Royal Prerogative." After months of wrangling over the excise, in January 1682 Dutton dissolved the assembly and purged the colony's commission of the peace of two of its five judges.[58]

Barbados was not the only colony where divisive political rhetoric became commonplace during the 1680s. Sir Thomas Lynch in Jamaica was also subject to a fair amount of political mudslinging. In large part this stemmed from his poor relationship with the old privateer Sir Henry Morgan and his cronies, who disliked Lynch's desire to promote the *asiento*. During the fall 1683 session of the assembly, Lynch managed to persuade the legislature to approve a new revenue bill, this time for twenty-one years. He also convinced the assembly to not petition the king with grievances about the African Company and the slave trade. Lynch's enemies, foremost among them Morgan, seized upon this and orchestrated rumors that the governor had been "bribed & partial to the R. Company." Lynch, who was frustrated with the company's inability to provide Jamaica with enough slaves to satisfy both local planters as well as Spanish merchants, vehemently denied the charge. Lynch then removed Morgan, Morgan's brother-in-law Robert Byndloss, and Morgan's son Charles from the colony's council. In explaining his actions to the Lords of Trade, Lynch described the political divisiveness that seemed to pervade Jamaican society. "[Sir Henry] and C. Morgan set up a particular Club," Lynch explained, "frequented only by 5 or 6 more, & here (especially when drunk) the Dissenters were cursed & Damned, & the whole Island provoked, & reflected on, by their assuming the name of the Loyal Club, & people began to take notice, that it looked as if hee designed to be thought Head of the Toryees, consequently I must be so of the Whiggs." Similar to Barbados, political labels had significant meaning in Jamaica as a kind of ideological code. In this case, Morgan and his privateering comrades presented themselves as loyal to the Crown by embracing the term "Tory" and labeling their political enemies "Whigs." Morgan portrayed the governor as a disloyal servant who threatened political order and stability. Such labels indicated how perceptions of ideological identity traveled beyond the confines of Westminster.[59]

Sometimes such political volatility spilled over into violence. The governor of the Leeward Islands, Sir William Stapleton, had survived the Whig onslaught against him during the Exclusion Crisis stemming from his Catholicism. But once the African Company's position became more politically secure, Stapleton faced a barrage of accusations that he inadequately protected the company's interests. In part, the company's campaign against Stapleton stemmed from a lack of a satisfactory resolution in the case of James Starkey, a company employee killed in an altercation involving illegal traders in Nevis in 1679. Stapleton immediately called a grand jury, and during the investigation it became apparent that many colonial officials in Nevis had been involved in protecting interlopers. The following summer the Nevis Admiralty Court issued indictments to four men for inciting a riot, and to another three for murder. In all but one case, the court issued an *ignoramus* verdict for lack of evidence, and in the sole case that went to trial, the defendant was found not guilty.[60] The colony's Admiralty Court judges, made up of planters and merchants who had little sympathy for the company, were unwilling to find in the company's favor, even when it involved the death of an employee.

Starkey's death highlighted the extremes colonial merchants and planters were willing to go to over the issues of forced labor and commercial regulation. It also underscored the violence that seemed endemic to the Leeward Islands, a frontier colony that was poor, poorly populated, and badly served by imperial authorities, including the African Company. The company, in fact, did not consider the Leeward Islands to be a significant market for slaves.[61] Such isolation bred resentment that often spilled over into violence. In fact, the Nevis assembly speaker, Philip Lee, one of the officials suspected of aiding interlopers, was involved in another altercation with the company's agents in June 1680, one month prior to the trial for Starkey's murder.[62] Further prosecution in this and the Starkey case, however, awaited the resurgence of the African Company's ability to exert its political influence in the aftermath of the Exclusion Crisis.

Stapleton's troubles were exacerbated by another brutal episode involving company agents and private merchants in June 1682. That month, an interloping ship was seized by Captain Christopher Billop, the commander of the king's ship *Deptford*, at Nevis. An altercation ensued, resulting in the death of one of the interlopers. Instead of turning the cargo of slaves and "African commoditys" over to the company's agents or to the colony's Admiralty Court, Billop and his crew seized the slaves and sold more than half for their own profit. Billop argued that because he and his crew had intercepted the cargo they were entitled to the proceeds. Stapleton had Billop court-martialed before the Admiralty Court, which prosecuted the captain and labeled him "one of the worst men that ever wee saw in the King's service." This outcome did not immediately satisfy the Crown or the company, however, because Billop was technically acting in the king's service. Billop escaped and made his way to London, where he appeared before the High Court of Admiralty and managed to convince them that Stapleton had illegally seized the *Deptford* from its rightful commander and encouraged interlopers.[63]

Stapleton soon found himself to be the target of the company's campaign against governors it deemed unfriendly to its interests. His agent in London, the merchant William Freeman, directly pleaded with the Duke of York regarding Stapleton's good character and intentions, and Blathwayt also spoke to York on Stapleton's behalf. Eventually, Stapleton's pleas and the appeals of Freeman and Blathwayt had an effect, and the Crown agreed to intervene and determined that Billop's accusations held no merit. But the case was significant because all sides claimed to be acting on behalf of the African Company, the king, and the royal prerogative. The episode demonstrated that even those governors who did not directly act against the interests of the company could be subject to its censure during the Tory Ascendancy.[64]

IMPERIAL TRIUMVIRS: STEDE, JOHNSON, AND ALBEMARLE

By James II's reign, all three of the English Caribbean colonies had governors selected for their support of prerogative authority in the colonies at the expense of local autonomy. In a move that indicated the African Company's resurgent influence over imperial affairs, Edwin Stede, the long-serving company agent in Barbados, became lieutenant governor of the most profitable slave colony in the English empire. Stede was a reliable Tory bureaucrat who understood his role in imperial administration: promoting the Crown's interests, especially the African Company, while maintaining deference to imperial authorities. His brief governorship, which almost exactly coincided with James II's reign, was the clearest representation of the king's imperial ideal. While governing Barbados, Stede retained his position as the company's chief factor on the island, and remained collector of the customs. He cracked down on interloping, which made him vulnerable to harassment. He relied on his friendship with Blathwayt for protection from "slanderers or backbiters, of which the world is too full, but will rest satisfied in your kind care of mee, hopeing you will be pleased timely to give mee notice of such persons and things that I may be the better able to assist in matters of my defense." Stede remained steadfast, however, in his dedication to James II and the African Company. After the Glorious Revolution, Stede "hoped that the throne of the King may be re-established, and the succession of the crown may be continued in the right line."[65] Not surprisingly, Stede's days were numbered after the Glorious Revolution; in the spring of 1689 he was replaced by a Barbados native and army officer, Sir James Kendall.

After Sir William Stapleton's death in 1686, a close ally of the king, Sir Nathaniel Johnson, was named governor-general of the Leeward Islands. Johnson had been a loyal servant to the king as a collector of the hearth tax, a linchpin of both Charles II's and James II's domestic agenda. As an outsider to the colony with a military background, Johnson was well positioned to keep the planters and merchants in line while at the same time maintaining peace and security with other European powers in the region. He was known for his steadfast support of James and his pro-French foreign policy, much to the consternation of the Leeward Islands colonists, who had lived in fear of French attacks for decades. Johnson was the first West Indies governor to be given instructions empowering him to punish and prosecute private merchants violating the African Company's monopoly. Despite Johnson's own inclinations to help the company, interloping remained a serious problem, as planters and merchants not only regularly purchased slaves from English interlopers but from Dutch slave traders as well, who frequently came to the islands to sell slaves in exchange for English colonial produce. It was bad enough that colonists obtained slaves illegally, but it was far worse that they purchased slaves from the Dutch, long the focus of James II's ideological animosity. As Johnson noted, "by the Trade of English Interlopers the company are principally the sufferers, but by what Trade of that or any other kind is with the Dutch, His Maty also is a sharer in the loss, it occasioning the convey-ance of our sugars and other produce to their Islands." The Lords of Trade ordered Johnson "not to permitt any Dutch merchant ship or vessell whatsoever to come unto any of his Matys Islands under your Government," except in cases of emergency or distress. The Privy Council similarly reminded the governor of his orders to punish all interlopers "severely."[66] In order for the English to succeed in dominating the slave trade, the ability of the Dutch to trade in the Caribbean had to be curtailed.

In addition to the persistence of interloping, the African Company's factors in the colony discovered that a number of high-placed officials directly profited from the illegal trade. The deputy governor of Nevis, Sir James Russell, was singled out for flagrantly ignoring the king's orders to seize interlopers because of his business dealings with Dutch merchants. Two members of the council of Saint Christopher were also accused of protecting interloping and removed from office. In order to better ensure compliance with the king's orders and agenda, Johnson decided a general purge of government offices was necessary. This ran parallel to a similar strategy in Britain orchestrated by James II, who wanted to maintain "ideological purity" among the judiciary and in local offices. In early 1688, Johnson launched a major investigation into the state of the colony's laws, courts, and government, and uncovered a distressing lack of uniformity "not onely in the different Islands but in the severall divisions or precincts of each particular colony." He took the opportunity to remove judges, council members, and other officials, and also attempted to alter land titles and patents in favor of quitrents for the king. In the midst of this turmoil came the news of the departure of James II in the Glorious Revolution. Johnson refused to recognize the revolution or the new monarchs and went even further and allowed a band of Irish Catholic servants on Saint Christopher to join the French and rebel against their English masters in 1689. Although he did eventually proclaim William and Mary in the Leeward Islands, shortly thereafter Johnson departed the colony with one hundred slaves and headed for the Carolina colony.[67]

Like the appointments of Stede and Johnson, the selection of the Duke of Albemarle as governor of Jamaica represented the realization of James II's imperial agenda in the West Indies. He was the son of George Monck, the first Duke of Albemarle, who had been instrumental in orchestrating the Restoration and had served Charles II for many years. The second duke, however, was a much less reliable royal servant than his father. Although he was Lord Lieutenant of Wiltshire, Albemarle failed to act decisively to suppress Monmouth's Rebellion in the summer of 1685, which contributed to a reputation for laziness. As a result, some historians have argued that James sent Albemarle to Jamaica to be rid of an irresponsible troublemaker.[68] But the selection of a duke to a colonial governorship was remarkable and indicated to some that the king had aspirations to consolidate the West Indies colonies under one powerful governor or viceroy, much like Sir Edmund Andros in the Dominion of New England.[69] Although plans to make Albemarle viceroy did not come to fruition, he was granted extensive executive powers, including the authority to suspend any council member, as well as the ability to administer an oath of allegiance to anyone he felt required it. As "Lieutenant General and General Governor of our Island of Jamaica," Albemarle had the authority to command "our forces within any of our Islands and Plantations in America where you shall pass or remain during your personal Residence within respective Island or Plantation." Before arriving in Jamaica, in fact, Albemarle stopped at Barbados and the Leeward Islands, inspected their militias, and consulted with officers and governors. Contrary to contemporary opinion, however, Albemarle did not have the power to declare war or muster other colonies' forces on his own. Albemarle was also ordered to help promote the *asiento* by ensuring that Spanish merchants in Jamaica "bee civilly treated and receive all fitting encouragement," and by halting any taxes the assembly might place on slaves reexported to foreign traders.[70] Albemarle's instructions reflected the three main pillars of James II's imperial designs in the West Indies: promoting prerogative authority, military supremacy, and the commercial and diplomatic interests of the African Company.

Armed with these extensive powers, Albemarle arrived in Jamaica in December 1687. He quickly formed a political alliance with Sir Henry Morgan and his buccaneering faction, including his avaricious lawyer Roger Elletson. Allying with Morgan and his cronies was more than just a pragmatic political move for an outsider governor like Albemarle; it appears that the duke had planned to orchestrate the alliance long before he arrived. In October 1686, a full year before he left England, Albemarle requested that Morgan and his brother-in-law Colonel Robert Byndloss be reinstated to the colony's council. The governor's decision to collaborate with Morgan seemed to be part of a larger plan to sponsor treasure-hunting voyages to salvage Spanish shipwrecks laden with bullion. This is where his alliance with Morgan and the buccaneers came in handy, both as experienced plunderers (or sponsors of plundering expeditions), and as longtime enemies of the Spanish. Of particular interest was a massive shipwreck off the coast of Hispaniola. Men from Jamaica, Barbados, the Leeward Islands, and Bermuda had been diving for treasure there months before Albemarle arrived. Treasure hunting for shipwrecks had the support of the king, who stood to gain from the ventures. The king gave Albemarle a patent, which granted the duke exclusive rights to all proceeds from the Hispaniola wreck after the king's "tenths and fifteenths," or guaranteed percentages of profit, had been delivered.[71] Although the Spanish disliked the idea of the English Crown profiting from their shipwrecks, the desire to salvage such wrecks did not represent the abandonment of James II's position regarding the Spanish in the New World. It was another way to siphon wealth away from Spain to England's benefit. Albemarle intended to grow rich as governor of Jamaica and had the blessing of his patron the king.

Albemarle's patent, not surprisingly, brought him into conflict with many political factions in Jamaica, most notably Molesworth and his merchant allies who were wary of annoying the Spanish and discouraging the *asiento*. Molesworth learned of Albemarle's patent before the new governor arrived, and he ordered all ships "fishing" at the Hispaniola wreck to return to Jamaica and forbade any further expeditions. Albemarle, however, did not trust Molesworth and soon after arriving demanded an account of all proceeds from the wreck. The duke was desperate for money, not only to line his own pockets but to cover the costs of the salvage operations, which owing to the patent belonged solely to him. For example, before allowing Molesworth to leave for England with the king's "tenths," Albemarle squeezed nearly £15,000 from the former governor. This still did not satisfy the duke's needs. In June 1688 he issued a proclamation forbidding anyone from "fishing" at the wreck without his permission and indicated to the Lords of Trade that because of the "vast expence in maintaining the ships and sloopes that will now be Imployd" in the operation, he hoped to get authorization to seek other wrecks to plunder. In a further desperate quest for funds, Albemarle ordered his attorney general to investigate private account books to see what colonists owed the king from "Quit Rents, fines, and forfeitures."[72]

In addition to fighting Molesworth on the issue of the shipwreck, Albemarle also actively opposed the *asiento* trade. Rather than stopping private individuals from seizing Spanish merchant ships that came into Port Royal as Molesworth had done, Albemarle turned a blind eye to this kind of vigilantism. This did not sit well with the African Company, whose directors grew increasingly disappointed with the duke. The company was especially displeased with an act the governor signed in the spring, which increased the value of the Spanish piece of eight, the main currency on the island, from five to six shillings. This had the effect of diminishing the value of debts on the island, and the company, one of the largest creditors in the colony, protested.[73] For the time being, however, the act stood.

As a result of his avarice, Albemarle's tenure as governor was marked by almost constant upheaval and factional strife, which in large part stemmed from his alliance with Morgan and Elletson. Within a few months of his arrival, Albemarle began purging members of the council as well as assistant judges from the colony's courts in order to place his and Morgan's cronies in office. When he attempted to name Elletson as chief justice, he faced a minor revolt from men who were unwilling to serve with him as assistant justices. Albemarle removed them from the council and proceeded to fill the judiciary with judges of his own choosing. He later removed John White from the council for being too closely connected to a major Spanish merchant resident in Port Royal. In May 1688 Albemarle suspended Attorney General Symon Musgrave and Provost Marshal Smith Kelly and replaced them with Sir Richard Derham and Thomas Waite, also allies of Morgan's. These purges not only alienated Albemarle from the governing classes in Jamaica but also raised the ire of the African Company, which especially disliked Waite's appointment, calling him "an indigent man" prone to "deale dishonestly" and against their interests. Like Johnson's purges of the judiciary in the Leeward Islands, Albemarle's actions ran parallel to those of his patron, James II in England.[74]

Albemarle's desire to remove enemies from government affected lawmaking as well. The assembly that met in the spring of 1688 was highly contentious, owing to the governor's purge of the council and courts. After dissolving the assembly, whose "private heats [were] growing more intolerable," Albemarle called new elections for July. Rather than let the polls run their course, however, the governor and his allies interfered to ensure their political enemies did not win reelection. In the parish of Clarendon to the west of Port Royal, this resulted in a near riot when Waite, the provost marshal, attempted to close the poll early and declare the winner Albemarle wanted. The new assembly met on July 20, 1688, packed with men loyal to Albemarle, and in a major coup, the governor secured the selection of Morgan's lawyer, Roger Elletson, as speaker. Not surprisingly, Albemarle reported that this assembly, filled with his cronies, "finished more business in two weeks they have sat than the last did in two months."[75]

Imperial authorities had already grown concerned about events in Jamaica even before word reached London of the irregular elections and accusations of political intimidation by the governor. Molesworth arrived in England in the summer of 1688 and informed the King-in-Council of the problems he had had with Albemarle. They also received complaints from the former deputy provost marshal that Elletson, Waite, and their associates had charged excessive fines and fees and falsely accused him of using seditious language. Imperial authorities were already aware of the African Company's many complaints against Albemarle and his administration. In addition, the King-in-Council had to reprimand the duke for obstructing the activities of the naval captain Sir Robert Holmes and his deputy in the region, Stephen Lynch, who had been charged with hunting pirates on behalf of the English Crown. Albemarle did not live long enough to experience the repercussions of these grievances, however. In October 1688, upon learning of the birth of the Prince of Wales earlier that summer, Albemarle, well known for his penchant for heavy drinking, in celebration drank himself to death. In the wake of Albemarle's death, the King-in-Council received a petition from some Jamaica merchants and planters resident in London, requesting that the king restore all men whom Albemarle had removed and the nullification of all laws passed during his governorship. In one of his last acts as king, James II ordered the removal of Elletson, Derham, and Waite from office and restored those who had been purged by Albemarle.[76]

CONCLUSION

The story of the Royal African Company and its confrontations with colonial governors, planters, and private merchants provides some insight into the nature of Stuart imperialism as it evolved over three decades. These conflicts demonstrated how important slavery and the transatlantic slave trade had become not only to the Caribbean colonies but to the English empire by the 1680s. During this decade, the power and influence of the company became a key component of Stuart policies of imperial control and consolidation. Colonial governors and assemblies who attempted to thwart the company's monopoly were seen to be in contempt of the king's sovereignty and the royal prerogative. The ruling in *East India Company v. Sandys* made it clear that royally granted corporate charters were extensions of the Crown and its authority. Undermining essential imperial policies would have opened the floodgates of rebellion as far as the Stuarts, the Lords of Trade, and the company were concerned. It is hardly surprising that much of the apprehension over the relationship of colonial governments to the Crown coincided with the uncertainty and upheaval of the Exclusion Crisis and its aftermath. The last thing the governments of Charles II or James II wanted was faraway colonies governed by men who openly questioned their policies or authority. As a result, the later Stuarts were interested not only in consolidating imperial administration, but in selecting servants and bureaucrats who would promote their interests. At the same time, the Crown learned that the best way to appease planters, and make colonial governance easier, was to occasionally compromise over the issue of the supply of slaves to the colonies.

The Tory Ascendancy could only last as long as its primary architect remained in power, however. In October 1688, James II warned colonial governors, "We have received undoubted advice, that a great and sudden invasion from Holland with an armed force of foreigners and strangers will speedily be made in a hostile manner upon this our Kingdom." He ordered governors to prepare for similar attacks in the colonies and "to hinder any landing or invasion that may be intended." News concerning the major events of the Glorious Revolution, from William of Orange's landing at Torbay in November 1688 to James II's flight to France that December, reached the colonies in subsequent months.[77] The following chapter examines the new regime's imperial agenda and how it dealt with affairs in the West Indies in relation to war and the slave trade. By the 1690s, the English government began to embrace slavery and the slave trade as tools of imperial management and governance, something learned in the previous decade.

6

————————◆◆————————

The 1690s: War, Unfree Labor, and Empire

In March 1689, one month after the coronation of William III and Mary II, Sir Robert Southwell, a prominent Protestant landowner in Ireland who served as a secretary to the Lords of Trade, wrote to Daniel Finch, the Earl of Nottingham. Southwell, a moderate Whig, offered Nottingham, a Tory and one of the new secretaries of state, his opinion regarding the imperial implications of the new alliance with the Dutch and the pending war against France. In general, Southwell viewed England's transatlantic empire as strong and worth maintaining. He was deeply concerned about the rebellions taking place in New York and New England and believed that "New England is going to be turn'd into a Common Wealth, to coine Money, to destroy our Act of Navigation, and to shake off all Dependence but what they think fitt. And that New York, New Jersey, &c. shall returne to their Old Intended Proprietors." According to Southwell, this would undermine the purpose of empire. In the West Indies, on the other hand, "the English have already the Governing Trade. The French are there but as great Interlopers, and the Dutch as small ones; While the Spaniard both in his Islands and his Continent lyes there as the great Carcass, upon which all the rest doe prey." But Southwell was wary of Dutch intentions and feared that "their true Interest seemes to be for Conquest." England, he argued, should focus on "bare defense and the keeping of what already wee have." Southwell asserted, "To me it appears we have already but too much Territory abroad, and to gett more, were but to drain England of People and to lose at home." He urged Nottingham to encourage the king to proceed with caution "before the Proceedings in Parliament run too far."[1]

Southwell's opinion on the state of the English Atlantic empire reveals a telling perspective on foreign policy and imperial administration in the wake of the Glorious Revolution. His wariness regarding England's imperial designs perhaps indicated some distaste for James II's policies of conquest, consolidation, and revenue extraction. For example, Southwell believed that "Trade lyes now under some Damp by the Late heavy Impositions on Sugar and Tobacco," referring to the 1685 plantation duties. Southwell was perhaps concerned that William III might continue this grandiose imperial agenda. On the other hand, the empire in North America and the West Indies was certainly worth keeping. After all, Southwell wrote, "There may be in these Parts about 3 or 400,000 subjects that furnish a full third of the whole Trade and Navigation of England. Here is a great Nursery of Our Sea Men, and the King's Customs depend mightily thereon."[2] Colonies, although potentially problematic, were at the same time beneficial to the realm. Southwell's ambivalent response to England's overseas empire, however, is revealing. He, like the critics of empire who had been so vocal during the 1670s and 1680s, was concerned that conquering more territory was not in the national interest. New colonies would provide opportunities for people to leave England at a time when the nation needed to maintain its workforce and a source of military strength. But rather than argue that the empire and its commercial and administrative apparatuses should be abandoned, Southwell and an increasing number of politicians and political economists who supported the revolution maintained that the empire should be preserved. This chapter explores what made this shift possible. The answer, in large part, has to do with the expansion of slavery in the colonies and England's involvement with the slave trade.

The Glorious Revolution resulted in a number of significant political, economic, and foreign policy transformations. Most important, it marked the end of the Tory Ascendancy. James II fled the kingdom, and the new regime drastically altered England's foreign policy goals and orientation. War against France was the immediate and most significant consequence of these transformations. On the surface, in terms of imperial administration, however, not much seemed to change. Initially, all colonial governors and officials were ordered to keep their positions until the new regime reached a satisfactory settlement. In addition, many Tory bureaucrats survived the revolution, including William Blathwayt, who assumed even more power and influence during the 1690s, becoming William's secretary at war. Although the Dominion of New England was abandoned, its main architects, Sir Edmund Andros and Sir Edward Randolph, found comfortable positions in the new regime. In addition, James II's tobacco and sugar duties were expanded, as were the Acts of Trade and Navigation in 1696. By 1700, a newly robust Board of Trade was investigating colonial charters and proprietary governments at Randolph's behest, and there was new a movement to unite many of the North American colonies under the rule of the Crown.[3]

Many of these apparent similarities with previous regimes, however, masked major transformations. In the wake of the revolution, various political institutions competed for power and influence in new ways. Parliament, especially the House of Commons, the Crown, the ministries at court, and entities such as the Lords (later Board) of Trade, the Admiralty, and the Treasury vied with one another in an uncertain environment as the terms and implications of the revolution's settlement were worked out. The status of the Royal African Company and its jurisdiction over the slave trade was one of the many elements of imperial authority to be seriously contested. With the departure of its governor and main advocate from the kingdom, the company's position at the center of England's imperial designs was in doubt, its monopoly was essentially null and void, and the slave trade was for all practical purposes open. In addition, charters that had been granted by the Stuart kings were now under intense scrutiny and in danger of being revoked. The African Company was fully aware of its precarious position, and throughout the 1690s its directors and allies tried to have its monopoly reaffirmed by Parliament. This campaign motivated the company's traditional enemies, such as private merchants and colonial planters, to lobby for the slave trade to remain open. Collectively, this group came to be known as the "separate trader" interest. In addition to petitioning Parliament, both sides published broadsides and pamphlets promoting their pro- and anti-monopoly positions, making the slave trade the focus of public debate throughout the 1690s.[4]

Scholars who have analyzed the slave-trade debates of the 1690s have tended to interpret them as simple disputes over commercial policy, representing classic mercantilist versus free trade disagreements, or as emerging from institutional and political changes unique to England after 1688.[5] Instead, this chapter will explore how public debates over the status of the slave trade contributed to the decline of the African Company's commercial viability, which was deeply ideological and connected to both partisan politics and competing understandings of empire and political economy, which had been evolving for decades. The opening of the slave trade during the 1690s was intimately tied to the fact that England was involved in a long and costly war in Europe. As a result, the debate over the proper management of the slave trade coincided with one of the most economically uncertain times in the seventeenth century. Many equated England's financial difficulties with the astronomical costs of the war against France, and throughout the decade, scores of writers and politicians offered assessments and criticisms of the costs and conduct of the war.[6] The slave-trade debates frequently overlapped and intersected with those concerning the war and its economic impact.

This chapter explores the intersection of war against France and the opening of the slave trade and subsequent expansion of slavery in the colonies. Prolonged war had a significant impact on the West Indies colonies, which the French sought to add to their own transatlantic empire.[7] But Jamaica, Barbados, and the Leeward Islands were left almost entirely on their own to defend themselves from the French threat. In part, this was not surprising: colonial governments traditionally relied almost exclusively on local militias for internal and external defenses. But protracted war threw a long-standing situation into stark relief: the diminishing number of white people in the English West Indies, especially when compared to the growing populations of African slaves. Colonial governors, forced to resort to arming slaves to protect the colonies, made vocal pleas for financial and military assistance from the metropolis. Yet there were only half-hearted attempts to address these grievances, and generally emigration from England to the colonies was discouraged by the state. In striking contrast, the African slave trade continued to be expanded and promoted, despite the increased dangers of trading during wartime and the apparent fears of slave uprisings.

THE ROYAL AFRICAN COMPANY AND THE SLAVE-TRADE DEBATES

The Royal African Company suffered commercially, politically, and financially in the aftermath of the Glorious Revolution. With its governor forced from the kingdom, its directors knew they could not rely on its old charter to defend its monopoly. Most significantly, the company was no longer at the center of imperial affairs influencing policies and appointments, and almost immediately its charter and monopoly were thrown into question. As a result, the African slave trade was effectively open to all who wished to participate and the company's market share began a precipitous decline that never recovered. Historians have usually attributed the company's commercial failure to long-standing structural inefficiencies, to competition from separate traders, and to the loss of its charter. The company's precarious commercial position was made worse by the spring 1689 decision at the King's Bench in the case *Nightingale v. Bridges*, which denied the company the right to seize the ships and cargoes of private traders, powers that had expanded during the 1680s.[8] Captain John Bridges, acting on behalf of the African Company, had seized a ship owned by Nightingale, who sued for an illegal seizure of private property. The plaintiff contended that the company's courts of judicature in Africa were beyond English jurisdiction and therefore illegal. Lord Chief Justice John Holt agreed and argued that although the king could grant a monopoly, he did not have the right to give any entity the authority to seize private property, even from those caught infringing on the given monopoly. Only an act of Parliament could confirm such rights, thereby conferring on Parliament the right to regulate overseas trade. This was potentially quite revolutionary, as the Crown had traditionally maintained its prerogative authority over trade, especially since the 1684 decision in *East India Company v. Sandys*. In the wake of this decision, the African Company's directors recognized they would need "an Act of Parliament to confirm this Company's Charter, by Reason of the limitation of the Royal Prerogative," and in January 1690 urged members to "use their Interest with their respective friends in the House." The company presented a petition that was read in the Commons later that month, which asked Parliament to reaffirm its charter and guarantee its right to maintain its "forts and castles" and other property holdings in Africa.⁹ The issue was sent to a committee, and a bill was introduced in the Commons in April reconfirming the 1672 charter.

The company's opponents organized themselves just as quickly, and over the next two parliamentary sessions in 1690 at least eleven petitions were read in opposition to the proposed bill. In addition to petitions from planters and independent merchants, Parliament heard from private traders whose ships and cargoes had been seized by the company and who sought restitution for their losses. Parliament also received petitions from wool manufacturers in Suffolk, Essex, and Devon who complained that the company's monopoly limited their ability to sell goods in Africa. In November 1690, the parliamentary committee issued a resolution that agreed about the necessity of forts and castles for trading in Africa but urged that the trade should instead be organized in a regulated company. The bill was rejected by the Commons on November 26, and a new bill establishing a regulated company was proposed, but the session ended without a decision on the bill.¹⁰ Despite this failure, the company tried to win parliamentary approval of its charter on at least four further occasions before 1698. In response, private merchants, colonial planters, and their merchant allies, known as the "separate trader" interest, lobbied for the slave trade to remain open. Parliament also heard from traders who had obtained licenses from the company to trade in West Africa but claimed the company consistently reneged on its financial obligations. One such petition triggered a parliamentary investigation of the company in 1694. In this case, as in most of these instances, the Commons resolved that forts and castles were indeed necessary to conduct trade in Africa and that a joint-stock company was the best means to organize the trade.¹¹ But Parliament never managed to reaffirm the company's charter.

The two sides also engaged in a lively pamphlet war, which, as historian Tim Keirn has shown, indicated a perceived necessity to appeal to the public regarding the economic benefits of the slave trade. During the 1690s, the company and its supporters produced a small number of pamphlets (about six) promoting the virtues of monopoly and the company's joint-stock structure. In contrast, the separate traders published at least thirty-four broadsheets and pamphlets criticizing the company's monopoly and trading practices. This numerical difference suggests a number of things. First, there was perhaps a greater willingness on the part of the separate traders to present their case to the public. The company's directors and supporters perhaps felt it was in poor taste to air these grievances openly and might have been concerned that such public discourse was disruptive to natural order and civil society. This is certainly in keeping with the company's conservative Tory orientation and reputation. The discrepancy might also indicate that there were more supporters of the separate traders' interest than the company's. It certainly demonstrated that the separate traders were far better organized to present their case to the public than the company and its supporters, and, as William Pettigrew has argued, were better suited to manipulate the "more open political culture" in the decade after the Glorious Revolution.[12]

The public debate revealed how the slave trade and African slavery were imagined as key elements of England's imperial economy. Publications on both sides emphasized the importance of the transatlantic colonies, and the slave trade on which they depended, to England's economic well-being by presenting slavery as a significant reason why colonies benefited the entire realm. "That it being of so great Importance to this Nation to Encourage and Support the Plantations," maintained one anti-company broadsheet, "it will be of absolute Necessity to have them plentifully supplied with Negroes, by whose Labour and Strength all the Commodities of those Countries are produced, which Production is all clear Gains to this Nation, and better than the Mines of Gold and Silver are to the Spaniard." One pro-company pamphlet declared, "The Trade to Africa is allowed to be of Consequence sufficient to deserve Extraordinary Care. The present Question," it continued, "is not whether it should be Preserved or not, but how it may be most Advantageous to England, and the Colonies." Both pro- and anti-monopolist polemics made the argument that not only did the colonies need slaves, but that those colonies with slaves were especially valuable to the empire.[13]

There were of course clear differences between the two sets of pamphlets. Tracts defending the company's interests echoed arguments presented in petitions to Parliament. The company's supporters claimed that opening up the trade by an act of Parliament would effectively take away property in West Africa that rightfully belonged to the company. Maintaining forts and castles, one leaflet claimed, was the only way England could preserve its foothold in the slave trade and "prevent the Designs of other *Europeans*, who have Forts and Castles on the same Coast: And if they could possess themselves of our Forts and Castles, would soon become Masters of the whole Trade, and exclude us." Monopoly was a natural consequence of this fierce international competition. The position of the Royal African Company in the 1690s was the same as it had been since its inception: whatever trade the English company lost, a foreign competitor necessarily gained. In addition, only a joint-stock company, with a guaranteed amount of capital resulting from limited sales of shares to "many Wealthy, Prudent, and Great Men," would protect the nation's interest. Interlopers, one pamphlet claimed, "while they pursue nothing but their private Interest, do cover themselves with the Mantle of pretended Zeal for public Liberties and Rights."[14] An open trade, with greater participation by less "prudent" merchants, would jeopardize England's prosperity.

In contrast, many of the anti-monopolist pamphlets called for the creation of a regulated company to manage the slave trade by appealing to natural law and a perceived right to an open trade. These tracts essentially reiterated the consequences of the *Nightingale v. Bridges* decision by underscoring that only Parliament had the power to limit such inclinations. As other historians have pointed out, in these debates the individual's right to trade became equated with the nation's economic interest. The anti-monopolists claimed that the profits derived from the West Indies plantations, and by extension the slave trade, were far more valuable to England's economic well-being than the stock of any trading company. "The Interest of the Plantations are of infinitely greater concern to be preserved," maintained one, "than any Company with a Joint-stock can pretend to." In addition, others claimed the company, despite its monopoly, had a poor track record when it came to supplying the colonies. Because a joint-stock company had a restricted number of subscribers, the economic benefit to the nation was also necessarily limited, and because of the company's monopoly, fewer merchants participated in the trade. This necessarily restricted the number of slaves on the market and resulted in higher prices.[15] A more-open slave trade, on the other hand, with greater merchant participation, would increase the number of slaves on the market and thereby reduce prices for colonial planters.

The debate over the African Company's monopoly was not limited to the metropolis. Colonial assemblies reiterated many of the same ideas articulated in printed pamphlets circulating in London. During the Nine Years' War against France (1689–1697) there were frequent complaints about the company's inability to supply the colonies with adequate numbers of slaves. Colonists also emphasized the important role the plantations played in the imperial economy. In the fall of 1693 the Barbados Assembly issued a report to the Lords of Trade arguing that the company's monopoly hindered navigation and limited the customs revenue. The assembly maintained that it was colonial planters' reliance on enslaved Africans that drove the imperial economy and kept people in England working in manufacturing trades. "This blessing will indisputably follow the laying open of this trade," the report continued, "for thereby more ships and seamen will be employed; more home commodities bought and exported; and more vastly imported by the full managery [*sic*] of the plantations; and thus the national wealth which ought to be diffusing will be every way promoted." This idea was also promoted in published pamphlets.[16] Slavery in the colonies, by promoting manufacturing jobs in England, brought profit to the empire. It made the colonies integral parts of the realm, rather than peripheral lands with alien societies, economies, and cultures.

AN INTEGRATED EMPIRE

The idea of an integrated empire based on the forced labor of African slaves had emerged as part of the planters' vision of empire as early as the 1670s. This ideal became more fully developed in the slave-trade debates of the 1690s. Perhaps the most well-known description of the planters' position in the late seventeenth century is Edward Littleton's pamphlet *The Groans of the Plantations*, originally published in 1689. Littleton, an absentee sugar planter from Barbados, took aim at some of the common conceptions about the colonies. Contrary to the idea that colonies were harmful to England's economic well-being, Littleton maintained that they were beneficial in a number of measurable ways. "The Plantations are not only not pernicious," Littleton wrote, "but highly beneficial, and of vast advantage to England." He asserted, "We by our Labour, Hazards, and Industry, have enlarged the *English* Trade and Empire, [and] the *English* Empire in *America,* whatever we think of it our selves, is by others esteemed greatly considerable." Littleton continued:

> Several Scores of Thousands are employed in *England*, in furnishing the Plantations with all sorts of Necessaries, and these must be supplied the while with Cloths and Victuals, which employs great numbers likewise. All which are paid out of Our Industry and Labour . . . How many Spinners, Knitters, and Weavers are kept at work here in *England*, to make all the Stockings we wear? . . . 'Tis strange we should be thought to diminish the People of *England*, when we do so much increase the Employments . . . But the *American* Plantations do both take off from *England* abundance of Commodities; and do likewise furnish *England* with divers Commodities of

value, which formerly were imported from foreign parts. Which things are now become our own: and are made Native. For you must know, and may please to consider, That the Sugar we make in the *American Plantations* (to instance only in that) is as much a native *English* Commodity, as if it were made and produced in *England*.

Littleton presented a concept of empire in which England's colonies were understood to be integral parts of England itself. This idea was based on a complicated web of trade and economic and political interdependence. According to this position, the colonies, as parts of England, should be allowed to prosper and flourish. For Littleton and many colonial planters, this meant opening the African slave trade because "Of all the things we have occasion for, *Negroes* are the most necessary, and the most valuable," he asserted. "And therefore to have them under a Company, and under a Monopoly, whereby their Prices are doubled; cannot but be most grievous to us." The reason why others were reluctant to understand colonies in this way, Littleton suggested, was because "there is a distance and space between *England* and the Plantations. So that we must lose our Countrey upon the account of Space, a thing little more then [*sic*] imaginary." Littleton's pamphlet embodied the planters' imperial ideal.[17] There was, however, an interesting slippage in Littleton's choice of words. Ultimately the "labours" that Littleton described in the cultivation of sugar were performed by enslaved Africans, not the planters themselves. But for Littleton and other big planters, that did not mean the colony or the commodity it produced were less "English." Colonies were extensions of the home country, and therefore the produce of the colonies, regardless of who did the work, was equally English.

Littleton was not alone in articulating this idea of an integrated empire during the slave-trade debates of the 1690s. The colonial merchant and slave trader Sir Dalby Thomas wrote in 1690 that popular opinion "take[s] for granted that the *American* Colonies occasion the decay both of the People and Riches of the Nation." But "upon a thorough examination, nothing can appear more Erroneous." The Bristol merchant and political economist John Cary maintained that "our Plantations are an Advantage to this Kingdom . . . as they take off our Product and Manufactures, supply us with Commodities . . . imploy our Poor, and encourage our Navigation; for I take England and all its Plantations to be one great Body." In a letter to a merchant in Antigua, Cary expressed a similar idea: "It must be allowed that the true interest of England is the interest of every particular English man wheresoever he be settled." This was the glue that held the empire together, according to Cary. "Now the true interest of England is its trade," he continued, "if this receives a battle, [then] England is neither able to support itself, nor the plantations that depend upon it, & then consequently they must crumble into so many distinct independent govern-ments, & thereby becoming weak will be a prey to any stronger power which shall attacque them." This imperial ideal, based on extensive trade and manu-facturing networks as well as political connections and traditions, inherently linked the colonies to metropolitan interests and vice versa. This was the kind of empire Sir Robert Southwell hinted at in his letter to Nottingham at the beginning of the war.[18] And it depended, at the end of the day, on slavery and the transatlantic slave trade.

This understanding of an integrated empire was based on mutual depen-dence and negotiated authority. This negotiation of authority between metrop-olis and the colonies had a long history. William Pettigrew, however, calls this imperial vision evident in the slave-trade debates a "new approach to empire" embraced by the separate traders that only emerged in the wake of the Glorious Revolution. But this image of an integrated empire was one that colonial gover-nors and assemblies had attempted to articulate in their negotiations with metropolitan authorities since the 1670s and 1680s, as argued in chapters 4 and 5. The separate traders, in emphasizing their anti-monopolistic vision of empire, refined arguments that had been evolving for decades. Central to it all, as it had been since the Restoration for West Indies planters and independent merchants, was a more-open slave trade. This negotiated authority, however, did not ulti-mately stem from conflicts over concepts of possessive individualism among colonial elites that the imperial state attempted to quash in its desire for greater commercial regulation and control, as Jack Greene has argued. Nor did these negotiations involve individuals or corporate bodies that were completely "separate from, rather than extensions of, the metropole's institutions," as Elizabeth Manke has suggested.[19] An integrated concept of empire based on negotiated authority was one of mutual dependence, and for colonial planters and their allies, reliance on the labor of enslaved Africans was a key component of this dependence. This deeply complicated the ideals of political freedom articulated by those who championed the Glorious Revolution.

This vision of an integrated empire addressed many of the concerns expressed by political economists during the 1670s and 1680s. For example, the idea that the sugar and tobacco trades did not make up for the loss in population caused by colonial settlement was directly disputed in the 1690s. "Every Negro that is sent into those Plantations, makes as much Tobacco yearly as pays from 30l. to 40l. Sterl. Customs," declared one pamphlet in 1698. African slaves, maintained John Cary, "are the hands whereby our plantations are improved, and 'tis by their labours such great Quantities of Sugar, Tobacco, Cotton, Ginger, and

Indigo, are raised, which being bulky Commodities employ great Numbers of our Ships for their transporting hither, and the greater number of ships employs the greater number of Handicraft trades at home." The Irish Whig Sir Francis Brewster argued in 1695, "The Foreign Plantations add to the Strength and Treasure of the Nation, even in that of People, which is generally thought our Plantations abroad consume; but if it were considered, That by taking off one useless person [from England], for such generally go abroad, we add Twenty Blacks in the Labour and Manufacturies of this Nation, that Mistake would be removed." In 1696 sugar bakers in Bristol argued that "the true ends of settling plantations abroad, & sparing our people to inhabit them, which was to give imployment to those who were left behind & that by raising new products there & promoting manufactures here, both might be enriched." In other words, the imperial economic system, by "sparing" English settlers, instead relied on enslaved African laborers. "It is well known, that the Riches of the Plantations consists in Slaves chiefly," declared the 1698 pamphlet quoted above, "by whose strength and labour all their Commodities . . . are produced, and the stronger they are to defend themselves against any Insults." It remarkably continued, "Neither can there be any more danger of being over-stockt with Negroes than there is that too much Tobacco, Sugar &c. should be sent to England; for it is a plain consequence, the more Negroes the more Goods will be produced, the more Goods the more Customs paid, and all those Commodities rendered here at home so cheap will enable this Nation to send them abroad cheap also."[20] According to the anti-monopolist position, this economic prosperity hinged on keeping the African slave trade free from excessive metropolitan control.

This emphasis on the importance of the West Indies colonies and on the perceived economic contributions of the forced labor of African slaves required a fundamental reimagining of the colonies not only as culturally, politically, and economically "English," but as fully integrated components of the realm. At the same time, slavery seemed to offer a "solution" to the population "problem" that the empire was alleged to have. By relying on slaves, planters demanded fewer servants from England. This made the West Indies, and increasingly the colonies in the Chesapeake and southern regions of North America, more acceptable to those who might otherwise have been critical of them. By the 1690s there was a widespread understanding that the existence of slavery in the colonies justified the empire's existence. And the transatlantic slave trade had become important to England's imperial economy by the late seventeenth century. Raw materials produced by slave labor dominated colonial imports. According to Nuala Zahedieh, in 1686 sugar constituted 87 percent of all imports from the English West Indies, worth about £586,528. Chesapeake tobacco, still mostly produced by white servants, was a distant second, at 68 percent of all imports from the North American colonies, worth about £141,606. In addition, colonial produce played an increasingly important role in England's economy. During the 1660s, colonial products made up approximately 12 percent of total imports into London; by 1700, that had increased to 18.5 percent. English merchants also exported growing numbers of manufactured goods to the colonies, especially to those like the West Indies that did not produce their own food, clothing, and other staples. And sugar planting was a profitable enterprise for English planters during the second half of the seventeenth century, with planters making anywhere from 10 to 50 percent profit returns.[21] As the slave-trade debates maintained, the colonies, especially those with slaves, were an increasingly important part of the imperial economy.

THE POLITICS OF THE AFRICAN COMPANY

The slave-trade debates of the 1690s not only revealed competing visions of empire and imperial governance but also highlighted significant ideological differences between the pro- and anti-company positions. Many of the anti-monopolist tracts appealed to the memory of the Glorious Revolution and reminded people of the close association the African Company had with the Stuarts, especially James II. One pamphlet claimed the company had been created "through the Countenance of the then Duke of York their Governour, and the strong Influence of the Beams of the then Prerogative, a Brood at length came forth to engage in a Design so apparently opposite to the Laws of the Land so destructive of the Native Liberty and Freedom of the Subjects of England, and so contrary to the true Interest of the Nation." Some even questioned Charles II's authority to have granted a monopoly in the first place. "These men have exercised an illegal Authority for Thirty Years, and now they would have it made legal," claimed one sheet. "They not only exercise the Illegal Powers granted them in their Charter," maintained another, "but scorn to be limited thereby, and become Sovereign Legislators themselves, and undertake Powers and Prerogatives not only not in the Crown to grant, but such as were not pretended to be granted them." Another sheet asked, "For if the Company have [previously] produced such Mischiefs by the Authority of a Charter only, What may be expected from them, if they should be established by a Law?"[22]

Many scholars have noted that for a decade after 1688, the African Company's opponents effectively argued that reestablishing the company's monopoly would be tantamount to reinstating Stuart imperial and commercial designs. But they have tended to downplay the ideological significance of this rhetoric and the role it played in isolating the company politically, as well as how effective it was in keeping the company commercially obsolete. But corporations like the African Company were never evaluated based solely on economic efficiency and profitability, but also in terms of political orientation and association. According to many historians of the African Company and late Stuart politics, by the mid-1680s the company had clear Tory political leanings. As Gary De Krey has shown, the majority of company shareholders who can be politically identified by the 1680s and 1690s were Tories. In contrast, most London-based colonial slave traders by the 1680s and 1690s, the overwhelming majority of whom did not own company stock, were Whigs or at least had Whiggish sympathies. Some historians have recently cautioned that attributing the company's decline after 1688 to its Tory association places too much emphasis on political labels that were extremely fluid, and that ultimately the company's demise had more to do with the fact that the separate-trader interest was better able to operate in a different political milieu that emerged after 1688.[23] It is certainly clear that the separate traders were better equipped to handle many of the political and institutional changes associated with the Glorious Revolution, at least during the 1690s, as the sheer volume of pamphlets they produced illustrated. Although there were Whigs involved in the company throughout its existence, and a number of Tories were represented among the ranks of the separate traders, the company's close relationship with the later Stuart monarchs cemented its Tory association and contributed not only to its political isolation but to its commercial obsolescence in the wake of the revolution. Regardless of the actual political affiliation, the perception that the company had a close connection to high Tory political ideology associated with the Stuarts, emphasized by the separate traders, contributed to its commercial decline.

Scholars of the African Company have tended to emphasize the economic and structural inefficiencies that led to its failure, but its financial difficulties during the 1690s are perhaps more surprising than it might at first seem. The company had substantial commercial and financial success during the 1670s and 1680s. It regularly managed to offer dividends to shareholders, and had as late as 1691 offered a bonus to each shareholder worth 300 percent of his or her stock. But all was not as it seemed, especially after 1688, when the patent protection offered by its royally granted charter disappeared and its market share in the slave trade began to shrink. K. G. Davies, the foremost historian of the company, has argued that it was hardly in a financial position to make the bonus in 1691. In order to make the offer, the company quadrupled its stock, thereby significantly depreciating the value of its shares. It was probably an attempt to raise much-needed capital through share transfers and resulted in a frenzy of stock transfers in the spring and summer of that year, which left the company extremely short of capital. In addition, the company suffered significant losses and disruptions of its trade during the war, as French privateers regularly seized company ships and cargoes.[24] As a result, the company experienced a chronic shortage of capital during the 1690s.

The African Company repeatedly attempted to deal with its cash-flow problems. It continued to sell licenses to private merchants and offered new stock issues to shareholders throughout the decade. But these efforts, while bringing in some money, never brought in the kind of capital acquired by other institutions of investment, such as the East India Companies or the Bank of England. For example, when the African Company offered its shareholders the opportunity to purchase more stock in 1693, it raised £72,340 in cash, which meant the company had about £183,440 in cash and £625,250 in stock as capital. A further stock issue in 1697 raised only £57,096 in cash, bringing the totals to £240,536 cash and £1,101,050 in stock. While these are not inconsiderable sums, the company's debts, combined with the poor state of its real assets, limited its actual capital accumulation. Unlike the old East India Company, the African Company could not entice many new subscribers by the 1690s. The slave trade had been open and profitable for some time, and fewer and fewer potential investors saw the company as necessary for the trade, as the separate traders had emphasized. As a result, the company sold its shares at such discounted prices and offered so many bonuses that it could never recoup its capital. Although shares tended to be valued at £100, they were often discounted to anywhere between £12 and £17 per share, especially from 1693 onward.[25] The value of shares declined as private traders increased control over the market. The company's finances never recovered, and the price of its shares never rebounded.

As a result of these financial difficulties, which stemmed in part from its ideological association with the Stuarts, the African Company was never in a position to gain political favor during the 1690s. Unlike the Bank of England or the East India Companies, for example, it never had enough capital to offer loans to the government. Offering loans to the government during the war became a primary means for joint-stock companies to win political favor and influence. In forging relationships with the government in the form of loans, joint-stock companies became associated as either "Whig" or "Tory," and at different moments were either winners or losers during the turbulent "rage of party" of the late seventeenth and early eighteenth centuries. As a result, people often made investment decisions based not only on the potential for financial return but also on the less "rational" concepts of political ideology. Again, actual political affiliation mattered less than perceptions. In the case of the Royal African Company, it was never in an economic position to offer the government much in return for reconfirming its charter. According to a Board of Trade report in 1698, the company had total capital in real money and property valued at £189,913. In contrast, the Bank of England and the East India Company had much more capital at their disposal, which could be turned into substantial loans to the government. When the Bank of England was established in 1694, sales of its shares brought in over £1 million in a ten-day period.[26] Granted, this was an open public sale of shares in a new company, as opposed to limited sales of stock in a previously existing company, but still, the contrast is impressive. This left the African Company financially, commercially, and politically isolated in the wake of the revolution.

The company faced opposition not only from its traditional Whig enemies. In fact, many of the separate traders who can be politically identified had Tory political leanings. This did not mean that partisan politics did not matter when it came to the African Company or the slave-trade debates, however, as some historians have suggested. Instead, these affiliations reflected the transformation of party politics that occurred in the wake of the Glorious Revolution. As David Hayton and Gary De Krey have argued, by the 1690s, the political concepts of "Tory" and "Whig," while maintaining a certain level of ideological purity from their origins in the Exclusion era, had in many ways changed. By the middle of the 1690s, rather than representing the opposition, Whigs, especially Court Whigs, were the party of the establishment.[27] As such, they promoted government interests, including King William's desire to maintain large armies to fight the war in Europe. This is why many of the so-called "Country Whigs," such as Robert Harley and Paul Foley, became outspoken critics of the Whig ministry and soon came to be seen as Tories. Men such as Chancellor of the Exchequer Charles Montagu, Secretary of State the Duke of Shrewsbury, and Thomas Wharton (who controlled Whig interests in the Commons) were accused of abandoning their true Whig sensibilities, which should have included a natural skepticism toward concentrated military and commercial power. Worse, because of their interests in financial institutions like the Bank of England, Court Whigs and their allies were seen as profiteering from the war. Tories, on the other hand, rather than naturally representing the court and traditional political power, became the party of opposition. They embraced many traditionally "Whiggish" ideologies, such as distrust of government, standing armies, and growing government debt. It is also therefore not surprising that Harley, as a "Country Whig," would come to the defense of the African Company and submit petitions on its behalf in early 1694.[28] It was probably a way to counterattack the interests of the Court Whigs and their merchant allies as much as it was a way to support the African Company's monopoly.

This does not mean, however, that Tories naturally advocated "free trade" while Whigs maintained the traditional "mercantilist" line of government regulation of overseas trade. Many Tories, most notably Harley and his associates, continued to embrace trading monopolies such as the South Sea Company in the eighteenth century. Rather, it was a political party's relationship to power that helped determine its attitude toward economic regulation. If political orientation helps determine investment decisions, economic philosophies are surely related to access to political power. This was especially true during the Nine Years' War, with government debt growing and new sources of extra-parliamentary funding desperately needed. The relationship of political power to economic regulation in the face of staggering war expenses might also explain why the Court Whigs, once in power, seemed to embrace "Tory" elements of imperial management, such as strengthening the Acts of Trade and Navigation and maintaining a standing army. While it might never have been in the Court Whigs' interest to have helped an old Tory institution like the African Company, one can certainly imagine that if the company had the capital to offer the government in the form of loans, those in power might have come to its aid and might have received a new charter.[29] But during the 1690s, few powerful politicians, Whig or Tory, were willing to come to the company's defense in any sustained or serious way. The ideological taint of its old association with the Stuarts, emphasized in the anti-monopolist tracts throughout the decade, seems to have played a role in not only politically isolating the company but contributing to its financial insignificance. One can safely assume that the issue of the African trade would have been settled before 1698 had leaders in the House of Commons or members of the king's ministry had any interest in doing so.[30]

THE TEN PERCENT ACT OF 1698

After nearly a decade of fighting in and out of Parliament, the debates over the status of the African slave trade resulted in the Act for the Settlement of the Trade to Africa, which became law in the spring of 1698. The act became known as the "Ten Percent Act" because it allowed private merchants to trade to Africa upon paying a 10 percent duty to the African Company on all cargoes shipped to and from Africa, with slaves and gold exempted. The money raised was to be used to help the company maintain its buildings on the coast. In passing the act, Parliament codified the position that forts and castles were necessary for maintaining the African trade. At the same time, the act indicated that Parliament did not believe a joint-stock corporation should have a monopoly on the slave trade. Although private merchants had to pay for the privilege, in theory the African trade was now legally an open, regulated one. Traditionally, the 1698 act has been interpreted as a victory for the separate-trader interest. In the long term, it certainly was; rather than improving the company's financial or political situation, the act forced it to compete more vigorously for a diminishing share of the market in African slaves. This perception was perpetuated by the company, which within a few years portrayed the act as a huge disappointment by claiming that the revenue it raised did not provide enough capital to maintain its buildings or its foothold in the slave trade.[31] But it is necessary to consider the passage of the act in the political context both of 1698 and the 1690s more broadly in order to understand not only why it passed but why it was by no means a triumph for the separate traders.

In late December 1697, the company once again petitioned the king, requesting that the African trade be settled. The petition proposed granting the company a monopoly on all trade in North Africa but opening the trade between Cape Mount and the Cape of Good Hope, the main slave-trading areas, to all merchants paying a 15 percent duty on all exports and a 15 shilling duty per head for each slave. After further negotiations, the "Bill for settling the Trade to Africa" was introduced in the Commons by Sir William Trumbull on February 12, 1698. Trumbull, a loyal if not particularly ideological Tory, had just resigned his position as secretary of state for the northern department in December 1697. He had long felt isolated within the Whig Junto ministry, which had dominated court politics since 1694, and had recently clashed with James Vernon, Shrewsbury's principal secretary, over the terms of the peace with France signed earlier in 1697. In fact, Vernon replaced Trumbull as secretary of state in early 1698. It is revealing that Trumbull would take up the cause of the African Company in the wake of this political turmoil.[32] The proposed act met with opposition in the form of petitions from colonial planters, merchants, and manufacturers in England, who feared the introduction of the new duty. But this time the separate traders could not prevent or delay action, and the bill ultimately passed the Commons in May and the Lords in June, and the king signed the act into law in July. Although the bill did not reaffirm the company's monopoly, it did provide a source of income and a confirmation of the company's property rights in West Africa and served as a potential financial lifeline at a desperate time. The company was willing to compromise after a decade of political isolation and near financial ruin. On the other hand, the act prevented company factors in the colonies from holding local political offices, which was clearly designed to undermine the traditional influence the company had over colonial administration. Despite this important provision, however, the separate traders were probably less happy with the bill, considering they had been trading to and from Africa for the better part of a decade without paying any duty at all.[33] Although the bill technically left the slave trade open, it did have a new and potentially expensive restriction enforceable by law. In the short term, it was by no means a straightforward victory for the separate traders.

Few scholars, even those who have studied the demise of the African Company's monopoly, have considered the origins of the Ten Percent Act. Some have posited that it passed amid "a wave of disgust at Whig corruption," while others maintain that an obsession with foreign competition and the need for an English presence on the coast of West Africa lay behind the act's passage.[34] But there is a case to be made that the passage of the Ten Percent Act in the spring of 1698 reflected the weakening political position of the Court Whigs after the Nine Years' War.

A comparison to the East India Company is instructive. In the spring of 1698, at the exact same time that the Commons extended a financial lifeline to the old Tory African Company, Parliament chartered the creation of a new East India Company. The act, signed into law in July, gave the old Tory East India Company three years to dissolve itself. The new company was controlled by many of the old company's enemies, including private merchants and former servants of the company. Many had connections to the Bank of England, most notably Sir Gilbert Heathcote, which gave the new company a Whiggish association. The survival of the African Company and the apparent demise of the old East India Company at the same moment was an indication of the political nature of trade and investment during the late seventeenth century. The backers of the new East India Company in 1698, like those of the Bank of England in 1694, practically guaranteed its creation with a promise of a £2,000,000 loan to the government with an 8 percent interest rate. Although the war was over, the national debt was staggering, and William III and his ministry were desperate for revenue. Although the old company attempted to counteroffer, it could not compete, and instead its directors adopted the policy of buying up as many shares as they could in the new company as a means to guarantee the old company's survival. The chartering of a new company was also significant because it represented the supremacy of Parliament, as opposed to the Crown, over foreign trade.[35]

Scholars of the East India Companies have maintained that the triumph of East India interlopers in 1698 was a victory for the Whig ministry under the direction of Chancellor of the Exchequer Montagu, who supported private merchants and had managed to gain widespread support for the project both in

Parliament and at court because of this loan offer.[36] The African Company's survival in 1698 did not depend on a similar offer of a substantial loan, however, and remains more of a puzzle. It is certainly important that because the Ten Percent Act did not confirm the African Company's monopoly, it was perhaps more palatable to its traditional Whig, planter, and merchant enemies. The survival of the company was acceptable so long as the slave trade remained open. In addition, it is possible that the Whig Junto and their allies were willing to support the bill despite separate-trader opposition because the African Company continued to be a source of gold from West Africa.[37] But it also might suggest that the Whig ministry was beginning to crumble. After the signing of the Treaty of Ryswick in the fall of 1697, growing discontent over the nation's war debt left the Whigs with a tenuous hold on power. The ministry and its leaders became increasingly isolated from the king, whose distrust of the Junto grew in the wake of the standing-army controversy that erupted after the war. William desperately wanted to maintain an army of at least thirty-five thousand men should Louis XIV decide to go on the offensive once again. But there was a long political tradition opposed to standing armies in England, as they were equated with absolutism, arbitrary government, and the loss of individual liberties. These associations did not dissolve with the removal of the Stuarts from power, and a major propaganda campaign launched by such astute political operatives as Paul Foley and Robert Harley severely weakened the king's case. In addition, this public campaign, which included the publication of dozens of pamphlets and broadsheets, attacked not only the idea of a standing army, but the ideological direction of the Court Whigs, who seemed to have abandoned their traditional position that was wary of such instruments of government control. Perhaps as an indirect result of these attacks, no one in the ministry took charge to organize for William's position.[38] The influence of the Whig Junto was therefore substantially weakened just as the African Company once again tried to get its status clarified.

The failure of the African Company to get its monopoly reaffirmed, however, was of course significant. The slave trade had been open for nearly a decade, and few—even steadfast Tory defenders of the company—had any real desire to restrict it to a monopoly once again. According to data collected by David Eltis, during the 1690s, approximately 70,643 African slaves arrived in the West Indies colonies in English ships. Although during the previous decade nearly 81,000 slaves had been delivered, considering the dangers of transatlantic trade during the Nine Years' War, these numbers are remarkable. They indicate not only the consistent demand for slaves in the colonies, but that plenty of independent merchants, many of whom had been trading illegally for decades, rushed to fill the void left by the erasure of the company's monopoly. And an open slave trade increased the volume of enslaved Africans being transported in British ships to the American colonies. This was despite the fact that the official opening of the slave trade increased the average prices for slaves in the decades after 1698.[39] The separate traders not only outbid the company for slaves in Africa but outperformed the company in terms of numbers of slaves successfully transported across the Atlantic. But separate-trader success in the long run should not obscure the fact that they were by no means the clear winners in 1698. What it revealed more than anything else was the total acceptance of slavery and the slave trade for England's economic well-being by merchants and politicians of every ideological stripe. The success of the separate traders indicated to most people involved that a monopoly over the slave trade made for bad imperial and commercial policy. The slave trade remained the one largely deregulated trade for the remainder of the eighteenth century.

WAR, SLAVERY, AND EMPIRE

There is another side of this story that has been largely ignored by scholars of the slave trade and the African Company's decline, and that is the role that ideas of political economy played in contributing to the expansion of the slave trade after 1688. The pleas for the economic well-being of the transatlantic colonies in the slave-trade debates coincided with one of the most tumultuous times in early modern England's economic history. For many contemporaries, a major cause of the economic uncertainty was the astronomical cost of England's military commitments during the Nine Years' War. Throughout the 1690s, scores of writers and politicians offered assessments and criticisms of the costs and conduct of the war against France. In pamphlets, books, and speeches, critics attacked William III's strategy of maintaining large land armies in Europe, not to mention the obvious lack of decisive victories for England and its allies. The interrelated questions of financing the war and changing strategy were central to the debate. One anonymous pamphleteer wrote in 1695, "Now we see all corners of Europe crouded with listed, disciplined and standing Armies in Pay, which . . . cannot be done without huge Funds of Money." Because "Money is now more than ever the Nerve of War," this writer continued, the question remained how best to secure the funds needed to win a large international conflict. He concluded that England should do its best to protect overseas trade and improve naval prowess, for "Trade [is] the great Minister of Wealth," and "Trade and Power at Sea are productive one of another."[40]

Many other writers came to the same conclusion: nations grew wealthy through trade, and therefore trade needed to be well managed to raise the money necessary to fight and win wars. In 1695 the Tory economic and political commentator Charles Davenant declared, "Trade, well secured, will bring in that Wealth by which [the war] may be fed and maintained." James Whitson argued in 1696, "So that it uncontroulably follows that a Foreign Trade Managed to the best Advantage, will make our Nation so Strong and Rich, that we may Command the Trade of the World, the Riches of it, and consequently the World it self." In order to have the wealth necessary to win the war, England had to better manage its foreign and colonial trades. By necessity, this included the transatlantic slave trade. The Whiggish John Cary wrote in the same book in which he criticized the African Company's monopoly that the war against France "may strain the Nerves and Sinews of our Treasure before it be ended, and therefore . . . 'tis Prudence to strengthen our Treasure, by advancing and securing our Trade which must bring it in."[41] Such ideas connected the debates over the costs of war to those on the status of the slave trade.

These writers offered a variety of proposals to improve trade and increase England's revenues to help pay for the war, revealing different strategies, agendas, and political philosophies. Several focused on the need to protect and defend England's overseas trade through the use of convoys. England's merchant marine in both the Atlantic and the Mediterranean was extremely vulnerable to French attack during the war, and English losses were high throughout the decade. In late 1692, a group of merchants petitioned Parliament claiming the French had taken at least fifteen hundred English ships, and three years later an anonymous merchant claimed that Barbados had lost at least fifty ships to the French.[42] A key corollary to these proposals was the necessity of focusing on England's navy rather than the army. In Parliament, this strategy was especially embraced by Tories and others who were critical of the Court Whigs and had grown wary of the costs of maintaining large armies in Europe. Although historians have noted the emergence of this nascent "blue water" ideology during the 1690s, few have connected it to contemporary debates about the importance of colonial trade or the regulation of the slave trade. In drawing attention to the need to better manage colonial trade and for greater naval protections, these critics, like the separate traders and the Royal African Company, emphasized the importance of the American colonies, especially the West Indies, to England's overall economic well-being. But despite these pleas, the government seemed unwilling or unable to provide the convoys, naval support, or manpower necessary to protect England's overseas trade or to defend its colonies. Few regiments were sent to the West Indies during the war, despite invasions and incursions by the French. In addition, inadequate supply often hindered progress when the government did attempt to send regiments across the Atlantic.[43]

The neglect of the colonial theater of war left the West Indies defenseless as far as colonial governors and officials were concerned. "Our militia is in a lamentable condition," Governor James Kendall of Barbados wrote to the Lords of Trade in the summer of 1690, "and unless we can have servants from England or Scotland it is impossible to make them more considerable." Although colonial governors had complained about the need for servants in previous decades, their pleadings took on a new urgency during the 1690s, as the Caribbean colonies transformed into full-blown slave societies. As table 1 illustrates, by 1690 Barbados had a population of approximately 47,800 black slaves and 20,000 white inhabitants. Although the most astonishing growth in the slave population occurred during the 1650s and 1660s, it continued to grow at a steady pace of between 2,000 and 4,500 per decade into the eighteenth century. In contrast, Barbados's white population stabilized at around 20,000 from the 1670s through the 1690s, and then began to decline to a low of about 13,000 during the 1710s. The white population began to increase once again by the 1720s, but because of the steady increases in the numbers of African slaves, the proportion of whites to blacks in Barbados remained heavily skewed. The other West Indies colonies followed roughly similar patterns. By 1690, Jamaica had 30,000 African slaves and 10,000 whites. Thereafter, the white population declined and stabilized to around 7,000 for many decades. In stark contrast, the black population grew exponentially, increasing to roughly 80,000 in just thirty years, by 1720.[44] The Leeward Islands, although lagging behind in terms of plantation development, more closely mirrored Barbados than Jamaica in terms of demographic change. By 1690, the Leewards had about 15,000 slaves and 8,700 whites. The white population mostly stabilized during the early eighteenth century, but the black slave population continued to grow significantly, increasing to roughly 41,700 by 1720. But there were few concerted efforts by imperial authorities to address these skewed population ratios during the Nine Years' War by encouraging migration, sending regiments, or transporting servants from the home country. In fact, it seemed the metropolitan government actively discouraged emigration from England during the 1690s. In contrast, the slave trade continued to expand, especially after the demise of the African Company's monopoly.

The situation in Barbados grew desperate by the summer of 1690. Earlier that year the King-in-Council repealed the laws in force in Barbados and Jamaica that had bound prisoners sent to those colonies in the aftermath of Argyll's and Monmouth's Rebellions in 1685 to ten-year terms of indentured service. In an

Table 1. Population of English Colonies, 1630–1720

Year	Barbados			Leeward Islands			Jamaica			Chesapeake (VA and MD)		
	White	Black	Total	White	Black	Total	White	Black	Total	White	Black	Total
1630	1,800			1,000						2,400	100	2,500
1640	14,000			15,000						8,000	100	8,100
1650	23,000	12,800	35,800	18,800						12,400	300	12,700
1660	19,000	27,100	46,100	17,100	2,000	19,100	3,000	500	3,500	24,000	900	24,900
1670	20,000	40,400	60,400	9,000	3,000	12,000	7,000	7,000	14,000	38,500	2,500	41,000
1680	20,600	44,900	65,500	10,000	9,000	19,000	12,000	15,000	27,000	55,600	4,300	59,900
1690	20,000	47,800	67,800	8,700	15,000	23,700	10,000	30,000	40,000	68,200	7,300	75,500
1700	15,000	50,100	65,100	7,800	20,000	27,800	7,000	40,000	47,000	85,200	12,900	98,100
1710	13,000	52,300	65,300	9,000	30,000	39,000	7,000	55,000	62,000	101,300	22,400	123,700
1720	17,700	58,800	76,500	11,300	41,700	53,000	7,100	80,000	87,100	128,000	30,600	158,600

Sources: Barbados and Leeward Islands white population, 1630–1700: Henry Gemery, "Emigration from the British Isles to the New World, 1630–1700: Inferences from Colonial Populations," *Research in Economic History* 5 (1980): 211, table A.1; white population, 1710–1720, and black population, 1650–1720: John J. McCusker and Russell R. Menard, *The Economy of British America, 1607–1789* (Chapel Hill: University of North Carolina Press, 1985), 153, table 7.1; Leeward Islands black population, 1660–1710, and white population, 1710: Richard S. Dunn, *Sugar and Slaves: The Rise of the Planter Class in the English West Indies, 1624–1713* (Chapel Hill: University of North Carolina Press, 1972), 312, table 26; Leeward Islands white and black populations, 1720: Alan Burns, *History of the British West Indies*, rev. 2nd ed. (London: George Allen & Unwin, 1965), 461; Jamaica, white and black populations, 1660–1710: Dunn, *Sugar and Slaves*, 312, table 26; white and black populations, 1720: George W. Roberts, *The Population of Jamaica* (Cambridge: Cambridge University Press, 1957; repr., Millwood, NY: Kraus Reprint, 1979), 33, table 4, and 36, table 5; Chesapeake (VA and MD), white and black populations: McCusker and Menard, *Economy of British America*, 136, table 6.4.

act of defiance, Kendall chose not to notify the colony's council or assembly of this order. He argued that not only was the labor of the rebel prisoners needed for plantations and militias, but because planters had lawfully purchased the prisoners' terms of service, it would be illegal and "dangerous to the safety of the island" to free them. Rather than reprimand Kendall for his failure to follow orders, however, the Lords of Trade informed him that he should introduce a bill in the assembly that would prevent the freed servants from leaving Barbados "without his Majesty's especial leave," which had the effect of giving the assembly the power to accept or reject the law on their own.[45] This episode illustrated that as far as imperial authorities were concerned, it was certainly easier and cheaper to maintain the white servant populations in the Caribbean colonies rather than undertake a significant effort to move people from England, Scotland, and Ireland. As a result, throughout the 1690s, officials in the West Indies continued to complain about the decreasing number of white people in their colonies and the apparent unwillingness on the part of London to do much about it.

As far as Governor Kendall was concerned, there were two main causes of the diminishing number of servants in Barbados. The first was the continued enforcement of the 1685 sugar duties. The second was the forced recruitment of such men to serve in the king's navy or in militias sent to protect other colonies, especially the Leeward Islands, which were by far the most vulnerable to French attack of all of the English West Indies. This was not only because of their proximity to the French islands of Martinique and Guadeloupe, but also because Saint Christopher was jointly occupied by the French and the English. The colony was also relatively sparsely populated in 1690. The English in fact lost Saint Christopher to the French when war broke out in the summer of 1689. A small fleet was then sent from England with a minor regiment to retake the island, but Kendall, who sailed with this contingent, was shocked to discover that "Never was a regiment so carelessly sent out or so extremely neglected." Little wonder colonial governors had to rely on each other's resources. The governor of the Leeward Islands, Christopher Codrington, only regained control of Saint Christopher the following year, with the help of men from colonies like Barbados. After successfully recapturing the island, Codrington continued to beg both Barbados and Jamaica to send men to maintain the security of the island. "Had I sufficient force in my own Government I should not ask for the aid of my neighbours."[46]

The situation did not improve as the war continued. In a 1692 memorandum to the Lords of Trade, the Barbados agents in London attempted to list the "extreme hazard both from the enemy, & Negroes, for want of [white] men." They lamented "the difficulties of getting white servants even in times of peace: but now since the war they are upon no terms to be had. For that sort of people that did use [*sic*] to go to the plantations go now into the Armies." In addition, they explained that those men who had been impressed to serve on the king's ships of war were frequently servants who still owed time to their masters or were planters with significant debts on the island. In March 1693, the agents made a formal request that a regiment be sent from England for the "defense and safety" of Barbados. The following year, a small regiment of about two hundred soldiers was sent to Barbados and remained there for two years. It was the only such regiment sent to the colony until the late eighteenth century.[47]

The problem was not simply one of regiments; it was about settling a servant population on a permanent basis. But more often than not, during the Nine Years' War, colonial officials and planters felt that their pleas fell on deaf metropolitan ears. This was especially true for Jamaica, which experienced extreme difficulties during the 1690s. In the summer of 1692, the city of Port Royal suffered a terrible earthquake. Newsletters in England reported that "houses that were 3 stories high were sunk severall yards under water & destroyed all the Platforms & Magazines," killing nearly two thousand people "in lesse then two minutes time." In the months following, Port Royal experienced severe outbreaks of malaria from lack of housing and poor sanitation. According to the island's council, the resulting population decline was exacerbated by the fact that servants no longer came to the colony in any significant numbers, which made them vulnerable to "the insurrection of slaves." Since the earthquake, the council continued, the Port Royal militia "is now reduced to about two hundred men," down from a muster of nearly two thousand. They urged the Lords of Trade to explain "the true state and condition of the island" to the king and queen so "that we may have at least one thousand men sent over hither." They warned that the French would attempt to take advantage of Jamaica's weakened state and "invade and ravage" the "remote parts of this island."[48]

These fears were realized when nearly three thousand French troops invaded and ransacked Jamaica in June 1694. Jamaica's governor, Sir William Beeston, reported that over the course of a six-week siege, the French "have done this country and people a spoil that cannot soon be estimated, they have wholly destroyed 50 sugar works besides many other plantations, and burnt all wherever they came and killed with barbarous inhumanity all the living creatures they could meet with." Despite this devastating incursion, the French were unable to conquer the vulnerable island. The Jamaican militia was successful in holding off the French because Beeston and his officers relied not only on indentured servants and former servants to fill the militia, but also on a number of slaves, or as Beeston put it, "Negroes as could be trusted." Just how many slaves were armed was unclear, but Beeston claimed that the colony suffered about one hundred casualties overall, including "Christians, Jews, and Negroes." Word of the victory as well as the governor's reliance on slaves circulated in newsletters in England, where it was reported that "severall letters which attribute all ye good success to the good conduct of the Governour whose promise to give freedome to any Negro that should take or kill a French man rendered them more serviceable than the soldiers."[49]

Relying on arming slave populations in times of war was both worrisome and costly for colonial governors. At a Jamaican Council of War meeting immediately prior to the French invasion, it was ordered that all officers announce "that any slave killing a Frenchman shall receive his freedom and further reward for good service." Because of such service, both servants and slaves were freed and their masters financially compensated. After the invasion, Beeston estimated that the war cost the colony £10,000 in "freeing Negroes and white servants that did service." "If therefore their Majesties be not pleased to send us relief by some money to the value of three or four thousand pounds," he pleaded, "these people that are ruined will leave the country, and that weakening will give occasion for others of more ability to do little, and by this means the island may be deserted." As far as Beeston was concerned, relying on slaves for protection from foreign enemies weakened the colony at an already vulnerable time. It threatened to undermine the regime of white supremacy that kept African slaves suppressed. The English government eventually responded by organizing a regiment to be sent to Jamaica in late 1694, but after many delays and obstructions, it did not leave for the colonies until the middle of 1695, long after the French had left the island.[50]

Although most North American and Caribbean colonies had laws prohibiting slaves and free blacks from owning and using weapons, such laws were frequently overlooked in times of war or internal emergencies, sometimes even during slave uprisings. Historians who have studied arming slaves in the colonies have tended to highlight shortages of manpower on the ground that made the practice necessary. Slaves outnumbered servants by wide margins in the West Indies, as these colonies developed into slave societies. In the face of an emergency, arming slaves remained a realistic if troubling option. Scholars have also rightfully stressed the contradictions and ambiguities inherent in giving weapons to slaves and ordering them to fight and defend a system of white mastery that kept them violently oppressed.[51] But it is also interesting to consider metropolitan events and concerns that contributed to the phenomenon in an imperial context. What did the use of slave soldiers mean militarily, politically, and economically in terms of the English empire? Why were there such shortages of manpower in the colonies during the Nine Years' War? Part of the explanation lies with the government's military priorities and was indicative of a burgeoning imperial fiscal-military state that was stretched to its limits fighting a war on two fronts. Despite the significant growth of the army and navy during the 1690s, England simply did not have the martial capability, let alone manpower, to supply a massive military effort in two far corners of the globe. Historians who have noted England's neglect of its colonial theater during the Nine Years' War have tended to emphasize the European priorities of William III's regime. Few scholars, however, have considered the question in terms of political economy, population management, and the rise of slavery.[52]

As far as Beeston was concerned, the fact that he had to rely on slaves to fill militias indicated that imperial authorities were unwilling to address the needs of the colonies. It represented metropolitan neglect and a fundamental misunderstanding of the dangers that the slave system posed for the white minority in Jamaica. Despite the perceived importance of England's overseas empire, the colonies were by and large left to their own devices to defend themselves from foreign invasion or internal threat. There was little political or economic will to alter this situation during the war. In contrast, as we have seen, the state was more than willing to embrace the opening of the slave trade. While colonial planters and officials in the West Indies were pleased with the opening of the slave trade, they were unhappy with the fact that the home government seemed to ignore their needs during wartime. This complicates Jack Greene's argument that the period after the Glorious Revolution witnessed a flowering of colonial autonomy that colonial elites by and large desired. Colonists and those with colonial interests saw themselves as integral to the empire and often wanted some level of assistance and even regulation from imperial authorities. This was what they expected in exchange for creating and maintaining a brutal and dangerous slave regime that economically benefited the entire realm. In this regard, Greene's overly Whiggish view of the Glorious Revolution and of the concept of Englishmen's love of "the sanctity of private and corporate rights" is overdrawn. Instead, a concept of mutual dependence and benefit, based on the expansion of slavery in the colonies, shaped the early English empire. Although Greene correctly notes that a "lack of troops" in the colonies indicated the empire was not held together by force, this did not indicate that colonial officials were pleased about it.[53]

THE POLITICS OF POPULATION AND THE BOARD OF TRADE

Another major reason why the state did not expand emigration to the colonies had to do with the politics of imperial administration. By the mid-1690s, as noted above, the governing Whig Junto underwent a major crisis. In addition to dealing with the fallout of the costs and conduct of the war, the country was convulsed by serious economic turmoil. For years there had been a widespread practice of "clipping" coins in order to extract silver, and as a result, coins circulating in England became increasingly devalued. The Whig Junto introduced legislation in November 1695 that removed clipped coins from circulation.[54] The immediate result was a severe shortage of cash circulating in the country, which hampered the war effort and exacerbated three years of bad harvests and inflationary food prices. This desperate situation led to rioting and instability in many parts of England.[55]

The matter of recoinage directly related to broader issues of trade and national wealth. Many of the pamphlets that were critical of the costs and conduct of the war also called for overhauling or replacing the existing administrative body in charge of trade and colonial affairs, the Lords of Trade, with a more professional and streamlined committee. While considering the issue of recoinage in 1695, the Lords Justices deliberated on the state of trade more generally and asked a number of prominent merchants, economic writers, and intellectuals to propose new ways of managing colonial and domestic trade. From their proposals emerged two possibilities for a reformed council of trade: one formed by Parliament and therefore subject to parliamentary scrutiny, or one that served as an arm of the Privy Council, like the existing Lords of Trade, and was subject only to the Crown's legal jurisdiction. By and large, Court Whigs supported the latter proposal, thinking parliamentary control of trade would restrict the king's prerogative authority. Many in the Commons, including a number of merchants and Tories, however, hoped to succeed in creating a board of trade controlled by Parliament, which added to political tensions in late 1695 at the height of the recoinage crisis. The issue of the Board of Trade became one of the many contests over prerogative authority that occurred in the wake of the revolution. A new council of trade could potentially influence major policy decisions regarding not only colonial trade but imperial administration and perhaps even the Royal Navy and the Treasury.[56] The stakes were incredibly high, especially during a time of war and economic turmoil.

The purview and authority of the new council were debated in the Commons during February and early March 1696, but ultimately the King-in-Council won a royally appointed committee. According to the foremost historian of the Board of Trade, Ian Steele, King William and his supporters in his ministry, especially Attorney General John Somers, succeeded in creating the board as a committee of the Privy Council because of revelations that emerged in late February 1696 of a Jacobite plot to assassinate the king. All other business, including Parliament's interest in creating a new council of trade, was put on hold while authorities investigated the conspiracy. In this environment, outward displays of disloyalty were risky. The king prorogued Parliament on April 30 and thereafter issued a royal warrant creating the new Board of Trade without parliamentary consideration or consent. Members of the new board included John Egerton, Earl of Bridgewater, who had been head of the Lords of Trade; Forde Grey, Earl of Tankerville, a Whig courtier who had participated in Monmouth's Rebellion in 1685; Sir Philip Meadows of the Excise Commission; Abraham Hill, a merchant and prominent member of the Royal Society, who also had ties to the African Company; John Pollexfen, a Whig political economist and merchant who was an outspoken opponent of the East India Company's monopoly; and Chancellor of the Exchequer Montagu. The final two regular members were John Locke and William Blathwayt; Locke's protégé William Popple served as secretary.[57] With the possible exception of Blathwayt, the new board was overwhelmingly Whig in political orientation.

The Board of Trade, created in this tense political atmosphere amid a serious economic crisis, did not have an auspicious beginning. Immediately, the board was forced to confront problems of colonial defense, trade, and population management. In September 1696, a number of prominent Jamaica merchants, including Sir Gilbert Heathcote and Bartholomew Gracedieu, known interlopers in the slave trade who also served as the colony's agents in London, sent a memorial proposing that the board should act to curb naval impressments in the colonies. Heathcote and Gracedieu, who worked closely with Governor Beeston, maintained that impressments weakened Jamaica by discouraging trade, driving up wages, and causing people to leave the colony altogether. They argued that colonial governors, as vice admirals, should have the power to block naval captains from impressing men into service, and indicated that corrupt officers were easily bribed into taking "debtors from the island contrary to the established laws of the place and to the great prejudice of his creditors." In December 1696 the merchants proposed to send fifteen hundred men to Jamaica and asked the board to request £500 from the king "to be paid out in procuring or encouraging such weavers or other poor tradesmen as are capable of doing service in case of an invasion." By the end of the month the scheme had been approved, "upon condition [the merchants] give security to restore the money in case they do not get the men accordingly."[58] Here was a plan the cash-strapped government could support. Although it would cost the Treasury some money, it was certainly cheaper to send over unemployed tradesmen than organized military regiments who required income and provisions for their service. The willingness of the board to accept Heathcote's plan indicated not only his political influence, but that ultimately the government was unwilling and unable to do anything to systematically improve supplies of servants to the Caribbean colonies. Instead, it relied on merchants, albeit powerful and wealthy merchants, to come up with plans to fill these needs.

Almost immediately, Heathcote and Gracedieu's plans hit serious road-blocks. The day after receiving a promise of aid from the king, the merchants indicated to the board "that they were doubtful whether they could be able to get men in time enough for their ships now intended to be sent." There was also trouble securing funds during the "present scarcity of money" in the wake of the recoinage. They had difficulties acquiring single men and could only get "some poor families, which including more women and children than men would not answer their ends." Secretary of State William Trumbull suggested sending "malefactors that are in Newgate," but the board doubted that Jamaica's merchants and planters would be amenable to such a plan. The main issue was the prohibitive cost of transporting men across the Atlantic during the war. Heathcote claimed that merchant captains informed him they would require £8 per person transported. During peacetime, the average cost of transporting an indentured servant to America was around £5–6. "Now the difficulty is how to get this money to pay the masters of the merchant men," Heathcote reported, "which I as a particular merchant cannot raise and when I talk with the rest they speak of their losses that I see no hopes of raising the money amongst ourselves or that This Business can be done unless it be by the Government."[59] Heathcote's last comment betrayed his frustration in the matter. The war and the recoinage left London's merchant community extremely cash poor, and therefore the only way for the colonies to be properly supplied with servants was with full financial support of the state. But he knew that this was something that the Board of Trade and the Whig Junto ministry were unwilling and unable to provide.

After receiving another proposal to send men to Jamaica from a merchant named Jeffrey Yellowton, the board suggested that all the merchants should work together and pool the money the king had promised for their scheme, something Heathcote and Gracedieu were unwilling to do. The board once again asked King William to step in, and the King-in-Council approved the new plan in April 1697 but sent it to be managed by the Admiralty rather than the Board of Trade. Upon learning of the involvement of the Admiralty in the affair, Heathcote backed out of the undertaking.[60] He and his allies were unwilling to allow the military to manage an enterprise they wanted to control for their own profit. In fact, as far as Heathcote and Gracedieu were concerned, the Admiralty had proven insensitive to the needs of the colonies, with its policy of impressments during the war. They considered the Admiralty to be part of the problem and could not reasonably be seen as part of the solution to Jamaica's population woes.

This episode represented the problematic and highly politicized nature of imperial administration during the Nine Years' War. Instead of answering the grievances of colonial governors regarding their declining servant populations with any serious plan, imperial authorities chose to leave such issues up to governors and merchants to settle themselves. In part, this was not surprising, given the use of such potential emigrants as recruits during the war. In addition, the costs of transporting people across the Atlantic during wartime had reached new heights. And as Heathcote and Gracedieu discovered, it was not an easy task to find people, especially single men with skills, willing to go to the colonies. A few months later, Heathcote informed the board that it was "the interest of England to improve [Jamaica] to the highest, as lying in the heart of the Spanish plantations, and producing very rich and valuable commodities." Heathcote emphasized, "But that must be done by the government itself, the planters that are now there will be content with their present circumstances and neither desire nor will they do any thing towards it."[61] Only state-sponsored efforts could have this desired effect, because planters could not be relied upon to maintain an adequate supply of white servants to maintain the militias.

The Board of Trade explored other ways to increase the white populations of the West Indies without relying heavily on emigration from England, including disbanding regiments of soldiers stationed in the colonies with the hope they would remain and settle there. Colonial officials tried to take matters into their own hands to encourage or even force planters to maintain adequate numbers of white servants. Beeston issued a proclamation in February 1698 ordering that "every owner of five Negroes shall have and maintain one white servant and for ten, two white servants and soe proportionably to ye number of their Negroes for every ten more, one white servant, which was ordained for ye peopling, strength and securing this island against any danger either foreign or domestick." The act was necessary because despite the fact that servants once again began to trickle into the West Indies colonies after the war, Beeston reported, "the people generally neglect the buying of them." Officials in Barbados pressed similar efforts to increase the number of white servants in that colony. In 1696 the assembly passed an act "to Encourage the bringing of Christian Servants to that Island," which offered payment from the island's treasury of £18 for each able-bodied white male adult servant brought to the island that could not be sold within ten days of his arrival in the colony, presuming he could work for four years. This was an unlikely scenario, as white servants arriving in Barbados by the end of the seventeenth century could demand fairly high wages.[62] But slavery had prevailed to such an extent that maintaining any kind of significant servant population proved extremely difficult. Ultimately, the English imperial state in the 1690s was unwilling to undertake any significant project of emigration from England to the colonies. It was far easier and far cheaper to leave such schemes up to private merchants who had the contacts and in theory the capital necessary for such enterprises. But even when white servants were available, plantation owners were not always willing to purchase their terms of service, despite laws ordering them to do so. Instead, they spent their money and credit purchasing slaves. That was what they demanded and expected, and that was what the state supported.

CONCLUSION

The total acceptance of slavery as a key element of English imperialism was indicated by two factors by the 1690s. The first was the ability of the separate-trader alliance to remove the Royal African Company permanently as a serious competitor in the slave trade. Second was the unwillingness on the part of the government to initiate any major emigration policy. The political and commercial decline of the African Company in the wake of the Glorious Revolution was related to its perceived ideological orientation as much as its financial and structural difficulties. The debates over the management of the slave trade revealed a widespread acceptance of the idea that the colonies, especially those that relied on African slavery, were integral parts of the realm. In addition, the apparent neglect of the colonial theater of war can be understood to be related to the acceptance of slavery by imperial authorities because it corresponded to demographic concerns at home. By understanding slave labor to be a key component of England's economy, the revolutionary regime indicated its acceptance of slavery as an institution, which worked to justify the empire's very existence. In fact, a report issued by the Board of Trade in December 1697 did not mention indentured servants at all. It emphasized that "the chief commodities of those plantations, to make them most advantageous for this nation and beneficial to the planters is best carried on by the labour of Negroes."[63] The English government's endorsement of an open trade for African slaves represented victory of the colonial planter vision of empire that had been evolving since the 1650s, which embraced a plantation-based empire. It depended upon the construction of a racialized slave system that was maintained through brutal forms of white mastery over blacks. Ultimately, the English state endorsed this as well. Over the course of confrontations and negotiations with imperial authorities during the late 1600s, this imperial vision helped to shape directives and ideologies emanating from the metropolis.

7

THE SLAVE TRADE, THE *ASIENTO*, AND THE NATIONAL INTEREST, 1698–1718

The 1690s had not been kind to the Royal African Company. Politically isolated, it no longer influenced colonial appointments or imperial policies. It also suffered financially, which was exacerbated by the way its enemies portrayed the company as a throwback to the worst of Stuart absolutism. Although the company hoped the Ten Percent Act of 1698 would improve its financial fortunes, it soon became apparent that any money it received from separate traders was offset by the increased costs of greater competition on the African coast. By 1707, it was clear to the company that the Ten Percent Act was not working to its advantage.[1] It spent the better part of the next five years trying to undo the act. From 1707 to 1712, the company presented its case to the Board of Trade and Parliament, which proved hostile to any attempts to reinstitute a monopoly on the slave trade. These attempts triggered a new wave of public interest in the status of the slave trade, and both the company's supporters and the separate traders and their allies appealed to the public in the form of published pamphlets and broadsides.

While the African Company continued to appeal to the public to support its position and regain its financial footing, it also focused on a venture in cooperation with a new joint-stock corporation. The South Sea Company was founded in the spring of 1711 by Queen Anne's trusted adviser and Lord Treasurer, Robert Harley, Earl of Oxford, in order to solve a looming credit crisis caused by the nation's enormous war debts. Creditors would exchange debt for stock in the new company. As an incentive to investors and creditors, Oxford gave the South Sea Company a monopoly on trade to and from Spanish America knowing full well that not only would peace soon be negotiated between Britain, Spain, and

France, ending the War of Spanish Succession, but that the terms of the peace would be commercially beneficial to Britain by including the *asiento*, the exclusive contract to provide the Spanish American colonies with African slaves.[2] The contract promised to be especially lucrative, because the Spanish appeared to have an insatiable need for slaves in their colonies but were not direct participants in the slave trade themselves. The British (and especially the African Company) had coveted providing the Spanish American colonies with slaves for decades. In 1713, the South Sea Company contracted with the Royal African Company to help fulfill the terms of the *asiento*. The African Company viewed this contract as a political and financial lifeline that could reverse its bad fortunes.

The creation of the South Sea Company with the explicit purpose of gaining the *asiento* was not merely the result of Oxford's inside information on the probable course of a peace settlement. It occurred at a time when the African slave trade had been at the center of national attention for decades. This chapter explores the relationship between the South Sea Company's procurement of the *asiento* and the slave-trade debates of 1707–1712, which highlighted the popular perception of the slave trade's importance to the British imperial economy. The new company's emergence in the midst of these popular debates was not coincidental, and it represented a key development in the evolution of the British dominance of the transatlantic slave trade. The South Sea Company's backers understood that there was a widespread perception among the British public that slavery and the slave trade provided significant economic benefits to the nation and could even solve a vexing and potentially dangerous credit crisis.[3] Although ultimately the *asiento* contract was not enough to save the African Company, in the end it represented the culmination of many decades of increased colonial dependence on slavery and the economic benefits that this dependence seemed to create, both in the colonies and in the metropolis.

THE CONSEQUENCES OF THE 1698 ACT

In the immediate aftermath of the Ten Percent Act becoming law, the African Company hoped that the 10 percent duty would help improve its financial condition. But the act soon proved disappointing. The company claimed that revenue collected did not provide enough capital to maintain its buildings or its foothold in the trade. Increased competition meant that African traders could raise prices because they now could sell slaves to the highest bidders. As a result, prices for slaves in the colonies rose so dramatically that colonial planters now complained about private traders. Governor William Beeston of Jamaica, a longtime enemy of the African Company, claimed in 1700 that private merchants came to the colony "under pretence they would supply Negroes more plentiful and cheap . . . and whereas the Royal Company usually supplied Negroes at 22 and 24 £ p head & gave 6, 8, & 12 months credit, now the [private] merchants sell for 34£ p head and give no credit at all."[4] Despite earlier protests about the African Company's monopoly, the opening of the trade made slaves more expensive and credit harder to obtain.

Despite the survival of the African Company in 1698, it was never able to regain its position either as a significant trading entity or as a key institution of imperial administration. Rather than improving the company's situation, the Ten Percent Act forced it to compete more vigorously for a dwindling share of the market in African slaves. The company ordered its agents in West Africa to do their best to prevent African traders from selling slaves to separate traders and foreign merchants. This proved to be a serious problem, because many company agents themselves frequently sold slaves for their own personal profit. The company worried that its access to slaves in West Africa had diminished to such a degree that its directors encouraged agents in Africa to cultivate trade in other commodities, especially gold and ivory. The company was so desperate to keep interlopers at bay that it even signed an agreement in 1707 with its main commercial rival, the Dutch West India Company, to work together to block illegal traders.[5]

Despite these efforts, the company continued to lose market share throughout the early 1700s. The separate traders not only outbid the company for slaves in Africa, but dramatically outperformed the company in terms of numbers of slaves transported across the Atlantic. Using a comprehensive database of transatlantic slaving voyages from the sixteenth to the nineteenth centuries, David Eltis has calculated perhaps the most accurate numbers to date on the transatlantic slave trade. As table 2 shows, Eltis estimates that from 1676 to 1700, approximately 243,300 Africans were forcibly taken across the Atlantic in British ships. From 1701 to 1725 British slavers brought about 380,900 slaves to the Americas. This is an increase of one-and-a-half times. Most telling, it has been estimated that between 60 percent and 80 percent of the market was controlled by interlopers by 1700. These numbers indicated not only the continued high demand for slaves in the colonies, but that many independent merchants took advantage of the end of the African Company's monopoly. Table 3, also taken from Eltis's calculations, illustrates the estimated arrivals of slaves in Barbados, the Leeward Islands, and Jamaica from 1662 to 1713. Although slave deliveries to Barbados seem to have peaked during the 1680s with approximately 39,000 slaves, deliveries of slaves to all three colonies remained high after the Glorious Revolution of 1688–1689, which could be an indication of separate-trader success in the trade.[6]

Table 2. Volume of Slaves Leaving Africa in English/British Ships

Year	Number of slaves
1601–1650	23,000
1651–1675	115,200
1676–1700	243,300
1701–1725	380,900
1726–1750	490,500
Total	1,252,900

Source: David Eltis, "The Volume and Structure of the Transatlantic Slave Trade: A Reassessment," *William and Mary Quarterly*, 3rd ser., 58, no. 1 (Jan. 2001): 43, table I.

Table 3. Estimated Arrivals of Slaves to English Colonies in English/British Ships

Year	Barbados	Leeward Islands	Jamaica
1662–1670	30,318	2,801	11,031
1671–1680	21,400	9,566	20,323
1681–1690	39,101	14,146	27,730
1691–1700	29,394	5,304	35,945
1701–1707	25,629	10,414	30,808
1708–1713	10,167	7,048	34,711
Total	156,009	49,279	160,548

Source: David Eltis, *The Rise of African Slavery in the Americas* (Cambridge: Cambridge University Press, 2000), 208, table 8.3.

By 1707, the African Company's directors decided to appeal to Parliament to urge the repeal or alteration of the Ten Percent Act. In December of that year, the company presented its case to Parliament and the Board of Trade, and that month the board opened an investigation into the state of the African trade. Just prior to the start of this inquiry, the Board of Trade experienced a significant overhaul in the midst of an ascendancy of Whigs in Queen Anne's ministry during the War of Spanish Succession (1702–1713), which influenced the direction and tone of the investigation. The ministry of Lord Godolphin as Lord Treasurer, the Duke of Marlborough as captain general of the queen's forces in Europe, and Robert Harley as speaker of the House of Commons and secretary of state for the northern department had attempted to govern through a broad coalition of moderates who supported the war effort and Marlborough's military strategies from 1704. But by the end of 1706, Whigs had begun to maneuver themselves into some of the most powerful ministerial positions, including Charles Spenser, third Earl of Sunderland (Marlborough's son-in-law), who was appointed secretary of state for the southern department. In the middle of 1707, he began to reshape the Board of Trade by removing remaining Tories and less-than-loyal Whigs. The most significant departure from the board was William Blathwayt, its longest-serving and most knowledgeable member. New members included the Earl of Stamford, Baron Herbert of Cherbury, Robert Monckton, John Pulteney, and Sir Charles Turner. Historian Ian Steele has characterized these men as Whig place-seekers with little regard for the inner workings of trade or imperial administration, who were appointed to secure Whig support in Parliament for the ministry's agenda. Just as the board's investigation into the state of African trade got under way, the Godolphin-Marlborough-Harley ministry shattered in January and February 1708 over mismanagement of the war effort and political affairs. Godolphin and Marlborough once and for all threw in their lot with the Whigs who embraced the ministry's continental war strategy and the necessity of preventing France from ruling Spain and Spanish America.[7] For the next two years, the Whig Junto, led by Sunderland, directed Britain's foreign, domestic, and imperial policy.

This was the political context that shaped the Board of Trade's investigation into the state of African trade. Historians have noted that the board's investigation was carried out in such a way that the African Company stood little chance of a fair hearing. Although the board requested information from the company about its finances and property holdings, it depended almost entirely on the opinions and testimony of the separate traders in its investigation. The board asked the separate traders about the necessity of forts and castles for carrying on the slave trade in Africa and also asked them if there "were any complaints against the said Company as to the ill management of that trade, what those complaints were, by whom made, and what done thereupon?" The board then requested the separate traders' opinions on the worth of the company's stock and property, the value of its imports and exports to and from Africa, and "What defects do you find in the constitution of their present charter?" In January 1708, the separate traders responded that they had little if any need to use the company's buildings and claimed to "carry on their commerce with the natives in safety and freedom without the protection of the forts and castles," many of which were in no condition to provide much protection in the first place. They also questioned the company's management of the revenue from the Ten Percent Act, and called for the African Company's financial books to be inspected. "We have reason to believe that part of their late adventures and dividends have been out of the sum of our Ten p Cent paid them, and not employed in the maintaining of their forts and castles as was intended." They blamed the company for neglecting Maryland and Virginia entirely and argued that a regulated company should take over the African trade. In presenting its case, the company emphasized that the 10 percent duty did not cover expenses for the upkeep of its forts and castles, and that increases in slave prices in the colonies were a direct result of the competition for market share in Africa created by the act.[8]

The board issued a report to Queen Anne in February 1708, which accepted the claims made by the separate traders almost entirely. The report agreed that the company misallocated its funds and argued that if the 10 percent revenue had properly been managed, the company would have plenty for the upkeep of its forts and castles. The board also agreed that the company's buildings provided little if any protection, and that "Cape Coast Castle is the only place of strength." The board argued that a joint-stock corporation should not be entrusted with such an "absolutely necessary" trade, because it would limit it to a particular area of the Gold Coast of Africa where its forts were concentrated, decrease the number of ships involved in the trade, and never provide the colonies with the numbers of slaves they demanded. The board agreed that the trade should instead be run by a regulated company.[9]

The Board of Trade continued its investigation throughout 1708, and late that year it drew up an act disestablishing the African Company and creating a regulated company in its place. Although Parliament did not take action on the proposed legislation, the board in conjunction with the House of Commons expanded its investigation during the next few years. In addition to their usual complaints, the separate traders now claimed that the company had agreed to "a collusive Neutrality with the French," so "that the Separate Traders should of consequence be either hindred from the Trade of those Parts or become a Prey to our Enemies." They noted that this design was especially treacherous while Britain was at war with France. The board asked colonial officials to provide accounts of how many slaves had been imported by the company and private traders between 1698 and 1707.[10] In response, the company's directors solicited petitions from British manufacturers and colonial planters, and even provided a sample petition for the planters to sign. The petition did not ask for a specific way of settling the slave trade but merely requested that the trade be settled so "that a sufficient number of Negroes may be had on ye Coast [of Africa] on moderate terms, by which your Petitioners may hope for a constant supply at reasonable prices." Planters from Barbados, Montserrat, and Nevis signed the petition on the African Company's behalf. The use of such petitioning and lobbying techniques suggests that the directors of the African Company by the early eighteenth century were more politically astute and in tune with structural political changes than some historians have suggested. The separate traders utilized the same strategy, and provided sample petitions to the colonies and to outlying ports and manufacturing towns and shires across England, many of which were answered requesting that the African trade "remain free and open."[11]

Although some planters were willing to sign petitions in support of the company's position, most responses from the colonies did not help the company's cause. According to the numbers provided by colonial governors, since the Ten Percent Act became law in 1698, separate traders had imported approximately 88,108 slaves to Barbados, Jamaica, and Antigua. The separate traders took advantage of this news and quickly published a pamphlet containing this information in 1709. Later that year the Board of Trade issued a report to the Commons, which stated the African Company claimed to have delivered 17,760 slaves to the colonies from 1698 to 1707. It also accepted the wildly overinflated claims of the separate traders that they had brought 160,950 slaves to the colonies during the same time period. Historian David Eltis maintains that the total number of slaves brought in British ships to the English West Indies for the period 1691–1707 probably totaled 137,494, so clearly these numbers were false. The board blamed the increased prices for slaves not on the Ten Percent Act but on the hazards of trading during wartime. Finally, the report determined that that although the exact state of the African Company's finances remained unclear (in part because the company hesitated to share such information with the board), based on the impressions of the separate traders, they proffered that the company "is reduced so very low, that it will be impossible (upon the Foot they now stand) for them to carry on that Trade." The African Company later complained "that the separate traders had formed a premeditated design, to impose upon the Lords Commissioners [of Trade] & consequently upon the whole nation . . . to magnify the value of their own yearly exports to Africa, & the number of Negroes yearly imported by them to the plantations, by fallacious computations, founded merely upon fictitious suppositions." Although the board made a few corrections to its calculations, it paid little heed to the company's concerns.[12]

THE PUBLIC DEBATE

The African Company and the separate traders also presented their cases to the public in the form of published pamphlets and broadsides. Like the debates of the 1690s, the public discussion over the slave trade in the early 1700s indicated significant popular interest in the politics of slavery and the slave trade's imperial ramifications. This time around, however, pamphlets in favor of reinstating the African Company's monopoly outnumbered those mobilized by the separate traders. From 1704 to 1714 approximately ninety-one publications were printed in support of the company and its monopoly, and about sixty-seven were published in opposition to the company's position, bringing the total for the decade to 158. In contrast, during the 1690s, only about forty pamphlets in total were published, six on behalf of the company and thirty-four by the separate traders and their allies.[13] This increase in overall numbers indicated that both sides recognized the importance of appealing to a broad public audience to promote their positions.

The flipped numerical difference between the pro- and anti-company positions by the early 1700s, however, brings into question some conclusions that scholars have made about separate-trader success in the wake of the Glorious Revolution. William Pettigrew has argued that the separate traders, as a group, were better able to respond to structural changes to political institutions in the wake of the revolution, such as the ascendancy of parliamentary rule, the rise of interest groups, and the use of political propaganda, and that this contributed to their commercial success. Although this might have been the case during the 1690s, the discrepancy in the numbers of pamphlets published by the two sides during the early 1700s indicates that the African Company and its supporters might have been less impervious to changes in political culture than it might at first appear. The company, after all, turned to such adept political propagandists as Charles Davenant and Daniel Defoe to promote its cause, illustrating a mature understanding of the nature of politics and the importance of public opinion by the time of Queen Anne's reign.[14] In addition, as noted above, the company embraced such modern political tools as lobbying and soliciting petitions from various constituencies. The fact that the company actively sought support from planters and manufacturers, who were usually counted among its traditional enemies, indicates that it was better prepared to adapt to the changing political landscape by the early 1700s. In addition, the company might have had greater financial resources available to have such publications written and printed by the 1700s. It was also possible that the African Company felt much more threatened by the 1700s and understood the need to present its case widely. But it is clear that the company's embrace of print and mobilizing prewritten petitions represented a greater readiness to come to terms with the new realities of British political culture, something the old Tory institution was by and large unwilling and unable to do in previous decades.

Scholars who have analyzed the slave-trade debates of the early 1700s have tended to lump them together with those of the 1690s. As in the 1690s, both sides in the early 1700s emphasized the importance of slavery to the colonies and of the colonies to the imperial economy. One pro-company pamphlet asserted in 1713, "Certainly the Plantation Trade is the most considerable Branch of the British Trade, that is the Sugar Plantations." It continued, "the more the Sugar Colonies are improv'd, the greater the Importation must be, and so by consequence more Wealth Accrue to the Nation." Also much as in the 1690s debates, the anti-monopolist side highlighted not only colonial reliance upon the home country, but an integrated vision of empire that emphasized mutual dependence and a kind of negotiated governance. Central to it all was colonial dependence on the forced labor of enslaved Africans, which drove the imperial economy. "The unspeakable Advantages that are continually flowing from her Majesty's *American* Colonies into *Great Britain*," one pamphlet claimed, "and how intirely the Prosperity of our *West-India* Plantations depend, beyond Exception, upon the *African* Trade, since they have no other way to occupy their Grounds, raise their Products, or manufacture their Commodities, but by hard Labour, and that not to be endur'd in such a sultry Climate by any but Negroes."[15]

Despite these similarities to the pamphlets of the 1690s, there were some significant differences between the two sets of publications. For example, pamphlets published on behalf of the African Company in the 1700s demonstrated a keen awareness of the political situation it faced during the Whig Ascendancy of 1708–1710. One pamphlet remarked that by reporting inflated numbers to the Board of Trade, the separate traders hoped to "prejudice the Company and to gain Applause from the Lords Commissioners for Trade," a recognition that the separate traders and the board acted together against the company's interests. Similarly, many pro-company pamphlets argued that the numbers presented by the separate traders were overinflated and false. "The Separate Traders affirm, in Seven Years, they imported into the Plantations 150,000 *Negroes*," read one pamphlet. This was pure fallacy. "No, if all those *Negroes* had been settled in the Plantations, there could have been no Complaint for want of Supply." Charles Davenant simply stated, "their Computations are grossly erroneous." In fact, he wrote, opening the trade had made it impossible to measure "how far (Nationally speaking) we may be either Gainers or Losers by [the slave trade]."[16]

Pro-company pamphlets in the early 1700s, like the few printed during the 1690s, emphasized the need to maintain forts and settlements in Africa to carry on the slave trade, especially because it was "the Practice of other Nations." By the 1700s, however, writers emphasized the "Treachery and Falsehood of the Natives" as a major underlying reason why this was the case. "The Necessity of Forts to carry on the Trade is *publickly owned*; that Necessity is apparent: For the Country is Barbarous, Perfidious, Bloody and Cruel." Forts and castles provided physical marketplaces to trade and form alliances with African traders in order to maintain "a constant co-ercive Power on the Coast, for curbing the natural Insolencies and Barbarity of the generality of their Tempers." Separate traders might claim that forts and castles were not necessary, but according to Davenant "that's but looking one way and rowing another; For if they speak their Minds plainly, it will be found that they slight these Forts merely with Design (if they could compass their ends with the Parliament) to get the Property of them, for little or nothing, to themselves."[17]

The other main difference between the two sets of pamphlets was that both sides had a decade of an open slave trade to remark upon since the passage of the 1698 act. Pro-company publications claimed that the act had the detrimental effect of dividing the interests of British traders in Africa and repeatedly highlighted a necessity for control, order, and discipline that only a joint-stock company licensed by the government could provide. "The unbounded Liberty allowed, by the said Act, to all Persons whatsoever to Trade to Africa," asserted one pamphlet, "without any uniform Influence, or pre-concerted Rules of Management, has rendered the British Interest on that Coast so divided, and the Consequences attending the different Methods of Trading there so very precarious." The result, it claimed, was "the Natives of Africa have thereby an Opportunity of imposing what [prices] they please, as well upon the separate Traders, as upon the Company, to the general Prejudice of the Kingdom." Daniel Defoe wrote in his defense of the company that in the wake of the Ten Percent Act, "The Coast of *Afric* was made a meer Common Fair, where every Ship's Company endeavouring to circumvent and undersell one another." The result, Defoe and numerous others maintained, was increased prices for slaves in Africa and in the colonies. One writer went so far as to claim that only a joint-stock company with a united interest could work to limit slave prices, and remarkably, slave mortality. "Are not the buying of them dear and the Mortality that frequently attends such Voyages too, much greater Causes of their high Prices, which a Company, being but one buyer, can only prevent."[18]

According to pro-company pamphlets, the fierce competition created by the Ten Percent Act resulted in violence on the African coast among British merchants. The need for order was so severe, one writer maintained, "that nothing but a united Power upon the Coast of *Africa* can secure this Trade: Power, *and the Purse, Force, and Merchandize must be united,* and put into *one* and the same Hand." Davenant went so far as to suggest that the African Company and the separate traders should form a united company, much like the two East India Companies had, in order to promote and better manage the trade without these divided interests. Not only did the Ten Percent Act promote chaotic conditions in West Africa, according to many pro-company pamphlets, it violated the company's property rights by opening up access to its forts and castles in the first place. It was especially galling to the author of one pamphlet that Parliament had felt it was within its jurisdiction to violate those rights that had been granted by the Crown in previous generations. Worse, the Ten Percent Act did not provide nearly enough money for the upkeep of the company's forts and castles. "It may be truly said," lamented Davenant, "that the Nation has lost so much, by not having the Trade settled on a fixed and solid Constitution all this time."[19]

Pamphlets produced in opposition to the company's monopoly directly attacked these claims. "The [African] Natives of the Country are not so Treacherous and False as represented, nor do they at any Time offer the first Affront, so that there's no need of Forts and Castles to keep them in Awe." It continued, "If the Blacks Insult the Company's Forts and Factories, and Detain their Provision, it is owing to the Companies Agents and Factors for Inraging them by their own Base Actions." If prices had increased it was because of the violence and treachery of African Company agents, who scared off other traders and made the slave trade more expensive than in previous decades. The African Company's claim that it needed buildings to form alliances with Africans was also dismissed as false. "'Tis fair Dealing with the Natives, and Justice," maintained one leaflet, "and not Alliances with one King, to make War on another, that is the Foundation of all Commerce in the World." Besides, these critics claimed, the company failed to properly maintain their buildings, despite the fact that the separate traders "pay so largely for the Protection of their Forts." In fact, claimed another pamphlet, rather than offering protection to the separate traders who paid the 10 percent duty, the company's agents in Africa offered "very ill Treatment" and "open Violence" to such an extent that the separate traders "dare not come near the English Settlements ashore; *but are forced to trade with the Natives out at Sea.*" Some suggested that ships of war rather than buildings would suffice to safeguard the trade.[20]

Some of the anti-company pamphlets also took on the idea that the African Company's property had been violated through the Ten Percent Act. One claimed that Cape Coast Castle, the main base of the slave trade and owned by the African Company since the 1660s, in fact belonged to the nation as a whole. Cape Coast Castle, "is undoubtedly the Nation's Property, being taken from the Dutch at the Nation's Charge; for tho King *Charles* granted this Company a Patent for the sole Trade, exclusive of all others, together with that Place, that Patent was disregarded by the Parliament in 1698 and all the Settlements in *Guinea* render'd free for all English Men to live in." Such claims seemed to confirm the African Company's fears that its right to property had been compromised by the Ten Percent Act. Others suggested that if the forts and castles were not already nationalized, they should be in the future. One even argued Parliament had the authority of eminent domain to make it happen.[21] This revealed a vision of the slave trade as not only in the national interest, but also so important as to be nationalized. According to this position, the company, through violent acts and poor management, had abdicated its authority over the trade and its own property.

The anti-monopolist pamphlets also disputed the argument that because other nations had forts and castles and joint-stock corporations to conduct trade in Africa, Britain should do the same. "The Practice of other Nations is like that of the English African Company, who use their Forts to the same Purpose," claimed one broadsheet, "that is, chiefly to hinder the rest of the People of their own Nation to Trade where ever they can prevent them." This practice, it was argued, should not be emulated by the British. Rather than actually doing something about Dutch or French competition, in fact, some anti-monopolist tracts claimed company agents protected "Dutch Interlopers, because I suppose they are well paid for their Pains." Some also reiterated the separate-traders' claim that the African Company had entered into a "neutrality" agreement with the French African company in 1704, alleging that the two companies had agreed to work together to suppress separate-trader access to African slave traders. Such "felonious Treaties" with "the open Enemies of Her Majesty" during wartime underscored the perception that the African Company, long associated with the Stuart monarchs and their connections to the court of the absolutist Louis XIV, had continued this perfidious union.[22]

Just as the separate traders had argued to the Board of Trade, anti-monopolist publications maintained that the African trade should not be managed by a joint-stock company. Some claimed the slave trade, "a Trade, upon the inlarging and improving whereof depends the Welfare of our *West-India* Plantations, and our Trade to *New Spain,*" was simply too important to be entrusted to a joint-stock company. In addition, the African Company had not provided the colonies with enough slaves, even at the height of its monopoly, and it continued to neglect the tobacco colonies of Virginia and Maryland. Limiting the African trade to a joint-stock company based in London would have the effect of neglecting outports, such as Bristol and Liverpool as well as all of Scotland. Some repeated the refrain that if a company was necessary for the trade, it should instead be organized as a regulated rather than a joint-stock company. "An open Trade," one pamphlet argued, "has as direct a tendency to enlarge and improve, as the other has to cramp and destroy whatever is valuable in this Article." Rather than promoting divided interests and a chaotic trading environment, anti-monopolist pamphlets emphasized that competition created by the Ten Percent Act was good for trade. "Nothing conduces so much to the Increase of Trade, as Emulation among Traders," claimed one sheet. "When Trade is confined to a few, who are in no Apprehension to be outdone by any Rival, they are not likely to take extraordinary Pains to improve it. Whereas when many carry on a Trade, their Industry and Ingenuity are always at work to out vie one another." Besides, claimed another, the African Company could hardly deny the fact that planters in the colonies "have always complained of this Monopoly, as a very burthensom Grievance, till laid open by Act of Parliament in 1698."[23] Such publications both for and against the African Company's position demonstrated widespread public interest in the slave trade and its place in Britain's imperial economy. For many, the imaginary of empire depended on the proper management of the slave trade.

THE POLITICS OF THE *ASIENTO* IN THE EARLY 1700S

For three years, the Whig-dominated Board of Trade sided with the separate traders and ensured that the Royal African Company would never again hold a monopoly on African trade or win more favorable terms than those provided by the Ten Percent Act. By 1710, however, Whig fortunes in the government began to change. Tories took advantage of popular dissatisfaction with another long, expensive war by focusing on the unevenness of military victories on the Continent. Most significantly, by 1709–1710 the country faced a significant credit crisis brought on by long-term debt and the increased costs of war. To fund the war effort, the government had to borrow money on increasingly poor terms. As Carl Wennerlind has argued, unlike previous credit crises, the financial emergency of 1709–1710 was especially troubling because of the new role public opinion played in the understanding and management of credit in Britain. At the same time, utilizing propaganda became an opportunity for politicians, financiers, and others to shape public opinion about credit according to their respective political and economic agendas. Whigs and Tories, as well as less obviously political groups, attempted to sway public opinion through the publication of books, pamphlets, and broadsides, and tried to place the blame for the crisis on their enemies and detractors.[24] The debates on the status of the African Company and the slave trade coincided with this larger debate on the state of the national debt, the health of public credit, and what needed to be done about the crisis. As a result, politics continued to play a major role in the discourse about the place of slavery and the slave trade in the British empire.

Not surprisingly, Tories and their allies blamed profiteering by Whig grandees in charge of the Bank of England and the new United East India Company, both of which provided significant loans to the government to finance the war effort, for working to prolong the war and exacerbating the credit crisis. By the summer of 1710, financial instability spilled over into the political realm. In June 1710 Queen Anne removed Sunderland as secretary of state, which triggered a backlash from establishment Whigs who were concerned about the state of public credit in the wake of such significant political change. The following day, Sir Gilbert Heathcote, the longtime colonial merchant and current governor of the Bank of England, requested an audience with the queen. The bank had granted the government an enormous loan in 1709 to fund the war, and Heathcote, along with a delegation from the bank, cautioned the queen that any further alteration of her ministry or dissolving the current Parliament would destabilize the nation's finances. For two months, Queen Anne made no further changes. In August, Heathcote, this time via Lord High Treasurer Godolphin, once again asked for an assurance that the ministry and Parliament would remain unchanged. This time his plan backfired, however, and Godolphin was summarily dismissed from office.[25] The Tory leader Sir Robert Harley, soon to be named Earl of Oxford, became chancellor of the exchequer, and the following year was named Lord High Treasurer.

It was not an auspicious time to take over the reins of government, with the credit crisis deepening and public support of the war effort waning. But Harley took advantage of popular anti-Whig fervor, war weariness, and "Church in danger" sentiment by engineering a resounding Tory victory in parliamentary elections that October. This hardly solved the credit problem, however, because as Heathcote and others had warned, the creation of a Tory ministry and majority in the Commons significantly undermined public confidence in government bonds, especially among the wealthy Whigs who held them. Harley did, however, have a two-pronged strategy to address the credit crisis. The first was to wrest control of the financial establishment away from its traditional Whig base. In April 1711, the Bank of England and the United East India Company, the bastions of the Whig financial establishment, held elections for their directorships. In the heated political environment, both Whigs and Tories, the latter encouraged by Harley, presented a "ticket" of twenty-four men deemed acceptable for director-ship positions. There was some overlap between the two tickets, and the lists did not represent a clear-cut Whig-Tory divide; as Gary De Krey and others have pointed out, there were a number of Whigs on the "Tory" slate endorsed by Harley. These Whigs, however, such as the merchants Sir James Bateman and Samuel Shepheard, had grown disaffected with the politics of the Whig estab-lishment. In the end, the anti-establishment, anti-Whig candidates were not successful in either case. Their failed attempt to thwart the Whig leadership, however, was not forgotten by Harley and his associates, who moved forward on the second part of his plan to counter the financial and political power of the Whigs while addressing the nation's credit crisis. One month prior to the directorship elections, Harley had introduced a proposal in the Commons for the creation of a joint-stock company that would absorb the government's short-term war debt. The day after he made this proposal, however, Harley was stabbed by the French spy the Marquis de Guiscard and forced to convalesce for weeks. After his recuperation and the failure to engineer a takeover of the Bank and East India Company, Harley reintroduced his scheme for a new trading company in Parliament.[26]

Harley's plan called for the creation by Parliament of a joint-stock company, the subscribers to which would be the holders of the nation's short-term war debt, which had been recently determined to be over £9.4 million. This group included not only larger bondholders and creditors, but also smaller creditors to the army and navy, including soldiers and sailors who were owed pay by the government. They would exchange their debt for shares in the company, which would serve as a conduit to swap "debt for equity" to keep creditors happy, credit afloat, and money circulating. As an incentive for creditors/investors, the government would pay a rate of 6 percent interest on the debt exchanged for stock, and the company would be granted a monopoly on all trade to Spanish America, including the *asiento*. The "South Seas" continued to have a powerful hold on the British imagination as a bottomless source of potential wealth. As early as 1710–1711, when preliminary peace negotiations with France began, Harley knew that Britain would likely be granted the *asiento* at the close of the war. As one supporter at the time remarked, "I must admit it to be an uncommon method to raise the public credit by exposing to the whole world the [nation's] immense debt, yet what ill consequence can it be, when the vast ocean of the South Seas, and the infinite treasures of America are (inter alia) assigned for that satisfaction?" Government creditors would earn money on their investments, and the nation's debt would be funded.[27]

The creation of the South Sea Company in 1711 was the culmination of a number of political and economic circumstances that came together under Harley's leadership. In the first instance, the company was meant to serve as a Tory counterweight to the power and influence of the wealthiest Whigs and their joint-stock companies, institutions from which Tories had largely been excluded. In order to keep Whigs out of directorships in the new company, Harley pushed for the first slate of directors to be appointed by the queen, which would essentially grant him and his associates the authority to choose the directors they wanted.[28] A number of unsuccessful candidates for the directorships of the Bank of England and East India Company in April 1711 found themselves or their family members with positions in the new venture. Initial directors of the South Sea Company included Sir Theodore Janssen, a Tory financier; Sir Richard Hoare, a Tory City of London populist; John Blunt and Sir George Caswall, Tory financiers who had tried unsuccessfully to compete with the Bank of England with the Sword Blade Company; Edward Harley, Robert's brother; Henry St. John, the Tory diplomat and politician soon to be appointed secretary at war; and Sir James Bateman and Samuel Shepheard, both London Whigs who had grown alienated by Heathcote's governorship at the Bank of England and had been unsuccessful candidates on the anti-establishment slate. Solidifying his political ascendancy, the same month he introduced the South Sea Company scheme, Harley was named the Earl of Oxford and Lord High Treasurer of the queen's ministry.[29]

The South Sea Company has been the focus of numerous historical and economic studies, most of which emphasize the infamous South Sea Bubble of 1720, in which the price of its stock skyrocketed on speculation of future profits and unceremoniously collapsed, with devastating effects on the British imperial economy. As a result, some scholars have downplayed the importance of trade, and especially the slave trade, to the reality of the scheme. This has changed in recent decades, as historians such as Colin Palmer, Carl Wennerlind, and Adrian Finucane have focused on the importance of the *asiento* to Britain's imperial project, the credit crisis, and the functioning of overseas trade.[30] They are right to emphasize that the company was not only founded with the explicit purpose of gaining access to lucrative Spanish American markets, but that it was established to manage the *asiento.* The government's interest in winning the exclusive contract to provide the Spanish colonies with slaves went as far back as the 1660s and was directly connected to the perceived centrality of the African slave trade to Britain's imperial economy, as well as the idea that Spanish American bullion could solve Britain's financial woes. Few scholars, however, have focused on the connections between the foundation of the South Sea Company and the *asiento* and the contemporaneous public debate on the status of the African Company. But it is important to note that the issue of the *asiento* frequently appeared in the slave-trade debate. Many pro–African Company publications emphasized the necessity of a joint-stock company not only to supply the British colonies with adequate supplies of slaves, but for "making any advantageous Contracts with the *Spaniards,* or *Portugueze,* to furnish them with *Negroes* in their *West Indies.*" On the other hand, many anti-monopolist tracts argued that because of the *asiento*'s economic importance, the slave trade to both British and Spanish colonies should remain open to all who wished to participate.[31]

In the midst of the public debate over the African trade, in fact, one particularly interesting pamphlet was published in 1709 called *Proposals for Raising a New Company for Carrying on the Trades of Africa and the Spanish West-Indies*. The author, who presented himself as "neither a *Guinea* nor *India* Party Man," saw the public debate and parliamentary investigation into the state of the African trade as an opportunity to reorganize the slave trade by "uniting the Trades to Guinea, and the Spanish West-Indies" into one company. "If we consider the Spanish Trade only," the author elaborated, "and of what vast Advantage to the Nation the keeping to our selves the *Assiento* may be, which is no other way to be preserved than by the Preservation of this Trade; this Consideration is of it self sufficient to obviate all Pretences. By that, we shall have a perpetual Supply of Gold, Silver, and other useful Commodities; and by them procure the Balance of Trade on our side, which must otherwise inevitably fall to our Neighbours." This was the political-economic position held by the Crown and the African Company since the Restoration. But instead of maintaining the old African Company, the author proposed the organization of "a new Fund, a new People, encouraged to be industrious, and united in one Bottom the better to reap the Fruits of their Industry."[32] According to this writer, it made sense to combine the interests and demands of the British and Spanish plantations into a new trading company whose primary concern was getting slaves across the Atlantic. The content of this pamphlet indicated that many in Britain recognized a connection between reorganizing the African trade and the opportunity that arose from the possibility of winning the *asiento* at the end of the war. Its appearance during the separate-trader debates indicates that the creation of the South Sea Company in 1711 with the explicit purpose of managing the *asiento* was implicated in wider popular discussions about the slave trade and the national interest.

Harley and his business associates in the South Sea Company understood that the slave trade was at the center of the nation's attention. They also hoped to take advantage of the popular image of Spanish America as an endless source of riches. The *asiento* in particular was viewed by many as a potential gold mine for whoever held the contract. The South Sea Company was granted a charter in September 1711, giving it a monopoly on all trade to Spanish America, or the "South Seas," even though neither Spain nor France, which now controlled much of New Spain, officially allowed foreigners to trade in their American territories. A few days later, the early peace negotiations to end the war were signed with France, and many in Oxford's circle knew that Britain would be granted the *asiento* in the final peace.[33]

Not surprisingly, considering the highly partisan environment of the final years of the war, Oxford's project met with serious opposition from a variety of constituencies. Many took issue with the riskiness of the venture and argued that despite the potential profitability of the Spanish American trade, "this New Company, as it stands constituted at present," would not guarantee safe returns. Others warned that the men behind the company were well-known fraudsters and that the entire scheme was potentially criminal. In response, South Sea Company backers presented a variety of political, diplomatic, and economic arguments to promote the scheme. In the first instance, the company, through the exchange of its stock for outstanding debt, would help solve the nation's looming credit crisis. Daniel Defoe, the Tory ministry's chief propagandist-for-hire, argued that if the ministry had not addressed the issue of government debt, credit would have been devastated and the economy ruined. One anonymous pamphleteer maintained that "The Provision made for the Payment of the National Debts [by the company's shares] cannot but produce a lasting Credit." This author also argued that gaining access to Spanish American trade would result in gains for Britain, especially "real Treasure, such as Gold and Silver."[34]

Many supporters also argued that the South Sea Company, by gaining access to the lucrative Spanish American market, would hinder Louis XIV's designs for universal monarchy. Therefore the South Sea Company represented the most patriotic anti-French aspirations of the British nation. Upon claiming the Spanish Crown and Dominions for his grandson in 1702, Louis XIV secured the *asiento* for France for a period of ten years. The *asiento* in French hands represented Louis XIV's most fearsome imperial designs and embodied the popular British perception of French perfidiousness. One pamphlet addressed the widespread Whiggish notion that the Tory ministry, which had risen to power on popular antiwar sentiment, would abandon Spain in peace negotiations and leave the Spanish Crown in French Bourbon hands. Nothing could be further from the truth, this writer claimed, trying to reassure an imaginary investor who contemplated selling his shares. "Be assur'd then, Sir, that the *Present Ministry* will never make any *Peace,* without the Concurrence of our Allies, nor without having *Spain* and the *Indies* restor'd to the [Habsburg] *Emperor.*"[35]

In a rhetorical move illustrating the connections between the origins of the South Sea Company and the debate over the status of the African Company, South Sea Company backers claimed that its control of the *asiento* would ultimately benefit the beleaguered African Company. Defoe maintained that only the African Company, because of its presence on the West African coast, "are capable to enter into Contracts for the supplying it [the *asiento*], and are alone capable of performing those Contracts."[36] This was exactly what Oxford seems to have had in mind. Although he entertained a proposal from the separate traders to execute a subcontract to procure slaves in late July 1713, in the end Oxford and the South Sea Company's directors chose to work with the African Company, believing its existing infrastructure and established contacts would benefit the *asiento*. According to the terms worked out in 1713, the company would provide Spanish colonies with a certain amount of slaves per year, paying a duty to the Spanish Crown on each slave for the privilege of a guaranteed sale. After Parliament approved the Treaty of Utrecht in the spring of 1713, the two corporations forged an agreement where the African Company arranged to provide the Spanish colonies with forty-eight hundred slaves annually on behalf of the South Sea Company. The official agreement between the two companies was signed on October 20, 1713.[37] The African Company no longer had a monopoly on the slave trade to Britain's colonies, but it made political and economic sense to Oxford and his associates to trust it with fulfilling the *asiento*.

THE ROYAL AFRICAN COMPANY AND THE *ASIENTO*

Not surprisingly, the African Company viewed the *asiento* as a financial and political lifeline and an occasion to attempt to reexert its influence over imperial affairs. The company's directors even agreed to "terms disadvantageous to themselves" in order to gain the contract. Nevertheless, hopes were high in the fall of 1713. "We shall omit no opportunity to strengthen our interest by Parliament or otherwise," the directors wrote to their agents at Cape Coast Castle in October 1713, "and we hope this agreement with the South Sea Company will have a good effect and that a right use will be made of it by all our servants towards the promoting & establishment of our interest both in Africa and America." And indeed, earlier that summer the African Company with the help of its new powerful ally convinced the House of Lords to reject a bill that had passed the Commons opening up the slave trade once and for all.[38]

It was significant, however, that Oxford created a new company to handle the *asiento* rather than granting it to the African Company in the first instance. This certainly demonstrated the African Company's political and structural weaknesses by 1711, and occurred despite the fact that Oxford and the Tory-dominated Parliament and ministry were by and large supportive of the old corporation. Although the South Sea Company agreed to contract with the African Company, which could be interpreted to mean that Oxford and his allies saw the scheme as a way to help the struggling corporation, William Pettigrew dismisses this as unlikely. It is crucial to keep in mind that the South Sea Company was founded first and foremost to solve the problem of government debt and the nation's credit crisis. As its financial difficulties of the 1690s demonstrated, the African Company could not have been used for such a massive undertaking; a new joint-stock company, with new incentives, had to be created. The *asiento*, while central to the scheme, was the means by which investors and creditors would be enticed into subscribing. In other words, the slave trade, and as Carl Wennderlind has recently argued, the place of the slave trade and the "South Seas" in the British popular imagination, was the means to attract creditors and solve the nation's debt and credit crisis.[39] Considering the African Company's dire financial straits, not to mention its ideological associations explored in the previous chapter, it was clear that Oxford could hardly trust his new scheme to save the nation's credit problems to the old African Company.

Some historians have argued that because the African Company was preoccupied by the prospects of the *asiento* trade, its directors were essentially "distracted" while the separate traders not only continued to chip away at the company's market share but also created a "legislative vacuum," ensuring the expiration of the 1698 Ten Percent Act in 1712. The African Company, however, hardly seemed "distracted" by the South Sea Company's overtures in 1711–1712. The first problem appears to be one of chronology. The official contract between the two companies for managing the *asiento* did not get approved until the spring of 1713, a year after the expiration of the Ten Percent Act. As Tim Keirn has noted, it was only "by 1713 [that] the African Company was concentrating its energies on gaining the subcontract" for the *asiento*. In addition, there is ample evidence to suggest that the African Company's supporters hoped that the Ten Percent Act would expire almost as much as the separate traders did. One pro-company pamphlet published in 1712, after outlining a litany of problems with the Ten Percent Act, concluded that "The Company humbly hope therefore, that their Long-sufferings and Oppression occasion'd by the aforesaid hard Law, shall now end and expire, and be buried with it." In addition, as soon as the act expired in July 1712, the African Company tried to take advantage of the resulting confusion to claim that "being now restored to their former Rights, [the company] do give notice and warning, that if any interlopers shall enter on the Company's possession of any of their lands, rivers, islands, ports or havens on the African Coasts," they would be prosecuted.[40]

Most important, however, the African Company secured legislation in June 1712 forming a "union" with a number of its major creditors, which helped the company's financial position. Daniel Defoe, admittedly hardly a neutral source in his role as African Company propagandist, went so far as to assert that it was the separate traders who were distracted by their own desire to establish a regulated company that allowed this legislation to pass. The separate traders, Defoe claimed, "took little Notice of this Bill, as being not at all concern'd in what the

Company and their Creditors might do together." Defoe insisted that "Upon this Act, as upon a steady Foundation, the present New Building of the Company stands fixt, and to the Disappointment of the Enemies of our Commerce is like to stand." Meanwhile, the separate traders' bill to create a regulated company "was thrown out." Defoe continued, "The *African* Company, standing still, and as may be said only looking on, saw themselves unexpectedly establish'd by the Defeat of their Enemies on a better Foundation than they were before."[41]

Defoe's account is obviously a biased and overly optimistic interpretation of events that transpired in the summer of 1712. But it is likely that the company's union with its creditors seemed to offer just as much hope as the *asiento* contract would the following year. The 1712 act, according to Defoe, put a stop to the separate traders' attempts to ruin the African Company. It was in part because of this alliance with its creditors, for example, that the company managed to urge the defeat of the bill opening the slave trade in June 1713, and it motivated the company to petition to gain the *asiento* subcontract. In 1714, two years after the agreement with the creditors, one pro-company propagandist noted that this "late Act of Parliament in Favour of their Creditors, . . . has revived [the company]." These actions and legislative successes, however sanguine, do not seem to have come from a company too distracted by the promise of the riches of the *asiento* to notice its declining fortunes. While it is certainly true that neither the union with its creditors nor its contract with the South Sea Company were enough to save the African Company financially or revive its role in the slave trade, this was not necessarily obvious to most interested parties during 1711–1714. The separate traders very well might have wanted a "legislative vacuum" and inaction to ensure the expiration of the Ten Percent Act to guarantee a deregulated slave trade. But the African Company hardly seems to have been caught off guard by the separate traders' strategy or the promise of the *asiento* by the turn of the eighteenth century.[42]

ASIENTO IN PRACTICE

The *asiento* scheme, however, never worked for either company. The contract began on May 1, 1713, but at first Spain ordered officials in its colonies not to recognize the contract until peace was officially declared, which did not happen until 1714. Governor Archibald Hamilton of Jamaica reported that as a result, Spanish merchants were unwilling to do business in his colony. The South Sea Company wanted to delay the official start of the contract until May 1, 1714, arguing that it should not have to pay the import duty on slaves if the peace had yet to be declared. The company, however, was unable to convince the Spanish

Crown to alter the terms of the contract. In addition, the company suffered temporary setbacks with the removal of Oxford from the ministry in the spring of 1714 and death of Queen Anne that August. The directors, however, managed to continue to convince investors that the company's trade would restore the nation's credit, and by the fall of 1714 it had regained some of its lost confidence. But the African Company was hardly in a position to help the South Sea Company fulfill the *asiento* contract. There were numerous bureaucratic and logistical difficulties, and arguments frequently erupted between the two companies over payments for shipments to and from Africa. They frequently had to hire arbitrators to settle financial disagreements, which resulted in a litigious mess.[43]

In addition to these logistical problems, there was sustained opposition to the *asiento* from planters in the British Caribbean colonies. There was a long tradition of resistance by colonial planters and privateers to the African Company's practice of selling slaves to the Spanish, and the *asiento* in British control did not change this pervasive attitude. According to colonial planters, the *asiento* trade diminished the number of slaves in British colonial markets, which resulted in raising prices for those few slaves that were available. Colonists frequently complained to imperial authorities that the company sold the most able Africans to the Spanish, leaving them with the "refuse." The main problem for colonists in Jamaica, however, was the fact that the *asiento* controlled by the South Sea Company significantly cut into their own market. Many Jamaican planters, merchants, and officials had achieved substantial profits from illegally selling slaves to the Spanish. This was the reason, according to some pro– African Company pamphlets, why many in that colony wanted the slave trade to remain open. South Sea Company's agents and directors agreed with this assessment and complained to imperial authorities that the contraband slave trade continued to flourish from Jamaica, despite the monopoly. In May 1715, the South Sea Company's Court of Directors asked Secretary of State James Stanhope to order "commanders of His Majesty's ships [to be] prohibited from carrying over Negroes to the Spanish Coast on any account whatsoever," unless they were South Sea Company ships.[44]

The South Sea Company's potential to cut into colonial merchant profits motivated the Jamaicans to obstruct the *asiento* in a variety of ways. The South Sea Company, like many of those who held the contract before it, used Jamaica as a depot to "refresh" slave cargoes with food, water, and medical care. Jamaica was also regularly used as a marketplace for Spanish merchants to come and purchase slaves to sell in New Spain. In December 1715 the assembly passed "a duty of forty shillings p head on all Negroes that shall be thence exported to the

Spanish Coast." Company directors quickly petitioned for its repeal and warned that if such duties remained in place, it "will be so very burdensome and destructive to the Company" that it would be forced to "proceed directly from Africa to the Spanish Ports with their Negroes altho' sickly to their damage," avoiding Jamaica or any other British colony altogether. According to the colony's agents in London, the assembly lowered the duty to twenty shillings, not wanting to hinder the trade. This duty, they insisted, had "generally [been] laid for twenty years past." If anyone had a right to complain, they continued, it was Jamaican merchants and residents who depended upon trade with the Spanish. The following fall the assembly renewed the duty, and in October 1717 the company petitioned George I to repeal the act. For their part, the men of the Jamaica Assembly contended that not only did the *asiento* take "merchantable" slaves away from British planters, but previous holders of the contract had willingly paid the duty for the privilege of trading on the island.[45]

The King-in-Council asked the Board of Trade to investigate, and in December 1717 the board concluded that although the Jamaican planters had the right to impose export duties in order to raise funds for the colony, "it cannot be reasonable that they should lay a tax upon Negroes landed there by the South Sea Company for refreshment, . . . nor can precedents of the like duty drawn from former times, whilst the *Assiento* was in the hands of foreigners." The King-in-Council repealed the act in January 1718 but indicated that Jamaica could pass an act imposing a duty on slaves exported from the island, just not on those who had been landed for "refreshment." Over the course of the next two years, Jamaica proved to be such a hostile environment for the South Sea Company that it moved its operations to Barbados by the end of the decade.[46]

Despite its inauspicious beginnings, the South Sea Company managed to transport a sizable proportion of slaves across the Atlantic during its early years, delivering between 14 percent and 25 percent of all slaves brought by English ships between the years 1714 and 1718. In addition, its stock price continued to slowly increase in value. But major difficulties remained. The main obstacle to success lay in icy relations between Britain and Spain, which resulted in war being declared again in 1718. This put a temporary stop to the *asiento* trade and left the South Sea Company in desperate financial straits, which at least one historian has argued left open the possibility for the South Sea Bubble in 1720.[47] But in the short term, Oxford's project succeeded in restoring confidence in the nation's credit. The reliance on popular understandings of the economic importance of the transatlantic slave trade as the means to achieve this goal was an indication of the central role slavery and the slave trade played in the British popular imagination as well as in important diplomatic, political, and economic policy decisions. Although Britain would hold the contract until 1739, the utter failure of the South Sea Company and its partner, the Royal African Company, to fulfill the terms of the *asiento* during its early years was a testament to the inability of the two joint-stock companies to operate effectively. It also indicated the determination of colonial planters and merchants and their allies in Britain to obstruct the South Sea Company's activities in British colonies and to keep the slave trade to the British and Spanish colonies free from monopolistic interference.

CONCLUSION

The South Sea Company's main purpose of solving the problem of the nation's staggering war debt by procuring the *asiento* indicated that slavery in the colonies and the transatlantic slave trade were perceived by a significant portion of the British public to be key to the economic well-being of the British empire by the early eighteenth century. Most important, British control of the *asiento* was a major indication of the British state's complete acceptance of slavery and the slave trade as central to the British imperial project. The creation of the South Sea Company in 1711 was connected to popular debates and discussions about slavery, the slave trade, and the status of the Royal African Company, which had been taking place since the 1690s. The separate traders and their colonial merchant-planter allies had successfully argued that an open slave trade to the British colonies was in the national interest. The British slave trade would remain the one large deregulated colonial trade for the remainder of the eighteenth century. But the slave trade to Spanish colonies, according to Tories like Oxford and his associates, needed monopoly control. The formation of the South Sea Company and the *asiento* represented Oxford's vision of empire, which was in some ways a holdover from the old Stuart imperial ideal, especially of relying on Spanish wealth for Britain's economic and imperial prosperity. The perceived importance of the *asiento* to Britain's economic well-being contributed to Britain's dominance of the transatlantic slave trade to all European colonies for the remainder of the eighteenth century.

CONCLUSION

The early modern English empire did not emerge free from conflict or controversy, nor did it occupy an unimportant or marginal place in the politics of late-seventeenth- and early-eighteenth-century England. The acquisition of the colonial empire and the prevalence of African slavery as the dominant labor force in the West Indies colonies were deeply connected to transatlantic ideological debates over the purpose of empire and the proper management of population and labor. Imperial concerns played an increasingly significant role in contributing to the divisive and ideological nature of early modern English political culture. The almost constant confrontation and negotiation that took place among colonial merchants, planters, and officials and their counterparts in London proved this. The deep anxiety on the part of the burgeoning imperial state over the integrity of the empire during such divisive events as the Exclusion Crisis and the Nine Years' War demonstrates that it is impossible to separate domestic from colonial concerns. The artificial separation between center and periphery that has persisted in scholarship on the early modern empire simply did not exist. Similarly, the prevalence of African slavery in the English West Indies colonies did not occur in isolation from events and affairs emanating from the metropolis, and it did not happen simply because of socioeconomic necessity on the part of colonial planters. Nor did English planters utilize and promote slave labor simply because they had been given the autonomy to do so. Although local issues certainly influenced colonial actors, African slavery did not emerge in a colonial vacuum but was deeply implicated in contemporary debates and disagreements on political economy and the purposes of an overseas territorial empire. The expansion of the Atlantic empire and the astronomic growth of slavery in the early modern period were deeply intertwined with metropolitan political concerns.

The power and influence of a cohesive group of London-based colonial merchants during the Commonwealth and Protectorate periods of the 1650s and the political-economic ideology they espoused provided the ideological foundations of the early English empire. Their imperial vision, which considered territorial expansion necessary for England to compete commercially and militarily with its rivals, was based on an overseas plantation empire supplied with indentured servants and African slaves. Also central to this ideal was the idea that England should utilize, through legal or illegal means, the wealth of the Spanish American colonies to promote its own imperial interests. Their imperial vision, with some modifications, continued to be supported by the restored monarchy of Charles II from the 1660s through the reign of James II in the 1680s. The Royal African Company became a key institution in the imperial designs of both Charles II and James II. Its royally granted charter, and therefore its very existence, was dependent on the royal prerogative and all of its political and economic associations. By limiting who could participate in the African trade through a state-controlled monopoly, it was thought that the benefits of the trade would come to England at the expense of other nations. The political influence exercised by the company over imperial administration demonstrated the important role institutions played in the evolution of the early modern empire. In addition, the African Company's position at the center of Restoration imperial affairs during the 1670s and 1680s represented the imperial state's commitment to promoting African slavery in the West Indies colonies.

After the Glorious Revolution of 1688–1689, the Royal African Company no longer held its guaranteed monopoly. The ensuing public debate over how the slave trade should be managed revealed a vision of empire shared by anti-monopolist colonial planters as well as the state: that African slavery in the West Indies was central to the functioning of the empire and that the empire was integral to England's overall economy and polity. By embracing an open slave trade, the English state not only promoted slavery in the colonies, it accepted the oppressive racial slave regimes in the colonies. Over the course of decades of confrontations with colonial interests over the Royal African Company's monopoly, the metropolitan government learned that the best way to placate West Indies planters and make them less likely to cause problems was to keep the slave trade open. It was hoped that West Indies planters would remain more compliant and complacent to imperial directives. In exchange, the English state also implicitly agreed to support and prop up the legal system of white mastery that planters in the colonies had constructed, in order to continue to reap slavery's economic rewards. In this sense, there absolutely was metropolitan complicity in the development and promotion of slavery in the English colonies.[1]

The English government, in promoting slavery, also seemed to take domestic demographic concerns into consideration, especially as war with France continued for the better part of two decades, beginning in the 1690s. War affected the Caribbean colonies in surprising ways, as many colonial governors and militia officers were forced to arm slaves in order to help defend the islands from French attacks. By relying on African slaves, English colonists demanded fewer and fewer servants from England. Slavery and the empire were each used to justify the existence of the other. By the turn of the eighteenth century, planters and others with colonial interests were willing to lose a certain level of autonomy in exchange for opening the slave trade. They were even willing to endanger themselves and the safety of their colonies for the sake of profit, and the imperial state wanted to share in those revenues. The inclusion of the *asiento* as part of the Treaty of Utrecht in 1713 was a further indication of the embracing of slavery and the slave trade by the imperial state. It demonstrated that dominating the transatlantic slave trade was understood by Robert Harley and his allies to be in the national interest.

In order to understand how and why it became acceptable to expand and maintain such a brutal and horrific system of labor in the English colonies requires not only a consideration of colonial labor demand and cultural and racial prejudices, but an analysis of how slavery became important to the English state. The emergence of African slavery as a key component of English imperialism occurred as a result of all of these factors, and it greatly influenced the ways in which the empire was understood by contemporaries. The interconnections between the growth of slavery and the evolution of English imperialism in the late seventeenth and early eighteenth centuries laid the foundations for British domination of the transatlantic slave trade in the eighteenth century, a defining feature of the modern British empire.

NOTES

INTRODUCTION

1. Roger Coke, *A Discourse of Trade* (London, 1670), 7; William Petyt, *Britannia languens, or a Discourse of Trade* (London, 1680), 154.

2. George Louis Beer, *The Old Colonial System, 1660–1754, Part I: The Establishment of the System, 1660–1688*, 2 vols. (New York: Macmillan, 1912), 1:vii; Charles M. Andrews, *The Colonial Period of American History* (New Haven, CT: Yale University Press, 1934–1938), vol. 4, *England's Commercial and Colonial Policy*, 2–3.

3. Stanley L. Engerman, "British Imperialism in a Mercantilist Age, 1492–1849: Conceptual Issues and Empirical Problems," *Revista de Historia Económica* 15 (1998): 195–234; Nuala Zahedieh, "Making Mercantilism Work: London Merchants and Atlantic Trade in the Seventeenth Century," *Transactions of the Royal Historical Society*, 6th ser., 9 (1999): 143–158; Kenneth Morgan, "Mercantilism and the British Empire, 1688–1815," in *The Political Economy of British Historical Experience, 1688–1914*, ed. Donald Winch and Patrick K. O'Brien (Oxford: British Academy, 2002), 165–191; Nuala Zahedieh, *The Capital and the Colonies: London and the Atlantic Economy, 1660–1700* (Cambridge: Cambridge University Press, 2010), 35–54. For recent discussions of the usefulness of mercantilism as an interpretive method of understanding the early modern British empire, see Steve Pincus, "Rethinking Mercantilism: Political Economy, the British Empire, and the Atlantic World in the Seventeenth and Eighteenth Centuries," *William and Mary Quarterly*, 3rd ser., 69, no. 1 (Jan. 2012): 3–34; Philip Stern and Carl Wennerlind, "Introduction," in *Mercantilism Reimagined: Political Economy in Early Modern Britain and Its Empire*, ed. Philip Stern and Carl Wennerlind (New York: Oxford University Press, 2014), 3–22.

4. Michael Kammen, *Empire and Interest: The American Colonies and the Politics of Mercantilism* (Philadelphia: J. B. Lippincott, 1970), 4; Andrews, *Colonial Period*, vol. 4, *England's Commercial and Colonial Policy*, 328; Edgar Furniss, *The Position of the Laborer in a System of Nationalism: A Study in the Labor Theories of the Later English Mercantilists* (Boston and New York: Houghton Mifflin, 1920), 7–8; D. C. Coleman, "Labour in the English Economy of the Seventeenth Century," *Economic History*

Review, n.s., 8, no. 3 (1956): 295; Richard Wiles, "Mercantilism and the Idea of Progress," *Eighteenth-Century Studies*, no. 1 (Autumn 1974): 56–74; Andrea Finkelstein, *Harmony and the Balance: An Intellectual History of Seventeenth-Century English Economic Thought* (Ann Arbor: University of Michigan Press, 2000), 251; Joyce Appleby, *Economic Thought and Ideology in Seventeenth-Century England* (Princeton, NJ: Princeton University Press, 1978).

5. David Armitage, *The Ideological Origins of the British Empire* (New York: Cambridge University Press, 2000), intro.; Stephen Saunders Webb, *The Governors General: The English Army and the Definition of Empire, 1569–1681* (Chapel Hill: University of North Carolina Press, 1979), xvi–xviii; Stephen Saunders Webb, "Army and Empire: English Garrison Government in Britain and America, 1569–1763," *William and Mary Quarterly*, 3rd ser., 34, no. 1 (1977): 2–3.

6. This stands in contrast to the work of Armitage, *Ideological Origins*, chaps. 5 and 6.

7. Richard S. Dunn, *Sugar and Slaves: The Rise of the Planter Class in the English West Indies, 1624–1713* (Chapel Hill: University of North Carolina Press, 1972), xxiii, 335. For a similar emphasis on colonial labor demand in the transition to slavery, see Edmund Morgan, "The First American Boom: Virginia 1618 to 1630," *William and Mary Quarterly*, 3rd ser., 28, no. 2 (Apr. 1971): 169–198; Edmund Morgan, *American Slavery, American Freedom: The Ordeal of Colonial Virginia* (New York: W. W. Norton, 1975); Russell Menard, *Sweet Negotiations: Sugar, Slavery, and Plantation Agriculture in Early Barbados* (Charlottesville: University of Virginia Press, 2006), 31, 44.

8. Eric Williams, *Capitalism and Slavery* 1944, repr. (Chapel Hill: University of North Carolina Press, 1994), 19; Winthrop Jordan, *White over Black: American Attitudes Toward the Negro, 1550–1812* (Baltimore, MD: Penguin Books, 1969), chaps. 1 and 2; David Brion Davis, *The Problem of Slavery in Western Culture* (New York: Oxford University Press, 1966), chaps. 3, 4, and 5.

9. David Eltis, *The Rise of African Slavery in the Americas* (Cambridge: Cambridge University Press, 2000), 58, 65, 55; Susan Dwyer Amussen, *Caribbean Exchanges: Slavery and the Transformation of English Society, 1640–1700* (Chapel Hill: University of North Carolina Press, 2007), 144.

10. Stephanie Smallwood, *Saltwater Slavery: A Middle Passage from Africa to American Diaspora* (Cambridge, MA: Harvard University Press, 2007); Trevor Burnard, *Mastery, Tyranny, and Desire: Thomas Thistlewood and His Slaves in the Anglo-Jamaican World* (Chapel Hill: University of North Carolina Press, 2004), 269–270.

11. Jack P. Greene, "Liberty, Slavery, and the Transformation of British Identity in the Eighteenth-Century West Indies," *Slavery and Abolition* 21, no. 1 (Apr. 2000): 1–31; Jack P. Greene, "The Jamaica Privilege Controversy, 1764–1766: An Episode in the Process of Constitutional Definition in the Early Modern British Empire," *Journal of Imperial and Commonwealth History* 22, no. 1 (1994): 16–53.

12. Christopher L. Brown, "The Politics of Slavery," in *The British Atlantic World*, ed. David Armitage and Michael Braddick (London: Palgrave Macmillan, 2002), 214–232.

13. This model of understanding England's early modern empire has been promoted especially by Atlantic World scholarship. See Alison Games, *The Web of Empire: English Cosmopolitans in an Age of Expansion, 1560–1660* (New York: Oxford

University Press, 2008), 7, 10–11; J. H. Elliott, *Empires of the Atlantic World: Britain and Spain in America, 1492–1830* (New Haven, CT: Yale University Press, 2006), xiv–xvii; April Hatfield, *Atlantic Virginia: Intercolonial Relations in the Seventeenth Century* (Philadelphia: University of Pennsylvania Press, 2004); Christian Koot, *Empire at the Periphery: British Colonists, Anglo-Dutch Trade, and the Development of the British Atlantic, 1621–1713* (New York: New York University Press, 2011); Kristen Block, *Ordinary Lives in the Early Caribbean: Religion, Colonial Competition, and the Politics of Profit* (Athens: University of Georgia Press, 2012).

14. As K. G. Davies writes, "it is safe to say that in no instance was the identification between the royal family and a trading monopoly so close as in the African Companies." K. G. Davies, *The Royal African Company* (London: Longmans, Green, 1957), 103.

1. UNFREE LABOR AND THE ORIGINS OF EMPIRE

1. Meeting of the King-in-Council, 1 June 1677, The National Archives (TNA), Colonial Office (CO) 153/2, pp. 219–222.

2. Lords of Trade to the king, 25 April 1678, TNA, CO 153/2, p. 281; Council of Saint Christopher to the Lords of Trade, 12 July 1680, CO 153/2, p. 449; Lords of Trade to William Stapleton, 5 March 1681/2, CO 153/3, p. 36; Stapleton to the Lords of Trade, 18 July 1682, CO 153/3, pp. 52–54; Col. Thomas Hill to the Lords of Trade, 13 February 1683/4, CO 153/3, pp. 134–136.

3. George Louis Beer, *The Origins of the British Colonial System, 1578–1660* (New York: Macmillan, 1908), chap. 2; Paul Slack, *Poverty and Policy in Tudor and Stuart England* (London: Longman, 1988), especially chap. 2; Joyce Appleby, *Economic Thought and Ideology in Seventeenth-Century England* (Princeton, NJ: Princeton University Press, 1978), 29.

4. Richard Hakluyt, *Discourse of Western Planting*, ed. David B. Quinn and Alison M. Quinn (London: Hakluyt Society, 1993), 120.

5. Robert Gray, *A Good Speed to Virginia* (London: Felix Kyngston, 1609), B3v; William Symonds, *Virginia: A Sermon Preached at White-Chapel* (London: I. Windet, 1609), 19; Ralph Hamor, *A True Discourse of the Present Estate of Virginia, and the successe of the affaires there till the 18 of June, 1614* (London: John Beale, 1615), 19; W. Crashaw, *A Sermon Preached in London before the right honorable the Lord Lawarre, Lord Gouernour and Captaine Generall of Virginea* (London: William Welby, 1610), E4v–F1r; *Nova Britannia: Offering Most Excellent fruites by Planting in Virginia* (London: Samuel Macham, 1609), D1r., D1v; R. Rich, *The lost Flocke Triumphant* (London: Edw. Allde, 1610), B3r.

6. J. M. Beattie, *Crime and the Courts in England, 1660–1800* (Princeton, NJ: Princeton University Press, 1986), chap. 9; J. M. Beattie, *Policing and Punishment in London, 1660–1750* (Oxford: Oxford University Press, 2001), chaps. 6 and 9; A. Roger Ekirch, *Bound for America: The Transportation of British Convicts to the Colonies, 1718–1775* (Oxford: Clarendon Press, 1987), 3, 19, 44; Joanna Innes, "The Role of Transportation in Seventeenth and Eighteenth-Century English Penal Practice," in *New Perspectives in Australian History*, ed. Carl Bridge (London: Menzies Centre for Australian Studies,

1990), 1–24; Cynthia Herrup, "Punishing Pardon: Some Thoughts on the Origins of Penal Transportation," in *Penal Practice and Culture, 1500–1900: Punishing the English*, ed. Simon Devereax and Paul Griffiths (New York: Palgrave, 2004), 121–137; Richard B. Morris, *Government and Labor in Early America* (New York: Harper & Row, 1965); Abbot Emerson Smith, *Colonists in Bondage: White Servitude and Convict Labor in America, 1607–1776* (Chapel Hill: University of North Carolina Press, 1947).

7. Richard Hakluyt, *Divers voyages touching the discouerie of America and the Ilands adiacent*, in *Works Issued by the Hakluyt Society*, ed. John Winter Jones, vol. 7 (London: Hakluyt Society, 1850), 8–9; Sir Thomas Dale to Lord Treasurer Salisbury, 17 August 1611, *Calendar of State Papers Colonial: North America and the West Indies, 1574–1739 (CSPC)*, ed. Karen Ordahl Kuperman, John C. Appleby, and Mandy Banton (London: Routledge, 2000), CD-ROM, 1:11–12. Quote from James I from Smith, *Colonists in Bondage*, 93.

8. Mildred Campbell, "'Of People either too Few or too Many': The Conflict of Opinion on Population and Its Relation to Emigration," in *Conflict in Stuart England*, ed. William Appleton Aiken and Basil Duke Henning (London: Jonathan Cape, 1960), 179. For the traditional view she is criticizing, see Beer, *Origins*, chap. 2.

9. Ted McCormick, "Population: Modes of Seventeenth-Century Demographic Thought," in *Mercantilism Reimagined: Political Economy in Early Modern Britain and Its Empire*, ed. Philip Stern and Carl Wennerlind (New York: Oxford University Press, 2014), 25–45.

10. Edmund Morgan, "The Labor Problem at Jamestown, 1607–1618," *American Historical Review* 73, no. 3 (June 1971): 595, 607–608; Alison Games, *The Web of Empire: English Cosmopolitans in an Age of Expansion, 1560–1660* (New York: Oxford University Press, 2008), 127–131; Robert Brenner, *Merchants and Revolution: Commercial Change, Political Conflict, and London's Overseas Traders, 1550–1653* (London: Verso, 2003), 145.

11. Wesley Frank Craven, *Dissolution of the Virginia Company: The Failure of a Colonial Experiment* (New York: Oxford University Press, 1932), 94–96; Robin Blackburn, *The Making of New World Slavery: From the Baroque to the Modern, 1492–1800* (London: Verso, 1997), 227, 233; Robert C. Johnson, "The Transportation of Vagrant Children from London to Virginia, 1618–1622," in *Early Stuart Studies*, ed. Howard S. Reinmuth, Jr. (Minneapolis: University of Minnesota Press, 1970), 137–151; Sir Edwin Sandys to Sir Robert Norton, 28 January 1619/20, in *Records of the Virginia Company of London*, ed. Susan Myra Kingsbury (Washington, DC: U.S. Government Printing Office, 1906–1935), 3:259.

12. Edmund Morgan, "The First American Boom: Virginia 1618 to 1630," *William and Mary Quarterly*, 3rd ser., 28, no. 2 (Apr. 1971): 170–171, 183, 195–198; Hilary McD. Beckles, *White Servitude and Black Slavery in Barbados, 1627–1715* (Knoxville: University of Tennessee Press, 1989), 5; Craven, *Dissolution of the Virginia Company*, 96; David Souden, "'Rogues, Whores and Vagabonds'? Indentured Servant Emigrants to North America, and the Case of Mid-Seventeenth-Century Bristol," *Social History* 3, no. 1 (Jan. 1978): 151.

13. Craven, *Dissolution of the Virginia Company*, chap. 10; Brenner, *Merchants and Revolution*, 93–102; David Souden, "English Indentured Servants and the Transatlantic

Colonial Economy," in *International Labour Migration: Historical Perspectives*, ed. Shula Marks and Peter Richardson (Hounslow, Middlesex, UK: Institute of Commonwealth Studies, 1984), 23, 29; Souden, "Rogues, Whores," 160, 166–167. Souden and others have shown how the emigration of indentured servants to the American colonies fit into broader patterns of migration within England. Souden, "Rogues, Whores," 151, 156; Souden, "English Indentured Servants," 27–28; Alison Games, "Migration," in *The British Atlantic World, 1500–1800*, ed. David Armitage and Michael J. Braddick (New York: Palgrave Macmillan, 2002), 31–50. For more on "vagrant" as a socioeconomic and legal category, see Paul Slack, "Vagrants and Vagrancy in England, 1598–1664," in *Migration and Society in Early Modern England*, ed. Peter Clark and David Souden (London: Hutchinson Education, 1987), 49–76.

14. E. A. Wrigley and R. S. Schofield, *The Population History of England, 1541–1870* (London: Edward Arnold, 1981), 208–209 (table 7.8); Roger Finlay, *Population and Metropolis: The Demography of London, 1580–1650* (Cambridge: Cambridge University Press, 1981), 51; Keith Wrightson, *Earthly Necessities: Economic Lives in Early Modern Britain* (New Haven, CT: Yale University Press, 2000), chaps. 5 and 6; Patrick Copland, *Virginia's God be Thanked, or A Sermon of Thanksgiving for the Happie Successe of the Affayres in Virginia this Last Yeare* (London: J. D., 1622), 31. The growth of London played a central role in shaping migration patterns within England, Britain, and across the Atlantic. See Games, "Migration," 35; John Wareing, "Migration to London and transatlantic emigration of indentured servants, 1683–1775," *Journal of Historical Geography*, 7, no. 4 (1981): 356–378.

15. Hilary McD. Beckles, "The 'Hub of Empire': The Caribbean and Britain in the Seventeenth Century," in *Oxford History of the British Empire*, vol. 1, *The Origins of Empire*, ed. Nicholas Canny (Oxford: Oxford University Press, 1998), 223; Beckles, *White Servitude*, 15–16, 34 (table 1.6), 35–37; Richard S. Dunn, *Sugar and Slaves: The Rise of the Planter Class in the English West Indies, 1624–1713* (Chapel Hill: University of North Carolina Press, 1972), 49, 56 (table 1); Vincent T. Harlow, *A History of Barbados, 1625–1685* (Oxford: Clarendon Press, 1926), 9–13; Blackburn, *Making of New World Slavery*, 225, 231.

16. Richard Ligon, *A True and Exact History of the Island of Barbadoes* (London, 1673), (originally published in 1657); James Hay, second Earl of Carlisle, *A Declaration by James Earl of Carlile, Lord of the Caribee Islands, or Province of Cariola* (London, 1647); Beckles, *White Servitude*, 17 (table 1.1); Gary A. Puckrein, *Little England: Plantation Society and Anglo-Barbadian Politics, 1627–1700* (New York: New York University Press, 1984), 72.

17. Michael Craton, "Reluctant Creoles: The Planters' World in the British West Indies," in *Strangers within the Realm*, ed. Bernard Bailyn and Philip D. Morgan (Chapel Hill: University of North Carolina Press, 1991), 315; Dunn, *Sugar and Slaves*, chap. 6; David Eltis, *The Rise of African Slavery in the Americas* (Cambridge: Cambridge University Press, 2000), 52.

18. Brenner, *Merchants and Revolution*, 115–166, 173–181; Blackburn, *Making of New World Slavery*, 231; Russell Menard, *Sweet Negotiations: Sugar, Slavery, and Plantation Agriculture in Early Barbados* (Charlottesville: University of Virginia Press, 2006), 25

(table 4), 52, 54, 59; J. E. Farnell, "The Navigation Act of 1651, the First Dutch War, and the London Merchant Community," *Economic History Review*, n.s., 16, no. 3 (1964): 443–444; Puckrein, *Little England*, 72.

19. Dunn, *Sugar and Slaves*, 19–20; Harlow, *History of Barbados*, 24; Blackburn, *Making of New World Slavery*, 230–231; Brenner, *Merchants and Revolution*, 586; Menard, *Sweet Negotiations*, 25 (table 4). On Dutch success in the Caribbean carrying trade and slave trade, see Jonathan Israel, *Dutch Primacy in World Trade, 1585–1740* (Oxford: Clarendon Press, 1989), 239–244; Johannes Menne Postma, *The Dutch in the Atlantic Slave Trade, 1600–1815* (Cambridge: Cambridge University Press, 1990), 17–21 (especially table 1.1). Traditionally, scholars have maintained that it was because of an influx of Dutch capital during the 1640s that English planters made the transition to sugar cultivation and began relying more heavily on the labor of enslaved Africans. Menard has questioned the role of the Dutch in financing the transition to sugar and slavery in Barbados and instead emphasizes English planter and merchant success with tobacco, indigo, and cotton, which helped finance the "sugar boom." Menard, *Sweet Negotiations*, chaps. 1–3.

20. James Horn and Philip D. Morgan, "Settlers and Slaves: European and African Migrations to Early Modern British America," in *The Creation of the British Atlantic World*, ed. Elizabeth Mancke and Carole Shammas (Baltimore, MD: Johns Hopkins University Press, 2005), 23; Games, "Migration," 32–33; Souden, "English Indentured Servants," 22; Menard, *Sweet Negotiations*, 44; Beckles, *White Servitude*, 123. Seventy thousand is an approximate total for all Europeans, but the vast majority would have come from England during this decade. Russell Menard has estimated that nearly thirty thousand European migrants, the bulk of whom were English, came to Barbados in the decade around 1650. Menard, *Sweet Negotiations*, 42, 114–115.

21. Richard S. Dunn, "Servants and Slaves: The Recruitment and Employment of Labor," in *Colonial British America: Essays in the New History of the Early Modern Era*, ed. Jack P. Greene and J. R. Pole (Baltimore, MD: Johns Hopkins University Press, 1984), 159–160; David Galenson, *White Servitude in Colonial America: An Economic Analysis* (Cambridge: Cambridge University Press, 1981), 124 (table 8.6), 125 (table 8.7).

22. Menard, *Sweet Negotiations*, 45; Betty Wood, *The Origins of American Slavery: Freedom and Bondage in the English Colonies* (New York: Hill and Wang, 1997), 55; Wrigley and Schofield, *Population History of England*, 207–215, 208–209 (table 7.8; total calculation mine); Wrightson, *Earthly Necessities*, 164–166, 235–236; Eltis, *Rise of African Slavery*, 44–47; Beckles, "'Hub of Empire,'" 232.

23. Eltis, *Rise of African Slavery*, 50–52; Richard Sheridan, *Sugar and Slavery: An Economic History of the British West Indies, 1623–1775* (Baltimore, MD: Johns Hopkins University Press, 1974), 236; Beckles, *White Servitude*, 46, 49; Menard, *Sweet Negotiations*, 44–45.

24. Smith, *Colonists in Bondage*, 156; Beckles, *White Servitude*, 53–54; Stephen Saunders Webb, *The Governors-General: The English Army and the Definition of Empire, 1569–1681* (Chapel Hill: University of North Carolina Press, 1979), 73; *Calendar of State Papers Domestic*, ed. Mary Anne Everett Green (London: Longmans, 1882), 1 March 1654/5, 7:62; 30 March 1655, 7:107; 30 March 1655, 7:107–108; "For the Council of

Scotland," 1655, in *A Collection of the State Papers of John Thurloe, Esq.*, 7 vols. (London, 1742): 3:497; "A Proposition for the Erecting of a West India Company, and the better securing the Interests of this Commonwealth in America," probably 1657, British Library (BL) Egerton 2395, fols. 87–88; Carla Gardina Pestana, *The English Atlantic in an Age of Revolution, 1640–1661* (Cambridge, MA: Harvard University Press, 2004), 185–190.

25. Beattie, *Policing and Punishment*, 291–292; *A Great Plot Discovered* (London: Printed for G. Horton, 1661); Webb, *Governors-General*, 84–86; Smith, *Colonists in Bondage*, 175; Beckles, *White Servitude*, 54; Peter Earle, *Monmouth's Rebels: The Road to Sedgemoor 1685* (New York: St. Martin's, 1978). Some transported political prisoners protested their situation. See *England's Slavery, or Barbados Merchandize* (London, 1659), 10.

26. Webb, *Governors-General*, 85; Herrup, "Punishing Pardon," 122–123, 132–133; Eltis, *Rise of African Slavery*, 50 (table 2.2). This table calculates numbers collected by Peter Wilson Coldham and estimates that approximately 8,282 prisoners, including both convicts and prisoners of war, were sent to the English colonies from 1650 to 1699. Eltis, however, thinks this probably did not account for all war prisoners sent. Peter Wilson Coldham, *The Complete Book of Emigrants in Bondage, 1614–1775* (Baltimore, MD: Genealogical Publishing, 1988). For contemporary evidence of the increased use of the royal pardon for transportation, see *His Majesties Most Gracious Pardon, to the Poor Prisoners in Newgate, on Friday the 26th of February. 1685/6* (London: E. Mallet, 1686).

27. Natalie Zacek, *Settler Society in the English Leeward Islands, 1670–1776* (New York: Cambridge University Press, 2010), 18, 48–49.

28. Stapleton to the Lords of Trade, 17 March 1674/5, TNA, CO 153/2, pp. 8–9; Petition from the Leeward Islands Assembly to Charles II, 26 March 1674, CO 1/31, no. 29; Stapleton to the Lords of Trade, 22 November 1676, CO 153/2, pp. 137–190 (esp. 181); Jeaffreson to Col. George Gamiell, 12 May 1677, and Jeaffreson to William Poyntz, 11 May 1677, in *A Young Squire of the Seventeenth Century*, ed. John Cordy Jeaffreson (London: Hurst & Blackett, 1858), 1:211–215, 207–209; William Freeman to Col. Philip Warner, 28 September 1678, in *The Letters of William Freeman, London Merchant, 1678–1685*, ed. David Hancock (London: London Record Society, 2002), 38.

29. Journal of the Lords of Trade, 14 June 1681 and 17 September 1681, TNA, CO 391/3, pp. 267, 283; Journal of the Lords of Trade, 30 September 1682, CO 391/4, pp. 62–63; Petition of Jeaffreson to the Lords of Trade [18 November 1682], CO 1/49, no. 107; Journal of the Lords of Trade, 18 November 1682, CO 391/4, p. 81; Jeaffreson to Edward Thorn, 25 November 1682, *A Young Squire*, 2:6.

30. Jeaffreson to Capt. Willet, 2 December 1682, *A Young Squire*, 2:13–14; Jeaffreson to Hill, 15 March 1682/3, *A Young Squire*, 2:44–48; Journal of the Lords of Trade, 17 April 1683, TNA, CO 391/4, pp. 139–140; Jeaffreson to Stapleton, 13 September 1683, *A Young Squire*, 2:73. William Freeman was of the opinion that prisoners were hardly worth the hassle and costs, "there being seldome above 4 or 5 [available] att a time." Freeman to Sir William Stapleton, 20 August 1678, *Letters of William Freeman*, 19.

31. Petition of Jeaffreson to the Lords of Trade, with List of Prisoners annexed, 4 June 1684, TNA, CO 1/54, nos. 119 and 119I; Journal of the Lords of Trade, 4 June 1684, CO

391/4, p. 304; Order of the King-in-Council, 13 June 1684, CO 153/3, pp. 162–163. Jeaffreson has been pressured by the Secretary of the Lords of Trade, William Blathwayt, to cease insisting on only transporting male prisoners. Jeaffreson to Hill, 12 February 1683/4, *A Young Squire*, 2:102.

32. Jeaffreson to Phipps, 30 June 1684, *A Young Squire*, 2:116; Jeaffreson to Hill, 25 August 1684, *A Young Squire*, 2:118–119; Letter to the Sheriffs of London from the King, 4 August 1684, TNA, CO 153/3, pp. 163–165; Jeaffreson to Hill, 8 September 1684, *A Young Squire*, 2:123–127; Richard S. Kay, "Jenner, Sir Thomas (1638–1707)," in *Oxford Dictionary of National Biography* (*ODNB*) (Oxford: Oxford University Press, 2004), http://www.oxforddnb.com/view/article/14753?docPos=3 (accessed 9 May 2014).

33. Jeaffreson to Hill, 28 March 1685, 22 April 1685, 9 December 1685; 2 March 1685/6; [spring 1686]; 4 June 1686, *A Young Squire*, 2:185; 2:194–201; 2:241–245; 2:271–276; 2:279–283; 2:292–299.

34. Beattie, *Policing and Punishment*, 290–297, 471; Beattie, *Crime and the Courts*, 479.

35. Beckles, *White Servitude*, 50–52; Smith, *Colonists in Bondage*, 67–69. John Wareing has found "only 238 spiriting cases from all London sources during the period 1642–1718." Wareing, "'Violently taken away or cheatingly duckoyed': The Illicit Recruitment in London of Indentured Servants for the American Colonies, 1645–1718," *London Journal* 26, no. 2 (2001): 9.

36. Journal of the Lords of Trade, 18 November 1682, TNA, CO 391/4, pp. 79–81; Jeaffreson to Phipps, 15 November 1682, *A Young Squire*, 1:318–319.

37. Petition of Edward Thompson to William III, 1 April 1689, TNA, CO 1/67, no. 68I; Petition of Edward Thompson to the Lords of Trade, April 1689, CO 1/67, no. 73; Attorney General's opinion read to King-in-Council, 21 November 1689, CO 323/1, no. 4; Christopher Guise to the Lords of the Treasury, 20 October 1690, CO 323/1, no. 5. For a history of servants' registries, see John Wareing, "Preventative and Punitive Regulation in Seventeenth-Century Social Policy: Conflicts of Interest and the Failure to Make 'Stealing and Transporting Children, and Other Persons,' a Felony, 1645–73," *Social History* 27, no. 3 (Oct. 2002): 288–308.

38. Smith, *Colonists in Bondage*, 70, 83–84; David Harris Sacks, *The Widening Gate: Bristol and the Atlantic Economy, 1450–1700* (Berkeley: University of California Press, 1991), 255, 301–302. Sacks has shown that this coincided with increased persecution of Quakers and other nonconformists in Bristol.

39. Dalby Thomas, *An Historical Account of the Rise and Growth of the West-India Collonies* (London: Jo. Hindmarsh, 1690), 41; Beattie, *Policing and Punishment*, 429–431; Souden, "English Indentured Servants," 31; Ekirch, *Bound for America*, 1; Coldham, *Complete Book of Emigrants*, ix. On some of the consequences of the Transportation Act of 1718/19, see Gwenda Morgan and Peter Rushton, *Eighteenth-Century Criminal Transportation: The Formation of the Criminal Atlantic* (New York: Palgrave Macmillan, 2004).

40. Proposals from Captain Jeaffreson, [December?] 1684, TNA, CO 1/55, no. 141; Jeaffreson to Stapleton, 6 December 1684, *A Young Squire*, 2:158; Jeaffreson to Hill, 17 January 1684/5, *A Young Squire*, 2:164; *A List of the Names of all the Adventurers of the Royal African Company of England* (London, 1681); K. G. Davies, *The Royal African Company* (London: Longmans, Green, 1957), 65–66.

41. Slack, *Poverty and Policy*, 30–31; Appleby, *Economic Thought and Ideology*, chap. 6; D. C. Coleman, "Labour in the English Economy of the Seventeenth Century," *Economic History Review*, n.s., 8, no. 3 (1956): 293–294; McCormick, "Population."

42. Beattie, *Crime and the Courts*, 480; Wrigley and Schofield, *Population History of England*, 207–215, esp. 208–209 (table 7.8); Roger Coke, *A Discourse of Trade* (London, 1670), 43.

43. [John Houghton], *England's Great Happiness: Or, a Dialogue between Content and Complaint* (London: J. M. for Edward Croft, 1677), 9; Anita McConnell, "Houghton, John (1645–1705)," in ODNB, http://www.oxforddnb.com/view/article/13868 (accessed 14 Oct. 2011); Samuel Fortrey, *England's Interest and Improvement, Consisting in the increase of the store, and trade of this kingdom* (Cambridge: John Field, 1663), 39; Perry Gauci, "Fortrey, Samuel (1622–1682?)," in ODNB, http://www.oxforddnb.com/view/article/9952 (accessed 23 Jan. 2012); William Petyt, *Britannia languens, or a Discourse of Trade* (London, 1680), 154; Carew Reynell, *The True English Interest* (London: Giles Widdowes, 1674), A7r–A7v.

44. Andrea Finkelstein, *Harmony and the Balance: An Intellectual History of Seventeenth-Century English Economic Thought* (Ann Arbor: University of Michigan Press, 2000), esp. pt. 3; Appleby, *Economic Thought and Ideology*; Richard Drayton, *Nature's Government: Science, Imperial Britain, and the "Improvement" of the World* (New Haven, CT: Yale University Press, 2000), chaps. 2 and 3; Paul Slack, "Material Progress and the Challenge of Affluence in Seventeenth-Century England," *Economic History Review* 62, no. 3 (Aug. 2009): 579–580; Carl Wennerlind, *Casualties of Credit: The English Financial Revolution, 1620–1720* (Cambridge, MA: Harvard University Press, 2012), chap. 2; Ted McCormick, *William Petty and the Ambitions of Political Arithmetic* (Oxford: Oxford University Press, 2009); Tom Leng, "Epistemology: Expertise and Knowledge in the World of Commerce," in Stern and Wennerlind, *Mercantilism Reimagined*, 97–116.

45. For political interpretations of this turn away from a zero-sum economic mentality during the mid-1600s, see Steve Pincus, "Neither Machiavellian Moment nor Possessive Individualism: Commercial Society and the Defenders of the English Commonwealth," *American Historical Review* 103, no. 3 (June 1998): 705–736; Steve Pincus, "From Holy Cause to Economic Interest: The Study of Population and the Invention of the State," in *A Nation Transformed: England after the Restoration*, ed. Alan Houston and Steven C. A. Pincus (Cambridge: Cambridge University Press, 2001), 272–298.

46. Henry Gemery, "Emigration from the British Isles to the New World, 1630–1700: Inferences from Colonial Populations," *Research in Economic History* 5 (1980): 180, 204–205, 216 (table A.6).

2. COMMONWEALTH AND PROTECTORATE IMPERIALISM

1. Blair Worden, "Oliver Cromwell and the Sin of Achan," in *History, Society, and the Churches*, ed. Derek Beales and Geoffrey Best (Cambridge: Cambridge University Press, 1985), 135–136; Richard S. Dunn, *Sugar and Slaves: The Rise of the Planter Class in the English West Indies, 1624–1713* (Chapel Hill: University of North Carolina

Press, 1972), 55; S. A. G. Taylor, *The Western Design* (London: Solstice Productions, 1969), chaps. 2–3; I. S., *A Brief and Perfect Journal of The late Proceedings and Successe of the English Army in the West-Indies* (London, 1655), 11–22; Lt. Col. Francis Barrington, Jamaica, to Sir John Barrington, 14 July 1655, British Library (BL) Egerton 2648, fols. 245–249; C. H. Firth, ed., *The Narrative of General Venables* (London: Longmans, Green, 1900), 14–39; "Narrative of the Expedition to San Domingo," in *The Clarke Papers. Selections from the Papers of William Clarke*, ed. C. H. Firth (London: Longmans, Green, 1899), 3:54–60.

2. Robert Brenner, *Merchants and Revolution: Commercial Change, Political Conflict, and London's Overseas Traders, 1550–1653* (London: Verso, 2003), chap. 10, especially 551–557. By dismissing the Western Design as unimportant, Brenner argues that this group of merchants lost political influence after the creation of the Protectorate in 1653. Brenner, "The Civil War Politics of London's Merchant Community," *Past and Present*, no. 58 (Feb. 1973): 107.

3. Brenner, *Merchants and Revolution*, 587, 597–598, 625–628; Tom Leng, *Benjamin Worsley (1618–1677): Trade, Interest and the Spirit in Revolutionary England* (London: Boydell Press, 2008), 70.

4. James Scott Wheeler, *Cromwell in Ireland* (New York: St. Martin's Press, 1999), 83–88, 94–100, 197–200, 228–230; Nicholas Canny, *Making Ireland British, 1580–1650* (Oxford: Oxford University Press, 2001), 557–559; Alison Games, *The Web of Empire: English Cosmopolitans in an Age of Expansion, 1560-1660* (New York: Oxford University Press, 2008), 263–264, 271–287; Nicholas Canny, *Kingdom and Colony: Ireland and the Atlantic World, 1560–1800* (Baltimore, MD: Johns Hopkins University Press, 1988), 108; T. C. Barnard, "Conclusion: Settling and Unsettling Ireland: The Cromwellian and Williamite Revolutions," in *Ireland from Independence to Occupation, 1641–1660*, ed. Jane H. Ohlmeyer (Cambridge: Cambridge University Press, 1995), 269. English attempts at subduing Ireland were not new by the mid-1600s; on earlier attempts, see Canny, *Making Ireland British*, chap. 9; Jane H. Ohlmeyer, "'Civilizinge of those Rude Partes': Colonization within Britain and Ireland, 1580s–1640s," in *Oxford History of the British Empire*, vol. 1, *Origins of Empire*, ed. Nicholas Canny (Oxford: Oxford University Press, 1998), 124–147. For contemporary accounts of the fall of Ireland, see Oliver Cromwell's pamphlets, including *Letters from Ireland, Relating the several great Successes* . . . (London: John Field for Edward Husband, 1649); *A Letter from the Lord Lieutenant of Ireland* . . . *Together with a Relation of the Taking in of Wexford* (London: John Field for Edward Husband, 1649); *A Letter from the Lord Lieutenant of Ireland* . . . (London: Edward Husband and John Field, 1649).

5. Allan Macinnes, *The British Revolution, 1629–1660* (New York: Palgrave Macmillan, 2005), 190–199. For an overview of the failed plans for union, see Allan Macinnes, *Union and Empire: The Making of a United Kingdom in 1707* (Cambridge: Cambridge University Press, 2007), chap. 3.

6. Gary Puckrein, *Little England: Plantation Society and Anglo-Barbadian Politics* (New York: New York University Press, 1984), 109–111; Robert M. Bliss, *Revolution and Empire: English Politics and the American Colonies in the Seventeenth Century* (Manchester, UK: Manchester University Press, 1990), 61–64, 86; Carla Pestana, *The*

English Atlantic in an Age of Revolution, 1640–1661 (Cambridge, MA: Harvard University Press, 2004), 87, 92–96, 100–101; Brenner, *Merchants and Revolution*, 593; *An Act Prohibiting Trade with the Barbada's, Virginia, Bermuda's, and Antego* (London: Edward Husband and John Field, 1650); *A Declaration Set forth by the Lord Lieutenant Generall the Gentlemen of the Councell & assembly occasioned from the view of a printed paper* (The Hague: Samuel Broun, 1651) (dated by Thomason as October 29, 1651), n. p. For a contemporary portrayal of Bell's neutrality, see A. B., *A Brief Relation of the Beginning and Ending of the Troubles of the Barbados* (London: Peter Cole, 1653), 1. For some parliamentarian propaganda, see Nicholas Foster, *A Briefe Relation of the late Horrid Rebellion Acted in the Island Barbadas . . .* (London: I. G., 1650). Foster was one of the planters exiled in London.

7. Bernard Capp, *Cromwell's Navy: The Fleet and the English Revolution, 1648–1660* (Oxford: Clarendon Press, 1989), 67–68; J. D. Davies, "Ayscue, Sir George (c.1615–1672)," in *Oxford Dictionary of National Biography (ODNB)* (Oxford: Oxford University Press, 2004), http://www.oxforddnb.com/view/article/956 (accessed 26 Feb. 2013); Puckrein, *Little England*, 120–123; Pestana, *English Atlantic*, 104–105, 108, 116; *Articles of Agreements, made, and concluded the 11th day of January, 1651* (London: Francis Coles, 1652), 4; Bliss, *Revolution and Empire*, 89. For the classic account of how English Civil War politics played out in Barbados, see N. Darnell Davis, *The Cavaliers and Roundheads of Barbados, 1650–1652* (Georgetown, British Guiana: Argosy Press, 1887). For a nuanced critique, see Puckrein, *Little England*, chap. 7. For a contemporary account of the events in Barbados during 1651–1652, see A. B., *Brief Relation*.

8. For the classic mercantilist interpretation of the early English empire, see C. M. Andrews, *The Colonial Period of American History* (New Haven, CT: Yale University Press, 1934–1938), vol. 4, *England's Commercial and Colonial Policy*, especially chap. 10. For the interplay of these various interests, see Bliss, *Revolution and Empire*, 58–60; Farnell, "The Navigation Act of 1651, the First Dutch War, and the London Merchant Community," *Economic History Review*, n.s., 16, no. 3 (1964): 452. Brenner's conclusions about the strong influence of these merchants over the passage of the Navigation Act of 1651 have been criticized, especially by Steven Pincus, *Protestantism and Patriotism: Ideologies and the Making of English Foreign Policy, 1650–1668* (Cambridge: Cambridge University Press, 1996), 12–13, 40.

9. Philopatris [Benjamin Worsley], *The Advocate* (London: William Du-Gard, 1651), 6, 12; Leng, *Benjamin Worsley*, 55–60, 75–79; Brenner, *Merchants and Revolution*, 625; Pincus, *Protestantism and Patriotism*, chaps. 2, 3, and 4; Richard Grassby, *The Business Community of Seventeenth-Century England* (Cambridge: Cambridge University Press, 1995), 211; Farnell, "The Navigation Act," 445; Bliss, *Revolution and Empire*, 59; Pestana, *English Atlantic*, 157. On the embracing of trade and commerce as primary interests of the state during the 1650s, see Steve Pincus, "From Holy Cause to Economic Interest: The Study of Population and the Invention of the State," in *A Nation Transformed: England after the Restoration*, ed. Alan Houston and Steven C. A. Pincus (Cambridge: Cambridge University Press, 2001): 272–298.

10. Macinnes, *The British Revolution*, 210; Michael J. Braddick, *State Formation in Early Modern England, c. 1550–1700* (Cambridge: Cambridge University Press, 2000),

213–221. According to notes written by Edward Montagu at a meeting of the Protector's Council in April 1654, Cromwell claimed that "Providence seemed to lead us" to declare war on Spain. *Clarke Papers*, 3:207, appendix B. Contemporary publications justifying the war utilized traditional rhetoric of a religious crusade against a Catholic enemy. See, for example, *A Dialogue, Containing a Compendious Discourse concerning the Present Designe in the West Indies* (London: R. Lownds, 1655). For more on Cromwell's providentialism as a motivating factor in the Western Design, see David Armitage, "The Cromwellian Protectorate and the Languages of Empire," *Historical Journal* 35, no. 3 (Sept. 1992): 536–538; Karen Ordahl Kuperman, "Errand to the Indies: Puritan Colonization from Providence Island through the Western Design," *William and Mary Quarterly*, 3rd ser., 45, no. 1 (Jan. 1988): 70–99. For Protectorate foreign policy toward Spain, see Pincus, *Protestantism and Patriotism*, 191; Steven Pincus, "England and the World in the 1650s," in *Revolution and Restoration: England in the 1650s*, ed. John Morrill (London: Collins & Brown, 1992), 129–147; Timothy Venning, *Cromwellian Foreign Policy* (New York: St. Martin's Press, 1995), chaps. 3–5.

11. "Edward Montagu's Notes on the Debates in the Protector's Council Concerning the Last Indian Expedition," in *Clarke Papers*, 3:203–205; Venning, *Cromwellian Foreign Policy*, 47–49, 72, 161–168; Kuperman, "Errand to the Indies," 90.

12. Venning, *Cromwellian Foreign Policy*, 74; Brenner, *Merchants and Revolution*, 157–159, 244; Sir Benjamin Rudyerd, *A Speech Concerning a West Indie Association* (n.p.: 1641), 4; Steven Pincus, "Neither Machiavellian Moment nor Possessive Individualism: Commercial Society and the Defenders of the Commonwealth," *American Historical Review* 103, no. 3 (June 1998): 705–736; Samuel Lambe, *Seasonable Observations humbly offered to his Highness the Lord Protector* (London, 1658?), A2r.

13. Newsletter from Gilbert Mabbott, Westminster, to William Clarke, 17 June 1654, in *The Clarke Papers: Further Selections from the Papers of William Clarke*, ed. Frances Henderson, Camden 5th ser., vol. 27 (Cambridge: Cambridge University Press, 2005), 190; Proceedings of the Council of State, 5 June 1654, *Calendar of State Papers Domestic Series, 1654 (CSPD)* (London: Longman, 1880), 200–201; John Paige to William Clerke, 27 May 1654, *Letters of John Paige, London Merchant, 1648–1658*, ed. George F. Steckley (London: London Record Society, 1984) 107; "Edward Montagu's Notes," in *Clarke Papers*, 3:207; Venning, *Cromwellian Foreign Policy*, 58–61.

14. Venning, *Cromwellian Foreign Policy*, 72–77. A number of "reformadoes," officers and soldiers discharged from the army resident in London awaiting their arrears, would in fact join the expedition. See Newsletter from John Rushworth, Lincoln's Inn, to William Clarke, 26 August 1654, and Newsletter from George Mabbott, Westminster, to William Clarke, 29 August 1654, in *Clarke Papers: Further Selections*, 204–205. For contemporary justifications for the war, see *A Declaration of His Highness, by the advice of His Council; setting forth, on the Behalf of this Commonwealth, the Justice of their Cause against Spain* (London: Henry Hills & John Field, 1655); Commission to General Venables, 4 December 1654, in *A Collection of the State Papers of John Thurloe, Esq.*, 7 vols. (*Thurloe*) (London, 1742), 3:16–17. On the ways English merchants tried to capitalize, legally and illegally, on Spanish American trade in the seventeenth century, see Stanley J. and Barbara H. Stein, *Silver, Trade and War: Spain*

and America in the Making of Early Modern Europe (Baltimore, MD: Johns Hopkins University Press, 2000), chap. 3.

15. "Mr. Andrew Riccard, &c. to the protector," 14 August 1654, in *Thurloe* 2:543; Cromwell's "Instructions unto General Penn, Collonell Venables . . . for managing the South Expedicion," 18 August 1654, in Firth, *Narrative of General Venables*, appendix A, 107–109. For more on Riccard, see Brian Weiser, *Charles II and the Politics of Access* (Woodbridge, Suffolk, UK: Boydell Press, 2003), 125–126. For the connections some of these merchants had to religious Independents, see Brenner, *Merchants and Revolution*, 517–528.

16. Stephen Saunders Webb, *The Governors-General: The English Army and the Definition of the Empire, 1569–1681* (Chapel Hill: University of North Carolina Press, 1979), 151–155. Webb does argue that Cromwell's understanding of the design involving territorial conquest from Spain through military superiority was absolutely imperial. Pincus has questioned the imperial nature of the design altogether. Pincus, "England and the World in the 1650s," 141. Newsletter from Gilbert Mabbott, Westminster, to William Clarke, 29 August 1654, in *Clarke Papers: Further Selections*, 205.

17. "Mr. Andrew Riccard, &c. to the protector," 14 August 1654, in *Thurloe*, 2:543; Modyford to John Bradshaw, 16 February 1652, *Calendar of State Papers Colonial: North America and the West Indies, 1574–1739* (CSPC), ed. Karen Ordahl Kuperman, John C. Appleby, and Mandy Banton (London: Routledge, 2000), CD-ROM, 1:373–374. For Modyford, see Dunn, *Sugar and Slaves*, 68–69, 81; Puckrein, *Little England*, 129; Webb, *Governors-General*, 225–234; Frank Cundall, *The Governors of Jamaica in the Seventeenth Century* (London: West India Committee, 1936), 21–30; Richard Ligon, *A True and Exact History of the Island of Barbadoes* (London, 1673), 22–23.

18. Cromwell's "Instructions unto General Penn, Collonell Venables . . . for managing the South Expedicion," 18 August 1654, in Firth, *Narrative of General Venables*, appendix A, 107–109; Webb, *Governors-General*, 39–42; Firth, *Narrative of General Venables*, preface, viii–ix; Capp, *Cromwell's Navy*, 67, 117, 293–294.

19. *To his Highness the Lord Protector: The Humble Petition of the Sea-men, belonging to the Ships of the Commonwealth of England* (London, 1654); Proceedings of the Council of State, 8 November 1654, *CSPD*, 1654,393; C. M. Andrews, *British Committees, Commissions, and Councils of Trade and Plantations, 1622–1675*, Johns Hopkins University Studies in Historical and Political Science, vol. 26, no. 1 (Baltimore, MD: Johns Hopkins Press, 1908), 50; Richard Sheridan, *Sugar and Slavery: An Economic History of the British West Indies, 1623–1775* (Baltimore, MD: Johns Hopkins University Press, 1973), 93. For provisions, see "A list of the ships provisions, presented to his highness" [August 1654], in *Thurloe*, 2:571–574.

20. "A paper of Col. Muddiford concerning the West Indies," December 1654, in *Thurloe*, 3:63–64. Cromwell also turned to Thomas Gage, a former Dominican friar who had lived in Central America, who provided traditional anti-Catholic arguments to go to war against the Spanish. See "Some briefe and true observations concerning the West Indies," 1654, in *Thurloe*, 3:59–61; Venning, *Cromwellian Foreign Policy*, 77–79; Kristen Block, *Ordinary Lives in the Early Caribbean: Religion, Colonial Competition, and the Politics of Profit* (Athens: University of Georgia Press, 2012), 113–118.

21. "Commission to the Commissioners for the West Indian Expedition," in Firth, *Narrative of General Venables*, 109–110; Commission to General Venables, 4 December 1654, in *Thurloe*, 3:16–17; Venning, *Cromwellian Foreign Policy*, 80; Capp, *Cromwell's Navy*, 162. Penn's instructions gave him far less authority over the operation as a whole. See "Instructions given unto General William Penn, Commander-in-chief of a Fleet of Ships into the parts of America," *The Writings and Speeches of Oliver Cromwell*, ed. Wilbur Cortez Abbott (Cambridge, MA: Harvard University Press, 1945), 3:530–532.

22. "Instructions unto General Venables," in Firth, *Narrative of General Venables*, 111–113; Venning, *Cromwellian Foreign Policy*, 81; Taylor, *Western Design*, 21.

23. "Extract of a Journal on the Conquest of Jamaica," BL Egerton 2395, fols. 60–61; Pestana, *English Atlantic*, 181; "Commission of the Commanders of the West Indian Expedition," 1 March 1655, *CSPC*, 12:628; Hilary McD. Beckles, *White Servitude and Black Slavery in Barbados, 1627–1715* (Knoxville: University of Tennessee Press, 1989), 26–29; Jonathan I. Israel, *Dutch Primacy in World Trade, 1585–1740* (Oxford, UK: Clarendon Press, 1989), 237, 239; Brenner, "Civil War Politics," 102–104. Menard argues that it was because of these claims made by Barbados planters in the 1650s that historians have overstated the importance of Dutch capital to Barbados's transition to sugar and slavery. Russell Menard, *Sweet Negotiations: Sugar, Slavery, and Plantation Agriculture in Early Barbados* (Charlottesville: University of Virginia Press, 2006), chaps. 1–3.

24. Edward Winslow, Barbados, to Thurloe, 16 March 1654/5, in *Thurloe*, 3:249–52; Puckrein, *Little England*, 132; "A collection of depositions of the captains of the Dutch ships found at Barbados," 8–25 February 1655, *CSPC*, 12:627–628; Firth, *Narrative of General Venables*, 10; I. S., *Brief and Perfect Journal*, 10; Lt. Col. Francis Barrington, Jamaica, to Sir John Barrington, 14 July 1655, BL Egerton 2648, fol. 46. This policy did not have the unqualified support of every commissioner. See, for example, Gregory Butler, Barbados, to Cromwell, 7 February 1654/5, in *Thurloe*, 3:142.

25. Puckrein, *Little England*, chap. 8; J. Berkenhead, Barbados, to Thurloe, 17 February 1655, in *Thurloe*, 3: 157–159.

26. Larry Gragg, *Englishmen Transplanted: The English Colonization of Barbados, 1627–1660* (New York: Oxford University Press, 2003), 55; Modyford to his brother (James?), 6 July 1655, in *Thurloe*, 3:620–622. Commissioner Edward Winslow indicated that this was what Venables had intended to do all along, and it was thanks to Modyford's efforts that they were able to proceed. Winslow to Thurloe, 16 March 1654/5, in *Thurloe*, 3:249–252.

27. Lt. Col. Barrington, Jamaica, to Sir John Barrington, 14 July 1655, BL Egerton 2648, fol. 245v; Modyford to his brother (James?), 6 July 1655, in *Thurloe*, 3:620–22; Searle to the Council of State, 19 September 1653, *CSPC*, 1:408–9; Winslow to Thurloe, 16 March 1654/5, in *Thurloe*, 3:249–52; Dunn, *Sugar and Slaves*, 79.

28. J. Berkenhead, Barbados, to Thurloe, 17 February 1654/5, in *Thurloe*, 3:159; Searle to Cromwell, 1 June 1655, in *Thurloe*, 3:499–500.

29. J. Daniels to Thurloe, 3 June 1655, in *Thurloe*, 3:504–508; Venables and Butler to Thurloe, 4 June 1655, in *Thurloe*, 3:509–511; Sedgwick to ?, 6 September 1655, The National Archives (TNA), Colonial Office (CO) 1/32, no. 25; Modyford to ?, 20 June 1655, in *Thurloe*, 3:565.

30. Webb, *Governors-General*, 155–156; Roger Hainsworth, *The Swordsmen in Power: War and Politics under the English Republic, 1649–1660* (Thrupp, Stroud, Gloucestershire, UK: Sutton Publishers, 1997), 198; Venables and Butler to Thurloe, 4 June 1655, in *Thurloe*, 3:509–511; Sedgwick to Cromwell, 5 November 1655, in *Thurloe*, 4:151–155; Sedgwick to Thurloe, 12 March 1655/6, in *Thurloe*, 4:604–606; "A Letter to Mr. Noel, 13 June 1655," in Firth, *Narrative of General Venables*, 49–50; Col. Richard Fortescue to the Protector, 21 July 1655, in *Thurloe*, 3:675–676; I. S., *Brief and Perfect Journal*, 15.

31. Modyford to ?, 20 June 1655, in *Thurloe*, 3:565; Webb, *Governors-General*, 164–167; Sedgwick to Cromwell, 5 November 1655, in *Thurloe*, 4:151–155. According to Webb, the success of Holdip's plantation led some of the other officers to oust him in a coup for fear that it would "tie them to pestilential Jamaica." This seems an overstatement, considering the efforts of the other officers to make Jamaica a permanent settlement colony.

32. In June, it was falsely reported that Venables had successfully taken Hispaniola "without the least opposition of the Spanyard or other inhabitants." Newsletter, 23 June 1655, in *Clarke Papers*, 3:44. A pamphlet published in April 1655 reported glorious victories by Venables and Penn and against the French, not the Spanish, on an unnamed island that the English took and became "Masters of no less then three and thirty gold and silver mines." *A Great and Wonderful Victory Obtained by English Forces, under the command of Gen. Pen and Gen. Venables* (London, 1655), 6. *Mercurius Politicus* reported the loss of Hispaniola and taking of Jamaica in the August 2–9 issue (no. 269), in Joad Raymond, ed. *Making the News: An Anthology of the Newsbooks of Revolutionary England, 1641–1660* (New York: St. Martin's Press, 1993), 287–288. The failure to take Hispaniola seems to have been common knowledge in the merchant community by that time. The London merchant John Paige indicated in August that by taking Jamaica instead of Hispaniola, "I fear our hopeful design will not be crowned with that victory as most men expected." Paige to William Clerke, 17 August 1655, *The Letters of John Paige, London Merchant, 1648–1658*, ed. George F. Steckley (London: London Record Society, 1984), 130–131. On the impact of the failure of the Western Design on Cromwell, see Worden, "Oliver Cromwell and the Sin of Achan"; Armitage, "Cromwellian Protectorate," 540–541.

33. "General Penn's account to the councill of his voyage to the West Indies," 15 September 1655, in *Thurloe*, 4:28–30; Firth, *Narrative of General Venables*, 73–75; Hainsworth, *Swordsmen in Power*, 199; *A Declaration of His Highnes by the Advice of His Council; Setting forth, On the Behalf of this Commonwealth, the Justice of their Cause against Spain* (London: Henry Hills and John Field, 1655), 115; Modyford to ?, 20 June 1655, in *Thurloe*, 3:565.

34. I. S., *Brief and Perfect Journal*, 11–12, 5; William Penn, Edward Winslow, and Gregory Butler to Governor Daniel Searle, 28 April 1655, in Firth, *Narrative of General Venables*, 30–31; Godfrey to ?, 30 April 1656, TNA, CO 1/32, no. 59; Newsletter from Jeremiah Smith to William Clarke, 20 September 1656, in *Clarke Papers: Further Selections*, 257–258.

35. "Proclamation of the Protector Relating to Jamaica," 1655, in *Thurloe*, 3:753; *By the Protector. A Proclamation Giving Encouragement to such as shall transplant themselves to Jamaica* (London: Henry Hills & John Fields, 1655); Searle to Cromwell, 8 January

1655/6, in *Thurloe*, 4:400; Goodson to the Governor of Bermuda, 24 September 1655, in *Thurloe*, 4:51–52; "Proclamation by Oliver Cromwell, Lord Protector, 25 March 1656," in Frank Cundall, *Governors of Jamaica*, plate between pp. xxxii and xxxiii; Goodson and Sedgwick to Cromwell, 12 March 1655/6, in *Thurloe*, 4:600–602.

36. Games, *Web of Empire*, 265–271; "Proposals of certain ships for the West Indies and other necessaries, for fleet and army humbly represented by Wm. Goodson," 1655, TNA, CO 1/32, no. 39; Broghill to Thurloe, 18 September 1655, in *Thurloe*, 4:41–42; Report concerning the Affaires of America made to Cromwell, 1656, BL Egerton 2395, fol. 123; *A True Description of Jamaica* (London: J. M., 1657), 4.

37. Vice Admiral Goodson to ?, 19 October 1656, TNA, CO 1/33, no. 12; Gookin to Thurloe, 24 January 1655/6, in *Thurloe*, 4:449; Julian de Castilla, *The English Conquest of Jamaica*, trans. and ed. Irene A. Wright, *Camden Miscellany*, vol. 13 (London: Camden Society, 1923), 29; Pestana, *English Atlantic*, 179–181; Venning, *Cromwellian Foreign Policy*, 87–88; "Report Concerning the Affaires of America made to Cromwell," 1656, BL Egerton 2395, fol. 123; Andrews, *British Committees*, 48; Grassby, *Business Community*, 206; D'Oyley to Thurloe, 6 October 1656, in *Thurloe*, 5:476.

38. Barry Coward, *The Cromwellian Protectorate* (Manchester, UK: Manchester University Press, 2002), 75; Cundall, *Governors of Jamaica*, 3–4; D'Oyley, *A Narrative of the Great Success God hath been pleased to give His Highness forces in Jamaica* (London: Henry Hills, 1658); Journal of Edward D'Oyley, 13 October 1656, BL, Additional Manuscripts (Add MS) 12423, fols. 26–27; Barrington to Sir John Barrington, 1 July 1657, BL Egerton 2648, fol. 302. For D'Oyley's pleas, see D'Oyley to Thurloe, 12 March 1655/6, in *Thurloe*, 4:602–603; D'Oyley to Thurloe, 20 June 1656, in *Thurloe*, 5:139; D'Oyley to Thurloe, 6 October 1656, in *Thurloe*, 5:476; D'Oyley to Cromwell, 12 September 1657, in *Thurloe*, 6:512; D'Oyley to the Council of State, 27 February 1657/8, in *Thurloe*, 6:833–834.

39. *A Dialogue, Containing a Compendious Discourse*, 2; *Hypocrisie Discovered* (London, 1655), 14.

40. *England's Remembrancers* (London, 1656), 8; *The Unparalleld Monarch* (London: T. C., 1656), 77–78; *An Appeale from the Court to the Country* ([London?], 1656), 4; Coward, *Cromwellian Protectorate*, 75–76; Armitage, "Cromwellian Protectorate," 532–535, 550.

41. Cromwell's Speech to Parliament, 17 September 1656, in *Writings and Speeches of Oliver Cromwell*, 4:261–264; G. M. D. Howat, *Stuart and Cromwellian Foreign Policy* (London: Adam & Charles Black, 1974), 88–90; Kuperman, "Errand to the Indies," 95–99; Games, *Web of Empire*, 230.

42. "A Proposition for the Erecting of a West India Company, and the better securing the Interests of this Commonwealth in America," probably 1657, BL Egerton MS 2395, fols. 87–88, 89, 90, 91–92, 103–104, 111; Brenner, *Merchants and Revolution* 158–159.

43. "Proposition for Erecting a West India Company," BL Egerton MS 2395, fols. 87–88.

44. John Bland, *Trade Revived, Or a Way Proposed to Restore, Increase, Inrich, Strengthen and Preserve the Decayed and even Dying Trade of this our English Nation* (London: Thomas Holmswood, 1659), 10, 3, 11; Lambe, *Seasonable Observations*, 5–6. For more on the origins of Lambe's pamphlet, see Brian Weiser, *Charles II and the Politics of Access* (Woodbridge, Suffolk, UK: Boydell Press, 2003), 122–123.

45. Andrews, *British Committees*, 53–55; Povey to Richard Povey, 29 October 1659, BL Add MS 11411, fols. 25–26; Povey to D'Oyley, late 1659 or early 1660, BL Add MS 11411, fols. 21–23.

3. RESTORATION IMPERIALISM

1. Colonel Edward D'Oyley to the Commissioners of the Admiralty, 24 January 1659/60, The National Archives (TNA), Colonial Office (CO) 1/33, no. 64; D'Oyley to the Commissioners of the Admiralty, 1 February 1, 1659/60, CO 1/33, no. 67; D'Oyley to the Council of Admiralty and Navy, 26 July 1660, CO 1/14, no. 26; Journal of the Proceedings of the Governor and Council of Barbados, 28–29 May 1660, CO 31/1, pp. 1–4; A. P. Thornton, *West-India Policy under the Restoration* (Oxford: Clarendon Press, 1956), 67–69; F. J. Routledge, *England and the Treaty of the Pyrenees* (Liverpool, UK: University of Liverpool Press, 1953), 7; Robert M. Bliss, *Revolution and Empire: English Politics and the American Colonies in the Seventeenth Century* (Manchester, UK: Manchester University Press, 1990), 138–139.

2. Report of the Committee of the Council on Foreign Plantations, 27 March 1660, British Library (BL) Egerton 2395, fols. 241–242.

3. Jack Sosin, *English America and the Restoration Monarchy of Charles II: Transatlantic Politics, Commerce, and Kinship* (Lincoln: University of Nebraska Press, 1980), 39, 48–49; Nuala Zahedieh, *The Capital and the Colonies: London and the Atlantic Economy, 1660–1700* (Cambridge: Cambridge University Press, 2010), 35–54; Nuala Zahedieh, "Making Mercantilism Work: London Merchants and Atlantic Trade in the Seventeenth Century," *Transactions of the Royal Historical Society*, ser. 6, 9 (1999): 143–158; Julian Hoppitt, *A Land of Liberty? England 1689–1727* (Oxford: Oxford University Press, 2000), 245–247; Bliss, *Revolution and Empire*, 104, 127, 138–145.

4. Brian Weiser, *Charles II and the Politics of Access* (Woodbridge, Suffolk, UK: Boydell Press, 2003), 121–122; George Frederick Zook, *The Company of Royal Adventurers Trading into Africa* (Lancaster, PA: New Era Printing, 1919), 16; Bliss, *Revolution and Empire*, 117; Steve Pincus, *1688: The First Modern Revolution* (New Haven, CT: Yale University Press, 2009), 377–378; Zahedieh, *Capital and Colonies*, 45; Thornton, *West-India Policy*, 17. On Charles II's nuanced view of the prerogative, see Gary S. De Krey, *Restoration and Revolution in Britain: A Political History of the Era of Charles II and the Glorious Revolution* (New York: Palgrave Macmillan, 2007), 24. On his brother the Duke of York's steadfast commitment to the prerogative, see John Callow, *The Making of King James II: The Formative Years of a Fallen King* (Thrupp, Stroud, Gloucestershire, UK: Sutton Publishing, 2000), 301; John Miller, *James II: A Study in Kingship* (Hove, East Sussex, UK: Wayland Publishers, 1977), 67–68; 124–125.

5. Thornton, *West-India Policy*, 144–145; Proclamation of Charles II on the Navigation Acts, 25 August 1663, TNA, CO 1/17, no. 72.

6. Thornton, *West-India Policy*, 5–6, 43; Richard Grassby, *The Business Community of Seventeenth-Century England* (Cambridge: Cambridge University Press, 1995), 206, 209; Weiser, *Charles II*, 129–130; Charles M. Andrews, *British Committees, Commissions, and Councils of Trade and Plantations, 1622–1675*, Johns Hopkins University Studies in

Historical and Political Science, vol. 26, no. 1 (Baltimore, MD: Johns Hopkins University Press, 1908), 67–68. Other members of both councils included Secretaries of State Sir Edward Nicholas and Sir William Morrice; Sir Anthony Ashley Cooper, who had served on the Protectorate Council of State and would soon be named chancellor of the exchequer; Sir William Coventry, who was the Duke of York's private secretary; and the governor of Barbados, Francis, Lord Willoughby. On Clarendon's importance to the Restoration settlement and to the structure of Restoration imperial designs more broadly, see Bliss, *Revolution and Empire*, chaps. 5 and 6.

7. Sosin, *English America*, 28; Bliss, *Revolution and Empire*, 114. In contrast, Andrews argued strongly that the merchant influence on the conduct and structure of these committees was quite strong. Andrews, *British Committees*, 67–68. On the presence of merchants and other "experts" on this Council of Trade, see Weiser, *Charles II*, 129–130; Thornton, *West-India Policy*, 6–7.

8. Zook, *Company of Royal Adventurers*, iii; Callow, *Making of King James II*, 240–241; *Select Charters of Trading Companies*, A.D. 1530–1707, ed. Cecil T. Carr, Publications of the Selden Society, vol. 28 (London: Bernard Quaritch, 1913), 174, 176–177. Other founding members included the Dukes of Buckingham and Albemarle and the Earls of Sandwich and Bath; John, Lord Berkeley, whose brother Sir William was governor of Virginia; William, Lord Craven, who was close to Prince Rupert and his mother, Queen Elizabeth of Bohemia, aunt to Charles II; and Sir George Carteret, a Royalist from Jersey who would become a founder of Carolina and East and West Jersey in the 1660s. For a full list, see *Select Charters*, 173–174.

9. Thornton, *West-India Policy*, 40–41; Povey's report to the Council on Foreign Plantations on the state of Jamaica, 9 April 1660, BL, Egerton 2395, fol. 244; "Considerations relating to the English Affaires in America," n.d., BL Egerton 2395, fols. 614–618.

10. "Capt. Linch his paper concerning Jamaica," about November 1660, TNA, CO 1/14, no. 54; "Considerations about the peopling & settling the Island Jamaica," probably 1660/1, BL Egerton 2395, fols. 283–288; Frank Cundall, *The Governors of Jamaica in the 17th Century* (London: West India Committee, 1936), 31.

11. "Proposals concerning Jamaica by James Earl of Marlborough," November 1660, TNA, CO 1/14, no. 56.

12. According to the diarist and future member of the Council of Trade John Evelyn, on September 27, 1660, "the King received the merchants' addresses in his closet, giving them assurances of his persisting to keep Jamaica." John Evelyn, *The Diary of John Evelyn*, ed. Austin Dobson (London: Macmillan, 1906; repr., London: Routledge/Thoemmes Press, 1996), 2:152. Stephen Saunders Webb highlights the continuity of personnel from the Protectorate, but equates it with a continuation of Cromwellian imperialism. Stephen Saunders Webb, *The Governors-General: The English Army and the Definition of the Empire, 1569–1681* (Chapel Hill: University of North Carolina Press, 1979), 199–200. In contrast, see Andrews, *British Committees*, 60.

13. "Copie of ye Royal Companies Patent," 10 January 1662/3, TNA, CO 1/17, no. 2; *Select Charters*, 177–181; Addendum to the Royal Company's patent, 20 January 1662/3, CO 1/17, no. 3. Bliss downplays investor interest in the slave trade in 1663. Bliss, *Revolution*

and Empire, 127. On the failure of the first company, see Callow, *Making of King James II*, 239–242; Zook, *Company of Royal Adventurers*, 10–12.

14. *Select Charters*, 180; Zook, *Company of Royal Adventurers*, iii; Steven Pincus, *Protestantism and Patriotism: Ideologies and the Making of English Foreign Policy, 1650–1668* (Cambridge: Cambridge University Press, 1996), 245–250; *The Several Declarations of the Company of Royal Adventurers of England Trading into Africa* ([London?], 1667), 1; Company of Royal Adventurers to the King, 26 February 1662/3, TNA, CO 1/17, no. 4. On Dutch dominance of the slave trade and the carrying trade in the Caribbean, see Jonathan Israel, *Dutch Primacy in World Trade, 1585–1740* (Oxford: Clarendon Press, 1989), 239–244; Johannes Menne Postma, *The Dutch in the Atlantic Slave Trade, 1600–1815* (Cambridge: Cambridge University Press, 1990), 17–21.

15. See, for example, Instructions to Sir Jonathan Atkins, 19 December 1673, TNA, CO 1/30, no. 93.

16. K. G. Davies, *The Royal African Company* (London: Longmans, Green, 1957), 43, 317, 326–329; Nuala Zahedieh, "The Merchants of Port Royal, Jamaica, and the Spanish Contraband Trade, 1655–1692," *William and Mary Quarterly*, 3rd ser., 43, no. 4 (Oct. 1986): 589; Zook, *Company of Royal Adventurers*, 93; Thornton, *West-India Policy*, 79–80; Colin Palmer, *Human Cargoes: The British Slave Trade to Spanish America, 1700–1739* (Urbana: University of Illinois Press, 1981), 4–5. On the centrality of Spanish trade to the African Company, see Nuala Zahedieh, "'The Wickedest City in the World': Port Royal, Commercial Hub of the Seventeenth-Century Caribbean," in *Working Slavery, Pricing Freedom: Perspectives from the Caribbean, Africa and the African Diaspora*, ed. Verene A. Shepherd (New York: Palgrave, 2002), 8–9; Company of Royal Adventurers to the King, 26 February 1662/3, TNA, CO 1/17, no. 4.

17. Company of Royal Adventurers to the King, 26 February 26, 1662/3, TNA, CO 1/17, no. 4; Charles II to Francis Willoughby, 26 February 1662/3, CO 1/17, no. 7 (nos. 5 and 6 are earlier drafts); Charles II to the Governor of Jamaica, 13 March 1662/3, CO 1/17, no. 13. On Dutch supremacy in the Spanish American slave trade, see Wim Klooster, *Illicit Riches: Dutch Trade in the Caribbean, 1648–1795* (Leiden: KITLV Press, 1998), 106–107.

18. Russell Menard, *Sweet Negotiations: Sugar, Slavery, and Plantation Agriculture in Barbados* (Charlottesville: University of Virginia Press, 2006), 25, table 4; Richard S. Dunn, *Sugar and Slaves: The Rise of the Planter Class in the English West Indies, 1624–1713* (Chapel Hill: University of North Carolina Press, 1972), 312, table 26.

19. Gary A. Puckrein, *Little England: Plantation Society and Anglo-Barbadian Politics, 1627–1700* (New York: New York University Press, 1984), 137–139; Bliss, *Revolution and Empire*, 142–143; Thornton, *West-India Policy*, 31–39.

20. Willoughby's Instructions, 10 June 1663, TNA, CO 1/17, no. 49 (instruction no. 12); Petition of the Royal Adventurers to the King, November 1663, CO 1/17, no. 93; Charles II to Francis Willoughby, 20 November 1663, CO 1/17, no. 94; Blank license issued by Charles II, 22 December 1663, CO 1/17, nos. 106 and 107.

21. Willoughby to Charles II, 4 November 1663, TNA, CO 1/17, no. 89; Willoughby to Charles II, 20 September 1664, CO 1/18, no. 104; Thornton, *West-India Policy*, 127–128; J. R. Jones, *The Anglo-Dutch Wars of the Seventeenth Century* (London: Longman,

1996), 36–37; Dunn, *Sugar and Slaves*, 124; Report of the Farmers of the Customs to the Council of Trade, 28 February 1664/5, CO 1/19, no. 31; Bliss, *Revolution and Empire*, 121.

22. Willoughby to Sir Henry Bennet (Lord Arlington), 20 May 1665, TNA, CO 1/19, no. 60; Willoughby to Sir Henry Bennet (Arlington), 20 May 1665, CO 1/19, no. 60; Willoughby to Charles II, 20 May 1665, CO 1/19, no. 58; Petition of the Barbados Assembly to Willoughby, 8 June 1665, CO 1/19, no. 78I; Willoughby to the King, 5 July 1665, CO 1/19, no. 77; Willoughby to the King, 8 August 1665, CO 1/19, no. 92; Vincent T. Harlow, *A History of Barbados, 1625–1685* (Oxford: Clarendon Press, 1926), 156–160. For accounts of the Dutch attempt on Barbados, see "A True relation of the fight at Barbadoes between the English and the Dutch, under De Ruyter, on April 20, 1665," CO 1/19, no. 50; Henry Willoughby to Arlington, 22 April 1665, CO 1/19, no. 51.

23. Harlow, *History of Barbados*, 155–156, 161–167; Thornton, *West-India Policy*, 28; Willoughby to Arlington, 15 July 1666, TNA, CO 1/20, no. 119; Willoughby to Charles II, 12 May 1666, CO 1/20, no. 92; Dunn, *Sugar and Slaves*, 124; Puckrein, *Little England*, 140. For an account of the hurricane, see Henry Willoughby to Joseph Williamson, 28 August 1666, CO 1/20, no. 140. For accounts of the French attack on Saint Christopher and English surrender, see "Relation of the loss of St. Christopher's," April 1666, CO 1/20, no. 51; "Articles betwixt the English and French on St. Christopher's," 11 April 1666, CO 1/20, no. 52; Willoughby to Charles II, 21 April 1666, CO 1/20, no. 58; "The humble desires of the Lord Willoughby to be presented to his most Excellent Majesty," April 1666, CO 1/20, no. 60. For some of the arguments between the governor and assembly in 1666, see Willoughby's Speech to the Assembly, 4 April 1666, CO 1/20, no. 40; Assembly's Response, 4 April 1666, CO 1/20, no. 41; Willoughby's Account, 20 April 1666, CO 1/20, no. 57.

24. Harlow, *History of Barbados*, 175; William Willoughby to the King, 8 December 1666, TNA, CO 1/20, no. 194. Puckrein points out that Willoughby failed to mention the possibility of arming slaves in this letter, despite the fact that this apparently occurred in Barbados during the Second Anglo-Dutch War. Puckrein, *Little England*, 140–141.

25. Dunn, *Sugar and Slaves*, 112; Menard, *Sweet Negotiations*, 114–115; David Galenson, *White Servitude in Colonial America: An Economic Analysis* (Cambridge: Cambridge University Press, 1981), 120, table 8.2; Richard S. Dunn, "The English Sugar Islands and the Founding of South Carolina," *South Carolina Historical Magazine* 72, no. 2, (Apr. 1971): 81–93; Jack P. Greene, "Colonial South Carolina and the Caribbean Connection," *South Carolina Historical Magazine* 88, no. 4 (Oct. 1987): 192–210.

26. Council of Barbados to Charles II, 29 September 1666, TNA, CO 1/20, no. 144; William Willoughby to the King, 8 December 1666, CO 1/20, no. 194; "Instructions to the New Lord Willoughby of Parham," 4 February 1666/7, CO 1/21, no. 15; William Willoughby to Charles II, July 1667, CO 1/21, no. 89.

27. Puckrein, *Little England*, 142.

28. Instructions to D'Oyley, Jamaica Entry Book, 8 February 1660/1, TNA, CO 138/1, pp. 6–8; "Instructions for Edward D'Oyley Esq. Governor of our Island of Jamaica," n.d., CO 1/15, no. 11; Richard Whiting to the "Officers of the Navy," 20 November 1661, CO 1/15, no. 90; Instructions to Thomas Lord Windsor, 21 March 1661/2, CO 138/1,

pp. 12–19; Windsor's Declaration in Barbados, June 1662, CO 1/16, no. 72; "An Act for the furtherance and encouragement of such persons as desire to go off this island," 15 July 1662, CO 1/16, no. 76; "A True & faithful narrative of the proceedings of the President and Council & Assembly of Barbados," 14 August 1662, CO 1/16, no. 89; Francis Willoughby to Charles II, 4 November 1663, CO 1/17, no. 89; Thornton, *West-India Policy*, 51; Cundall, *Governors of Jamaica*, 11.

29. Charles II's order to William Willoughby, January 1663/4, TNA, CO 1/18, no. 6; Charles II's Proclamation enclosed in letter from Modyford to Sir Henry Bennet, 20 March 1663/4, CO 1/18, no. 37I; Modyford to ?, 30 June 1664, CO 1/18, no. 83; "A Journal kept by Colonel Beeston, from his first coming to Jamaica," in *Interesting Tracts, Relating to the Island of Jamaica* (Saint Jago de la Vega, Jamaica: Lewis, Lunan & Jones, 1800), 282; Joseph Martin to Bennet, 26 June 1664, CO 1/18, no. 80; William Willoughby to Sir Henry Bennet, 27 June 1664, CO 1/18, no. 81. In November, the Crown issued a warrant to pay Modyford £1,200 for "transporting 1,000 people" to Jamaica, which probably explains his enthusiasm for the project. Warrant, 17 November 1664, *Calendar of State Papers Colonial: North America and the West Indies, 1574–1739* (*CSPC*), ed. Karen Ordahl Kuperman, John C. Appleby, and Mandy Banton (London: Routledge, 2000), CD-ROM, 5: 255, no. 853. According to Webb, while Modyford was governor, Jamaica's white population increased by about ten thousand. Webb, *Governors-General*, 227–228.

30. E[dmund] H[ickeringill], *Jamaica Viewed* (London, 1661), 16–17, 80; E. A. Wrigley and R. S. Schofield, *The Population History of England, 1541–1870: A Reconstruction*, Studies in Social and Demographic History (London: Edward Arnold, 1981), 207–215; David Eltis, *The Rise of African Slavery in the Americas* (Cambridge: Cambridge University Press, 2000), 46–47; Menard, *Sweet Negotiations*, 44–45; Hilary McD. Beckles, *White Servitude and Black Slavery in Barbados, 1627–1715* (Knoxville: University of Tennessee Press, 1989), 123; I. S., *A Brief and Perfect Journal of The late Proceedings and Successe of the English Army in the West-Indies* (London: 1655), 6.

31. For a different view, see Christian Koot, "A 'Dangerous Principle': Free Trade Discourses in Barbados and the English Leeward Islands, 1650–1689," *Early American Studies* 5, no. 1 (Spring 2007): 132–163.

32. Petition from the Barbados Assembly to Charles II, 5 September 1667, TNA, CO 1/21, no. 102; *An Answer of the Company of Royal Adventurers of England trading into Africa* ([London], 1667), 9, 11, 18; Sir Ellis Leighton to Charles II, 23 January 1667/8, CO 1/22, no. 21; Order of the Royal Adventurers, January 1667/8, CO 1/22, no. 22. Christian Koot also emphasizes these differences of opinion but de-emphasizes their political significance far too much. Koot, "'Dangerous Principle,'" 150.

33. Abstract of a letter from John Bushell and Francis Bond, Barbados, to Edward Bushell, 20–27 April 1668, *CSPC*, 5:561, no. 1734; Harlow, *History of Barbados*, 192–193; "Address of the Merchants and Planters of Barbados now in London," 16 June 1668, TNA, CO 1/22, no. 123; Barbados Assembly to Charles II, 3 August 1668, CO 1/23, no. 33; William Willoughby to Charles II, 11 August 1668, CO 1/23, no. 36. Koot does not see this petition as particularly political in nature. Koot, "'Dangerous Principle,'" 155.

34. Gentlemen Planters to the Barbados Assembly, 14 December 1670, TNA, CO 31/2, pp. 15–17; Gentlemen Planters to the Barbados Assembly, 17 February 1670/1, CO 31/2,

pp. 35–37; Gentlemen Planters to the Barbados Assembly, 17 November 1670, CO 31/2, pp. 12–13; Dunn, *Sugar and Slaves*, 102; Koot, "'Dangerous Principle,'" 156; Harlow, *History of Barbados*, 197–205; Gentlemen Planters to the Barbados Assembly, 1 May 1671, CO 31/2, pp. 45–49; Thornton, *West-India Policy*, 142–143. Included in this group were Sir Peter Colleton, the former African Company agent in the colony; Henry Drax, a major plantation owner since the 1650s; Philip Bell, probably a son of the former governor; planters Constantine Sylvester, John Bawden, and Thomas Wardall; Thomas Middleton, a naval officer with substantial estates in Barbados and Antigua; John Searle, probably a relative of the former governor Daniel Searle; and Fernando Gorges, son of the colonial promoter.

35. "Proposition humbly offered to the Council by the Refiners of sugar in England," 4 July 1671, TNA, CO 31/2, pp. 50–52; "Reasons Humbly Offered By the Refiners of Sugars in England . . .," 4 July 1671, CO 31/2, pp. 68–72; "The Case Between the English Sugar Plantations and the Refiners Stated," 4 July 1671, CO 31/2, pp. 56–58. Other committee members included the Earls of Bridgewater, Berkshire, Essex, Anglesey, Halifax, and Rochester.

36. Gentlemen Planters to the Barbados Assembly, May 1, 1671, TNA, CO 31/2, pp. 45–49; "House of Lords Journal, Volume 12: 12 April 1671," *Journal of the House of Lords: Volume 12: 1666–1675* (1767–1830), 485–489, http://www.british-history.ac.uk/report.aspx?compid=12794 (accessed 27 September 2011); "House of Lords Journal, Volume 12: 17 April 1671," *Journal of the House of Lords: volume 12: 1666–1675* (1767–1830), 493–499, http://www.british-history.ac.uk/report.aspx?compid=12798 (accessed 27 September 2011); "House of Commons Journal, Volume 9: 22 April 1671," *Journal of the House of Commons: Volume 9: 1667–1687* (1802), 238–244, http://www.british-history.ac.uk/report.aspx?compid=27338 (accessed 18 August 2011); Gentlemen Planters to the Barbados Assembly, 1 May 1671, CO 31/2, pp. 45–49; "The State of the Case of the Sugar Plantations in America," May 1671, CO 1/26, no. 57; Harlow, *History of Barbados*, 205; Thornton, *West-India Policy*, 143–144.

37. For a different view, see Zahedieh, "'Wickedest City in the World,'" 15.

38. "Report of the Council for Foreign Plantations to his Majesty," July 1661, *CSPC*, 5:47, no. 130; *By the King. A Proclamation for the Encouraging of Planters in his Majesties Island of Jamaica in the West-Indies* (London: John Bill and Christopher Barker, 1661); "Further additional instructions for Thomas Lord Windsor," 23 April 1662, TNA, CO 1/16, no. 49; Jon Latimer, *Buccaneers of the Caribbean: How Piracy Forged an Empire* (Cambridge, MA: Harvard University Press, 2009), 128.

39. Webb, *Governors-General*, 204–208; Orders in Council of Jamaica by D'Oyley, 3 July 1661, TNA, CO 140/1, pp. 17–20; Dunn, *Sugar and Slaves*, 155, table 16. For discussions of the code in Barbados and its significance, see Beckles, *White Servitude*, chap. 5; Edward B. Rugemer, "The Development of Mastery and Race in the Comprehensive Slave Codes of the Greater Caribbean during the Seventeenth Century," *William and Mary Quarterly* 70, no. 3 (July 2013): 429–458.

40. "A particular narrative of ye buying & forfeiture of ye ship of Negroes in Jamaica," 14 June 1661, TNA, CO 1/15, no. 63; Richard Whiting to the Navy, 10 March 1661/2, CO 1/16, no. 30; Cundall, *Governors of Jamaica*, 8.

41. Latimer, *Buccaneers of the Caribbean*, 132–137; Thornton, *West-India Policy*, 46; Webb, *Governors-General*, 209–210, 213; Sean Kelsey, "Windsor, Thomas, first earl of Plymouth (*c.* 1627–1687)," in *Oxford Dictionary of National Biography* (ODNB) (Oxford: Oxford University Press, 2004), http://www.oxforddnb.com/view/article/29726 (accessed 18 August 2011); Cundall, *Governors of Jamaica*, 10; Instructions to Thomas Lord Windsor, 21 March 1661/2, TNA, CO 138/1, pp. 12–19; "An Additional instruction to Thomas Lord Windsor," 8 April 1662, CO 138/1, p. 19; "Journal kept by Colonel Beeston," 276–277; Nuala Zahedieh, "'A Frugal, Prudential and Hopeful Trade': Privateering in Jamaica, 1655–89," *Journal of Imperial and Commonwealth History* 18, no. 2 (1990): 148. Windsor's conduct led Samuel Pepys to famously conclude "these young Lords are not fit to do any service abroad." *The Diary of Samuel Pepys*, ed. Robert Latham and William Mathews (London: G. Bell and Sons, 1970), 4:41, 13 February 1663.

42. Thornton, *West-India Policy*, 56–57, 76, 79–80; Davies, *Royal African Company*, 43, 317, 326–329. As Nuala Zahedieh has shown, the profits from privateering helped fund the growth of the city of Port Royal and eventually Jamaica's transition to a plantation colony. Nuala Zahedieh, "Trade, Plunder, and Economic Development in Early English Jamaica, 1655–89," *Economic History Review*, 2nd ser., 39, no. 2 (May 1986): 205–222; Zahedieh, "Merchants of Port Royal, Jamaica," 570–593.

43. Webb, *Governors-General*, 218; Cundall, *Governors of Jamaica*, 16; Order of the King to Sir Charles Lyttleton, 28 April 1663, TNA, CO 1/17, no. 23; Sir Henry Bennet to Lyttleton, 29 April 1663, CO 1/17, no. 26; "Journal kept by Colonel Beeston," 277–278, 280; Lyttleton to Sir Henry Bennet, 15 October 1663, CO 1/17, no. 80; Thornton, *West-India Policy*, 80–82.

44. Petition of the Royal Company of Adventurers, 1663, TNA, CO 1/17, no. 93; Zook, *Company of Royal Adventurers*, 74; Cundall, *Governors of Jamaica*, 21; Webb, *Governors-General*, 225–226.

45. Instructions to Modyford, 18 February 1663/4, TNA, CO 138/1, pp. 29–34; Modyford's Commission, 15 February 1663/4, CO 1/18, no. 20.

46. "Journal kept by Colonel Beeston," 282; Modyford to Sir James Modyford, 10 August 1664, TNA, CO 1/18, no. 95; Dr. Henry Stubbs to William Godolphin, 3 October 1664, CO 1/18, no. 116; Thornton, *West-India Policy*, 85–88; Jones, *The Anglo-Dutch Wars*, 89–91; Weiser, *Charles II*, 132–136; Pincus, *Protestantism and Patriotism*, chap. 16.

47. Sir George Downing to the Earl of Clarendon, The Hague, 17/27 March, 1664/5, *Calendar of the Clarendon State Papers Preserved in the Bodleian Library*, ed. F. J. Routledge (Oxford: Clarendon Press, 1970), 5:474; Israel, *Dutch Primacy in World Trade*, 240–243; Order of the King-in-Council, 25 November 1664, CSPC, 5:257, no. 864; "Report of the Committee for the Affayres of Jamaica," 7 November 1664, TNA, CO 1/18. no. 133; Thornton, *West-India Policy*, 85–86, 92–93; Modyford to Bennet, 20 February 1664/5, CO 1/19, no. 27; Modyford to Bennet, February 1665, CO 1/19, no. 29; Latimer, *Buccaneers of the Caribbean*, 147–148; Modyford to Bennet, 20 April 1665, CO 1/19, no. 69; Col. Theodore Cary to Albemarle, 23 August 1665, CO 1/19, no. 97; Modyford to Arlington (Henry Bennet), 16 November 1665, CO 1/19, no. 127. Lynch, now resident in England, reported that the English captured at least eighteen hundred

slaves and resold them in neighboring Saint Christopher. Lynch to Arlington, 13 October 1665, CO 1/19, no. 111. Many thanks to Dan Richter for this reference.

48. Modyford to Arlington, 16 November 1665, TNA, CO 1/19, no. 127; "A True and Perfect Narrative by Col. Theodore Cary," November 1665, CO 1/19, nos. 130 and 130I; Minutes of the Council of Jamaica sent to the Duke of Albemarle, 22 February 1665/6, CO 1/20, no. 24I; and CO 140/1, pp. 143–147; Modyford to Albemarle, 1 March 1665/6, CO 1/20, no. 22; Modyford to Albemarle, 1 June 1666, CO 1/20, no. 24; Modyford to Arlington, 8 March 1665/6, CO 1/20, no. 26; Modyford to Arlington, 16 June 1666, CO 1/20, no. 100; Thornton, *West-India Policy*, 93–94, 98; Webb, *Governors-General*, 235–236.

49. Modyford to Arlington, 21 August 1666, TNA, CO 1/20, no. 134; Modyford's "Reasons why the private men of war are advantageous to the island of Jamaica," Summer 1666, CO 1/20, no. 135; "A Narrative of Sir Thomas Modyford Baronett, Governour of His Majesties Island of Jamaica . . .," 23 August 1669, CO 1/24, no. 81; Webb, *Governors-General*, 232; Thornton, *West-India Policy*, 99.

50. Lynch to Bennet, 25 May 1664, TNA, CO 1/18, no. 68; Zook, *Company of Royal Adventurers*, 22–24; Davies, *Royal African Company*, 57–59. On the poor economic state of the company by 1665, caused at least in part by the war, see Petition of the Royal Company to the King, early 1665, CO 1/19, no. 5; Petition of the Royal Company to the King, 1665?, CO 1/17, no. 110.

51. Orders of a Council of War on board the *Jersey*, 7 May 1664, TNA, CO 1/18, no. 63; Callow, *Making of King James II*, 247–248.

52. Apparently Modyford never received official word of the peace. Petition of Charles Modyford, January 1668, TNA, CO 1/22, no. 31; Modyford to Albemarle, 1 October 1668, CO 1/23, no. 59; Webb, *Governors-General*, 241, 247–248. On the 1667 treaty, which was silent on the issue of conflicts in the Americas, see Thornton, *West-India Policy*, 101–102; Stanley J. and Barbara H. Stein, *Silver, Trade, and War: Spain and America in the Making of Early Modern Europe* (Baltimore, MD: Johns Hopkins University Press, 2000), 63; Latimer, *Buccaneers of the Caribbean*, 162–163.

53. "Journal kept by Colonel Beeston," 286–287; Latimer, *Buccaneers of the Caribbean*, chaps. 9–10; Thornton, *West-India Policy*, 110; Peter Earle, *The Sack of Panamá: Sir Henry Morgan's Adventures on the Spanish Main* (New York: Viking Press, 1981), chap. 11; Minutes of the Council of Jamaica, 29 June 1670, TNA, CO 1/25, no. 44; Modyford's Commission to Morgan, 2 July 1670, CO 1/25, no. 45; Morgan's Instructions, 2 July 1670, CO 1/25, no. 46; Additional Instructions to Morgan, 1 August 1670, CO 1/25, no. 50. Morgan was the nephew of Edward Morgan, who had led raids against the Dutch islands in 1665.

54. Earle, *Sack of Panamá*, 176–179, 217, 237–242; Latimer, *Buccaneers of the Caribbean*, 205, 210–221; Stein and Stein, *Silver, Trade, and War*, 64; Thornton, *West-India Policy*, 114, 118–119, 122–123; Morgan's Account to the Council of Jamaica, 20 April 1671, TNA, CO 138/1, pp. 121–128; Revocation of Modyford's commission, 4 January 1670/1, CO 1/26, no. 1; CO 138/1, p. 86; Draft memorandum of instructions to Sir Thomas Lynch, January 1670/1, CO 1/26, no. 16; Instructions to Sir Thomas Lynch, 31 December 1670, CO 1/25, no. 107. Zahedieh argues that another reason why the English state began to turn against privateering was diminishing returns; by 1670–1671, privateering was

simply not as profitable as it had once been. Nuala Zahedieh, "'A Frugal, Prudential and Hopeful Trade,'" 145, 156–157. News of the raid appeared in the *London Gazette*, July 3–6, 1671.

4. POLITICIZED EMPIRE

1. Modyford to Arlington, 20 September 1670, The National Archives (TNA), Colonial Office (CO) 1/25, no. 59; Modyford to Arlington, 20 September 1670, CO 1/25, no. 59III.
2. Philip S. Haffenden, "The Crown and Colonial Charters, 1675–1688: Part I," *William and Mary Quarterly*, 3rd ser., 15, no. 3 (July 1958): 299; A. P. Thornton, *West-India Policy under the Restoration* (Oxford: Clarendon Press, 1956), 19; Jack P. Greene, *Peripheries and Center: Constitutional Development in the Extended Polities of the British Empire and the United States, 1607–1788* (Athens: University of Georgia Press, 1986), 13; Richard S. Dunn, "Imperial Pressures on Massachusetts and Jamaica, 1675–1700," in *Anglo-American Political Relations, 1675–1775*, ed. Alison Gilbert Olson and Richard Maxwell Brown (New Brunswick, NJ: Rutgers University Press, 1970), 59–60; Richard Johnson, *Adjustment to Empire: The New England Colonies, 1675–1715* (New Brunswick, NJ: Rutgers University Press, 1981), 26; Stephen Saunders Webb, *The Governors-General: The English Army and the Definition of the Empire, 1569–1681* (Chapel Hill: University of North Carolina Press, 1979), 268–269; Robert M. Bliss, *Revolution and Empire: English Politics and the American Colonies in the Seventeenth Century* (Manchester, UK: Manchester University Press, 1990), 178.
3. J. R. Jones, *Country and Court: England, 1658–1714* (Cambridge, MA: Harvard University Press, 1978), 101, 160; Bliss, *Revolution and Empire*, 161–162; Barry Coward, *The Stuart Age: England, 1603–1714*, 2nd ed. (London: Longman, 1994), 301; Thornton, *West-India Policy*, 133–140; Brian Weiser, *Charles II and the Politics of Access* (Woodbridge, Suffolk, UK: Boydell Press, 2003), 138; Report of the Council of Trade to the King, 4 December 1668, TNA, CO 1/23, no. 93.
4. Instructions for the Council of Plantations, 20 July 1670, *Coventry Papers of the Marquis of Bath at Longleat* (Washington, DC: American Council of Learned Societies, Library of Congress Photoduplication Service), (*Coventry Papers*), microfilm, vol. 76, fols. 191–195. Other members of the council included Lord Gorges, Lord Allington, the poet Edmund Waller, and Henry Slingsby, the master of the mint. In 1671 the Duke of York, Prince Rupert, the Dukes of Buckingham and Ormond, Lord Culpepper, and Sir George Carteret joined the council. Charles M. Andrews, *British Committees, Commissions, and Councils of Trade and Plantations, 1622–1675*, Johns Hopkins University Studies in Historical and Political Science, vol. 26, no. 1 (Baltimore, MD: Johns Hopkins University Press, 1908), 96–100.
5. John Callow, *The Making of King James II: The Formative Years of a Fallen King* (Thrupp, Stroud, Gloucestershire, UK: Sutton Publishing, 2000), 247–250; K. G. Davies, *The Royal African Company* (London: Longmans, Green, 1957), 43–44, 57–59; George Frederick Zook, *The Company of Royal Adventurers Trading into Africa* (Lancaster, PA: New Era Printing, 1919), 22–24; Petition of the Royal Company of Adventurers, n.d., but in 1669/70 papers, TNA, CO 1/25, no. 12.

6. Callow, *Making of King James II*, 251; *Select Charters of Trading Companies*, A.D. 1530–1707, ed. Cecil T. Carr, Publications of the Selden Society, 28 (London: Bernard Quaritch, 1913), 192; Davies, *Royal African Company*, 98–99, 156. Other founding members included William, Lord Craven, Sir John Shaw, and Sir Charles Modyford (Thomas's brother), Lords Bath and Berkeley, Sir George Carteret, Sir William Coventry, Sir Peter Colleton (a "Gentleman Planter" whose brother John had been a founding member of the Adventurers), and Sir Nicholas Crispe, the longtime merchant to Africa. For a full list, see *Select Charters*, 187–189; Minute Book of the General Court of the Royal African Company, 27 October 1671, TNA, Treasury (T) 70/100, fols. 5–8.

7. K. H. D. Haley, *The First Earl of Shaftesbury* (Oxford: Clarendon Press, 1968), chaps. 12–15; E. E. Rich, "The First Earl of Shaftesbury's Colonial Policy," *Transactions of the Royal Historical Society*, 5th ser., 7 (1957): 66–67; Callow, *Making of King James II*, 251. For Shaftesbury's rise to the presidency of the council, see John Evelyn, *The Diary of John Evelyn*, ed. Austin Dobson (London: MacMillan, 1906; repr., London: Routledge/Thoemmes Press, 1996), 2:353, 24 October 1672. Other members included Viscount Halifax and Sir Thomas Osborne, the future Earl of Danby. Thornton, *West-India Policy*, 148, n. 3

8. John Spurr, *England in the 1670s: "This Masquerading Age"* (Oxford: Blackwell, 2000), 26–27; Bruce Carruthers, *City of Capital: Politics and Markets in the English Financial Revolution* (Princeton, NJ: Princeton University Press, 1996), 61–69. On the pro-French, anti-Dutch orientation of the court in the lead-up to the Third Anglo-Dutch War, see Gary S. De Krey, *Restoration and Revolution in Britain: A Political History of the Era of Charles II and the Glorious Revolution* (New York: Palgrave, 2007), 93–98; Coward, *Stuart Age*, 306–307; Davies, *Royal African Company*, 61–62; Callow, *Making of King James II*, 252. Not all of these men knew all of the details of the secret treaty, by which Charles II promised to convert to Catholicism and encourage its promotion in England. Only York, Clifford, and Arlington, of those listed above, knew at this stage. Spurr, *England in the 1670s*, 11–12.

9. Ann M. Carlos and Jamie Brown Kruse, "The Decline of the Royal African Company: Fringe Firms and the Role of the Charter," *Economic History Review* 49, no. 2 (1996): 310, 293; De Krey, *Restoration and Revolution*, 24; Callow, *Making of King James II*, 252, 301; John Miller, *James II: A Study in Kingship* (Hove, East Sussex, UK: Wayland Publishers, 1977), 67–68; 124–125.

10. Richard S. Dunn, *Sugar and Slaves: The Rise of the Planter Class in the English West Indies, 1624–1713* (Chapel Hill, NC: University of North Carolina Press, 1972), 124; Council of Trade Report to the King, 17 November 1670, TNA, CO 153/1, pp. 2–3; Instructions for William Lord Willoughby, 30 April 1672, *Calendar of State Papers Colonial: North America and the West Indies, 1574–1739* (CSPC), ed. Karen Ordahl Kuperman, John C. Appleby, and Mandy Banton, 45 vols. (London, 2000), CD-ROM, 7:352–353, no. 812; Commission to William Lord Willoughby, 30 April 1672, CSPC, 7:351–352, no. 811; Vincent T. Harlow, *A History of Barbados, 1625–1685* (Oxford: Clarendon Press, 1926), 208. For a petition requesting separation from Barbados, see "Petition of the Planters of the Leeward Islands to have a Governour not depending on the Barbados," 22 September 1670, CO 153/1, p. 1; Harlow, *History of Barbados*, 210.

11. Commission to Sir Jonathan Atkins, 19 December 1673, TNA, CO 1/30, no. 92; Thornton, *West-India Policy*, 154; Atkins to the Council of Trade, 1 December 1673, CO 1/30, no. 84; Harlow, *History of Barbados*, 217–218; John Locke to Arlington, 6 January 1674, CO 1/31, no. 3. For more on the importance of "outsider governors" to imperial governance, see Nuala Zahedieh, *The Capital and the Colonies: London and the Atlantic Economy, 1660–1700* (Cambridge: Cambridge University Press, 2010), 48.

12. Bevin and Stede to the Council of Trade, n.d., TNA, CO 1/30, no. 96; Harlow, *History of Barbados*, 219.

13. Petition of Edwin Stede to Charles II, 1673, TNA, CO 31/2, p. 158; CO 1/30, no. 82; Harlow, *History of Barbados*, 216; Bliss, *Revolution and Empire*, 173–174; David S. Lovejoy, *The Glorious Revolution in America*, rev. ed. (Middletown, CT: Wesleyan University Press, 1987), 10–11; Nuala Zahedieh, "Overseas Expansion and Trade in the Seventeenth Century," in *Origins of Empire*, ed. Nicholas Canny, vol. 1, *Oxford History of the British Empire* (Oxford: Oxford University Press, 1998): 406; Thornton, *West-India Policy*, 164–165, 182; Atkins to Sir Joseph Williamson, 20/30 April 1675, CO 1/34, no. 57; Lt. Col. Edward Thornburgh to the Barbados Assembly, 1 April 1673, CO 31/2, pp. 123–124.

14. Royal African Company to Charles II, n.d., TNA, CO 324/2, p. 89; Stede[?] to the Royal African Company, 26 November 1675, CO 324/2, pp. 90–92; Charles II to Atkins, 10 March 1675/6, CO 324/2, pp. 83–85; Atkins to the Lords of Trade, 6/16 September 1677, CO 29/2, pp. 185–191. For other complaints about interlopers in Barbados from the company, see Stede and Gascoigne to Robert Southwell[?], 15 September 1675, CO 1/35, no. 19; Royal African Company to Charles II, 22 November 1676, CO 1/38, no. 60.

15. *Great Newes from the Barbadoes. Or, a True and Faithful Account of the Grand Conspiracy of the Negroes against the English* (London: Printed for L. Curtis, 1676), 9, 11–12; *A Continuation of the State of New-England; being a Farther Account of the Indian Warr . . . Together with an Account of the Intended Rebellion of the Negroes in the Barbadoes* (London: T. M. for Dorman Newman, 1676), 19–20; Atkins to Williamson, 3/13 October 1675, TNA, CO 1/35, no. 29; Gary Puckrein, *Little England: Plantation Society and Anglo-Barbadian Politics* (New York: New York University Press, 1984), 162–164; Jerome S. Handler, "Slave Revolts and Conspiracies in Seventeenth-Century Barbados," *New West Indian Guide / Nieuwe West-Indische Gids* 56, no. 1/2 (1982): 17–18; Jerome S. Handler, "The Barbados Slave Conspiracies of 1675 and 1692," *Journal of the Barbados Museum and Historical Society* 36, no. 4 (1982): 316–317; Russell Menard, *Sweet Negotiations: Sugar, Slavery, and Plantation Agriculture in Barbados* (Charlottesville: University of Virginia Press, 2006), 25, table 4.

16. Draft memorandum of instructions to Sir Thomas Lynch, January 1670/1, TNA, CO 1/26, no. 16; Instructions to Sir Thomas Lynch, 31 December 1670, CO 1/25, no. 107; Instructions to Lynch, 31 January 1670/1, CO 138/1, pp. 88–95; Frank Cundall, *The Governors of Jamaica in the Seventeenth Century* (London: West India Committee, 1936), 32; "A Journal kept by Colonel Beeston, from his first coming to Jamaica," in *Interesting Tracts, Relating to the Island of Jamaica* (Saint Jago de la Vega, Jamaica: Lewis, Lunan & Jones, 1800), 288–289; Webb, *Governors-General*, 251–253; Lynch to Arlington, 27 June 1671, and Lynch to Sandwich, 20 August 1671, British Library (BL), Additional Manuscripts

(Add MS) 11410, fols. 180–184 and 185–191. Interestingly, Lynch did not receive orders to arrest Henry Morgan until October 1671. Dudley Pope, *The Buccaneer King: The Biography of Sir Henry Morgan, 1635–1688* (New York: Dodd, Mead, 1977), 257–259.

17. James Bannister to Arlington, 14 August 1671, TNA, CO 1/27, no. 19; Proclamation of Sir Thomas Lynch, 15 August 1671, CO 1/27, no. 20; Kris E. Lane, *Pillaging the Empire: Piracy in the Americas, 1500–1750* (Armonk, NY: M. E. Sharpe, 1998), 123; Webb, *Governors-General*, 255; *Journals of the Assembly of Jamaica*, 14 May 1672 (Wilmington, DE: Scholarly Resources, microfilm), 6.

18. Lynch to Joseph Williamson, 20 November 1674, TNA, CO 1/31, no. 77; Lynch to Williamson, 13 January 1671/2, BL Add MS 11410, fols. 222–226; Lynch to the Council of Trade, 4 April 1673, CO 1/30, no. 19; Lynch to Arlington, 20 August 1671, CO 1/27, no. 22; Nuala Zahedieh, "The Merchants of Port Royal, Jamaica, and the Spanish Contraband Trade, 1655–1692," *William and Mary Quarterly*, 3rd ser., 43, no. 4 (Oct. 1986): 575; Thornton, *West-India Policy*, 215–217; Jon Latimer, *Buccaneers of the Caribbean: How Piracy Forged an Empire* (Cambridge, MA: Harvard University Press, 2009), 225–226; Benjamin Worsley to Lynch, 8 October 1672, CO 1/29, no. 35. For an account of Spanish reprisals against the logwood cutters, see Richard Browne, Bristol, to Williamson, 28 September 1672, CO 1/29, no. 33.

19. Nuala Zahedieh, "Trade, Plunder, and Economic Development in Early English Jamaica, 1655–89," *Economic History Review*, 2nd ser., 39, no. 2 (May 1986): 218–219; Nuala Zahedieh, "'The Wickedest City in the World': Port Royal, Commercial Hub of the Seventeenth-Century Caribbean," in *Working Slavery, Pricing Freedom: Perspectives from the Caribbean, Africa and the African Diaspora*, ed. Verene A. Shepherd (New York: Palgrave, 2002), 8–9; Zahedieh, "Merchants of Port Royal," 579; Nuala Zahedieh, "Regulation, Rent-seeking, and the Glorious Revolution in the English Atlantic Economy," *Economic History Review* 63, no. 4 (2010): 878.

20. Lynch to the Council of Trade, 5 July 1672, TNA, CO 1/29, no. 5; Council of Trade to the King, 2 July 1672, CO 1/29, no.1; Lynch to Williamson, 9 October 1672, CO 1/29, no. 36; Benjamin Worsley to Lynch, 2 November 1672, CO 1/29, no. 41; Thornton, *West-India Policy*, 218; Webb, *Governors-General*, 260–261; Minutes of the Council of Jamaica, 9–12 May 1673, CSPC, 7:488–489, no. 1089; *Journals of the Assembly of Jamaica*, 11 May 1672, 12–16 May 1673, 1:6; Lynch to Benjamin Worsley, 8 July 1673, CO 1/30, no. 49.

21. Spurr, *England in the 1670s*, 43, 47; Pope, *Buccaneer King*, 265–268; Latimer, *Buccaneers of the Caribbean*, 226; Memorial of Col. Morgan to Charles II, August 1673, TNA, CO 1/30, no. 56; *Diary of John Evelyn*, 20 October 1674, 2:372; Thornton, *West-India Policy*, 219.

22. Lane, *Pillaging the Empire*, 124; Thornton, *West-India Policy*, 218; Cundall, *Governors of Jamaica*, 77.

23. Cundall, *Governors of Jamaica*, 77–79; Commission to Lord Vaughan, 3 April 1674, TNA, CO 138/3, pp. 1–11; Instructions to Lord Vaughan, 3 December 1674, CO 138/3, pp. 12–27; Coventry to Vaughan, 31 December 1674, BL Add MS 25120, fols. 43–45; Vaughan to the Lords of Trade, 24 March 1674/5, CO 1/34, no. 31; Vaughan to the Lords of Trade, 20 January 1675/6, CO 1/36, no. 13; Vaughan to Williamson,

20 September 1675, CO 1/35, no. 20. Coventry wrote that because the government was unwilling to take a stand on the issue of logwood cutting, the cutters "must consider their own hazards themselves" and therefore could not rely on any official support or protection. Coventry to Vaughan, 28 July 1675, BL Add MS 25120, fols. 47–49; Coventry to Vaughan, 26 September 1675, BL Add MS 25120, fols. 59–60.

24. Bliss, *Revolution and Empire*, 183; Thornton, *West-India Policy*, 219–220; Latimer, *Buccaneers of the Caribbean*, 226–229. For the traditional "planter vs. privateer" dynamic in Jamaica, see Dunn, *Sugar and Slaves*, 156–160, 177–182; Webb, *Governors-General*, 250–254.

25. *Journals of the Assembly of Jamaica*, 15 May 1675, 1:10–11; Minutes of the Lords of Trade, 11 August 1675, TNA, CO 138/3, pp. 27–32; Vaughan to Williamson, 18 May 1675, CO 1/34, no. 81; Coventry to Vaughan, 30 July 1675, BL Add MS 25120, fols. 51–54; Coventry to Morgan, 24 August 1675, BL Add MS 25120, fols. 57–58; Coventry to Vaughan, 29 March 1676, BL Add MS 25120, fols. 69–71; Coventry to Morgan, 29 March 1676, BL Add MS 25120, fols. 72–73; Coventry to Vaughan, 8 June 1676, BL Add MS 25120, fols. 74–75; Coventry to Morgan, 8 June 1676, BL Add MS 25120, fols. 76–78; Minutes of the Jamaica Council, 10 November 1676, CO 138/3, pp. 94–106; Bliss, *Revolution and Empire*, 183; Thornton, *West-India Policy*, 222; Webb, *Governors-General*, 263–275.

26. Rich, "Shaftesbury's Colonial Policy," 67–68; Halcy, *First Earl of Shaftesbury*, 343; Spurr, *England in the 1670s*, 49–56; Coward, *Stuart Age*, 311; Steven Pincus, "From Botterboxes to Wooden Shoes: The Shift in English Popular Sentiment from Anti-Dutch to Anti-French in the 1670s," *Historical Journal* 38, no. 2 (1995): 333–361.

27. Andrews, *British Committees*, 111–112; Thornton, *West-India Policy*, 157–158; Haley, *First Earl of Shaftesbury*, 233–234, 262–263, 330, 336–337, 403–406; Rich, "Shaftesbury's Colonial Policy," 70; Stephen Saunders Webb, *1676: The End of American Independence* (New York: Knopf, 1984), 191; Callow, *Making of King James II*, 253; Royal African Company Subscriptions and Transfers, 1671–1677, TNA, T 70/100, fols. 48–100; Davies, *Royal African Company*, 65.

28. Greene, *Peripheries and Center*, 13–14; Haffenden, "Crown and Colonial Charters, Part I," 298–299; Thornton, *West-India Policy*, 159; A. M. Whitson, *The Constitutional Development of Jamaica, 1660 to 1729* (Manchester, UK: Manchester University Press, 1929), 70; Lovejoy, *Glorious Revolution in America*, 13; Weiser, *Charles II*, 142–143; Andrew Browning, *Thomas Osborne, Earl of Danby and Duke of Leeds, 1632–1712* (Glasgow: Jackson & Son, 1944–1951), 1:146, 149, 325. On Danby's influence and governing style, see De Krey, *Restoration and Revolution*, 125–134; Tim Harris, *Politics under the Later Stuarts: Party Conflict in a Divided Society, 1660–1715* (London and New York: Longman, 1993), 57–58; Bliss, *Revolution and Empire*, 176–179; Webb, *1676*, 179–180, 188–189.

29. Other members included men who had served on the previous committees and councils and had longtime colonial interests, including George Savile, Viscount Halifax; and John Lord Berkeley. Ralph Paul Bieber, *The Lords of Trade and Plantations 1675–1696* (Allentown, PA: H. Ray Haas, 1919), 23, 32.

30. Atkins to Williamson, 3/13 October 1675, TNA, CO 1/35, no. 29; Petition of the Barbados Council and Assembly to Charles II, n.d., CO 1/66, no. 93I; Petition of the Barbados Council and Assembly, 24 November 1675, CO 1/35, no. 45II; Atkins to

Coventry, 20/30 April 1675, *Coventry Papers*, vol. 76, fol. 343; Atkins to the Lords of Trade, 4/14 July 1676, CO 1/37, no. 23.

31. Minutes of the Lords of Trade, 26 October 1676, TNA, CO 391/1, pp. 234–236; Minutes of the Lords of Trade, 31 October 1676, CO 391/1, pp. 238–239; Thornton, *West-India Policy*, 187–188; Harlow, *History of Barbados*, 226–227. Christian Koot interprets this contest to be exclusively about commercial regulations and argues that it did not have wider political or ideological implications. Christian Koot, "'A Dangerous Principle': Free Trade Discourses in Barbados and the English Leeward Islands, 1650–1689," *Early American Studies* 5, no. 1 (Spring 2007): 157–158.

32. Report of the Lords of Trade to the King, 7 November 1676, TNA, CO 1/38, no. 31; Charles II to Atkins, 9 December 1676, CO 29/2, fols. 70–72; Minutes of the Lords of Trade, 24 November 1676, CO 391/1, p. 256. Atkins attempted to defend himself in light of this reprimand. Atkins to Williamson, 22 January 1676/7, CO 1/39, no. 9; Atkins to the Lords of Trade, 17/27 April 1677, CO 1/40, no. 47.

33. Lovejoy, *Glorious Revolution in America*, 20; Lords of Trade to Atkins, 21 December 1676, TNA, CO 1/38, no. 94; Bliss, *Revolution and Empire*, 180; Harlow, *History of Barbados*, 224–225; Coventry to Atkins, 28 November 1676, BL Add MS 25120, fols. 96–99; Coventry to Atkins, 21 November 1677, BL Add MS 25120, fols. 120–122.

34. The imperial implications of Bacon's Rebellion and King Philip's War are discussed in Webb, *1676*, 169–247.

35. Peter Beckford to Sir Joseph Williamson, 2 April 1676, TNA, CO 1/36, no. 38; Symon Musgrave to the Admiralty Court of Jamaica, 23 March 1675/6, *Coventry Papers*, vol. 74, fols. 225–229; Vaughan to the Lords of Trade, 4 April 1676, CO 138/3, pp. 52–54; Jamaican Admiralty Court ruling, 23 March 1675/6, *Coventry Papers*, vol. 74, fol. 221; Vaughan to Henry Coventry, 29 April 1676, *Coventry Papers*, vol. 74, fol. 269; Morgan to Coventry, 16 April 1676, *Coventry Papers*, vol. 74, fols. 241–242. The act "for dividing his Majesty's Island of Jamaica into several parishes and precincts," which had the effect of altering the Admiralty's jurisdiction, passed in April 1675; "Forty-five Acts . . . of Jamaica," 26 April 1675, *CSPC*, vol. 9, no. 538.

36. Minutes of the Lords of Trade, 22 June 1676, TNA, CO 391/1, pp. 148–149; Report of Richard Lloyd to the Lords of Trade, 4 July 1676, CO 1/37, no. 21; "Royal Company Negroes at Jamaica, 1676," 13 July 1676, CO 1/37, no. 31. *CSPC*, vol. 9, no. 987, indicates that this paper was "probably the opinion of the Attorney General." Many thanks to Roy Ritchie for pointing out this reference.

37. Memorandum, July 1676, TNA, CO 1/37, no. 32; Minutes of the Lords of Trade, 13 July 1676, CO 391/1, pp. 165–167.

38. Coventry to Vaughan, 31 July 1676, BL Add MS 25120, fols. 84–85; Morgan to Coventry, 31 May 1677, *Coventry Papers*, vol. 75, fols. 182–183; Vaughn to Coventry, 28 May 1677, *Coventry Papers*, vol. 75, fols. 180–181; "Journal kept by Colonel Beeston," 26 July 1677, p. 292. Coventry sent Vaughan advance notice of his replacement in May 1677. Coventry to Vaughan, 31 May 1677, BL Add MS 25120, fols. 110–111.

39. Spurr, *England in the 1670s*, 56, 75; Webb, *Governors-General*, 70, 276; Whitson, *Constitutional Development*, 79; Cundall, *Governors of Jamaica*, 86; Gordon Goodwin, rev. by Sean Kelsey, "Charles Howard, first earl of Carlisle," in *Oxford*

Dictionary of National Biography (ODNB) (Oxford: Oxford University Press, 2004), http://www.oxforddnb.com/view/article/13886?docPos=3 (accessed 9 May 2014).

40. "Journal kept by Colonel Beeston," 19 July 1678, pp. 294–295; *Journals of the Assembly of Jamaica*, 4 September 1678, 1: 25; Instructions to the Earl of Carlisle, 30 March 1678, TNA, CO 138/3, pp. 216–241; Report of the Lords of Trade, 13 November 1677, CO 138/3, pp. 161–162; Bliss, *Revolution and Empire*, 182–186. Council members' names would be included in the governor's private instructions but not his public commission. For further alterations to Carlisle's instructions in the fall of 1677, see CSPC, vol. 10, no. 412, 11–12 September 1677; no. 457, 25 October 1677; no. 461, 28 October 1677. In July 1677, Sir Thomas Lynch had suggested to the Lords of Trade that the governor of Jamaica be given "ye title of Viceroy of Jamaica, New England, or America, or ye like," in order to more effectively engage with the Spanish. Lynch, "Reflections on ye State of ye Spanyard & ye island of Jamaica in America," 20 July 1677, CO 1/40, no. 111. For the history of Poynings' Law in Ireland, see James Kelly, *Poynings' Law and the Making of Law in Ireland, 1660–1800* (Dublin, IR: Four Courts Press, 2007). Emphasis in the original.

41. Bliss, *Revolution and Empire*, 176; Webb, 1676, 179–180; Lovejoy, *Glorious Revolution in America*, 55–56; Dunn, "Imperial Pressures," 60–64; Dunn, "The Downfall of the Bermuda Company: A Restoration Farce," *William and Mary Quarterly* 20 (1963): 487–512; Haffenden, "Crown and Colonial Charters, Part I," 297–311; Haffenden, "The Crown and Colonial Charters, 1675–1688: Part II," *William and Mary Quarterly*, 3rd ser., 15, no. 4 (Oct. 1958): 452–466. Other historians have noted the probable connections between the case of the *St. George* and the attempted overhaul of Jamaica's laws two years later. See Whitson, *Constitutional Development*, 76; Bliss, *Revolution and Empire*, 182. However, neither explores the role that the African Company played in the longer-term trajectory of this imperial plan.

42. Report of the Lords of Trade, 13 November 1677, TNA, CO 138/3, pp. 161–162; Bliss, *Revolution and Empire*, 184.

43. Lovejoy, *Glorious Revolution in America*, 56–57; "Royal Company Negroes at Jamaica, 1676," 13 July 1676, TNA, CO 1/37, no. 31. Webb has estimated that Bacon's Rebellion cost the government well over £200,000 in direct expenditures and lost revenues. Webb, 1676, 189.

44. Roger Coke, *A Discourse of Trade* (London, 1670), 44; William Petyt, *Britannia languens, or a Discourse of Trade* (London, 1680), 70; [Slingsby Bethel], *The Present Interest of England Stated* (London: D. B., 1671), 9, 18, 28–30; Carew Reynell, *The True English Interest* (London: Giles Widdowes, 1674), 9, 71–72. Many of these pamphlets were part of a larger public debate on the "imbalance" of trade between England and France, which contributed to growing anti-French sentiment. Spurr, *England in the 1670s*, 60–61.

45. "Debates in 1675: November 8th–9th," *Grey's Debates of the House of Commons: Volume 3* (London, 1769), 417–435, http://www.british-history.ac.uk/report.aspx?compid=40380 (accessed 15 November 2011). For more on William Coventry, who was the brother of Secretary of State Henry Coventry, see Sidney Lee, "Coventry, Sir William (*bap.* 1627, *d.* 1686)," rev. by Sean Kelsey, in ODNB, http://www.oxforddnb.com/view/article/6485 (accessed 15 November 2011).

46. Joyce Appleby, *Economic Thought and Ideology in Seventeenth-Century England* (Princeton, NJ: Princeton University Press, 1978), 135; Coke, *Discourse of Trade*, 10; *The Character and Qualifications of an Honest and Loyal Merchant* (London: Robert Roberts, 1686), 13; Petyt, *Britannia languens*, 176; Reynell, *True English Interest*, 88; Richard C. Wiles, "Mercantilism and the Idea of Progress," *Eighteenth-Century Studies* 8, no. 1 (Autumn 1974): 62–66.

47. Spurr, *England in the 1670s*, 176–177. For the story behind the proclamation and its quick withdrawal, see Steven Pincus, "'Coffee Politicians Does Create': Coffeehouses and Restoration Political Culture," *Journal of Modern History* 67 (Dec. 1995): 807–834.

48. John Callow, "Coke, Roger (ca. 1628–1704x7)," in *ODNB*, http://www.oxforddnb.com/view/article/5829 (accessed 14 October 2011); V. E. Chancellor, "Reynell, Carew (1636–1690)," in *ODNB*, http://www.oxforddnb.com/view/article/23397 (accessed 14 October 2011); Gary S. De Krey, "Bethel, Slingsby (*bap.* 1617, *d.* 1697)," in *ODNB*, http://www.oxforddnb.com/view/article/2303 (accessed 14 October 2011); Melinda Zook, *Radical Whigs and Conspiratorial Politics in Late Stuart Britain* (University Park: Pennsylvania State University Press, 1999), 8–9; Jonathan Scott, *Algernon Sidney and the Restoration Crisis, 1677–1683* (Cambridge: Cambridge University Press, 1991), 63–64.

49. Koot, "'Dangerous Principle,'" 132–163.

5. EXCLUSION, THE TORY ASCENDANCY, AND THE ENGLISH EMPIRE

1. Blathwayt to Atkins, 15 January 1677/8, *The William Blathwayt Papers at Colonial Williamsburg 1631–1722* (*Blathwayt Papers*) (Frederick, MD: UPA Academic Editions, 1989), microfilm, vol. 29, folder 1, Barbados; Sir Robert Southwell to Atkins, draft letter, 23 April 1678, The National Archives (TNA), Colonial Office (CO) 1/42, no. 61; Atkins to the Lords of Trade, 17/27 April 1679, CO 1/43, no. 47; Vincent T. Harlow, *A History of Barbados, 1625–1685* (Oxford: Clarendon Press, 1926), 230–234; Barbara Murison, "The Talented Mr. Blathwayt: His Empire Revisited," in *English Atlantics Revisited: Essays Honouring Professor Ian K. Steele*, ed. Nancy L. Rhoden (Montreal, QC, and Kingston, ON: McGill-Queen's University Press, 2007), 33–58; Matthew Carl Underwood, "Ordering Knowledge, Re-Ordering Empire: Science and State Formation in the English Atlantic World, 1650–1688," (Ph.D. diss., Harvard University, 2010), 217–244.

2. Journal of the Lords of Trade, 26 June 1679, TNA, CO 391/3, pp. 30–37; Petition of Colonel Strode and Partners to the Lords of Trade, read 18 June 1679, CO 1/43, no. 73I; A. P. Thornton, *West-India Policy under the Restoration* (Oxford: Clarendon Press, 1956), 189; Harlow, *History of Barbados*, 236; Lords of Trade report on Barbados, 4 July 1679, CO 1/43, no. 85; Lords of Trade to Atkins, 26 June 1679, CO 324/2, pp. 148–150; Order of the King-in-Council, 24 July 1679, CO 324/2, pp. 151–152; Journal of the Lords of Trade, 13 January 1679/80, CO 391/3, pp. 114–18; Coventry to Atkins, 25 July 1679, British Library (BL), Additional Manuscripts (Add MS) 25120, fol. 143;

Atkins to the Lords of Trade, 26 March 1680, CO 1/44, no. 45; Order of the King-in-Council, 12 December 1679, CO 324/4, pp. 72–74.

3. John Miller, *Popery and Politics in England, 1660–1688* (Cambridge: Cambridge University Press, 1973), 155–159; John Kenyon, *The Popish Plot* (London: Phoenix Press, 2000), chaps. 3–5; Tim Harris, *Restoration: Charles II and His Kingdoms, 1660–1685* (London: Penguin, 2006), 136–139, 146–163; Gary S. De Krey, *Restoration and Revolution in Britain: A Political History of the Era of Charles II and the Glorious Revolution* (New York: Palgrave Macmillan, 2007), 145–151; Michael Mullett, *James II and English Politics, 1678–1688* (London: Routledge, 1994), chap. 2; Mark Knights, *Politics and Opinion in Crisis, 1678–81* (Cambridge: Cambridge University Press, 1994), chap. 2; J. R. Jones, *The First Whigs: The Politics of the Exclusion Crisis, 1678–1683* (New York: Oxford University Press, 1961).

4. Harris, *Restoration*, 204, 411; John Spurr, *England in the 1670s: "This Masquerading Age"* (Oxford: Blackwell Publishers, 2000); Knights, *Politics and Opinion in Crisis*; Melinda Zook, *Radical Whigs and Conspiratorial Politics in Late Stuart Britain* (University Park: Pennsylvania State University Press, 1999); Jonathan Scott, *Algernon Sidney and the Restoration Crisis, 1677–1683* (Cambridge: Cambridge University Press, 1991); Tim Harris, *Politics under the Later Stuarts: Party Conflict in a Divided Society, 1660–1715* (London: Longman, 1993), 80–82.

5. J. R. Jones, *Country and Court: England, 1658–1714* (Cambridge, MA: Harvard University Press, 1978), 219–220; Barry Coward, *The Stuart Age: England, 1603–1714*, 2nd ed. (London: Longman, 1994), 334; Harris, *Restoration*, chap. 5; Paul D. Halliday, *Dismembering the Body Politic: Partisan Politics in England's Towns, 1650–1730* (Cambridge and New York: Cambridge University Press, 1998), chap. 6; Ann M. Carlos and Jamie Brown Kruse, "The Decline of the Royal African Company: Fringe Firms and the Role of the Charter," *Economic History Review* 49, no. 2 (1996): 310.

6. Ralph Paul Bieber, *The Lords of Trade and Plantations, 1675–1696* (Allentown, PA: H. Ray Haas, 1919), 25; Thornton, *West-India Policy*, 188–189; Philip S. Haffenden, "The Crown and the Colonial Charters, 1675–1688: Part I," *William and Mary Quarterly*, 3rd ser., 15, no. 3 (July 1958): 300–301; Stephen Saunders Webb, *The Governors-General: The English Army and the Definition of the Empire, 1569–1681* (Chapel Hill: University of North Carolina Press, 1979), 283; Miller, *Popery and Politics*, 172; Harris, *Restoration*, 171–183; Knights, *Politics and Opinion*, 27–28, 193–199; De Krey, *Restoration and Revolution*, 152–153.

7. William Freeman to William Stapleton, 9 December 1678, 10 March 1678/9, 24 April 1679, 6 June 1679, 19 December 1679, in *Letters of William Freeman, London Merchant, 1678–1685*, ed. David Hancock (London: London Record Society, 2002), 49, 72, 84–85, 88, 136. For more on Wheeler, see Natalie Zacek, *Settler Society in the English Leeward Islands, 1670–1776* (New York: Cambridge University Press, 2010), 45; Richard S. Dunn, *Sugar and Slaves: The Rise of the Planter Class in the English West Indies, 1624–1713* (Chapel Hill: University of North Carolina Press, 1972), 124.

8. Edward Raymond Turner, "The Privy Council of 1679," *English Historical Review* 30, (1915): 251–270; De Krey, *Restoration and Revolution*, 155; Harris, *Restoration*, 190;

Lords of Trade to the Governor and Council of Jamaica, 14 January 1679/80, TNA, CO 138/3, pp. 353–355.

9. K. G. Davies, *The Royal African Company* (London: Longmans, Green, 1957), 106–108; Royal African Company Court of Assistants records, 8–28 May 1679, TNA, T (Treasury) 70/78, fols. 82–87; *Journal of the House of Commons*, vol. 9, 28 April 1679, http://british-history.ac.uk/report.aspx?compid=27761#s8 (accessed 18 October 2013); *Journal of the House of Commons*, vol. 9, 17 May 1679, http://british-history.ac.uk/report.aspx?compid=27779#s7 (accessed 18 October 2013); *Journal of the House of Commons*, vol. 9, 27 May 1679, http://www.british-history.ac.uk/report.aspx?compid=27787 (accessed 21 June 2010); William Freeman to Henry Carpenter and Robert Helme, 14 September 1679, *Letters of William Freeman*, 121–122; Atkins to the Lords of Trade, 26 October 1680, TNA, CO 29/3, fols. 45–50; Blathwayt to Joseph Crisp, 23 October 1680, *Blathwayt Papers*, vol. 39, folder 1, Leeward Islands; Blathwayt to William Stapleton, 22 October 1680, *Blathwayt Papers*, vol. 37, folder 3, Leeward Islands.

10. *Certain Considerations Relating to the Royal African Company of England* (London, 1680), 1, 5, 6. For more on this pamphlet, see John Callow, *The Making of King James II: The Formative Years of a Fallen King* (Thrupp, Stroud, Gloucestershire, UK: Sutton Publishing, 2000), 255; Davies, *Royal African Company*, 107–108. The previous publication was *The Several Declarations of the Company of Royal Adventurers of England Trading into Africa* (London, 1667).

11. Witham to Blathwayt, 29 July 1680, *Blathwayt Papers*, vol. 35, folder 1, Barbados.

12. Blathwayt to the Earl of Carlisle, 9 July 1680, *Blathwayt Papers*, vol. 22, folder 3, Jamaica; Dunn, *Sugar and Slaves*, 86–87; Harlow, *History of Barbados*, 239. For an informative discussion of the 1680 census and what it revealed about Barbadian society, see Dunn, *Sugar and Slaves*, chap. 3.

13. Thornton, *West-India Policy*, 188–189; Bieber, *Lords of Trade*, 25. Underwood makes a compelling case that it was Atkins's failure to send information requested by the Lords of Trade that led to his recall. Underwood, "Ordering Knowledge," 243–244.

14. Carlisle to Coventry, 14 August 1678, *Coventry Papers of the Marquis of Bath at Longleat* (Washington, DC: American Council of Learned Societies, Library of Congress Photo Duplication Service), (*Coventry Papers*), microfilm, vol. 75, fol. 270; Carlisle to Coventry, 14 August 1678, TNA, CO 138/3, pp. 244–246; Bryan Edwards, ed., *The History, Civil and Commercial, of the British Colonies in the West Indies*, 2 vols. (London, 1794), 1:262–263; Carlisle to the Earl of Danby, 12 August 1678, BL Egerton 3340, fols. 177–178; Carlisle to Coventry, 11 September 1678, *Coventry Papers*, vol. 75, fol. 272; Carlisle to Coventry, 11 September 1678, CO 138/3, pp. 249–251; *Journals of the Assembly of Jamaica*, 13 September 1678 and 14 September 1678 (Wilmington, DE: Scholarly Resources, microfilm), 1:27–29.

15. Assembly of Jamaica to Carlisle, n.d., *Coventry Papers*, vol. 75, fol. 277; *Journals of the Assembly of Jamaica*, 4 October 1678, 1:36–37. For a similar interpretation regarding a petition from Virginia's House of Bugesses in 1684, see David S. Lovejoy, *Glorious Revolution in America*, rev. ed. (Middletown, CT: Wesleyan University Press, 1987), 66. For a discussion of "English liberties" in the colonies, see Carla Gardina Pestana, *The English Atlantic in an Age of Revolution, 1640–1661* (Cambridge, MA: Harvard University Press, 2004), 164–170.

16. Edward Rugemer, "The Development of Mastery and Race in the Comprehensive Slave Codes of the Greater Caribbean during the Seventeenth Century," *William and Mary Quarterly* 70, no. 3 (July 2013): 449–450; Dunn, *Sugar and Slaves*, 155, 169, 312, table 26; Richard Sheridan, *Sugar and Slavery: An Economic History of the British West Indies, 1623–1775* (Baltimore. MD: Johns Hopkins University Press, 1974), 212.

17. Carlisle to the Lords of Trade, 24 October 1678, TNA, CO 1/42, no. 136; Carlisle to the Lords of Trade, 15 November 1678, CO 1/42, no. 145; "A Journal kept by Colonel Beeston, from his first coming to Jamaica," in *Interesting Tracts, Relating to the Island of Jamaica* (Saint Jago de la Vega, Jamaica: Lewis, Lunan & Jones, 1800), 1 May 1679, 296; Webb, *Governors-General*, 283. After dissolving the session in late October, Carlisle arranged to send his secretary, Mr. Atkinson, to plead the colony's case in London. Atkinson died before departing, and in May 1679 Carlisle sent his associate Sir Francis Watson, the island's major general.

18. A number of historians have pointed out that there was a six-week delay from the time the Lords of Trade learned of the Jamaican assembly's recalcitrance in February and the beginning of the inquiry in April, and they have suggested that domestic issues were considered to be far more urgent than imperial problems at the time. Webb, *Governors-General*, 283; A. M. Whitson, *The Constitutional Development of Jamaica, 1660 to 1729* (Manchester, UK: Manchester University Press, 1929), 89; Thornton, *West-India Policy*, 190. I suggest that a six-week delay was hardly unusual for early modern administration, and the fact that during that time a new Privy Council and Lords of Trade were created, both of which had a direct impact on imperial policy and the direction of the Jamaican crisis, suggests that imperial affairs were hardly being ignored.

19. Report of the Lords of Trade, 28 May 1679, BL Add MS 12429, fols. 88a–92b; Edwards, *History, Civil and Commercial*, 1:273–278; *Acts of the Privy Council of England, Colonial Series* (Hereford, UK: Anthony Brothers for His Majesty's Stationery Office, 1908), 1:826–33. This scathing report was never endorsed by the entire committee, however, which has been interpreted as an indication of disagreement among members over its tone. Thornton, *West-India Policy*, 191–192.

20. Blathwayt to Carlisle, 31 May 1679, *Blathwayt Papers*, vol. 22, folder 1, Jamaica; Blathwayt to Carlisle, 2 October 1679, *Blathwayt Papers*, vol. 22, folder 2, Jamaica; Charles II to Carlisle, 31 May 1679, in *Calendar of State Papers Colonial: North America and the West Indies, 1574–1739* (CSPC), ed. Karen Ordahl Kuperman, John C. Appleby, and Mandy Banton, 45 vols. (London, 2000), CD-ROM, vol. 10, no. 1011; Lovejoy, *Glorious Revolution in America*, 56. On Blathwayt's attitude toward the royal prerogative in imperial administration, see Murison, "Talented Mr. Blathwayt," 34–39. For implications for other colonies, see Robert M. Bliss, *Revolution and Empire: English Politics and the American Colonies in the Seventeenth Century* (Manchester, UK: Manchester University Press, 1990), 185.

21. *Journals of the Assembly of Jamaica*, 28 August 1679, 1:46; "Journal kept by Colonel Beeston," 27 August 1679, 297; Edward Long, *History of Jamaica* (London, 1774), 1:199; Webb, *Governors-General*, 288–291; Carlisle to the Lords of Trade, 15 September 1679, TNA, CO 138/3, pp. 327–331; Edwards, *History, Civil and Commercial*, 1:281; Carlisle to Coventry, 15 September 1679, *Coventry Papers*, vol. 75, fols. 328–330; Carlisle to

Coventry, 15 September 1679, CO 138/3, pp. 331–338; Whitson, *Constitutional Development of Jamaica*, 95–96; Carlisle to Coventry, 18 February 1679, CO 138/3, pp. 288–290; Carlisle to Lords of Trade, 20 April 1679, CO 1/43, no. 48.

22. Long, a plantation owner and former Cromwellian soldier, had been in the colony since the late 1650s and had served in the assembly and council since Modyford's governorship. Beeston, a merchant, had also served in the assembly and council for over a decade. Webb presents Long, Beeston, and their allies as longtime opponents of "monarchical authority." Webb, *Governors-General*, 221–222. For more on Beeston, who was appointed governor in 1692, see Frank Cundall, *The Governors of Jamaica in the Seventeenth Century* (London: West India Committee, 1936), 143–165.

23. Petition of the Council and Assembly of Jamaica to the Duke of York, October 1679, TNA, CO 1/43, no. 148. For similar petitions, see Petition of the Barbados Council and Assembly to Charles II, n.d. (but ca. 1675), CO 1/66, no. 93I; Petition of Jamaica Merchants and Planters, received 20 January 1682/3, CO 1/51, no. 20; Petition of Jamaica Planters and Merchants, received 14 August 1683, CO 1/52, no. 55.

24. Trevor Burnard, "Who Bought Slaves in Early America? Purchasers of Slaves from the Royal African Company in Jamaica," *Slavery and Abolition* 17, no. 2 (Aug. 1996): 70, 77; *Journals of the Assembly of Jamaica*, 10 November 1679, 1:49; Carlisle to Coventry, 23 November 1679, *Coventry Papers*, vol. 75, fols. 336–337. Webb maintains the militia bill took precedence. Webb, *Governors-General*, 292.

25. Blathwayt to Carlisle, 22 December 1679, *Blathwayt Papers*, vol. 22, folder 2, Jamaica; Harris, *Restoration*, chap. 4; De Krey, *Restoration and Revolution*, 173–175. Carlisle claimed to have the king's "Verbal leave" and permission to depart, in a letter in April: Carlisle to the Lords of Trade, 23 April 1680, TNA, CO 138/3, pp. 400–403; Long, *History of Jamaica*, 201. Interestingly, in October 1680 the African Company issued congratulations to Carlisle on his safe return to England. Court of Assistants' Minute Books, 26 October 1680, T 70/78, pp. 222–223. Long and Beeston were accused of treason for having omitted the king's name from the 1675 revenue bill. Webb, *Governors-General*, 306–307. On Carlisle's decision to send Long to London, see Carlisle to Coventry, 23 November 1679, CO 138/3, pp. 369–373; for Carlisle's charges against Long, see CO 138/3, pp. 418–422.

26. Journal of the Lords of Trade, 12 October 1680, 14 October 1680, 18 October 1680, 21 October 1680, 27 October 1680, 28 October 1680, 30 October 1680, TNA, CO 391/3, pp. 212–213, 214–216, 217, 219–220, 220–221, 222–223, 223–224; Webb, *Governors-General*, 299–312; Edwards, *History, Civil and Commercial*, 1:309–319. Carlisle was urged to do his best to pass a perpetual revenue bill, but his private instructions indicated that a seven-year bill would be acceptable. Private Instructions to the Earl of Carlisle, 3 November 1680, CO 138/3, pp. 453–454; Royal Instructions to Lord Carlisle, 3 November 1680, CO 138/3, pp. 447–453. For the legal correspondence that does survive, see CO 138/3, pp. 375–377 (11 March 1679/80); 380–381 (27 April 1680); 396–397 (10 July 1680). For suggestions that the justices' opinions did not favor the Crown's position, see Bliss, *Revolution and Empire*, 186; Webb, *Governors-General*, 303–304; Robert C. Ritchie, *The Duke's Province: A Study of New York Politics and*

Society, 1664–1691 (Chapel Hill: University of North Carolina Press, 1977), 167; Whitson, *Constitutional Development of Jamaica*, 104–108.

27. Planters of Jamaica to the Lords of Trade, 4 November 1680, TNA, CO 268/1, pp. 81–87; Lords of Trade Meeting Minutes, CO 1/46, no. 32; Planters of Jamaica to the Lords of Trade, read 28 October 1680, CO 138/3, pp. 442–443. A week later, the Lords received another petition, which focused primarily on legal and constitutional issues. See "An humble motion in the behalfe of Jamaica," 12 November 1680, CO 1/46, no. 43. Webb focuses on this petition, and rightly points out that proposals contained therein were by and large rejected by the Lords of Trade. But he does not consider the petition from 4 November. Webb, *Governors-General*, 307–308.

28. Planters of Jamaica to the Lords of Trade, 4 November 1680, TNA, CO 268/1, pp. 81–87; Christopher L. Brown, "The Politics of Slavery," in *The British Atlantic World, 1500–1800*, ed. David Armitage and Michael J. Braddick (New York: Palgrave Macmillan, 2002), 220.

29. Journal of the Lords of Trade, 11 November 1680, 16 December 1680, TNA, CO 391/3, pp. 231–232, 239–241; Journal of the African Company's Court of Assistants, 6 November 1680, T 70/78, fol. 225; "Report touching some Proposals concerning Jamaica made by ye Merchants & Planters," 18 December 1680, CO 138/3, pp. 455–456.

30. Thomas Barker, Danzig, to [?], 18 December 1680, Edmund Poley Papers, James Marshall and Marie-Louise Osborn Collection, Beinecke Rare Book and Manuscript Library, Yale University, Osborn Manuscripts (OSB MSS) 1, folder 2; Harris, *Restoration*, 148, 171; Knights, *Politics and Opinion*, 80–84; Callow, *Making of King James II*, 283; Davies, *Royal African Company*, 103. York had been first sent to Edinburgh in October 1679. On York's political weakness at this time in relation to governing his colony of New York, see Ritchie, *Duke's Province*, 164.

31. Haffenden notes that an initial campaign against the charter of the Massachusetts Bay Colony was dropped at this time for similar reasons. Haffenden, "Crown and Colonial Charters, Part I," 303; Webb, *Governors-General*, 301.

32. Jones, *Country and Court*, 219–220; Harris, *Restoration*, chap. 5, pp. 293, 323; De Krey, *Restoration and Revolution*, 202–210; Grant Tapsell, *The Personal Rule of Charles II, 1681–85* (Woodbridge, Suffolk, UK: Boydell Press, 2007), 62.

33. Halliday, *Dismembering the Body Politic*, esp. chap. 6; Richard Johnson, *Adjustment to Empire: The New England Colonies, 1675–1715* (New Brunswick, NJ: Rutgers University Press, 1981), 28–29, 56; Tapsell, *Personal Rule*, 10.

34. Lovejoy, *Glorious Revolution in America*, 63; Thornton, *West-India Policy*, 210; Bieber, *Lords of Trade*, 32–35.

35. Bliss, *Revolution and Empire*, 221; Murison, "Talented Mr. Blathwayt," 34–35, 39; Stephen Saunders Webb, "William Blathwayt, Imperial Fixer: From Popish Plot to Glorious Revolution," *William and Mary Quarterly*, 3rd ser., 25, no. 1 (Jan. 1968): 3–21; Thornton, *West-India Policy*, 204. For Blathwayt as auditor general, see William Blathwayt Papers, James Marshall and Marie-Louise Osborn Collection, Beinecke Library: Thomas Martyn, Port Royal, to the Lords of Trade, 10 November 1680, box 6, folder 123; Nathaniel Bacon, Virginia, to Blathwayt, 10 July 1683, box 1, folder 6; Thomas Ryves, Port Royal, to Blathwayt, 25 September 1686, box 8, folder 164; Ryves to Blathwayt,

12 March 1686, box 8, folder 164; Henry Brograve, Antigua, to Blathwayt, 15 July 1685, box 2, folder 47; Warrant to Edward Randolph, February 1691, box 1, folder 26.

36. Stephen Saunders Webb, *1676: The End of American Independence* (New York: Knopf, 1984), 173–182; Philip S. Haffenden, "The Crown and the Colonial Charters, 1675–1688, Part II," *William and Mary Quarterly*, 3rd ser., 15, no. 4 (Oct. 1958): 452; Callow, *Making of King James II*, 271–282; Bliss, *Revolution and Empire*, chap. 9; Steve Pincus, *1688: The First Modern Revolution* (New Haven, CT: Yale University Press, 2009), 155.

37. Lords of Trade Meeting Minutes, 3 March 1684/5, TNA, CO 391/5, pp. 101–102; Johnson, *Adjustment to Empire* 52–56; Bliss, *Revolution and Empire*, 233–236; Lovejoy, *Glorious Revolution in America*, 67–69, 171–172; Ritchie, *Duke's Province*, 167, 178. Contrast Ritchie's interpretation with Callow, *Making of King James II*, 271–272.

38. Circular letter of James II, 4 July 1685, TNA, CO 138/5, pp. 80–83; Dunn, *Sugar and Slaves*, 101; Molesworth to Blathwayt, 29 August 1685, CO 1/58, no. 44; Barbados Assembly to Blathwayt, 16 September 1685, CO 31/3, pp. 131–133; Deputy-Governor, Council, and Assembly of Barbados to the Lords of Trade, 14 September 1685, CO 1/58, nos. 56, 56I; "A Moderate calculation of the annual charge and produce of a Plantation in Barbados," 14 September 1685, BL Sloane 3924, fols. 214–217; Edwyn Stede to the Lords of Trade, 10 March 1687/8, CO 1/64, no. 33; "The Address of the Barbados Assembly & Council to the King," 14 February 1687/8, BL Sloane 3924, fols. 223–224, and CO 1/64, no. 33III.

39. Haffenden, "Crown and Colonial Charters, Part II," 465; "Proposal for a South American Company," BL Sloane 3984, fols. 210–211v; "An Essay of the Interest of the Crown in American Plantations & Trade computed about the year 1685," BL Add MS 47131, fols. 22–28. Colonial planters and officials were aware of and uneasy about the plan: Edwyn Stede to the Lords of Trade, 19 October 1687, TNA, CO 1/63, no. 45.

40. "An Essay of the Interest of the Crown in American Plantations & Trade computed about the year 1685," BL Add MS 47131, fols. 22–28; William Blathwayt's Reflections on a Paper Concerning America, ca. 1685, Blathwayt Papers, Huntington Library, San Marino, CA, box 2, BL 416.

41. David Eltis, "The British Transatlantic Slave Trade before 1714: Annual Estimates of Volume and Direction," in *The Lesser Antilles in the Age of European Expansion*, ed. Robert L. Paquette and Stanley L. Engerman (Gainesville: University Press of Florida, 1996), 183, and table 10–1; Ann M. Carlos and Jamie Brown Kruse, "The Decline of the Royal African Company: Fringe Firms and the Role of the Charter," *Economic History Review* 49, no. 2 (1996): 293, 310; Callow, *Making of King James II*, 252; W. R. Scott, *The Constitution and Finance of English, Scottish and Irish Joint-Stock Companies to 1720* (Cambridge: Cambridge University Press, 1910), 2:21.

42. Stapleton to the Lords of Trade, 1 July 1680, TNA, CO 1/45, no. 33; "Part of a letter to the Royal Company from their factors at Nevis," 16 July 1680, CO 1/45, no. 57; Lynch to the Lords of Trade, 29 August 1682, CO 138/4, pp. 78–91; Blathwayt to the Attorney General, 18 January 1682/3, CO 138/4, p. 104; Opinion of Attorney General Sawyer, 23 January 1682/3, CO 138/4, p. 106.

43. Blocking interloping ships before they had left England was a new strategy adopted by both the East India and African Companies during the 1680s. Christopher Jeaffreson to

Edward Thorn, 1 March 1682/3, in *A Young Squire of the Seventeenth Century: Christopher Jeaffreson*, 2 vols., ed. John Cordy Jeaffreson (London: Hurst & Blackett, 1878), 2:36–39.

44. "*East India Company v. Sandys*," in *A Complete Collection of State Trials*, compiler T. B. Howell, vol. 10 (London: T. C. Hansard, 1816), 532–535; Philip J. Stern, *The Company-State: Corporate Sovereignty and the Early Modern Foundations of the British Empire in India* (New York: Oxford University Press, 2011), 46–58; Petition of the Royal African Company to James II, 18 October 1686, TNA, T 70/169, pp. 73–75; Instructions to Sir Nathaniel Johnson, 28 November 1686, CO 153/3, pp. 225–226; Instructions to the Duke of Albemarle, 15 March 1687, CO 138/5, p. 281; Royal Instructions to Lieutenant-Governor Stede, 5 December 1686, CO 29/3, pp. 395–396. On some of the imperial implications of the *Sandys* case, see Pincus, 1688, 376–381.

45. Instructions to Sir Thomas Lynch, 8 September 1681, TNA, CO 138/4, pp. 17–39; Sir Henry Morgan to Leoline Jenkins, 4 October 1681, CO 1/47, no. 67. To encourage Lynch's allegiance to its agenda, the company presented the governor with a parting gift "in plate to such value as hath been given other governors." African Company Court of Assistants, 13 September 1681, TNA, T 70/79, fol. 49v. It is unclear which "other governors" also received this kind of gift.

46. Lynch's speech to the Assembly of Jamaica, 21 September 1682, TNA, CO 1/49, no. 59; *Journals of the Assembly of Jamaica*, 21 September 1682, 58–59; Lynch to the Lords of Trade, 29 September 1682, CO 138/4, pp. 92–96; Lynch to the Lords of Trade, 8 October 1682, CO 138/4, pp. 96–98; Lynch to the Lords of Trade, 29 August 1682, CO 138/ 4, pp. 78–91; Sir Henry Morgan to Leoline Jenkins, 2 July 1681, CO 1/47, no. 25.

47. Council and Assembly of Jamaica's Address to the King, 6 October 1682, TNA, CO 138/4, pp. 99–101; Lynch's Speech Proroguing the Jamaica Assembly, 7 October 1682, CO 1/49, no. 77; Lynch to the Lords of Trade, 29 September 1682, CO 138/4, pp. 92–96. The key speeches and addresses of this episode were published in *A Narrative of Affairs lately Received from his Majesties Island of Jamaica* (London, 1683), which is included in the colonial state papers, CO 1/49, no. 78.

48. Petition of the Royal African Company to Charles II, 12 January 1682/3, TNA, CO 138/4, pp. 102–103; Blathwayt to Lynch, 5 March 1682/3, *Blathwayt Papers*, vol. 23, folder 4, Jamaica. The response of the planters and merchants can be found at CO 1/51, no. 20.

49. Petition of Jamaica Merchants and Planters to the Lords of Trade, August 1683, TNA, CO 268/1, pp. 94–95; Lynch to Blathwayt, 15 April 1683, 26 April 1683, 5 June 1683, 9 June 1683, *Blathwayt Papers*, vol. 24, folder 1, Jamaica; Lynch to Blathwayt, 23 July 1683, *Blathwayt Papers*, vol. 24, folder 2, Jamaica; Lords of Trade Meeting Minutes, 14 February 1682/3, CO 391/4, pp. 122–124.

50. Lynch to Blathwayt, 23 July 1683, *Blathwayt Papers*, vol. 24, folder 2, Jamaica; Petition of the Merchants and Planters of Jamaica to the Lords of Trade, 3 October 1683, TNA, CO 1/53, no. 2; Petition of the African Company to the Lords of Trade, 23 October 1683, CO 1/53, no. 19; Lords of Trade Meeting Minutes, 30 October 1683, CO 391/4, pp. 226–227; Draft of "An Act for the incouragement of the Royal African Company of England to import Negros into his Majesty's island of Jamaica," 14 November 1683, CO 1/53, no. 52; Lords of Trade Meeting Minutes, 13 May 1684, CO 391/4, pp. 292–293; Order of the King-in-Council, 15 May 1684, CO 268/1, pp. 116–117; Charles II to Lynch,

1 June 1684, CO 389/9, pp. 194–95; Draft of the "Act Concerning Negroes," 1 June 1684, CO 389/9, pp. 196–200.

51. Lynch to the Lords of Trade, 28 February 1683/4, TNA, CO 1/54, no. 41; Lynch to Blathwayt, 25 February 1683/4, *Blathwayt Papers*, vol. 24, folder 4, Jamaica; Lynch to the Lords of Trade, 29 August 1682, CO 138/4, pp. 78–91; Lynch to the Lords of Trade, 29 September 1682, CO 1/49, no. 66; CO 138/4 pp. 92–96; Lynch to Blathwayt, 21 October 1683, *Blathwayt Papers*, vol. 24, folder 3, Jamaica; Lynch to Blathwayt, 15 April 1683, *Blathwayt Papers*, vol. 24, folder 1, Jamaica; Lynch to the Lords of Trade, 6 May 1683, CO 1/51, no. 106.

52. Matthew Meverell to the Lords of Trade, 9 May 1684, TNA, CO 138/4, pp. 262–263; Lynch to the Lord President, Earl Radnor, 20 June 1684, CO 1/54, no. 132; Lynch to Blathwayt, 20 June 1684, *Blathwayt Papers*, vol. 24, folder 6, Jamaica. Morgan was removed from office after he allowed four Spanish ships that had been captured by the Elector of Brandenburg's ships in the region to be condemned and sold in Jamaica, triggering a diplomatic mess. Blathwayt to Edmund Poley, 5 April 1681; and Earl of Conway to Poley, 12 April 1681, Edmund Poley Papers, Beinecke Library, OSB MSS 1, folder 8; Conway to Poley, 6 September 1681, Edmund Poley Papers, Beinecke Library, OSB MSS 1, folder 13; Conway to Poley, 22 November 1681, Edmund Poley Papers, Beinecke Library, OSB MSS 1, folder 15; "Representation of Sir Henry Morgan," 1682, CO 1/56, no. 145; Revocation of Morgan's Commission, 7 September 1681, CO 389/8, p. 88; Order of the King-in-Council, 14 October 1681, CO 1/47, no. 75.

53. Molesworth to Blathwayt, 25 September 1685, TNA, CO 138/5, pp. 103–112; Molesworth to Blathwayt, 15 November 1684, CO 1/56, no. 75; Molesworth, Charles Penhallow, & Walter Rudding to the African Company, 7 April 1684, T 70/16, fol. 79; Molesworth to Blathwayt, 19 September 1684, *Blathwayt Papers*, vol. 25, folder 1, Jamaica; Molesworth to Blathwayt, 3 February 1684/5, *Blathwayt Papers*, vol. 25, folder 2, Jamaica; Molesworth to Blathwayt, 16 January 1685/6, CO 138/5, pp. 128–139; Molesworth to Blathwayt, 3 February 1684/5, *Blathwayt Papers*, vol. 25, folder 2, Jamaica; Molesworth to Sunderland, 15 March 1684/5, CO 138/5, pp. 34–37; Molesworth to Sunderland, 24 April 1685, CO 1/57, no. 100; Molesworth to Blathwayt, 6 July 1685, CO 138/5, pp. 71–77; Journal of the Council of Jamaica, 23 March, 1684/5, CO 140/4, pp. 72–74; Molesworth to the Lords of Trade, 24 March 1684/5, CO 138/5, pp. 42–48. For Molesworth's connections to the *asiento*, see Lynch to the Lords of Trade, 28 February 1683/4, CO 138/4, pp. 236–255; Dunn, *Sugar and Slaves*, 160; Cundall, *Governors of Jamaica*, 95–96; Nuala Zahedieh, "Regulation, Rent-seeking, and the Glorious Revolution in the English Atlantic Economy," *Economic History Review* 63, no. 4 (2010): 878–879.

54. Molesworth to Blathwayt, 25 September 1685, TNA, CO 138/5, pp. 103–112; Molesworth to Sunderland, 28 April 1686, CO 1/59, no. 63; Molesworth to Blathwayt, 2 November 1685, *Blathwayt Papers*, vol. 25, folder 2, Jamaica; Molesworth to Blathwayt, 27 November 1685, CO 138/5, pp. 119–121; Molesworth to Blathwayt, 17 July 1686, CO 138/5, pp. 171–175.

55. Molesworth to Blathwayt, 29 August 1685, TNA, CO 138/5, pp. 87–102; Molesworth to Blathwayt, 25 March 1686, *Blathwayt Papers*, vol. 25, folder 3, Jamaica; Molesworth's

Speech to the Assembly, 1 June 1686, CO 1/59, no. 96; "Colonel Molesworth's Speech to the Assembly of Jamaica," in *Interesting Tracts Relating to the Island of Jamaica*, pp. 200–204; Molesworth to Blathwayt, 15 June 1686, CO 138/5, pp. 158–161; Molesworth to Blathwayt, 15 June 1686, *Blathwayt Papers*, vol. 25, folder 4, Jamaica; Molesworth to Blathwayt, 17 July 1686, CO 138/5 pp. 171–175. For accounts of some of the bloodier episodes of the uprising, see Molesworth to Blathwayt, 16 February 1686, *Blathwayt Papers*, vol. 25, folder 3, Jamaica; Molesworth to Blathwayt, 12 March 1687, *Blathwayt Papers*, vol. 25, folder 5, Jamaica.

56. Molesworth to Blathwayt, 5 July 1686, TNA, CO 138/5, pp. 161–167; Molesworth to the Lords of Trade, 5 November 1686, CO 1/60, no. 98; Molesworth's Speech to the Assembly, 24 September 1686, CO 1/60, no. 56; Molesworth to Blathwayt, 31 August 1686, CO 138/5, pp. 191–196; Molesworth to Blathwayt, 28 September 1686, CO 138/5, pp. 185–191; Molesworth to Blathwayt, 16 June 1687 and 24 June 1687, *Blathwayt Papers*, vol. 25, folder 5, Jamaica. In early 1685 the king had announced Sir Philip Howard would be the new governor in chief of Jamaica. But Howard died in April 1685 before leaving England, leaving Molesworth's status even more uncertain. Molesworth felt that news of his pending replacement had rendered him powerless in the face of the assembly's obstructions. Molesworth to [?], 15 June 1686, CO 138/5, pp. 158–161.

57. Tapsell, *Personal Rule*, 198; Webb, *Governors-General*, 470–471; Dunn, *Sugar and Slaves*, 100; Harlow, *History of Barbados*, 244; Dutton to Jenkins, 14 June 1681, TNA, CO 29/3, pp. 72–75; Dutton to Blathwayt, 14 June 1681, *Blathwayt Papers*, vol. 30, folder 2, Barbados.

58. Harris, *Restoration*, 323; "A general view of the affairs of the Island of Barbados, by John Witham, Deputy Governor," 6 August 1683, TNA, CO 1/52, no. 48; Witham to the Lords of Trade, 31 October 1683, CO 1/53, no. 30; Blathwayt to Dutton, 22 August 1681, *Blathwayt Papers*, vol. 30, folder 2, Barbados; Dutton to Jenkins, 2 February 1681/2, TNA, CO 1/48, no. 19; Dunn, *Sugar and Slaves*, 100; Harlow, *History of Barbados*, 241–267.

59. Lynch to the Lords of Trade, 2 November 1683, TNA, CO 138/4, pp. 180–192; Lynch's Speech Proroguing the Assembly, 19 October 1683, CO 138/4, pp. 194–201; Lynch to Jenkins, March 1683/4, CO 1/54, no. 46; Bliss, *Revolution and Empire*, 230.

60. Verdict of the Coroner's Jury, 10 September 1679, TNA, CO 1/54, no. 73XIX; Copy of Proceedings at the Admiralty Court at Nevis, 12 July 1680, CO 1/45, no. 45. The depositions can be found in CO 1/54, no. 73IV–XVIII.

61. The company had agents stationed only at Nevis, much to the consternation of the other islands, and only delivered approximately five thousand slaves to the colony from 1672 to 1679. Zacek, *Settler Society in the English Leeward Islands*, 57; Eltis, "British Transatlantic Slave Trade," table 10–1, 198. Total calculation is mine.

62. Council of Montserrat to the Lords of Trade, 13 July 1680, TNA, CO 153/2, pp. 434–437; Council of St. Christopher to the Lords of Trade, 12 June 1680, CO 153/2, pp. 444–452; "Part of a letter to the Royal Company from their factors at Nevis dated 16 July 1680," CO 1/45, no. 57; Stapleton to the Lords of Trade, 1 July 1680, TNA, CO 1/45, no. 33.

63. Stapleton to Blathwayt, 7 June 1682, TNA, CO 153/3, p. 42. An investigation determined that the company had promised Billop "a fourth part" of the seized slave cargo

"for encouragement" to pursue interlopers, but he and his crew proceeded to take all they could. Stapleton to the Lords of Trade, 18 June 1682, CO 153/3, pp. 45–48; Governor and Council of Nevis to the Lords of Trade, 6 July 1682, CO 153/3, pp. 53–54; Freeman to Stapleton, 26 November 1682, *Letters of William Freeman*, 316; Christopher Jeaffreson to Edward Thorn, 1 March 1682/3, in *Young Squire*, 2:36–39.

64. Freeman to Stapleton, 14 September 1682 and 27 September 1682, *Letters of William Freeman*, 295–296, 304; Blathwayt to Stapleton, 29 September 1682, *Blathwayt Papers*, vol. 37, folder 3, Leeward Islands; Murison, "Talented Mr. Blathwayt," 39; Stapleton to the Lords of Trade, 20 December 1682, TNA, CO 153/3, pp. 80–83; Report of the King's Attorney & Advocate General, 5 June 1683, CO 153/3, p. 96; Jeaffreson to Phipps, 12 February 1683/4, in *Young Squire*, 2:99; Jeaffreson to Hill, 10 March 1683/4, in *Young Squire*, 2:111–112. Stapleton remained in office until he voluntarily left for England in 1685.

65. Stede to Blathwayt, 16 May 1687, *Blathwayt Papers*, vol. 32, folder 3, Barbados; Stede to Blathwayt, 23 July 1687, *Blathwayt Papers*, vol. 32, folder 3, Barbados; Stede to Blathwayt, 16 March 1688/89, *Blathwayt Papers*, vol. 32, folder 5, Barbados; Dunn, *Sugar and Slaves*, 101.

66. Lord President to the Lords of Trade, 7 August 1686, TNA, CO 153/3, p. 200; Dunn, *Sugar and Slaves*, 133; Petition of Nicholas Lynch to Johnson, 23 November 1687, CO 1/63, no. 70; Johnson to the Lords of Trade, 3 March 1688, CO 153/3, pp. 302–317; Instructions to Sir Nathaniel Johnson, 28 November 1686, CO 153/3, pp. 225–226; Petition of the Royal African Company to the Lords of Trade, April 1687, CO 1/62, no. 33; Royal African Company agents in Nevis to the Company, 9 July 1686, CO 1/59, no. 132; Johnson to the Lords of Trade, 2 June 1688, CO 1/64, no. 71; Lords of Trade to Johnson, 18 June 1687, CO 153/3, pp. 264–265; Privy Council to Johnson, 30 July 1687, CO 153/3, p. 271.

67. Capt. Loe's Information on the State of Nevis, 19 July 1687, TNA, CO 1/62, no. 92; Johnson to the Lords of Trade, 2 June 1688, CO 1/64, no. 71; Pincus, *1688*, 154–155; Johnson to the Lords of Trade, 3 March 1688, CO 153/3, pp. 302–317; Representation of Col. Edward Powell, Lieutenant Governor of Antigua, read 8 February 1688, CO 153/3, pp. 288–289; Deputy Governor John Netheway of Nevis, June 27, 1689, CO 153/3, pp. 427–431; K. G. Davies, "The Revolutions in America," in *The Revolutions of 1688: The Andrew Browning Lectures 1988*, ed. Robert Beddard (Oxford: Clarendon Press, 1991), 251–252; Dunn, *Sugar and Slaves*, 133–134. Johnson became governor of South Carolina in 1710.

68. Webb, *Governors-General*, 480; Dunn, *Sugar and Slaves*, 160. In her "pindarick" to Albemarle written on the occasion of his appointment, Aphra Behn noted that in accepting the post, Albemarle "breaks the Lazy Chains." Aphra Behn, *To the Most Illustrious Prince Christopher, Duke of Albemarle, on his Voyage to his Government of Jamaica* (London, 1687), 3.

69. Haffenden, "Crown and Colonial Charters, Part II," 465; Christopher Jeaffreson to Col. Hill, n.d. but 1686, in *Young Squire*, 2:280; William Bridgeman to Sir Richard Bulstrode, 16 April 1686, Harry Ransom Center, University of Texas at Austin, MS 1416. Many thanks to Brent Sirota for this reference.

70. Commission to the Duke of Albemarle, [November?] 1686, TNA, CO 138/5, pp. 220–241; King's Order to Albemarle, July 1687, CO 138/5, pp. 333–334; *Jamaica in 1687: The Taylor Manuscript at the National Library of Jamaica*, ed. David Buisseret (Kingston, Jamaica: University of the West Indies Press, 2010), 298–299; Albemarle to the Lords of Trade, 19 December 1687, CO 138/6, pp. 74–80; Instructions to the Duke of Albemarle, 15 March 1686/7, CO 138/5, pp. 261–296.

71. "A List of the Council of Jamaica, as desired by the Duke of Albemarle," 20 October 1686, TNA, CO 1/60, no. 76; "A Memorandum concerning the D. of Albemarl's Dispatch," read 24 October 1686, CO 138/5, pp. 246–247. Albemarle reiterated his request after arriving, and the Lords of Trade agreed to reappoint Morgan in April 1688. Albemarle to the Lords of Trade, 19 December 1687, CO 138/6, pp. 74–80; Albemarle to Blathwayt, 11 February 1687/8, *Blathwayt Papers*, vol. 21, folder 1, Jamaica; Minutes of the Lords of Trade, 10 April 1688, *CSPC*, vol. 12, no. 1694; Governor Sir Robert Robinson, Bermuda, to Sunderland, 10 August 1687, *CSPC*, vol. 12, no. 1385; Affidavit of the Mariners of the Sloop *Anne*, Barbados, 22 October 1687, *CSPC*, vol. 12, no. 1471; Nathaniel Johnson to the Lords of Trade, 20 February 1688, CO 153/3, pp. 296–300; Proclamation of Molesworth, 27 July 1687, CO 1/62, no. 86; "Circular Letter touching the Lord High Admiral's Moiety of Wrecks," 22 October 1687, CO 138/6, pp. 47–49.

72. Zahedieh, "Regulation, Rent-seeking," 880; Minutes of the Council of Jamaica, 17 November 1687, TNA, CO 1/63, no. 68; Molesworth to Blathwayt, 7 December 1687, CO 138/6, pp. 68–74; Albemarle to the Lords of Trade, 11 February 1688, CO 138/6, pp. 83–87; "Copy of recognizances taken from Masters of vessels going to the wreck," 31 January 1688, CO 1/64, no. 14; Molesworth to the Lords of the Treasury, 28 February 1688, CO 1/64, nos. 26 and 26I; Albemarle to the Lords of Trade, 6 March 1688, CO 1/64, no. 30; Molesworth to the Lords of the Treasury, 30 April 1688, CO 1/64, no. 56; Albemarle to the Lords of Trade, 11 May 1688, CO 138/6, pp. 118–122; Proclamation of the Duke of Albemarle, 4 June 1688, CO 1/65, no. 1; Albemarle to the Lords of Trade, 6 June 1688, CO 1/65, no. 2; Order of the Duke of Albemarle, 7 June 1688, CO 1/65, no. 4.

73. Petition of the Royal African Company to the King, 3 July 1688, TNA, T 70/169, fol. 54v; Petition to King William III, 28 March 1689, T 70/169, fols. 57–58.

74. Albemarle to the Lords of Trade, 6 March 1688, TNA, CO 138/6, pp. 88–93; Col. John Bourden to the Lords of Trade, 7 March 1688, CO 138/6, pp. 102–104; Albemarle to the Lords of Trade, 16 April 1688, CO 138/6, pp. 109–116; "Samuel Barry's Petition to the King," in *Interesting Tracts Relating to Jamaica*, 212; Albemarle to the Lords of Trade, 8 August 1688, CO 1/65, no. 38; Albemarle to the Lords of Trade, 11 May 1688, CO 138/6, pp. 118–122; "Case of Smith Kelly, late Provost Marshal of Jamaica," [May] 1688, CO 1/64, no. 65; "Memoriall of the African Company," [19 July 1688], CO 1/65, no. 26; Pincus, 1688, 156–159.

75. Albemarle to the Lords of Trade, 16 April 1688, TNA, CO 138/6, pp. 109–116; Deposition of Richard Swanson, 7 July 1688, CO 1/65, no. 38v; Deposition of Thomas Waite, Provost Marshal, 7 July 1688, CO 1/65, no. 38viii; Report of Sir Richard Derham, n.d., CO 1/65, no. 38xiv; "List of Persons fined together with the fines sett on them in his Maties Surpream Court," August 1688, CO 1/65, no. 45; Albemarle to the Lords of Trade, 8 August 1688, CO 1/65, no. 38; Albemarle's Speech to the Assembly, 20 July

1688, CO 1/65, no. 29; Albemarle to the Lords of Trade, 8 August 1688, CO 138/6, pp. 139–143; "Speech of the Speaker of the Assembly of Jamaica," 20 July 1688, CO 1/65, no. 30.

76. Petition of Hender Molesworth to the King, 12 October 1688, TNA, CO 1/65, no. 68A; Order of the King-in-Council, 12 October 1688, CO 1/65, no. 70; Petition of Charles Sadler, read 12 October 1688, CO 1/ 65, no. 70I; "Memoriall of the African Company," [19 July 1688], CO 1/65, no. 26; James II to Albemarle, 4 September 1688, CO 138/6, pp. 129–132; Minutes of the Council of Jamaica, 29 November 1688, *CSPC*, vol. 12, no. 1939; Dunn, *Sugar and Slaves*, 161; Petition of Planters and Merchants trading to Jamaica to the King, November 1688, CO 1/65, no. 87; Petition to King William III, 28 March 1689, T 70/169, fols. 57–58; Petition of the Royal African Company to the Lords of Trade, received 23 August 1689, CO 137/2, no. 22; Order of the King-in-Council, 1 December 1688, CO 138/6, p. 145.

77. James II to Stede, 16 October 1688, TNA, CO 29/4, pp. 2–3; J. Mackleburne to Sir Thomas Montgomery, Attorney General of Barbados, 7 February 1688/89, CO 28/1, no. 2.

6. THE 1690S

1. Sir Robert Southwell to the Earl of Nottingham, 23 March 1688/9, Blathwayt Papers, Huntington Library, San Marino, CA, box 3, BL 418; Toby Burnard, "Southwell, Sir Robert (1635–1702)," in *Oxford Dictionary of National Biography* (ODNB)(Oxford: Oxford University Press, 2004), http://www.oxforddnb.com/view/article/26066 (accessed 2 May 2007).

2. Southwell to Nottingham, 23 March 1688/9, Blathwayt Papers, Huntington Library, box 3, BL 418.

3. G. C. Gibbs, "The Revolution in Foreign Policy," in *Britain after the Glorious Revolution, 1689–1714*, ed. Geoffrey Holmes (London: Macmillan, 1969), 57–79; Steve Pincus, *1688: The First Modern Revolution* (New Haven, CT: Yale University Press, 2009), chap. 11; Richard R. Johnson, "The Revolution of 1688–9 in the American Colonies," in *The Anglo-Dutch Moment: Essays on the Glorious Revolution and Its World Impact*, ed. Jonathan I. Israel (Cambridge: Cambridge University Press, 1991), 230; Stephen Saunders Webb, "William Blathwayt, Imperial Fixer: Muddling through to Empire, 1689–1717," *William and Mary Quarterly*, 3rd ser., 26, no. 3 (July 1969): 373–415; I. K. Steele, *Politics of Colonial Policy: The Board of Trade in Colonial Administration 1696–1720* (Oxford: Clarendon Press, 1968), chap. 4.

4. Philip J. Stern, *The Company-State: Corporate Sovereignty and the Early Modern Foundations of the British Empire in India* (New York: Oxford University Press, 2011), 145; Alison Gilbert Olson, *Making the Empire Work: London and American Interest Groups, 1690–1790* (Cambridge, MA: Harvard University Press, 1992), 9–11, chap. 3; William A. Pettigrew, "Free to Enslave: Politics and the Escalation of Britain's Transatlantic Slave Trade, 1688–1714," *William and Mary Quarterly*, 3rd ser., 64, no. 1 (Jan. 2007): 3–38; Tim Keirn, "Monopoly, Economic Thought, and the Royal African Company," in *Early Modern Conceptions of Property*, ed. John Brewer and Susan Staves (London: Routledge, 1995), 427–466.

5. These are the principal arguments of George L. Cherry, "The Development of the English Free-Trade Movement in Parliament, 1689–1702," *Journal of Modern History* 25, no. 2 (June 1953): 103–119; Keirn, "Monopoly, Economic Thought"; and Pettigrew, "Free to Enslave."

6. Gary S. De Krey, *A Fractured Society: The Politics of London in the First Age of Party, 1688–1715* (Oxford: Clarendon Press, 1985), 192–193; Craig Rose, *England in the 1690s: Revolution, Religion and War* (Oxford: Blackwell, 1999), 122–130.

7. On the impact of the Glorious Revolution in the American colonies, see David S. Lovejoy, *The Glorious Revolution in America*, rev. ed. (Middletown, CT: Wesleyan University Press, 1987); K. G. Davies, "The Revolutions in America," in *Revolutions of 1688: The Andrew Browning Lectures 1988*, ed. Robert Beddard (Oxford: Clarendon Press, 1991), 246–270; Johnson, "Revolution of 1688–9," 215–240; Jack P. Greene, *Negotiated Authorities: Essays in Colonial Political and Constitutional History* (Charlottesville, VA: University Press of Virginia, 1994), chap. 4; Richard S. Dunn, "The Glorious Revolution and America," in *Oxford History of the British Empire*, vol. 1, *Origins of Empire*, ed. Nicholas Canny (Oxford: Oxford University Press, 1998), 445–466.

8. K. G. Davies, *The Royal African Company* (London: Longmans, Green, 1957), 122–151; David Galenson, *Traders, Planters, and Slaves: Market Behavior in Early English America* (Cambridge: Cambridge University Press, 1986), 148–150; Ann M. Carlos and Jamie Brown Kruse, "The Decline of the Royal African Company: Fringe Firms and the Role of the Charter," *Economic History Review* 49, no. 2 (1996): 293; Pettigrew, "Free to Enslave," 11; W. Darrell Stump, "An Economic Consequence of 1688," *Albion* 6, no. 1 (Spring 1974): 28–29.

9. *Nightingale and others against Bridges, Michaelmas Term, 1 Will & Mary, Roll 397*, in *Reports of the Cases Adjudged in the Court of King's Bench*, ed. Sir Bartholomew Shower (London: W. Clarke & Son, 1794), 131–139; Stump, "Economic Consequence," 28–32; James Bohun, "Protecting Prerogative: William III and the East India Trade Debate, 1689–1698," *Past Imperfect* 2 (1993): 66, 68; Pincus, *1688*, 385–386; Douglass C. North and Barry R. Weingast, "Constitutions and Commitment: The Evolution of Institutions Governing Public Choice in Seventeenth-Century England," *Journal of Economic History* 49, no. 4 (Dec. 1989): 803–832; Minute Book of the General Court of the Royal African Company, 15 January 1689/90, The National Archives (TNA), Treasury (T) 70/101, fols. 24–25; *Journals of the House of Commons*, 27 January 1689/90, 10:345, http://british-history.ac.uk/report.aspx?compid=28986#s8 (accessed 19 October 2013).

10. *Journals of the House of Commons*, 21 April 1690, 10:381–383; 22 April 1690, 10:383–385; 30 April 1690, 10:394–396, http://british-history.ac.uk/source.aspx?pubid=115&month=4&year=1690 (accessed 19 October 2013); 21 October 1690, 10:447–449; 22 October 1690, 10:449–450; 30 October 1690, 10:455–457, http://british-history.ac.uk/source.aspx?pubid=115&month=10&year=1690 (accessed 19 October 2013); 26 November 1690, 10:483–485, http://british-history.ac.uk/report.aspx?compid=29089#s3 (accessed 19 October 2013).

11. Davies, *Royal African Company*, 122–135; Keirn, "Monopoly, Economic Thought," 434; Pettigrew, "Free to Enslave," 12–13; W. R. Scott, *The Constitution and Finance of*

English, Scottish and Irish Joint-Stock Companies to 1720 (Cambridge: Cambridge University Press, 1910), 2:22; *Journals of the House of Commons*, 2 March 1694, 11:113–115, http://british-history.ac.uk/report.aspx?compid=38985 (accessed 19 October 2013).

12. Keirn, "Monopoly, Economic Thought," 428–429; Pettigrew, "Free to Enslave," 8, 10. These estimates are based on a comprehensive list gathered by Keirn in appendix II, 458–466.

13. *Considerations Humbly Offered To the Honourable House of Commons, by the Planters, in relation to the Bill to settle the Trade to Africa* (London, [1697?]); William Wilkinson, *Systema Africanum: or a Treatise, Discovering the Intrigues and Arbitrary Proceedings of the Guiney Company* (London, 1690), 7–8; D. T. [Dalby Thomas], *Considerations on the Trade of Africa, Humbly Offer'd to the Most Honourable House of Lords* (London, 1698), 1; *Reasons Humbly Offered in behalf of the Plantations, against the Bill for Settling the Trade to Affrica* (London, [1698?]); *Some Considerations: Humbly Offered to Demonstrate how prejudicial it would be to the English Plantations, Revenues of the Crown, the Navigation and general Good of this Kingdom, that the sole Trade for Negroes should be granted to a Company with a Joynt-Stock exclusive to all others* (London, [1698?]), 1; Keirn, "Monopoly, Economic Thought," 431; Pettigrew, "Free to Enslave," 25.

14. D. T. [Dalby Thomas], *Considerations on the Trade of Africa*, 2, 1; Gentleman in the city, *That the Trade to Affrica, is only Manageable by an Incorporated Company and a Joynt Stock* (London, [1690?]), 1; Keirn, "Monopoly, Economic Thought," 439.

15. *Considerations Concerning the African-Companies Petition* ([London], 1698); *Some Considerations Humbly Offered, against Granting the Sole Trade to Guiny from Cape Blanco to Cape Lopez, to a Company with a Joint Stock, exclusive of others* ([London], 1693), 1; Pettigrew, "Free to Enslave," 15–16; William A. Pettigrew, *Freedom's Debt: The Royal African Company and the Politics of the Atlantic Slave Trade, 1672–1752* (Chapel Hill: University of North Carolina Press, 2013), 85–90; *Considerations Humbly Offered To the Honourable House of Commons*; *Reasons Humbly Offered in behalf of the Plantations*; Dalby Thomas, *An Historical Account of the Rise and Growth of the West-India Collonies* (London: Jo. Hindmarsh, 1690), 51; Edward Littleton, *The Groans of the Plantations: Or, a True Account of their Grievous and Extreme Sufferings By the Heavy Impositions upon Sugar* (London: M. Clark, 1689), 6; *The Case of the Late African Company, and the Trade to Guiny, and other Parts within the said Company's Patents* (n.p., [1694?]), 3.

16. Council and Assembly of Barbados to the Board of Trade, July 1696, TNA, Colonial Office (CO) 28/3, no. 6; Agents of Barbados to the Board of Trade, 18 November 1696, CO 28/3, no. 18; Remonstrance of the Barbados Assembly, 14 November 1693, CO 31/3, pp. 357–360; *Reasons Humbly Offered in behalf of the Plantations*; Wilkinson, *Systema Africanum*, 2–3.

17. Littleton, *Groans of the Plantations*, 23–26, 7, 21; emphasis in the original. Jack Greene offers a similar interpretation of Littleton's pamphlet but overemphasizes concepts of "free trade" and "private enterprise." Greene, *Negotiated Authorities*, 59–60.

18. Thomas, *Historical Account*, 1; John Cary, *An Essay on the State of England in Relation to its Trade* (Bristol: W. Bonny, 1695), 66–67; Cary to Thomas Long, Antigua, 19 August 1696, British Library (BL), Additional Manuscripts (Add MS) 5540, fol. 76;

Southwell to Nottingham, 23 March 1688/9, Huntington Library, Blathwayt Papers, box 3, BL 418.

19. Pettigrew, "Free to Enslave," 27; Greene, *Negotiated Authorities*, chaps. 1 and 3; Jack P. Greene, "Transatlantic Colonization and the Redefinition of Empire in the Early Modern Era," in *Negotiated Empires: Centers and Peripheries in the Americas, 1500–1820*, ed. Christine Daniels and Michael V. Kennedy (New York and London: Routledge, 2002), 267–282; Elizabeth Manke, "Negotiating an Empire: Britain and Its Overseas Peripheries, c. 1550–1780," in *Negotiated Empires*, 235–265.

20. *Some Considerations: Humbly Offered to Demonstrate*, 2, 1; Cary, *Essay on the State of England*, 74–75; Sir Francis Brewster, *Essays on Trade and Navigation in Five Parts: The First Part* (London: Tho. Cockerill, 1695), 70; Sugar Bakers of Bristol to Thomas Day and Robert Yate, 15 January 1695/6, BL Add MS 5540, fol. 95.

21. Nuala Zahedieh, "Overseas Expansion and Trade in the Seventeenth Century," in *The Origins of Empire*, ed. Nicholas Canny (Oxford: Oxford University Press, 1998), 410, table 18.7; Nuala Zahedieh, "London and the Colonial Consumer in the Late Seventeenth Century," *Economic History Review* 47, no. 2 (1994): 242, table 2; J. R. Ward, "The Profitability of Sugar Planting in the British West Indies, 1650–1834," *Economic History Review* 31, no. 2 (May 1978): 208.

22. *The Case of the Late African Company*, 1, 2; *Considerations Concerning the African-Companies Petition*; *Some Considerations Humbly Offered, against Granting the Sole Trade*, 1.

23. Pettigrew, "Free to Enslave," 8, 11, 17, 35; Pettigrew, *Freedom's Debt*, 91; Davies, *Royal African Company*, 104, 133; John Callow, *The Making of King James II: The Formative Years of a Fallen King* (Thrupp, Stroud, Gloucestershire, UK: Sutton Publishing, 2000), 253; Keirn, "Monopoly, Economic Thought," 434; Pincus, *1688*, 375; De Krey, *A Fractured Society*, 137–141. I owe the overarching argument in this paragraph to a conversation with Brent Sirota.

24. Davies, *Royal African Company*, 81–83, 205; Galenson, *Traders, Planters, and Slaves*, 150; Carlos and Brown Kruse, "The Decline of the Royal African Company," 293, 311–312; Scott, *The Constitution and Finance*, 2:26; Keirn, "Monopoly, Economic Thought," 432–433. Davies estimates the company's losses from French privateer attacks to have amounted to about £300,000.

25. Davies, *Royal African Company*, 84–85; Scott, *The Constitution and Finance*, 2: 26–27, 33; Pettigrew, "Free to Enslave," 11; Bruce G. Carruthers, *City of Capital: Politics and Markets in the English Financial Revolution* (Princeton, NJ: Princeton University Press, 1996), 149.

26. Carruthers, *City of Capital*, 6–8, 18, 137; Scott, *The Constitution and Finance*, 1:321, 362; Geoffrey Holmes, *British Politics in the Age of Anne*, rev. ed. (London and Ronceverte, WV: Hambledon Press, 1987), 26–27.

27. Pettigrew, "Free to Enslave," 17; David Hayton, "The 'Country' Interest and the Party System, 1689–c.1720," in *Party and Management in Parliament, 1660–1784*, ed. Clyve Jones (New York: St. Martin's Press, 1984), 45; De Krey, *A Fractured Society*, chap. 5; Holmes, *British Politics*, 55, 58–63. De Krey calls the Whig transformation "the apostasy of the City Whigs."

28. Hayton, "'Country' Interest," 55–57; *Journal of the House of Commons*, 24 January 1694, 11: 68–69, http://british-history.ac.uk/report.aspx?compid=38954#s5 (accessed 19 October 2013); Pincus, *1688*, 595, n. 21; Pettigrew, "Free to Enslave," 28.

29. Nuala Zahedieh, "Regulation, Rent-seeking, and the Glorious Revolution in the English Atlantic Economy," *Economic History Review* 63, no. 4 (2010): 882; Carruthers, *City of Capital*, 152–153; Stump, "Economic Consequence," 35; Bohun, "Protecting Prerogative," 69, 75.

30. Pettigrew rightly points out that with "continued political backing, the company could have been economically successful." But he dismisses the role political ideology played in obstructing the company's financial livelihood. Pettigrew, "Free to Enslave," 7.

31. Davies, *Royal African Company*, 134–135, 139; Keirn, "Monopoly, Economic Thought," 435.

32. Davies, *Royal African Company*, 132–133; *Journal of the House of Commons*, 11 February 1698, 12:97, http://british-history.ac.uk/report.aspx?compid=39552#s13 (accessed 19 October 2013); Rose, *England in the 1690s*, 93; A. A. Hanham, "Trumbull, Sir William (1639–1716)," in *ODNB*, http://www.oxforddnb.com/view/article/27776 (accessed 6 March 2012). Trumbull does not appear to have owned shares in the African Company, but he did serve as governor of the Hudson's Bay Company from 1696 to 1700, another old Stuart/Tory commercial institution.

33. Davies, *Royal African Company*, 133–135; Keirn, "Monopoly, Economic Thought," 435; Zahedieh, "Regulation, rent-seeking," 883.

34. Zahedieh, "Regulation, Rent-seeking," 883; Davies, *Royal African Company*, 134. Neither Keirn nor Pettigrew explore the origins of the bill or why it passed when it did.

35. Stern, *The Company State*, 156; Henry Horwitz, "The East India Trade, the Politicians, and the Constitution: 1689–1702," *Journal of British Studies* 17, no. 2 (Spring 1978): 11; Bohun, "Protecting Prerogative," 79–80.

36. Horwitz, "East India Trade," 11.

37. Robin Hermann, "Money and Empire: The Failure of the Royal African Company," in *The Empire of Credit: The Financial Revolution in the British Atlantic World, 1688–1815*, ed. Daniel Carey and Christopher J. Finlay (Dublin: Irish Academic Press, 2011), 97–119.

38. Rose, *England in the 1690s*, 93–99; Lois Schwoerer, *"No Standing Armies!": The Antiarmy Ideology in Seventeenth-Century England* (Baltimore, MD: Johns Hopkins University Press, 1974), 157, 172; Hayton, "'Country' Interest," 57–59.

39. David Eltis, *The Rise of Slavery in the Americas* (Cambridge: Cambridge University Press, 2000), 208, table 8.3; Davies, *Royal African Company*, 124; Keirn, "Monopoly, Economic Thought," 433. Zahedieh suggests that collusion among merchants drove up prices. Zahedieh, "Regulation, Rent-seeking," 883.

40. Robert Yard to Edmund Poley, 6 November 1691, Edmund Poley Papers, James Marshall and Marie-Louise Osborn Collection, Beinecke Rare Book and Manuscript Library, Yale University, Osborn Manuscripts (OSB MSS) 1, folder 94; Rose, *England in the 1690s*, 122–130; *Considerations Requiring greater Care for Trade in England* (London: Printed for S. Crouch, 1695), 1, 3, 4.

41. [Charles Davenant], *An Essay upon the Ways and Means of Supplying the War* (London, 1695), 29; James Whitson, *The Causes of our Present Calamities In reference to the Trade of the Nation fully discovered* (London: Printed for Ed. Poole, 1695/6), 3; Cary, *Essay on the State of England*, betw. A3 and A4.

42. Robert Yard to Edmund Poley, 19 February 1691/2, Edmund Poley Papers, James Marshall and Marie-Louise Osborn Collection, Beinecke Library, OSB MSS 1, folder 98; James Vernon to Blathwayt, 2 June 1693, William Blathwayt Papers, James Marshall and Marie-Louise Osborn Collection, Beinecke Library, OSB MSS 2, folder 196; J. R. Jones, *Country and Court: England, 1658–1714* (Cambridge, MA: Harvard University Press, 1978), 158–159; Rose, *England in the 1690s*, 126; Newsletter, 17 November 1692, Newsletters Addressed to Madam Pole, James Marshall and Marie-Louise Osborn Collection, Beinecke Library, OSB MSS 60, box 2, folder 31; West-India Merchant, *A Brief Account of the Present Declining State of the West-Indies* (London: John Harris, 1695), 4, 6–7; Whitson, *The Causes of our Present Calamities*, 10; Cary, *Essay on the State of England*, 27. For reports of French disruption of English trade during the war, see Newsletters, 13 August 1692 and 17 December 1693, Newsletters Addressed to Madam Pole, James Marshall and Marie-Louise Osborn Collection, Beinecke Library, OSB MSS 60, box 1, folder 25, and box 2, folder 46.

43. John Brewer, *The Sinews of Power: War, Money and the English State, 1688–1783* (Cambridge, MA: Harvard University Press, 1988), 168–172; Daniel Baugh, "Maritime Strength and Atlantic Commerce: The Uses of a 'Grand Marine Empire,'" in *An Imperial State at War: Britain from 1689 to 1815*, ed. Lawrence Stone (London: Routledge, 1994), 185–223; Daniel Baugh, "Great Britain's 'Blue-Water' Policy, 1689–1815," *International History Review* 10, no. 1 (Feb. 1988): 33–58; Hayton, "'Country' Interest," 59; West-India Merchant, *A Brief Account*, 3; Shrewsbury to Blathwayt, 28 September 1694, Charles Talbot, Duke of Shrewsbury's Letters to William Blathwayt, James Marshall and Marie-Louise Osborn Collection, Beinecke Library, Osborn b 317.

44. Kendall to the Lords of Trade, 22 August 1690, TNA, CO 28/1, no. 48. For most of the eighteenth century, Jamaica's demographic reality made it stand out, even in comparison to the other British slave colonies in the region. Trevor Burnard, "A Failed Settler Society: Marriage and Demographic Failure in Early Jamaica," *Journal of Social History* (Fall 1994): 63–82; Trevor Burnard, *Mastery, Tyranny, and Desire: Thomas Thistlewood and His Slaves in the Anglo-Jamaican World* (Chapel Hill: University of North Carolina Press, 2004), 17.

45. Order of the King-in-Council, 9 January 1689/90, TNA, CO 324/5, pp. 114–116; Kendall to Shrewsbury, 26 June 1690, CO 28/1, no. 48; Report Concerning Monmouth Rebels, 3 November 1690, CO 324/5, pp. 137–140; Lords of Trade to Kendall, 20 November 1690, CO 29/4, fols. 120–121; Privy Council to Governors of Barbados, Leeward Islands and Jamaica, 20 November 1690, CO 324/5, pp. 140–142. For a petition to the king asking that colonial governors be forced to finally free the rebels as per the order, see CO 323/1, no. 6, 13 November 1690.

46. "Annexed observations on the effects of the sugar duty sent to the King and Queen," 8 October 1689, TNA, CO 31/3, pp. 199–203; Kendall to Earl of Shrewsbury, 26 June 1690, CO 28/1, no. 41; Henry Gemery, "Emigration from the British Isles to the New

World, 1630–1700: Inferences from Colonial Populations," *Research in Economic History* 5 (1980): 211, table A.1; Richard S. Dunn, *Sugar and Slaves: The Rise of the Planter Class in the English West Indies, 1624–1713* (Chapel Hill: University of North Carolina Press, 1972), 312, table 26; G. H. Guttridge, *The Colonial Policy of William III in America and the West Indies* (Hamden, CT: Archon Books, 1966), 62–63; Codrington to the Lords of Trade, 3 August 1690, *Calendar of State Papers Colonial: North America and the West Indies, 1574–1739* (CSPC), ed. Karen Ordahl Kuperman, John C. Appleby, and Mandy Banton (London: Routledge, 2000), CD-ROM, 13:303–306. In 1691, Codrington noted that "we have so worn out our strength that we have not as many men in the whole of the Islands as we had two years ago in Nevis alone." Codrington to the Lords of Trade, 13 July 1691, *CSPC*, 13:507.

47. Edward Littleton and William Bridges to the Lords of Trade, 7 September 1692, TNA, CO 28/1, no. 89; Littleton and Bridges to the Lords of Trade, 15 March 1693/2, CO 28/2, no. 9; Petition from Barbados Planters to William III, 30 November 1693, CO 28/2, no. 32I; Memorial of the Barbados Agents, December 1693, CO 28/2, no. 39; Jerome S. Handler, "Freedmen and Slaves in the Barbados Militia," *Journal of Caribbean History* 19, no. 1 (1984): 1.

48. Newsletter 9 August 1692, Newsletters Addressed to Madam Pole, James Marshall and Marie-Louise Osborn Collection, Beinecke Library, OSB MSS 60, box 1, folder 25; Robert Yard to Edmund Poley, 12 August 1692, Edmund Poley Papers, James Marshall and Marie-Louise Osborn Collection, Beinecke Library, OSB MSS 1, folder 103; Dunn, *Sugar and Slaves*, 163; Council of Jamaica to the Lords of Trade, 13 September 1692, TNA, CO 140/5, p. 216; Council of Jamaica to Nottingham, 24 December 1692, CO 140/5, pp. 233–234.

49. Sir William Beeston to Sir John Trenchard, 23 June 1694, TNA, CO 138/7, pp. 192–196; "A Narrative by Sir William Beeston of the Descent on Jamaica by the French," 23 June 1694, BL Add MS 12430, fols. 4–13; Dunn, *Sugar and Slaves*, 163; Guttridge, *Colonial Policy of William III*, 69; Beeston to the Lords of Trade, 7 August 1694, CO 137/1, fols. 190–191; Shrewsbury to William Blathwayt, 30 October 1694, Charles Talbot, Duke of Shrewsbury's Letters to William Blathwayt, James Marshall and Marie-Louise Osborn Collection, Beinecke Library, Osborn b 317; John Oldmixon, *The British empire in America, containing the history of the discovery, settlement, progress and state of the British colonies on the continent and islands of America* (London, 1741), 2:331; Peter M. Voelz, *Slave and Soldier: The Military Impact of Blacks in the Colonial Americas* (New York: Garland Publishing, 1993), 30; Newsletters, 18 October 1694, 18 August 1694, and 21 August 1694, Newsletters Addressed to Madam Pole, James Marshall and Marie-Louise Osborn Collection, Beinecke Library, OSB MSS 60, box 3, folders 67 and 70. For more on Beeston, see Frank Cundall, *The Governors of Jamaica in the Seventeenth Century* (London: West India Committee, 1936), 143–165; Webb, *The Governors-General: The English Army and the Definition of the Empire, 1569–1681* (Chapel Hill: University of North Carolina Press, 1979), 231, 292.

50. Minutes of the Council of War of Jamaica, 31 May 1694, *CSPC*, 14:291, no. 1074; Beeston to Blathwayt, 7 August 1694, *The William Blathwayt Papers at Colonial*

Williamsburg 1631–1722 (Frederick, MD: UPA Academic Editions, 1989), microfilm, vol. 21, folder 3, Jamaica; Beeston to the Lords of Trade, 26 August 1694, TNA, CO 138/8, pp. 14–19; Beeston to the Lords of Trade, 7 August 1694, CO 137/1, fols. 190–191; Shrewsbury to Blathwayt, 28 September 1694, Charles Talbot, Duke of Shrewsbury's Letters to William Blathwayt, James Marshall and Marie-Louise Osborn Collection, Beinecke Library, Osborn b 317; James Vernon to Lexington, 1 January 1694/5, Lexington Papers, BL Add MS 46527, fols. 39–40.

51. Philip D. Morgan and Andrew Jackson O'Shaughnessy, "Arming Slaves in the American Revolution," in *Arming Slaves: From Classical Times to the Modern Age*, ed. Christopher Leslie Brown and Philip D. Morgan (New Haven, CT: Yale University Press, 2006), 180–208; Voelz, *Slave and Soldier*, esp. chap. 2; Handler, "Freedmen and Slaves"; Benjamin Quarles, "The Colonial Militia and Negro Manpower," *Mississippi Valley Historical Review* 45, no. 4 (Mar. 1959): 643–652; Susan Dwyer Amussen, *Caribbean Exchanges: Slavery and the Transformation of English Society, 1640–1700* (Chapel Hill: University of North Carolina Press, 2007), 168; Burnard, *Mastery, Tyranny, and Desire*, 176–177.

52. Brewer, *Sinews of Power*, 29–32, 171; Allan Macinnes, *Union and Empire: The Making of the United Kingdom in 1707* (Cambridge: Cambridge University Press, 2007), 182, 184, 193; Rose, *England in the 1690s*, 126–130; Bruce P. Lenman, "Colonial Wars and Imperial Instability, 1688–1793," in *The Eighteenth Century*, ed. P. J. Marshall, vol. 2, *The Oxford History of the British Empire* (New York: Oxford University Press, 1998), 151–168. Among those cited here, the exception is Macinnes, who considers imperial policies during the Nine Years' War in relation to political economy and population, although he does not consider colonial slavery.

53. Beeston to the Board of Trade, 4 July 1696, TNA, CO 137/4, no. 8; Greene, *Negotiated Authorities*, 84–86.

54. Peter Laslett, "John Locke, the Great Recoinage, and the Origins of the Board of Trade: 1695–1698," *William and Mary Quarterly*, 3rd ser., 14, no. 3 (July 1957): 374–392; Patrick Kelly, "'Monkey' Business: Locke's 'College' Correspondence and the Adoption of the Plan for the Great Recoinage of 1696," *Locke Studies* 9 (2009): 139–165; Steele, *Politics of Colonial Policy*, 10; Jones, *Country and Court*, 271; Rose, *England in the 1690s*, 137; Vernon to Lexington, 29 November 1695, Lexington Papers, BL Add MS 46527, fol. 95.

55. Rose, *England in the 1690s*, 138, 141; De Krey, *A Fractured Society*, 192–193. For evidence of the scarcity of money in the wake of this legislation, see John Ellis to Lord Lexington, 10 July 1696, Lexington Papers, BL Add MS 46525, fols. 67–68; James Vernon to Lexington, 6 October 1696, Lexington Papers, BL Add MS 46527, fol. 118.

56. *Considerations Requiring greater Care for Trade*, 15; Whitson, *Causes of our Present Calamities*, 5–7; Cary, *Essay on the State of England*, 139–141; Brewster, *Essays on Trade and Navigation*, 37–40. Those asked to present their ideas included John Locke, now at his height of influence over the Whig ministry (although he did not hold an official government position); Sir Christopher Wren; Sir Isaac Newton; Sir Josiah Child; Charles Davenant; and Sir Gilbert Heathcote. Steele, *Politics of Colonial Policy*, 11–18; Laslett, "John Locke, the Great Recoinage," 375–376, 384–385, 389; John

Ellis to Lexington, 3 January 1695/6, Lexington Papers, BL Add MS 46525, fol. 63; Blathwayt to Lexington, 3/13 January 1695/6, Lexington Papers, BL Add MS 46528B, fol. 9.

57. James Vernon to Lexington, 3 March 1695/6, and March 6, 1695/6, Lexington Papers, BL Add MS 46527, fol. 112–113; John Ellis to Lexington, 13 March 1695/6, Lexington Papers, BL Add MS, fol. 66; Steele, *Politics of Colonial Policy*, 16–23; "Clauses in the Commission for Trade," ca. 1696, William Blathwayt Papers, James Marshall and Marie-Louise Osborn Collection, Beinecke Library, OSB MSS 2, folder 76. For Bridgewater's papers and notes from Board of Trade meetings, see Huntington Library, Ellesmere Collection, Americana, EL 9571–9881; for Abraham Hill's papers, see BL Sloane MS 2902.

58. "Proposals of the Jamaica merchants for the better carrying on and securing the trade of Jamaica," 18 September 1696, TNA, CO 138/9, pp. 2–4; Journal of the Board of Trade, 18 September 1696, CO 391/9, pp. 115–119; Beeston to Blathwayt, 19 June 1696, CO 137/4, no. 7; Journal of the Board of Trade, 2 October 1696, CO 391/9, pp. 151–153; "A Memorial from the Jamaica merchants & planters representing the weak state of that island," 16 December 1696, CO 137/4, no. 38; and 11 December 1696, CO 391/9, p. 227; Journal of the Board of Trade, 25 November 1696, CO 391/9, pp. 249–250; Jamaica Entry Book, Board of Trade, 3 December 1696, CO 138/9, pp. 53–57; Journal of the Board of Trade, 7 December 1696, CO 391/9, pp. 266–267; Journal of the Board of Trade, 10 December 1696, CO 391/9, pp. 271–272 and 1 January 1696/7, CO 391/9, pp. 318–319; Board of Trade to William III, Jamaica Entry Book, 19 December 1696, CO 138/9, pp. 59–61; Order of the King-in-Council, 31 December 1696, CO 137/4, no. 40. Gracedieu had traded to and from Jamaica since at least 1686; he was a nonconformist and a Whig who served on the City of London's Common Council and was Jamaica's agent in London from 1693 to 1704. Perry Gauci, "Gracedieu, Sir Bartholomew (*c*.1657–1715)," in *ODNB*, http://www.oxforddnb.com/view/article/49752 (accessed 9 May 2014).

59. Journal of the Board of Trade, 1 January 1696/7, 6 January 1696/7, 15 January 1696/7, 25 January 1696/7, TNA, CO 391/9, pp. 318–319, 329–330, 350–351, 366–367; Heathcote to William Popple, 18 March 1696/7, CO 137/4, no. 50.

60. Petition from Jeffrey Yellowton to the Board of Trade, 8 March 1696/7, TNA, CO 137/4, no. 48; "Opinion of the Agents of Jamaica upon Mr. Wellowton's Proposal," n.d., CO 137/4, no. 48I; Journal of the Board of Trade, 8 March 1696/7, 15 March 1696/7, 19 March 1696/7, 16 April 1697, CO 391/10, pp. 10, 28, 37–38, 75.

61. Journal of the Board of Trade, 22 October 1697, TNA, CO 391/10, pp. 322–324.

62. Journal of the Board of Trade, 28 June 1697, TNA, CO 391/10, pp. 135–136; Board of Trade to the Lords Justices of England, Jamaica Entry Book, 6 July 1697, CO 138/9, p. 113; Proclamation of Governor Beeston and the Council of Jamaica, 25 February 1697/8, CO 140/6, pp. 78–79; Act of the Governor, Council, and General Assembly of Barbados, June 1696, CO 28/3, no. 44I; Council of Barbados to the Board of Trade, 12 July 1698, CO 28/3, no. 68. Such laws had existed in Barbados since the creation of the 1661 servant and slave codes. I owe this point to a conversation with Jessica Luther.

63. "Copy of a Representation of ye Commissioners for Trade & Plantations relating to ye general state of the Trade of this Kingdom," 23 December 1697, BL Add MS 46542, fols. 24–33.

7. THE SLAVE TRADE, THE *ASIENTO*, AND THE NATIONAL INTEREST

1. K. G. Davies, *The Royal African Company* (London: Longmans, Green, 1957), 140; D. A. G. Waddell, "Queen Anne's Government and the Slave Trade," *Caribbean Quarterly* 6, no. 1 (1960): 7–10.

2. Elizabeth Donnan, "The Early Days of the South Sea Company, 1711–1718," *Journal of Economic and Business History* 2, no. 3 (May 1930): 419–450; John Carswell, *The South Sea Bubble* (London: Cresset Press, 1961), chap. 3.

3. Carl Wennerlind, *Casualties of Credit: The English Financial Revolution, 1620–1720* (Cambridge, MA: Harvard University Press, 2011), chap. 6.

4. Royal African Company to agents Buckeridge, Cooper, and Browne, 7 July 1698, The National Archives (TNA), Treasury (T) 70/51, fols. 5–6; Davies, *Royal African Company*, 139; Letter from the Royal African Company to its agents in the West Indies, n.d., T 70/58, fol. 149; William Beeston to the Board of Trade, 5 January 1699/1700, Colonial Office (CO) 137/5, no. 13. David Eltis has estimated that in Barbados the average cost of one slave in 1689 was approximately £14; by 1700 the price had risen to £25. Eltis, *The Rise of African Slavery in the Americas* (Cambridge: Cambridge University Press, 2000), 152, table 6-I. Nuala Zahedieh argues that collusion among merchants drove up prices. Nuala Zahedieh, "Regulation, Rent-seeking, and the Glorious Revolution in the English Atlantic Economy," *Economic History Review* 63, no. 4 (2010): 883.

5. Royal African Company to Buckeridge, Freeman, and Wallis, Cape Coast Castle, 29 August 1699, TNA, T 70/51, fols. 21–23; 27 February 1699/1700, T 70/51, fols. 48–49; 11 June 1700, T 70/51, fols. 61–63; Royal African Company to Freeman, Peck, and Hicks, 8 January 1701/2, T 70/51, fols. 109–113; Royal African Company to Browne, Peck, and Hicks, 23 July 1702, T 70/51, fols. 131–133; Royal African Company to Gresham, Gile, and Rayner, 3 December 1700, T 70/51, fols. 74–76; Royal African Company to Seth Grosvenor, Winneba, 26 June 1707, T 70/52, fol. 98.

6. David Eltis, "The Volume and Structure of the Transatlantic Slave Trade: A Reassessment," *William and Mary Quarterly*, 3rd ser., 58, no. 1 (Jan. 2001): 43, table 1; Tim Keirn, "Monopoly, Economic Thought, and the Royal African Company," in *Early Modern Conceptions of Property*, ed. John Brewer and Susan Staves (London: Routledge, 1995), 433; Ann Carlos and Jamie Brown Kruse, "The Decline of the Royal African Company: Fringe Firms and the Role of the Charter," *Economic History Review* 49, no. 2 (1996): 311. The separate traders' ability to outperform the company did not go unnoticed by its directors: Royal African Company to Sir Dalby Thomas, 12 October 1705, TNA, T 70/52, fols. 54–55.

7. Davies, *Royal African Company*, 140; Waddell, "Queen Anne's Government," 7–10; John Perry to the Board of Trade, 5 December 1707, TNA, CO 389/20, pp. 28–29; Angus McInnes, "The Appointment of Harley in 1704," *Historical Journal* 11, no. 2 (1968): 255–271; Julian Hoppit, *A Land of Liberty? England 1689–1727* (Oxford: Oxford

University Press, 2000), 294–295; Ian K. Steele, *Politics of Colonial Policy: The Board of Trade in Colonial Administration 1696–1720* (Oxford: Clarendon Press, 1968), 110–114, 132; Stephen Saunders Webb, "William Blathwayt, Imperial Fixer: Muddling Through to Empire, 1689–1717," *William and Mary Quarterly*, 3rd ser., 26, no. 3 (July 1969): 413–414; Godfrey Davies, "The Fall of Harley in 1708," *English Historical Review* 66, no. 259 (Apr. 1951): 246–254; G. S. Holmes and W. A. Speck, "The Fall of Harley in 1708 Reconsidered," *English Historical Review* 80, no. 317 (Oct. 1965): 673–698.

8. William A. Pettigrew, "Free to Enslave: Politics and the Escalation of Britain's Transatlantic Slave Trade, 1688–1714," *William and Mary Quarterly*, 3rd ser., 64, no. 1 (Jan. 2007): 17; Steele, *Politics of Colonial Policy*, 127; William A. Pettigrew, *Freedom's Debt: The Royal African Company and the Politics of the Atlantic Slave Trade, 1672–1752* (Chapel Hill: University of North Carolina Press, 2013), 40; Keirn, "Monopoly, Economic Thought," 436; William Popple to John Perry, 15 December 1707, TNA, CO 389/20, pp. 38–39; Popple to the Separate Traders, 15 December 1707, CO 389/20, pp. 40–44; "Response of the Separate Traders to the Board of Trade's Queries," 2 January 1707/8, CO 389/20, pp. 61–75; Benjamin Way to the Board of Trade, 2 January 1707/8, CO 389/20, pp. 76–92; Royal African Company to the Board of Trade, 18 December 1707, CO 389/20, pp. 52–53 and T 70/ 175, fol. 6; Davies, *Royal African Company*, 140.

9. Pettigrew, "Free to Enslave," 16; Board of Trade's Report on African Trade to Queen Anne, 3 February 1707/8, TNA, CO 389/20, pp. 115–46; Steele, *Politics of Colonial Policy*, 127–128.

10. Great Britain, Parliament, *An Act for the Better Improvement of the Trade to Africa, by Establishing a Regulated Company* ([London?]: J. Tonson, 1708); Steele, *Politics of Colonial Policy*, 128; "Memorial of the Separate Traders to Africa," 8 December 1708, TNA, CO 389/20, pp. 232–239; Report of the Separate Traders, 29 November 1709, CO 389/20, pp. 487–495; "Circular letter to the Governors of Several Plantations," Board of Trade Entry Books, 15 April 1708, CO 324/9, pp. 165–170, and copy in CO 389/20, pp. 301–304, as part of the January 1709 report; Pettigrew, "Free to Enslave," 22.

11. Sample Petition to Barbados, n.d., TNA, T 70/58, pp. 167–168; Royal African Company to Agents in Barbados, 20 April 1708, T 70/58, pp. 168–169. The company had solicited petitions from the colonies since at least 1707 (see T 70/58, pp. 139 and 149). For pro-company petitions signed by planters, see T 70/175, fols. 39, 43–44, 45. A printed version of the Barbados petition appeared in 1711: *To the Queen's Most Excellent Majesty, The humble Petition of several Planters, and other the Inhabitants of your Majesty's Island of Barbadoes* (n.p., [1711]). For anti-company petitions to Parliament, see T 70/175, fol. 78 (Dartmouth), f. 80 (Lancaster), fol. 83 (Whitehaven), fol. 83 (Plymouth), fol. 84 (Bridgewater), fol. 88 (Birmingham), fols. 88–89 (London), fol. 90 (Bristol), fol. 90 (London). For a different view of the African Company's ability to adapt to the changing political culture, see Pettigrew, "Free to Enslave," 8–10; Pettigrew, *Freedom's Debt*, chap. 5.

12. *An Account of the Number of Negroes delivered in to the Islands of Barbadoes, Jamaica, and Antego, from the Year 1698 to 1708, since the Trade was Opened, taken from the Accounts sent from the respective Governours of those Islands to the Lords Commissioners of Trade* . . . (London, [1709?]); Davies, *Royal African Company*, 143, n. 1; Board of Trade's Report on the African Trade to the House of Commons, 27 January 1708/9,

TNA, CO 389/20, pp. 275–313; Eltis, *The Rise of African Slavery*, 208, table 8.3; "Some general observations and particular remarks on the report made by the Lords Commissioners for Trade & Plantations," 3 January 1708/9, T 70/175, fols. 47–51; Board of Trade to John Perry, 27 January 1708/9, CO 389/20, pp. 274–275.

13. I have calculated these numbers from Tim Keirn's list of pamphlets at the end of his article. Keirn, "Monopoly, Economic Thought," 438, 458–466.

14. Pettigrew, "Free to Enslave," 7–10; Pettigrew, *Freedom's Debt*, 19; Waddell, "Queen Anne's Government," 9. The company's enemies derided this practice by referring to "the Hackney Scriblers of the *African Company*" and the "Suggestions cook'd up by the mercenary Writers of the Town, and daily given out in the lobby," on the part of the company. *Observations On Some of the African Company's late Printed Papers* ([London?], [1709?]), 1; *The African Trade in no Danger of being Lost, Otherwise than by the Designs of the Company* (London, [1711?]), 1.

15. *The Present State of the Sugar Plantations Consider'd; But more especially that of the Island of Barbadoes* (London: John Morphew, 1713), 25; *A Letter to a Member of Parliament Concerning the African Trade* (n.p., [1709?]), 3; *The Case of the Separate Traders to Africa With Remarks on the African-Company's Memorial* (n.p., [1709?]), 2; *A True State of the Present Difference Between the Royal African Company, and the Separate Traders* (London: 1710), 32.

16. *Some Observations on Extracts taken out of the Report from the Lords Commissioners for Trade and Plantations* ([London], [1708]), 2; A Planter, *Some Observations Shewing the Danger of Losing the Trade of the Sugar Colonies* (London, 1714), 14; *The Scandalous Political Arithmetick (as they term it) of the Private Traders detected* ([England?], [1708?]) (printed copy in TNA, T 70/175, f. 19); [Charles Davenant], *A Clear Demonstration, from Points of Fact, That the Recovery, Preservation and Improvement of Britain's share of the Trade to Africa, is wholly owing to the Industry, Care and Application of the Royal African Company* ([London?], [1709?]), 4; [Charles Davenant], *Several Arguments proving, that our Trade to Africa, cannot be preserved and carried on effectually by any other Method, than that of a considerable Joint-Stock, with exclusive Privileges* ([London], [1709?]), 3. Pettigrew argues that the main difference between the two sets of pamphlets was the inclusion of complaints about the African Company from tobacco planters and merchants in the 1700s. Pettigrew, "Free to Enslave," 23.

17. *The British Interest on the Coast of Africa Consider'd, with the Interest of other Europeans, and the Politicks they used for Carrying on that Trade* (London, 1708); *A Memorial touching the Nature and present State of the Trade to Africa* ([1709?]), 2, 7; *Some Considerations on the Late Act of Parliament, for Setling the Trade to Africa* (London, [1709?]); *An Explanation of the African-Company's Property in the Sole Trade to Africa, Making their Right equal with any Subject's Right to his Freehold* (London, 1712), 5; [Charles Davenant], *Several Arguments*, 1; [Davenant], *A Clear Demonstration*, 3.

18. *Memorial touching the Nature*, 4; Daniel Defoe, *A Brief Account of the Present State of the African Trade*, in *The Political and Economic Writings of Daniel Defoe*, vol. 7, *Trade*, ed. John McVeagh (London: Pickering & Chatto, 2000), 62; *Some Considerations On the Late Act of Parliament; A few Remarks proper to be regarded in the Establishment of the African Trade* (n.p., [1709?]), 1; *The British Interest on the Coast of Africa*

Consider'd; Present State of the Sugar Plantations Consider'd, 28; A Planter, *Some Observations*, 13, 8.

19. A Planter, *Some Observations*, 7, 8; [Davenant], *Several Arguments*, 2, 3; *The Case of the Royal African Company* (n.p., [1709?]), 1, 2; *Reasons against the Bill for the better Improvement of the Trade to Africa, by Establishing a Regulated-Company* ([1709?]), 1; *Some Considerations on the Late Act of Parliament* (London, [1709?]); [Davenant], *A Clear Demonstration*, 4.

20. *The African Companies Considerations on the Late Act of Parliament for Settling the Trade to Africa, Answer'd Paragraph by Paragraph* (London, [1708?]); *The Case of the Separate Traders to Africa. With Remarks on the African-Company's Memorial* ([1709?]), 1, 2; *A Letter from a Merchant in Bristol. touching the Trade to Africa, as it relates to the Out-ports of Great Britain* ([London], 1711), 1; *True State of the Present Difference*, 19, 22; *Some Remarks on a Pamphlet*, 15.

21. *Case of the Separate Traders to Africa*, 1; *Letter to a Member of Parliament touching the African Trade*, 1; *A Second Letter to a Member of Parliament, relating to the settling the trade to Africa* (London, 1710), 1.

22. *African Companies Considerations; True State of the Present Difference*, 29; *The African Company's Property to the Forts and Settlements in Guinea, Consider'd; and the Necessity of establishing the Trade in a Regulated Company, Demonstrated* (1709), 3; *Letter to a Member of Parliament Concerning the African Trade*, 1; *Considerations upon the Trade to Guinea* (London, 1708), 16.

23. *Considerations upon the Trade to Guinea*, 13–14, 19, 21–22; *True State of the Present Difference*, 34; *A Letter to a Member of Parliament Concerning the African Trade*, 2; *African Companies Considerations; Case of the Separate Traders to Africa*, 1; *Reasons for Establishing the African Trade under a Regulated Company* (n.p., 1709), 1; *Letter from a Merchant in Bristol; Some Remarks on a Pamphlet*, 6, 30; *Reasons for Establishing the African Trade under a Regulated Company*, 2; *Letter to a Member of Parliament*, 3.

24. Gary S. De Krey, *A Fractured Society: The Politics of London in the First Age of Party, 1688–1715* (Oxford: Clarendon Press, 1985), 213–215; Geoffrey Holmes, *British Politics in the Age of Anne*, rev. ed. (London: Hambleton Press, 1987), 172–174; Wennerlind, *Casualties of Credit*, 161–166.

25. De Krey, *Fractured Society*, 223–224; Holmes, *British Politics*, 174; Wennerlind, *Casualties of Credit*, 167.

26. Hoppit, *A Land of Liberty?*, 302–306; Wennerlind, *Casualties of Credit*, 168, 195–196; De Krey, *Fractured Society*, 239–241; John G. Sperling, *The South Sea Company: An Historical Essay and Bibliographical Finding List* (Boston: Baker Library, Harvard Graduate School of Business Administration, 1962), 7; Bruce G. Carruthers, *City of Capital: Politics and Markets in the English Financial Revolution* (Princeton, NJ: Princeton University Press, 1996), 153.

27. Sperling, *South Sea Company*, 3; Carruthers, *City of Capital*, 152–154; Carswell, *South Sea Bubble*, 53; Wennerlind, *Casualties of Credit*, 197, 200–201; Donnan, "Early Days of the South Sea Company," 422; "Remarkes upon the Act *None Annae R.* for Erecting a Corporation for carrying on a Trade to the South Seas," n.d., but probably late 1711, British Library (BL), Harley MS 6393, pp. 3–6; "Explanatory Observations on the South Sea

Trade and Company," n.d., but likely 1711, fols. 239–246, BL Additional Manuscripts (Add MS) 70163; *A True Account of the Design, and Advantages of the South-Sea Trade* (London: J. Morphew, 1711).

28. This point was hotly debated in the Commons and was strongly opposed by a small group of staunch Whigs, led by Robert Walpole, who understood Harley's plan to keep them out of positions of power. J. G. Sperling, "The Division of 25 May 1711, on an Amendment to the South Sea Bill: A Note of the Reality of Parties in the Age of Anne," *Historical Journal* 4, no. 2 (1961): 191–202; Carruthers, *City of Capital*, 153.

29. De Krey, *Fractured Society*, 241–243; Carruthers, *City of Capital*, 152–154; Holmes, *British Politics*, 174–175, 197; Wennerlind, *Casualties of Credit*, 189–190; Carswell, *South Sea Bubble*, 57–58 and chap. 2 more generally; Sperling, *South Sea Company*, 5–6. For more on the "clashing financial interests" of Whigs and Tories during Anne's reign, see Holmes, *British Politics*, chap. 5.

30. Carswell, *South Sea Bubble*; P. G. M. Dickson, *The Financial Revolution in England: A Study in the Development of Public Credit, 1688–1756* (London: Macmillan, 1967), chaps.5–6; Sperling, *South Sea Company*, 11–12, 25–38; Richard Dale, *The First Crash: Lessons from the South Sea Bubble* (Princeton, NJ: Princeton University Press, 2004); Colin Palmer, *Human Cargoes: The British Slave Trade to Spanish America, 1700–1739* (Urbana: University of Illinois Press, 1981); Wennerlind, *Casualties of Credit*, chap. 6; Adriane Finucane, "The South Sea Company and Anglo-Spanish Connections, 1713–1739," (Ph.D. diss., Harvard University, 2010). For a corrective on the significance of the South Sea Bubble, see Julian Hoppit, "The Myths of the South Sea Bubble," *Transactions of the Royal Historical Society*, 6th ser., 12 (2002): 141–165.

31. *Memorial Touching the Nature*, 6. Davenant made the same argument, using almost the same wording, in *Several Arguments*, 2–3. A Planter, *Some Observations*, 9–10; *An Address relating to the African Company, to be presented to Her Majesty* (London, 1711), 1; *Observations on Some of the African Company's late Printed Papers*, 1; *True State of the Present Difference*, 33.

32. *Proposals for Raising a New Company for Carrying on the Trades of Africa and the Spanish West-Indies, Under the Title of The United Company* (London: John Morphew, 1709), 3, 4, 5, 7–8. One pro–African Company pamphleteer took issue with this proposal. See *Some short Remarks, on two Pamphlets lately Printed* (London, 1709).

33. Wennerlind, *Casualties of Credit*, 205–206; Donnan, "Early Days of the South Sea Company," 424.

34. *Some Observations upon a late Pamphlet, Intitled, A Modest Representation of the Past and Present State of Great Britain* (London: A. Baldwin, 1711), 10; *Some Queries, Which being Nicely Answered May Tend Very Much to the Encouragement of the South-Sea Company* (1711); Daniel Defoe, *The True State of the Case between the Government and the Creditors of the Navy, &c. As it Relates to the South-Sea-Trade* (London: J. Baker, 1711), 10–11; *A Letter to a Member of Parliament, on the Settling a Trade to the South-Sea of America* (London: J. Phillips, 1711), 4, 8. For more on Defoe's pamphlet, see Wennerlind, *Casualties of Credit*, 211.

35. "Explanatory Observations on the South Sea Trade and Company," n.d., but likely 1711, fols. 239–246, BL Add MS 70163, Portland Papers, Papers of Robert Harley, First

Earl of Oxford. This manuscript matches Defoe's pamphlet *A True Account of the Design, and Advantages of the South-Sea Trade* (London, J. Morphew, 1711). Robert Allen, *Essay on the Nature and Methods of Carrying on a Trade to the South-Sea* (London: John Baker, 1712), 21, 22; *Letter from an Exchange Broker to a Country Gentleman, Concerning Peace and South-Sea Stock* (London, 1711), 14.

36. Defoe, *True Account of the Design, and Advantages*, 20; Defoe, *Brief Account of the Present State of the African Trade*, 75.

37. "An Account of the Proceedings of the Court of Directors of the South Sea Company from their first institution in relation to Trade," fols. 13–16v, minutes for 10 June, 11 June, 17 June, 19 June, 21 July, 22 July, 28 July, 29 July, 13 August, and 20 October 1713, BL King's MS 73; Donnan, "Early Days of the South Sea Company," 428–429, 432; *The Assiento; or Contract, for Allowing the Subjects of Great Britain the Liberty of Importing Negroes into the Spanish America* (London: John Baskett, 1713); Finucane, "South Sea Company," chap. 1.

38. Resolution of the Royal African Company, 11 September 1713, enclosed in a letter from Oxford to James Bateman, 15 September 1713, BL Add MS 25562, fol. 6; Royal African Company to Grosvenor, Phipps, and Bleau, Cape Coast Castle, 22 October 1713, TNA, T 70/52, fols. 177–179; "The humble Proposition of the Royal African Company of England & of their creditors united with them," 26 June 1713, BL Add MS 70165, no. 82.

39. Pettigrew, "Free to Enslave," 28–29; Wennerlind, *Casualties of Credit*, chap. 6.

40. Pettigrew, "Free to Enslave," 29–30; Keirn, "Monopoly, Economic Thought," 437; *An Explanation of the African-Company's Property in the Sole Trade to Africa* (London, 1712), 13; Advertisement of the Royal African Company, 9 July 1712, TNA, T 70/58, f. 214.

41. Pettigrew, "Free to Enslave," 27–28; Minute Book of the General Court of the Royal African Company, 18 June 1712, TNA, T 70/ 101, fols. 141–142; Defoe, *Present State of the African Trade*, 64, 65.

42. Defoe, *Present State of the African Trade*, 66, 69; "The humble Proposition of the Royal African Company of England & of their creditors united with them," 26 June 1713, BL Add MS 70165, no. 82; John Lade, Andrew Hopegood, and Thomas Pindar of the Royal African Company to Lord Oxford, 27 June 1713, BL Add MS 70165, no. 81; A Planter, *Some Observations, Shewing the Danger of Losing the Trade of the Sugar Colonies*, 14; Pettigrew, "Free to Enslave," 30–32. Tim Keirn suggests that the African Company "abandoned all pretences of regaining its privileges after 1712, and saw its future as subordinate to the more dynamic and politically viable projects promoted by the Tory leadership." Keirn, "Monopoly, Economic Thought," 437.

43. Archibald Hamilton to the Board of Trade, 22 March 1713/14, TNA, CO 137/10, pt. 2, no. 51; James Bateman to Bolingbroke, 30 September 1713, BL Add MS 25559, fols. 20v–21v; Palmer, *Human Cargoes*, chap. 3; Wennerlind, *Casualties of Credit*, 221; Memorandum from Royal African Company to South Sea Company, 27 July 1714, T 70/38, no page number; Donnan, "Early Days of the South Sea Company," 449. For a narrative of the activities and problems of the South Sea Company in relation to the *asiento* during its first years, see Papers of the South Sea Company, BL King's MS 73.

44. Petition of the Council and Assembly of Jamaica to the Queen, 24 December 1713, TNA, CO 137/10, pt. 2, no. 45I; Zahedieh, "Regulation, Rent-seeking," 877–881; *Present*

State of the Sugar Plantations Consider'd, 29; J. Ury to James Stanhope, 25 May 1715, BL Add MS 25559, fol. 50v.

45. Palmer, *Human Cargoes*, 62–66; James Bateman and Samuel Shepheard to James Stanhope, 28 February 1715/16, BL Add MS 25559, fols. 58–58v; Francis March, John Carver, Ezekiel Gomersall, and W. Hering to the Board of Trade, 8 March 1715/16, TNA, CO 137/11, no. 7; South Sea Company petition to the King-in-Council, read 31 October 1717, CO 137/12, pt. 2, no. 92I, and BL Add MS 25559, fols. 66–66v; Board of Trade report to the King-in-Council, 21 December 1717, CO 138/16, pp. 32–43.

46. Board of Trade report to the King-in-Council, 21 December 1717, TNA, CO 138/16, pp. 32–43; Order of the Privy Council, 9 January 1717/18, BL Add MS 25562, fols. 76v–77; Donnan, "Early Days of the South Sea Company," 442.

47. Wennerlind, *Casualties of Credit*, 222–223; Finucane, "South Sea Company," 88–92; Donnan, "Early Days of the South Sea Company," 450.

CONCLUSION

1. Jack P. Greene, "Liberty, Slavery, and the Transformation of British Identity in the Eighteenth-Century West Indies," *Slavery and Abolition* 21, no. 1 (Apr. 2000): 1–31.

INDEX